PLOUGHING
SAND

Other books by the author

Wilfrid Israel
The Zealous Intruders
The Mayor and the Citadel
Alarms and Excursions
A Price Below Rubies
The Russians in Israel

PLOUGHING SAND

British Rule in Palestine
1917–1948

Naomi Shepherd

JOHN MURRAY
Albemarle Street, London

First published in 1999
by John Murray (Publishers) Ltd,
50 Albemarle Street, London W1X 4BD

A catalogue record for this book is available from the British Library

ISBN 0-7195-5707 0

Typeset in Sabon by Servis Filmsetting Ltd, Manchester
Printed and bound in Great Britain by The University Press, Cambridge

For Josh, Sarah, Isaac and their partners

Contents

Illustrations   ix
Maps   xi

Preface: The Cenotaph and the House   1
1. The Genesis of the Mandate   5
2. From Conquest to Colony: Palestine 1917–1922   20
3. The Law Factory: Legislation and Evasion   74
4. Patching up Palestine: Health and Education   126
5. Iron Gloves: The Resort to Violence   179
Postscript   244

Sources and Acknowledgements   248
Notes   251
Index   283

Illustrations

(between pages 146 and 147)

1. The Jerusalem cenotaph today
2. The surrender of Jerusalem, 9 December 1917
3. General Allenby
4. Colonel Ronald Storrs with local workmen, April 1918
5. Herbert Samuel with T. E. Lawrence and Arab leaders, 1921
6. A meeting at Government House, 1922
7. British show of force, August 1929
8. Sir John Chancellor inspecting Arab Boy Scouts
9. Humphrey Bowman as Scoutmaster with Arab schoolboys
10. Sir Arthur Wauchope, Edward Keith-Roach and Stewart Perowne, October 1933
11. The donkey race 'Grand National' during the Second World War
12. The Right Reverend George Francis Graham-Brown
13. The Peel Commission, 1936
14. The Arab Higher Committee
15. Ruhi Bey Abd'el Hadi, 1937
16. Sir Arthur Wauchope with his ADC outside Government House, 1937
17. 'Destruction to property in Jaffa during the Arab Revolt'
18. A derailed train on the sabotaged railway
19. A British army convoy ambushed on the Jenin Road, 1936
20. British guardsmen in the Via Dolorosa, winter 1938–9
21. Sir Harold MacMichael, relaxing with his pipe
22. The King David Hotel after a bomb attack, July 1946
23. Jewish illegal immigrants, August 1946
24. Lieutenant-General Sir Alan Cunningham at Lydda airfield, November 1945

The author and publisher would like to thank the following for permission to reproduce photographs: plates, 2, 3, 4, 5, 11, 17, 18, 19, 20, 21, 22, 23 and 24, Imperial War Museum, London; 7, 13 and 14, Walid Khalidi and the Institute for Palestine Studies; 9, Humphrey Bowman, *Middle East Window*, Longmans Green & Co., 1942; and 6, 8, 10, 12, 13, 14, 15 and 16, Middle East Centre, St Antony's College, Oxford.

Maps

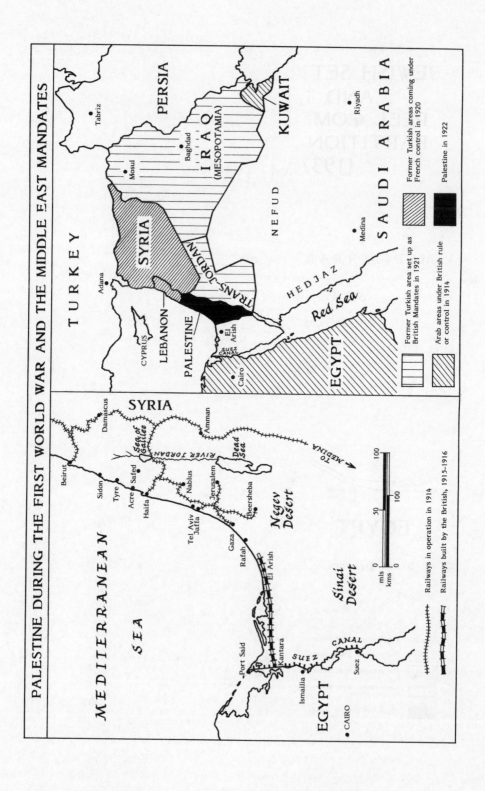

PALESTINE DURING THE FIRST WORLD WAR AND THE MIDDLE EAST MANDATES

Railways in operation in 1914

Railways built by the British, 1915–1916

Former Turkish area set up as
British Mandates in 1921

Arab areas under British rule
or control in 1914

Former Turkish areas coming under
French control in 1920

Palestine in 1922

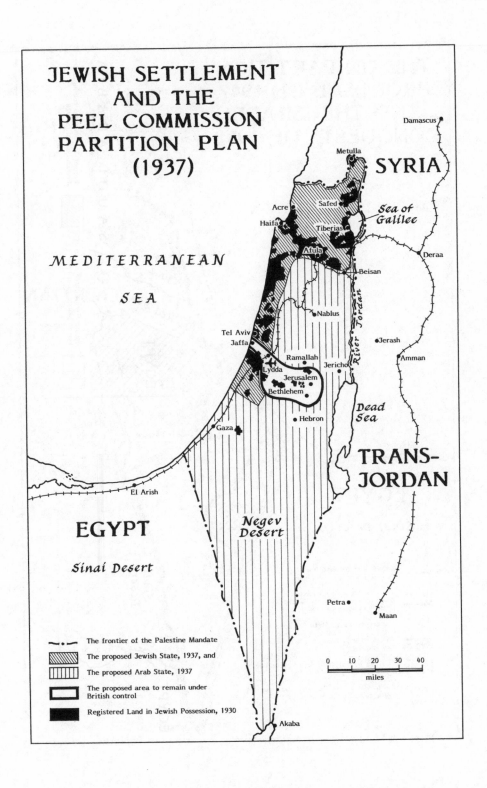

JEWISH SETTLEMENT AND THE PEEL COMMISSION PARTITION PLAN (1937)

SYRIA

Damascus

Metulla

Acre
Safed
Haifa
Sea of Galilee
Tiberias

MEDITERRANEAN

Afula

Deraa

SEA

Beisan

Nablus

River Jordan

Jerash

Tel Aviv
Jaffa

Amman

Ramallah
Lydda
Jericho
Jerusalem
Bethlehem

Dead Sea

Hebron

Gaza

TRANS-JORDAN

El Arish

EGYPT

Negev Desert

Sinai Desert

Petra
Maan

The frontier of the Palestine Mandate

The proposed Jewish State, 1937, and

The proposed Arab State, 1937

The proposed area to remain under British control

Registered Land in Jewish Possession, 1930

| 0 | 10 | 20 | 30 | 40 |

miles

Akaba

THE UN PARTITION
PROPOSAL OF 1947
AND THE ISRAELI
CONQUESTS OF 1948

LEBANON

Tyre

• Kuneitra

SYRIA

Nahariya
Acre
• Safed

Sea of
Galilee

Haifa
Tiberias
Nazareth

MEDITERRANEAN

SEA

Hadera
• Bet Shean
(Beisan)

Jenin

Netanya
• Tulkarm

• Nablus

Tel Aviv
Jaffa

THE WEST
BANK

JORDAN

River

Lydda
Ramla

Jordan

• Amman

• Jericho

Jerusalem

• Hebron

Gaza

Ein
Gedi

Dead
Sea

Beersheba

El Arish •

EGYPT

Sinai Desert

Negev
Desert

Boundary of the British
Palestine Mandate, 1922–1948

The territory of the State of
Israel as proposed by the United
Nations in November 1947

The proposed Arab State

Jerusalem and its suburbs; to be an
international zone

Territory beyond the United Nations line
conquered by Israel, 1948–1949

The frontier of the State of Israel according
to the Armistice agreements of 1949

0   10   20   30   40
miles

Eilat •
• Akaba

Preface:

The Cenotaph and the House

THE LITTLE cenotaph shares a playground with painted slides and seesaws and a battered tin horse, in a backwater between the Jerusalem bus station and the television studios. The legend running round its base reads: 'Near this spot the Holy City was surrendered to the 60th London Division, 9th December 1917. Erected by their comrades to those officers, NCOs and men who fell in fighting for Jerusalem.' There were doubts after the Great War about how to commemorate this sacrifice. The final, modest design of the cenotaph was chosen only after grander memorials, including one to rival Nelson's Column in Trafalgar Square, had been rejected as offensive to Muslim taste. Even the British lions in the final plan by Lutyens and Wallcousins were thought too assertive, and the only decorations engraved on the stone are the repeated outlines of Knight-Crusaders, faceless but in full armour.[1]

The former Government House, on a hill to the south of Jerusalem, is now the headquarters of the United Nations. Construction of the building, also the Residence, was long delayed, and the first three High Commissioners ruled Palestine for ten years from the former German army headquarters in a converted hospice. It was only after the ceiling fell into the High Commissioner's bed during an earthquake in 1927 – His Excellency being absent on leave – that the Treasury funded a new building. The veranda was designed to overlook the Judean desert and the Old City, now hidden behind a tangle of unpruned trees and bushes. The sunken English garden has survived, but the water courses and the fountains are dry, the tennis courts are framed by advertisements for Rollerblade skates, and blue UN shirts hang drying on the terraces. In the entrance hall, photographs show UN soldiers under fire during the Six Days War of 1967, when the building was overrun in turn by Jordanian and Israeli troops. The regimental plaques lining the corridors, like the flags overlooking the council chamber, are those of UN member states. All that remains of the original furnishings, looted in the wars, is a tall chimneypiece of blue Armenian tiles. The former ballroom is a staff lounge and bar, and a fluorescent strip lights what was once the minstrel's gallery.

Unwept, unhonoured and off the tourist map, the cenotaph and Government House are relics of an episode in late colonial history which was controversial from the start and ended in a stark admission of failure. Together with seventy indestructible police forts at strategic crossroads, a few inscriptions, street names, red pillar boxes and manhole covers which still carry the names of Midlands' plumbing firms, they are all that is now visible of thirty years of British rule in Palestine.

The Israel–Arab conflict has brought this period under microscopic scrutiny. There is a vast scholarly literature, almost all of which, whether in English, Hebrew or Arabic, centres on high policy and its effects. Far less has been written about the men who actually governed Palestine.

British officials in Palestine – and their critics – described themselves repeatedly as umpires, 'holding the ring', between Arabs and Jews. That even-handedness has been disputed, or rather inverted. Jewish and Arab polemic presented neatly symmetrical cases against British rule. Britain was indicted for double treachery, for betraying a dual obligation: self-determination for the Arabs, a National Home for the Jews. The Arabs accused Britain of promising Palestine to both sides (the question of whether the 1916 McMahon letters, which promised the Arabs self-rule across the Middle East, did or did not include Palestine). The Jews blamed Britain for reneging on its promises to the Zionists. The Arabs were incensed by British encouragement of Jewish immigration, the Jews by the imposition of immigration quotas. The Arabs protested at the suppression of the Arab Revolt, the Jews were outraged by the naval blockade of immigrant ships during the Nazi period and after the Holocaust. British officials were accused of favouring one or the other side – a policy, it was argued, that underlay every administrative act. Palestinian Arabs accused British officials of deliberately keeping their children in a state of ignorance, in order to advance Jewish interests and delay Palestinian national development. Jews argued that the same officials deliberately created chaos at the end of the Mandate in order to assist an Arab invasion. Neither argument has any documentary basis, though there was a rationale behind British neglect of Arab education, and the Mandate ended in disorder.[2] But propaganda and polemics were essential weapons in the battle for Palestine, waged in the parliaments and press in the West long before it was fought out in the cities and countryside of Palestine.

The officials of the Mandate had to carry out policies about which they often had misgivings, and sometimes (in the case of Jews and Arabs in the administration) divided loyalties, according to a colonial code inappropriate to both the period and the place, on a financial shoestring. How they did so has rarely been the object of enquiry. The only High Commissioner to have rated a properly documented biography is Herbert Samuel, since he was a British politician whose chequered term of office as a colonial ruler was only a chapter in a longer career.[3] The few studies which have appeared on subjects like the land question, health policies and rural government are highly specialized, and make little reference to the cultural and social context of colonial rule, or to the education, experience and background of Palestine's rulers. Memoirs and diaries of the period – many published years later, or posthumously – remind us forcibly that we no longer share any of the beliefs which enabled colonial officials to govern foreign peoples for their supposed benefit.

This book is an attempt to penetrate beyond the familiar claims and counter-claims, indictments and defences, and to try to put together a portrait of British rule in Palestine from the moment in early 1917 when Commonwealth soldiers struggled up the coast from the desert, until the last High Commissioner, Sir Alan Cunningham, having delivered a final address – an apology for British rule rather than a defence – left for England in the spring of 1948. It is, inevitably, selective in its approach. The first chapter looks at the genesis of the Mandate and the problems it posed for the British colonial official. The second describes the experiences of the soldiers who conquered Palestine, the

interim rule of the military and the emergence of a colonial administration staffed chiefly by men whose training had not prepared them
for the complexities of Palestine. Chapter 3 looks at how they tried to
cope with the two main subjects of conflict between Arabs and Jews:
immigration and land. The fourth chapter describes the patchy record
of the Mandate in promoting welfare in two key areas: health and education. The fifth shows how – together with the Army and Navy – the
Mandate government used coercion when legislation and diplomacy
failed to control nationalist rebellion. I have tried to keep to an overall
chronology, though there are inevitable overlaps.

In surveying this history I have kept my focus almost entirely on
British officials in Palestine and used their reports, papers, diaries,
letters, minutes and memoirs as sources; it is their experience, their
views of the rival communities, their reflections on the problems of the
country which I describe. Jews and Arabs appear primarily through
British eyes. British government policy on Palestine, so often analysed,
is merely outlined. Examining the familiar history of the Arab–Israel
conflict from this angle suggests, I think, additional reasons why the
Jews in Palestine were able to turn numerical and political weakness
into strength, and for the catastrophe which overtook the Palestinian
Arabs.

I

The Genesis of the Mandate

PALESTINE WAS one of a number of territories entrusted – 'mandated' – to British rule by the League of Nations after the First World War, to be governed until their peoples were judged capable of governing themselves. By 1947 it was the only such territory in the Middle East not to have won independence, since no step towards self-government was acceptable to both Palestine's Arab majority and Jewish minority.[1] The strategic advantages in prolonging British control of Palestine were eventually outweighed by the problems of controlling it. The Mandate was abandoned six months after the United Nations vote to partition Palestine in November 1947, in what was probably the most shamefaced British withdrawal from any of its colonies, protectorates and mandates. The purpose of the Mandate was never entirely clear to most of those serving in Palestine, for there was as much reluctance to spell out British interests clearly as there had been to portray symbols of British power openly on the cenotaph.

The Mandate system of government in the Middle East was a compromise between annexation based on military conquest and the granting of independence to the peoples of the former Ottoman Empire. In the political climate following the First World War, that of Wilson's Fourteen Points and the right of self-determination for subject peoples, conquest no longer meant the right to govern in perpetuity land occupied in war. Britain's reason for being in Palestine, apart from preparing it for independence, was the encouragement, under British protection, of Jewish settlement; on the rare occasions when British officials in Palestine and the Colonial Office tried to formulate their ultimate objective, they argued that they were creating a 'composite state', Arab and Jewish, or, in the spirit of the League of Nations, 'a trial of internationalism'.[2]

But within twenty years, the recognition of unbridgeable divisions between the peoples of Palestine led to a British proposal to partition the country. As this could only have been imposed by force, the idea was gradually abandoned, and Britain finally handed over responsibility to the United Nations.

Britain saw the control of Palestine as a strategic necessity in the imperial context. It was also probably more intimately known – in the physical sense – than any country in the Empire. English travellers, scholars and soldiers had charted every corner of the Holy Land long before the defence of Suez, and protection of the route to India, defined Britain's regional ambitions more clearly. During the nineteenth century, antiquarianism, the passion for authenticating the Bible, and Evangelical hopes for the conversion of the Jews, had all inspired British visitors and missionaries. By the twentieth, these concerns were largely irrelevant. Archaeologists had replaced the antiquarians, and provided the ordnance maps which guided the soldiers of 1917. Theories about the racial characteristics of ancient peoples had become more popular than Bible studies. Missionaries reported despondently that few souls were to be saved in Palestine; their work in schools and hospitals had to be its own reward. Yet it was still a country which evoked a proprietary, paternalist interest in British travellers and scholars and, in 1917, in the soldiers and colonial officials who succeeded them.

Edmund Allenby, the soldier under whose command Palestine was conquered, attempted to identify the sites of his battles (sometimes wrongly) by reference to biblical campaigns. Edward Keith-Roach, who became one of Palestine's longest-serving colonial officials, found that a tombstone at the entrance to the Holy Sepulchre commemorated a Crusader ancestor of his by marriage, and determined 'to dedicate himself to the service of the city'. The members of the Bishopric established eighty years earlier with the hope of bringing the Anglican faith to a Muslim-dominated Holy Land, now looked forward eagerly to a Christian regime in Palestine. The Knight-Crusader was sketched on the cenotaph – if only in outline.

The realities of Palestine swiftly dispelled these associations. Allenby's military administration had little sympathy with the Zionist

Jews, who took their Palestinian ancestry literally. Keith-Roach ended his service with bitter criticism of the 'uninspired' leadership he blamed for the failure of the Mandate; and in 1933 the Bishop in Jerusalem, George Graham-Brown, reported: 'Islam is endeavouring to make it a stronghold. 60% of the population of Jerusalem is Jewish. The forces of Islam and Judaism have invaded the stronghold of Christianity.'[3]

The strategic interests behind British rule in Palestine remained constant throughout the Mandate. Palestine provided a foothold – the only one apart from Cyprus – in the Eastern Mediterranean. It was a buffer between the Suez Canal and enemies to the north. It was a reserve base near Egypt but independent of Anglo-Egyptian relations, and it provided an overland route to Iraq and its oil reserves. Developments during the Mandate – from the Italian invasion of Ethiopia in 1935 to the German North African campaign during the Second World War – underscored its importance as a military base. After the war, the British Chiefs of Staff strongly opposed any withdrawal from the country, which they saw as 'vital to all Commonwealth defence strategy'.[4]

The official reason for British rule, as expressed in 1917, was far less straightforward. The Balfour Declaration, the first document to define Britain's intentions in Palestine, was issued by the British government on 2 November 1917, a few weeks before Allenby's entry into Jerusalem. The Declaration, issued by the British Foreign Secretary, was both a propaganda move, inspired by the needs of the moment, and a statement of policy based on Britain's longterm aims in the Middle East. Because of its ambivalent and contradictory phrasing, as well as its controversial nature, it was to be the subject of dispute during the entire period of the Mandate.

The Declaration committed Britain to the establishment of a 'National Home' for the Jews in Palestine, without compromising either the rights of those Jews who were citizens of other countries or the 'civil and religious' rights of 'the non-Jewish communities in Palestine' – a reference to the Palestine Arabs. According to Lloyd George, then Prime Minister, the Declaration was intended, in the short term, to secure the support of the Jews both in the Allied and the enemy camps. The thinking behind it had evolved over the previous two years, and related to the need for a reliable client population in a region of strategic importance. Britain was not prepared to tolerate possible French control of the area along the Canal, the Arabian peninsula and the Persian Gulf.

November 1917 was a critical moment in the First World War. The trench war in France was deadlocked; the United States had entered the war in April, but it took many months of training before its troops were ready to fight in Europe. The Tsar's forces, Britain's Russian allies, had been beaten back by the Germans and, after the March Revolution, it was feared that they were no longer reliable partners. The Turks were still in the field under German command.

British intelligence had learned that the Germans were courting the Zionists – the Jewish nationalist movement – with promises of post-war support. Though the Zionist Jews resident in Palestine were a tiny minority, their colonizing skills were impressive, and the military Intelligence they had provided to Britain had proved valuable. But there were also other, less clearly defined concepts behind the framing of the Balfour Declaration.

The British politicians and diplomats who made the Zionists their clients in 1917 shared two assumptions: the first was that 'world Jewry' was a powerful force which could affect the fortunes of war; and the second, that most Jews were active supporters of Zionism. The first assumption originated in myth and prejudice, rather than rational assessment. The second was an exaggeration. While the idea of the return to Zion pervaded Jewish religious tradition, the Zionist movement had recruited few members in the Jewish communities in countries outside Eastern Europe. Assimilated Jews in England were often vociferously anti-Zionist, fearing that to identify with the new creed would call their loyalty in question and endanger their own rights (a fear well known to the British government and therefore explicitly addressed in the Declaration's reference to Jews in other countries).

Some eighty years earlier, Lord Palmerston had established the Anglican Bishopric in Jerusalem after he was told that the Jews, whose conversion would both hasten the Second Coming and enable Britain to win a foothold in Palestine, were on the verge of returning to the Holy Land. This rumour had been spread by two missionaries who had misinterpreted the echo of a Jewish theological debate accessible only to the initiate. The much more important decision to anchor British rule in Palestine on Zionism was based on more varied sources of information, and also, paradoxically, on prejudices about the Jews in general.

Belief in the 'international power of the Jews', as Robert Cecil at the Foreign Office termed it, and allegedly widespread Jewish support for the Zionist idea, recur frequently in the British diplomatic dispatches of the period. Prominent Jews in Germany, Turkey, Russia and the United States were all seen not only as capable of influencing the high policy of the country of which they were citizens, but also as belonging to a shadowy, international network working for specific Jewish interests. Gerald Fitzmaurice, the Chief Dragoman of the Constantinople Embassy and adviser on Turkish matters to Reginald Hall, head of Intelligence at the Admiralty, held strong views on the Jews as a political force, manipulating the great powers in the Jewish interest and working for the creation of an autonomous Jewish state in Palestine. A paper by Hall, written in 1916, suggested that Palestine's importance for the Jews could make them useful allies. Their power was sometimes ludicrously exaggerated: Hugh O'Beirne, a senior official in the Foreign Office, argued: 'If we could offer the Jews an arrangement as to Palestine, we might . . . conceivably be able to strike a bargain with them as to withdrawing their support for the Young Turk government, which would automatically collapse.'[5]

The country where Jewish support was seen as most important to the Allied cause at the time of the Declaration was Russia. Russian Jews had suffered greatly from the Tsar's regime during the war, with over three million driven from their homes. Many of them regarded the Germans, naturally enough, as liberators. Jews in Western Europe, serving in armies on the other side, saw the Germans as enemies. But to the British official mind, whether hostile or sympathetic, Jews were part of one brotherhood. The British Ambassador in St Petersburg, Buchanan, had recommended that the Tsar moderate his policies, as Jews 'exercised powerful influence on the money markets of the world'. The Tsar did not respond, but the Russian Revolution of March 1917 suggested another role for 'world Jewry' in the minds of British politicians, who had noted that many members of the revolutionary leadership were Jews. By April 1917 Robert Cecil, Arthur Nicholson and Ronald Graham, leading officials at the Foreign Office, were all suggesting using Zionism – Jewish nationalism – to counteract what they believed to be the growing influence of Jewish

Communist leaders in Russia. By October, they were urging the British government to support the Zionist cause publicly so that the Jews of Russia, whose sufferings had 'deepened and intensified their national aspirations' could spearhead a 'powerful active pro-ally propaganda throughout the world'.[6]

By November 1917, therefore, it was believed that to neutralize Jewish power as a potentially destructive force linked with Communism, it was necessary to divert it to a safer goal: Zionism. This idea was to survive the war. Its classic expression was in an article by Winston Churchill, in the *Illustrated London Herald* in February 1920, in which he wrote of the 'struggle for the soul of the Jewish people' between Communism and Zionism. However, the Russian Jews who supported Communism were violent enemies of Zionism and were unmoved by the Declaration; in any case, five days after its publication, the Bolsheviks seized power and took Russia out of the war. Yet the belief in the power of the Jews, whether as revolutionaries or financiers, continued. Ronald Graham now suggested that by offering 'the Jew' Palestine, it might be possible to persuade Russian Jews to obstruct German exploitation of the grain resources of the Ukraine. Charles Webster made the same point to British delegates at the Paris Peace Conference. Once more, this misread the options of the Jewish minority in Russia. Those Jews who were prominent in the grain trade could scarcely risk opposing an occupying power which had treated them far better than their previous rulers. All in all, there was never any rational indication that Jewish minorities in Allied and enemy countries, given totally different political affiliations and options, could act in concert. In British eyes, however, American–Jewish capitalist financiers, Russian–Jewish entrepreneurs in the grain trade, Communist politicians, Jewish supporters of the Young Turk regime – all belonged to one group, one coherent, calculating entity with its hidden agenda: 'world Jewry'.

Though there was no real foundation for this belief, there had indeed been evidence of the international solidarity of several Jewish families and organizations during the half-century preceding the First World War. Jewish financiers, the Rothschilds in particular, provided valuable services to the rulers of the countries of which they were citizens. During the Russo-Japanese war, Jewish bankers had objected *en masse* to lending financial help to Tsarist Russia, which had instituted anti-Jewish legislation and condoned much violence against the Jews. During the First World War, the American–Jewish banker Jacob Schiff, of Kuhn Loeb, refused to underwrite any loan from which Russia – home of the pogroms – would benefit. (Yet another prominent Jew with different priorities, Rufus Isaacs – later, as Lord Reading, to become British Viceroy of India – raised a $500 million loan in the US for this purpose in 1915.[7]) In 1860, the Alliance Israelite Universelle had been established, an organization which provided support, both diplomatic and educational, from the Jews of the West to less privileged Jews in Eastern Europe and the Ottoman Empire. Without the support of the Alliance, the earliest Jewish colonies would never have succeeded in establishing a foothold in Palestine in the last part of the nineteenth century.

But the Alliance, like other international Jewish organizations, stood for the integration of the Jews into their host countries, and for their political emancipation, not for the creation of a separate Jewish state. When delegates from the Alliance and other Jewish organizations appeared at the Paris Peace Conference, they succeeded in having safeguards for Jewish minorities written into the treaties that recognized the newly independent and reconstituted states of Eastern and Central Europe, not in pleading for a separate Jewish homeland. It was perhaps not surprising, however, that British diplomats did not distinguish between international Jewish organizations of this kind and the very different Zionist movement.

What appears to have confirmed belief in Jewish power irrevocably, where the British government was concerned, was the skilful rhetoric of the Zionist leadership and its supporters. Zionism, at this stage of its development, was scarcely two decades old as a political movement. It had few financial resources; most of the assimilated and wealthy Jews of Europe and the United States were indifferent, if not hostile, to its message. Much depended on the ability of its leaders, Chaim Weizmann in particular, to convince Western governments not only of the vulnerability of the Jews in many parts of the world and of their need for a country of their own, but also of their potential usefulness to whichever power would provide them with one. They certainly did not point out that 'international Jewish power' was a myth. It has been observed that: 'Weizmann possessed a personal magnetism that could win over Balfour and Lloyd George and persuade them in defiance of reality that behind him stood a great force, "world Jewry", which could help sway the political balance in Russia and America decisively in Britain's favour.'[8] Given their prior beliefs, British Intelligence officers were easily seduced by this message, particularly since Bolshevism was regarded as a direct threat to the Empire.

Weizmann and leading American Zionists encouraged the British belief that the Jews of southern Russia could block German access to vital grain supplies. To Israel Rosov, head of the Zionist Central Committee in Petrograd, Weizmann cabled: 'Considering the great influence our people have in these branches, we appeal to you to use all your influence and energy at whatever cost preventing the Germans from accomplishing this scheme.' A similar appeal was made by the American Zionist leader Stephen Wise. Copies of these cables were sent to the Foreign Office, and were the subject of a War Office memorandum on the importance of Zionist support for the war effort. There is no evidence that the appeals could have had any result, but this was irrelevant.[9]

Richard Meinertzhagen, Chief Political Officer to the British military administration in Palestine, and a confidant of Chaim Weizmann, was certainly persuaded that Zionism was 'constructive Bolshevism' and said that Weizmann agreed with him. After the war, the Zionist leader had simultaneously to alarm and to allay the fears of the British regarding the Bolshevik bogey. In a letter written in late 1919 to General Clayton, Chief Political Officer during the Palestine campaign and in charge of Intelligence in Egypt, Weizmann pointed out that whatever the prominence of a handful of Jews in the revolutionary movement, the Jews of Russia were overwhelmingly anti-Bolshevik. But in the same letter, he suggested that they might yet be driven to Bolshevism by despair:

> The world will never be at peace as long as there are fifteen million intelligent people who have bled in this war . . . and will be exposed . . . to the same sufferings and humiliations as before. If the Jews are disappointed this time there will be too much bitterness produced in the new world, and instead of a valuable constructive element, especially in the Near East, they will be driven into anarchy and Bolshevism.[10]

The Zionist representatives at the Paris Peace Conference had an agenda which fitted the notion of the Jews as an international force.

They spoke in the name of Jews everywhere, they claimed to represent an entire nation dispersed throughout the world, and, as has been pointed out, they 'insisted on the existence of a Jewish people independent of citizenship, and could therefore be expected to render services which depended upon international connections and an international point of view'.[11] Zionist polemic confirmed the beliefs of those who thought of the Jews as a world power which it could be advantageous to recruit. It was not until the rise of Nazism, twenty years later, that this belief was revealed to be grotesquely mistaken. Neither Jewish international organizations, nor influential individuals, nor the Jewish community in Palestine under British rule (since immigration was not under their control) were able to save more than a few thousand Jews from their Nazi persecutors. But the supposed strength of 'international Jewry' became the ideological basis for genocide in Nazi propaganda. As a historian of Jewish politics of the period has written:

> The belief in Jewish power, exaggerated to the level of myth, had permitted Jewish organisations and advocates to intervene at crucial moments and at the highest government levels . . . to win grandiose promises with regard to the future. Few realised just how much this myth, albeit a source of political strength, was still more – given the essential weakness it disguised – a source of danger without limit.[12]

One more important factor appears to have influenced the British decision to adopt the Zionists as British wards. During the First World War the support for Zionism of several prominent British Jews, unexpected as it was both to the British Cabinet and to the (mainly Russian Jewish) Zionist leadership, buttressed the view that the Zionists could be useful allies, a reliable client population in a volatile region of strategic importance. Chief among the British Jews championing this view was Herbert Samuel (Postmaster-General and, later, Home Secretary), who in 1915 had submitted an emotional memorandum to the Cabinet expounding Zionism to his colleagues. Samuel wrote of 'twelve million Jews looking towards Zion' (actual members of the Zionist movement at this stage numbered some hundred thousand). While in political terms Samuel's 1915 memorandum was premature, after the Sykes–Picot Agreement of 1917 – in which Britain and France partitioned the Middle East into their spheres of influence – and in a rewritten form stressing the British interest in supporting Zionism, it became essential. The Prime Minister in 1915, Asquith, had concluded from Samuel's impassioned memorandum only that – quoting Disraeli – 'race is everything'. Lloyd George, the Prime Minister in 1917, was more impressed by the practical benefits Samuel suggested would be gained for Britain by supporting Zionism, and Samuel was duly appointed first High Commissioner to Palestine.

The nature of the 'National Home' to be set up in Palestine was left undefined, and neither side was concerned to elaborate. British and Zionist leaders rarely spoke at this time of the creation of a Jewish state in Palestine. Britain wanted to prolong colonial rule there for as long as possible; the Zionists, to increase their meagre numbers by immigration, and their territorial base by land purchase. Both therefore had an interest in procrastinating on the issue of self-government – the question for whom, exactly, Palestine was to be held in trust.

For there was another set of obligations involved in the Palestine Mandate. The Mandate system evolved after the war was over held out the promise of eventual self-government for subject peoples in Africa and Asia. Britain had made commitments to the Arabs of the Middle East; but because of the conflicts and pressures surrounding the creation of the League, not all the political implications of the Mandates were spelled out – least of all in the case of Palestine. In Article 22 of the League Covenant, on which the entire system of Mandatory Territories were based, the Balfour Declaration was ignored or overlooked. The stipulation that the wishes of the various communities be 'a principal consideration' in the selection of the Mandatory Power was similarly passed over.

The author of the Declaration saw quite clearly the contradiction of Britain's position on self-government where Palestine was concerned. Nor was Balfour under any illusions as to the reaction of the Arabs of Palestine. As he had written to Lloyd George in 1917: 'Zionism is more important than the "desires and prejudices" of the 700,000 Arabs who now inhabit it.' In 1919 he added: 'The weak point of our position of course is that in the case of Palestine we deliberately and rightly decline to accept the principle of self-determination . . . our justification is that we regard Palestine as absolutely exceptional, as the Jews outside Palestine are of world importance.' The historic claim of the Jews would predominate, wrote Balfour, 'provided that a home can be given them without either dispossessing or oppressing the present inhabitants'.[13]

The conceptual basis to the Mandate was therefore that the Jews (as a historic world body) were to reclaim their ancestral homeland – an essentially active role. The Palestine Arabs were to be protected, and not to be dispossessed or oppressed – a passive role. International control of this process was to be ensured by requiring that the Mandatory Power report yearly to the League of Nations. But the articles of the Mandate gave the administrators very little guidance as to how Palestine was actually to be governed.

The Mandate idea was associated primarily with the partition of the African continent, and its main concerns were allegedly the welfare of the indigenous inhabitants and the protection of free trade. The former Turkish possessions in the Middle East, including Palestine, all fell into the highest – 'A' – of three categories of Mandates, graded according to Western assessment of their maturity and fitness for eventual independence. There was no obvious relevance, in the definitions of the Mandatory responsibilities as described in the Covenant, to Palestine or other ex-Turkish territories. The Mandates were framed to prevent such abuses of African colonial rule as the continuance of slavery and the slave trade, the use of forced labour for private advantage, and the use of colonial territories and colonial manpower to reinforce the armed strength of the colonial power. These, it has been observed, were all basically negative injunctions, while the positive recommendations were far vaguer. They included the obligation to 'undertake to promote to the utmost the material and moral well-being and social progress of the inhabitants'; rather strikingly, there was no reference to the training of the subjects of the Mandatory in the exercise of political responsibility.

The idea of governing beneficiaries as 'a sacred trust for civilization' – the words of Article 22 – may have meant, as has been cynically argued, to ensure access to raw materials by the industrial nations of the West. But Palestine had none of these: as against its strategic value, its only eventual economic importance was that it became the terminus of the oil pipeline from Iraq. Britain's sole investment in Palestine, apart from the railways, a road system and the police forts (all contributions to security), was to be, in the mid-1930s, the Haifa port which served both the Army and the oil refineries nearby. There was only a limited market for British goods.[14]

Hence the reluctance of the Treasury to invest in the country, its determination to squeeze the people of Palestine, Arabs and Jews alike, for every penny possible, to save on services and, perhaps most important in the political sense, to encourage Zionist investment as an alternative to financing the development of Palestine at the British taxpayers' expense. In adopting this policy, the British government set Mandate economic principles aside. Under the terms of the Mandate Palestine was supposed to be financially autonomous; the Mandatory was to bear the cost of defence only provisionally; and the Mandatory Power was supposed to guarantee loans for the development of the territory. While Palestine had a separate budget, and its own currency, the currency system was restricted, and the Treasury controlled the budget for the best part of two decades.[15] It was argued by the second High Commissioner, Lord Plumer, an experienced soldier, that the system set up to defend Palestine and ensure the rapid passage of British forces was not primarily in the interests of the Palestinians – Arabs and Jews at that time – who had to shoulder much of the cost. But the British Treasury, in line with general colonial policy, demanded that Palestine balance its budgets. It made Mandatory attempts to extend development projects or social services as difficult as possible, and rarely granted development loans. Even the Residence, symbol of colonial power, had to double as Government House, with many offices housed in a wing of the King David Hotel. Though often planned, a proper government centre was never built.

The more general provisions of Article 22 of the League Covenant were incorporated, together with the Balfour Declaration, into the articles of the Mandate in 1922. The Jews were given an advisory role in government through a body to be known as the Jewish Agency, which represented not only Palestine but also world Jewry, or the Jews outside Palestine, hence bringing a large, somewhat ill-defined partner into all discussions and policy decisions on the running of the country. The Palestinian Arabs, who were not seen as a discrete historical or political community by the British, were given no such representation, nor did any article of the Mandate refer specifically to them. In keeping with the 'historical' aspect of the Declaration, Article 21 went into enormous detail, in eight separate subclauses, as to what was to be done regarding antiquities, their preservation, and the licensing of archaeologists. Antiquity was spoken for. The Arab population of Palestine was not.

Such was the brief handed to the British administrators of Palestine, to cope with as best they could. Seven High Commissioners, and many longterm colonial Civil Servants who spent two decades or more of their official lives in Palestine, as well as others whose stay was shorter, were to try to resolve its ambiguities. It became rapidly apparent to the Mandate administration that the Palestine Arabs were totally opposed to Zionist settlement and its support by Britain. As this called in question the very validity of the Mandate, repeated attempts were made to reformulate its provisions and to make some explicit reference to the Palestine Arabs as candidates for self-government. In 1919, and again in 1921, when responsibility for Palestine passed from the Foreign Office to the newly constituted Middle East Department of the Colonial Office, statements were made in London to the Arabs promising eventual representation in a legislative assembly. In 1923 and again in 1935 the respective High Commissioners – Samuel and Wauchope – made proposals for the setting up of such a body, in which Arabs and Jews would participate and thus share in the government of the country. The first attempt was scuttled by the Arab leadership, the second by the Jews. The Arabs refused to give any legitimacy to the Jews in 1923, the Jews refused proportional representation and insisted on parity in 1935. The result was that Palestine, though it was an 'A' Mandate on paper, remained in effect a Crown Colony.

Since no representative institutions emerged, Palestine was governed according to the 1922 Order in Council which conferred absolute power on the High Commissioner, and ensured that all operative decisions remained in the hands of Mandate officials. Legislation was the prerogative of the High Commissioner and his advisers: the government of Palestine. The special status accorded the Jewish Agency enabled the Jews, both inside Palestine and outside it, to make their views and suggestions constantly known to the administration. Inevitably, therefore, the Mandate government had to offer some compensation to the Arabs. It attempted to deflect Arab opposition on the two key questions of Jewish immigration and Arab land. The immigration laws were repeatedly reframed to limit the parameters of the 'National Home' in accordance with what was known as the 'economic absorptive capacity' of the country – a formula much disputed between the Mandatory and the Jews; and a series of laws, the 'Protection of Cultivators' ordinances, aimed to restrict the effects of

Jewish land purchases on the rural population. Ultimately these laws antagonized the Jews without satisfying the Arabs and were evaded or infringed by Arabs and Jews alike, often in collusion.

The chief problem for the administration in promoting the welfare of both the Arabs and the Jews of Palestine was the enormous difference between post-Ottoman Arab society and that of the immigrant Jews. In no part of the Empire had British administrators to govern two such different communities, divided not only by politics, religion, language and culture but by their economic and social organization and their political expectations and ambitions. The Arab urban élite, formerly represented in the Ottoman administration, was organized on traditional family and religious lines; the Zionist leadership, within the framework of Jewish political parties which originated in Eastern Europe. The Arab rural masses lived in a pre-industrial society, on what was primarily subsistence agriculture; Jewish farmers introduced advanced methods of farming and communal settlements based on European socialist theory. At the outset of the Mandate no modern institutions for the organization of labour or social security existed among the Arabs, while within a few years, the Jews had established a tightly organized society on Western lines, with its own educational, health and labour facilities financed largely by the Zionist organization outside Palestine and by communal self-taxation. Under these circumstances, the administration's main responsibility was to the Arabs. While Arab health improved dramatically, the outstanding failure was in education. Despite Arab pleas and protests, only 65 per cent of Arab boys were at school by the end of the Mandatory period, and two thirds of the Arab population were still illiterate – most of them peasant women. Facilities for technical training were few, and there was no Arab university.

British rule of Palestine began with a military administration, and many ex-soldiers stayed on after the civil administration began. Six of the seven High Commissioners were former soldiers. The garrison of Palestine had to be reinforced repeatedly, notably after the Arab attacks on Jews of 1929 and during the Arab Revolt of 1936–9. At that time, British training of Jewish military units began. It expanded during the Second World War, particularly during the period when a German invasion seemed near. Palestine became an important military centre, which boosted the local economy and led to a temporary truce in the Arab–Jewish conflict.

The Mandate ended in civil war between Arabs and Jews. Violence was never far from the surface and its suppression never far from the concerns of the Palestine government. Martial law was rarely introduced as such ('military control' was the euphemistic alternative), but successive Emergency Regulations replaced the rule of law. The decline of the British-led bi-national police force was a clear indication of the breakdown of the idea of Jewish–Arab co-operation. The suppression of the Arab Revolt, and later conflicts with Jewish militants and terrorists, brought the Mandate administration, in its last decade, into a head-on confrontation with both the subject peoples. Too late, it became clear that British interests depended on the resolution of a conflict which – in the framing of the Mandate – had been ignored.

2

From Conquest to Colony

THE PRICE of British rule in Palestine was more than thirteen thousand British and Commonwealth soldiers' lives, lost in the Palestine campaign of the First World War. At the war's end, the British and Commonwealth forces left behind, as victims both of battle and disease, 12,640 men: in graves on the Sinai coast and outside Gaza and Beersheba, in Jerusalem on Mount Scopus (with a small, separate cemetery for Indian soldiers to the south of the city) and in Ramle and Haifa to the north. Numbers of Turkish soldiers lay among them; 499 bodies were never found. John Burnet, the designer of the Scopus cemetery, made gestures to the 'oriental' in his Palestine war cemeteries and memorial chapels, in the use of local stone, chiselled by Arab masons. He also planned the Scopus chapel, with its dome, to resemble the Hagia Sofia Byzantine church in Istanbul – a nod to Eastern Christianity. In his report on the Scopus cemetery, Burnet mentioned the need to take into consideration the fact that Palestine was 'the country of another faith'. In case all these conciliatory gestures were misunderstood, the cemeteries were surrounded by high protective walls.[1]

The Palestine campaign ended four hundred years of Turkish and Muslim rule over the area demarcating Arabia from Africa – from 1902 known as the Middle East. Victory ensured British control of Suez and the route to India, and pre-empted French domination of the region. In the histories of the First World War, the campaign figures as a sideshow to the European theatre, as the Turks, under their German commanders, were dislodged from one vital stronghold after another. Early in the war the capture of Basra secured the Persian Gulf. After many setbacks, Baghdad, the centre of oil-rich Mesopotamia (later

Iraq), followed in early 1917. The British official press representative accompanying the Army wrote that now: 'British prestige was maintained among the races governed. They were more influenced through the Mesopotamian campaign than that taking part in France; the occupation of Baghdad was more important than the Hindenburg line.' This 'saved the Empire much anxiety over our position in the Tigris and Euphrates valleys and probably prevented unrest on the frontiers of India'.[2]

Palestine was the focus of the next Allied drive, by the Egyptian Expeditionary Force made up of British, Australian, New Zealand and Indian troops. A Turkish attack through Sinai on the Suez Canal had long been feared by the British Army in Egypt, and was only finally blocked when troops moved into the Sinai desert in the spring of 1917. They were supported by a labour corps which included the Egyptian fellahin, who extended the British railway northwards, and the Raratonga islanders, who unloaded supplies arriving at the Jaffa roadstead at skilled and muscular speed.

The battle for Palestine was to be long drawn out – the whole country was brought under British control only a short time before the end of the war itself – and nowhere more than in the desert. Gavin Richardson of the King's Own Scottish Borderers reported that walking in the sand of Sinai was, for a Highlands shepherd, like walking in snow: two steps forward and one back. The infantry wore detachable wire soles over their boots, like snowshoes. They were weighed down with haversacks, ammunition pouches, water bottles, trenching spades, bayonets and rifles, with only one thin blanket for covering for the cold desert night. To meet the political deadline of 'Jerusalem by Christmas' – Lloyd George's instruction to Allenby – the same men were to be sent up into the Judean hills in mid-winter, in rain and sleet, wearing the same thin desert tunics. Greatcoats had been left behind at the Suez Canal, with all heavy equipment, for greater mobility. Jerusalem was a symbolic prize to raise Allied morale, not a strategic necessity. The last European to invade Palestine, Napoleon, had bypassed it altogether.

In the desert the soldiers endured heat, thirst and septic sores from sand abrading the skin and then entering the wounds. Some of the battalions, like the British Yeomanry, farmers and tenants together with their horses, had no more than a week or two of military training behind them. The historian of the British cavalry, the Marquess of Anglesey, deplores their general 'unfitness for service' and 'lack of officer material'. The yeomen themselves tell a different story. J. W. Wintringham of the Lincolnshire Yeomanry describes in his memoir how the English horses arrived with legs swollen from the sea voyage, and suffered badly from the heat and flies. Each horse carried up to seventeen stone of equipment, stumbling and rearing when metal shoes caught in the rabbit netting which had been laid down across the sand. The Ford cars driven by officers did better. Both the English and the Australian horses – hardier and more suited to the terrain – which survived were sold off or abandoned after the campaign, to the abiding grief of their owners. Some efforts were made to save them from being sold to Egyptian gharri drivers and farmers, but 'most had to be left in a harsh foreign land, no longer in the care of British animal lovers but in the hands of a greedy and cruel race of people'. At a ceremony later in the war the yeomen handed over the remaining horses to the Indian cavalry, their spurs and saddlery were buried, and a memorial was erected. 'For cavalry they said there is no room, So we buried our spurs in a desert tomb', as the soldiers' jingle went. 'We got £38 14s. 8d. for four years' service,' Wintringham recorded bitterly.[3]

Once across the desert and moving up the coast of Palestine, the infantry fought desperate battles against the Turks, who were better armed and supplied, and well dug in. There were two unsuccessful attempts to break the siege of Gaza, which repeated the horrors of trench warfare in Europe – the command too far in the rear while suicidal attacks were ordered across open ground in broad daylight. In the trenches round Gaza, a first wave of sixty-five officers and men were blown up by four contact mines. 'The second wave passed over the bodies of their comrades without a moment's check into the trenches,' a survivor reported. The 4th Royal Scots, who had seen the mutilated condition of some of their dead left in Turkish hands at El Arish, took retribution at what the Army called Umbrella Hill, near Gaza, where few Turks captured remained alive. Between Sheria and Huj, further east, the Warwick and Worcester Yeomanry: 'sabred every artilleryman at his piece so that the guns all fell silent together'. One quarter of the Yeomanry died in these battles; the Scots had already lost two-thirds of their number in Gallipoli. At Huj, Robert Henley Wilson of the Berkshire Yeomanry, the son of a farmer, recorded a milder revenge on 'Johnny Turk': after eating fruit and quail they had found in the fields, the yeomen stole into the Turkish lines and removed lances and stirrups from the cavalry. Wilson took Zeiss fieldglasses from a Turkish cavalry officer and did not hand them in. He was indignant when, 'at the very first point-to-point I attended after the war, some crook pinched them out of their case'. Still suffering from malaria, he had returned to England to find that 'profiteering farmers at home had exploited the absence of others'.[4]

The deadlock round Gaza was eventually broken by Allenby, who replaced the high-handed Murray as head of the Expeditionary Force. Allenby had learned from his mistakes on the European front, moved his headquarters to the battlefield, and devised a new strategy which ended the suicidal onslaughts.[5] From then on, there was mobile warfare with a minimum of casualties. The Australian Light Horse under Chauvel won every one of its thirty-six battles, and lost few men. Australian, New Zealand and British cavalrymen swept round in an arc through Beersheba, cutting off the Turks in Gaza from their main supply route. In this campaign, and later in the north, Allied airmen, using a technique first tried against rebels in the Sudan, were active in reconnaissance and in pursuit, flying very low and emptying their machine-guns into the retreating enemy columns.

The combination of cavalry and airpower was unique in military history: 'The newest and the oldest arms met and mingled, and the result was a victory that will live in history,' wrote the correspondent of *The Nation*. The airmen who attacked the Turkish columns, exhilarated by their new skills, sometimes flew only seventy feet above ground, so low that, leaning from their cockpits, they could sometimes smell the meat cooking in towns below. They dropped bombs from only 1,500 feet, and strafed the retreating Turks with machine-gun fire. One pilot was shot down while trying to reignite his engine with his one remaining match. When flying over the battlefield, the airmen were so horrified at the look of the Turkish and German corpses their bombs had torn apart that they asked to be relieved from further sorties. The request was granted; perhaps an indication of the privileges of certain airmen, but also of the novelty of air warfare, and its lack of guidelines.

After the desert ordeal, and the battles for Gaza, the pastoral quality of Palestine's coastal plain was a relief. The Jewish settlements in the coastal plain, cottages with red-tiled roofs and white walls, reminded them of Europe. At Rishon le Zion, where the first Jewish colonists had settled thirty years earlier as viniculturists, under the patronage of the Baron Edmond de Rothschild, they were welcomed with 'buckets' of wine. It was an 'up to date place, with a barber, cafés, butcher, synagogue, and a huge distillery', Wilson recalled, the first 'civilized' place they had seen in eighteen months. The *Kia-Ora Coo-ee*, the Australian and New Zealand official magazine, reported the men's pleasant impression of the coastal plain, where Arab farmers grew crops of wheat and barley, and tended the orange orchards dotting the landscape.[6] A number of members of the Expeditionary Force, recalling the opportunities offered soldiers in South Africa after the Boer War, wanted to register as settlers. They were reminded that the ultimate ownership of Palestine had not yet been decided, and that war no longer won the victors the right to settlement. For several years after the war, none the less, the Treasury and the Colonial Office encouraged the immigration of Jewish ex-servicemen with 'special sentimental reasons for desiring to go to Palestine, and who were likely, politically and otherwise, to be a valuable element in the Palestine community'.[7]

The soldiers were not to linger in the pleasant landscape of the coast, and neither cavalry nor aircraft were of use during the painful winter ascent to Jerusalem, as the force made its way up the mountain tracks, dislodging loose boulders, in rain, cold and mud. The soldiers' boots fell apart at the soles and were tied on again with string. Deprived of tobacco, the men smoked tea leaves and cactus hedge roots. They barely glimpsed the enemy, for there were no pitched battles; the Turks emerged from behind the rocks, in the mist, only to snipe at them. The Judean hills reminded the Scots of the remotest parts of the Highlands, as the 'roads' marked on their maps turned out to be mere tracks between boulders. Half the ambulance carts of the mobile medical unit were soon broken, their wheels and axles twisted, and had to be abandoned; from then on, the unit relied on the camels – little seen before in the mountains – and mules, which carried supplies, guns and stretchers, and progressed at no more than half a mile an hour.

Throughout the campaign, an additional enemy was the insidious anopheles mosquito, which spread malaria. The sources of the swarms tormenting the soldiers ranged from the marshes on the coast and in the Jordan valley to the uncovered cisterns which provided Jerusalem and the other hill towns with their only water supply. The susceptible British and Commonwealth troops were prostrated in such numbers that special squads were sent out, as the fighting continued, to drain and clean swamps. Nets, repellents, clothing and drugs were distributed as routinely as ammunition; malarial diagnosis stations were set up, and treatment was given on the march. The narrow Auja river and its tributaries near Jaffa, occupied in 1918 after fierce fighting, were drained, filled and covered with oil by British and Sikh units. While cisterns were treated, a pipeline was laid from springs near Bethlehem to Jerusalem – the first outside water supply in the city's history since Roman times. Even so, there were thousands of primary cases of malaria in front-line troops between April and November 1918, and the New Zealand General Chaytor's force, dispatched to the Jordan valley, was infected as soon as it moved out of the protected area.[8]

Though the high season of imperalism was over, the Crusader image was still evoked in speeches and field sermons. On the eve of the second, disastrous battle for Gaza, a sermon was delivered to the Yeomanry by Reverend Spence, the Minister of Southdean Parish, who quoted the Twentieth Psalm ('Some trust in chariots, and some in horses'), and told them: 'In the Middle Ages you remember how the armies of Christendom came to this land to fight against the infidels for the possession of the Holy Places. And we too are Crusaders, soldiers of the Christian faith, fighting so that the spirit and teaching of Jesus Christ may prevail throughout the world.'[9]

But most of these new Crusaders never even saw Jerusalem – political and international considerations meant that no battles were fought within the city, in order to protect the Holy Places – and its formal surrender by the infidels, commemorated on the Jerusalem cenotaph, was not quite a state occasion. The Turkish Governor had given the elderly Arab mayor of the city, Hussein Bey el Husseini, a document of surrender to present to the British. But the mayor feared that he might be accused of collaboration, should the Turks return. He locked the document in a safe and, carrying a bedsheet taken from an Italian mission hospital – the 'large white flag' mentioned in many accounts – went out to look for the British forces and deliver the city by word of mouth. The first soldiers to spot him were Private Church and Sergeant Andrew of the 52nd London Infantry, out foraging for supplies; they alerted two sergeants, who in their turn looked for a superior officer capable of accepting, with all due ceremony, the surrender of the Holy City. The procedure took so long, in the December chill, that el Husseini caught cold, and died of pneumonia three weeks later.[10]

Allenby's subsequent entrance into Jerusalem was famous for its appearance of humility. He left his staff car and entered the Old City on foot; the car, parked at a discreet distance, flew only the tiniest of Union Jacks. Those soldiers who visited Jerusalem were not quite so respectful. The city had enchanted from a distance, but the Protestants' sense of decorum was offended by the commerce around the Holy Sepulchre: 'one mass of gaudiness', wrote Wilson; 'dozens of flags with rubbishy designs, paper flowers, horrible trashy waxworks, spoiled by money-grabbing Greeks and Armenians'.[11]

W. T. Massey, the official correspondent accompanying Allenby, wrote that the result of the occupation of the Holy Land would be an 'awakening' in Palestine not merely of Christians and Jews but of Muslims too, who would see their lives improved under British protection. The improvement was not immediately obvious. Those local Arabs and Jews who had participated in the Palestine campaign were variously rewarded. The Egyptian labour force of 120,000 fellahin had been coerced into service with the Army, torn away, some soldiers remembered, from the arms of their women and children. Many remained in Palestine when the military occupation was over, finding temporary employment with the railways before swelling the numbers of the post-war unemployed, unless they were lucky enough to find work as domestic servants to British officials. A Palestinian–Jewish espionage group provided information on Turkish dispositions, including essential data on the location of wells and springs around Beersheba, for the Allied cavalry, thus helping to ensure the success of the third attempt on Gaza. Sarah Aaronsohn, one of the group, caught and tortured by the Turks, committed suicide rather than reveal information; her brother Aaron Aaronsohn, an agronomist, won important support for Zionism in intelligence and political circles in London.[12]

Jewish soldiers also played a symbolic role in the conquest of Palestine, despite many obstacles. In the autumn of 1917, the British Cabinet had responded to the demand by the more militant Zionist leaders for a Jewish unit to take part in the fighting. A regiment consisting of four battalions of the Royal Fusiliers was made up of Jews recruited from England, Egypt and Palestine. Some were the survivors of the Zion Mule Corps, a group of former Russian Jews from Palestine and from Egypt, which had served as a supply unit at Gallipoli. Among the newer recruits, too, were Russian immigrants from the East End of London. Calls for volunteers among these Jews (to fight on the same side as their recent oppressors, the Tsars) evoked a feeble response. Those who were not British subjects were threatened with deportation by Sir Herbert Samuel (then Home Secretary and later High Commissioner in Palestine), should they fail to volunteer.[13] The Mule Corps was led by an old India hand and veteran of the Boer War, Colonel James Patterson. An old-style believer in the Jewish Return, Patterson resented the opposition of influential British Jews to the formation of a Jewish regiment, and the preference of most British Jews for service in regular units. Among those he claimed to have recruited was the American sculptor Jacob Epstein – who, however, appealed to every influential friend he had in the art and social world to avoid service in the Jewish unit. Army headquarters in Cairo did not like the idea of a Jewish regiment, and suggested breaking it up and sending the Jews to labour units, like the fellahin; most of the Jews refused to go. Patterson took charge of one battalion, whose men he called the Judeans, which was attached to one brigade after another, ending up in the Jordan valley. The Judeans were stationed in a ravine near the Dead Sea, on the extreme right flank of the British Army, with the Turks on three sides, and their function was to take part in a bluff suggesting an attack on the east while the advance took place elsewhere. 'We had the most exposed piece of front to guard which it is possible to conceive,' wrote Patterson later, 'and we were so badly supported by guns, etc., that had the Turks made a determined attack in force, we would probably have been annihilated. It was an extraordinarily risky position in which to place a raw battalion.' The Jews were reduced to a fifth of their original number by illness. Their reward, at the war's end, was that they were forbidden to enter Jerusalem during Passover 1918 by the Army High Command, which feared friction with the Muslims.[14]

Palestine had been devastated by the war – countryside and town alike. Turkish forced conscription had deprived many of the villages of their men, who slowly filtered back home in the chaos of the post-war period. The Turks had confiscated the peasants' livestock either to feed their troops or as pack animals, and had cut down all trees within a ten-mile radius of the railway, including oak, eucalyptus and at least half the country's olive trees, to provide fuel for the Turkish locomotives. As olive trees needed a dozen years and more until they could bear fruit, there was damage to soap production (one of Arab Palestine's few modest industries) as well a shortage of olive oil – a staple of the local diet. A locust invasion had ravaged the crops in 1915. In the towns, many were starving and typhus had broken out among the thousands of refugees; Turkish prisoners-of-war were suffering from pellagra. The low-lying Jordan valley was largely wasteland, inhabited by malaria-ridden fellahin who lived in mud huts. 'Large areas of their lands were uncultivated and covered with weeds. There were no trees, no vegetables . . . there was little public security, and the fellahin's lot was an alternation of pillage and blackmail by their neighbours the Bedouin,' reported one of the first British surveys. The Bedouin tribes, who had tribal territory and grazing rights on both sides of the Jordan, and in the southern desert, observed no frontiers and, when their animals lacked fodder, still staged raids into Palestinian villages.

Until July 1920, when the civil administration took over, soldiers ruled Palestine – the Occupation of Enemy Territories Administration (OETA). The overall authority was in Cairo with Allenby, who was responsible to the War Office. After the fight against malaria – a military necessity – other rehabilitation measures followed in an effort to control infectious diseases, ensure a supply of food, and heal the scarred land. Public medicine had been neglected under Ottoman rule, and during the war there had been only two Turkish infirmaries in the entire country (in Jaffa and Jerusalem), and five Arab doctors in rural areas. To supplement the hard-pressed mission and Jewish hospitals, fifteen government hospitals and clinics were opened in Jerusalem, Jaffa, Hebron and other smaller towns.[15] The administration was helped by American and Jewish voluntary bodies, among whose members was a Jewish woman doctor from Lithuania, Helena Kagan, who had treated sick children in Jerusalem for years, in defiance of the Turkish refusal to grant a woman a licence. A relief committee was set up by the Anglican Bishop of Jerusalem, Rennie MacInnes. Egyptian Muslims contributed to a free medical dispensary and soup kitchen for

Muslim refugees. In an effort to control the spread of venereal disease among the troops, some supervised red-light districts in Jerusalem, Bethlehem, Gaza and Jaffa were permitted to men off duty, but later severe penalties were imposed on infected prostitutes caught with soldiers, and on both women and men soliciting; young male prostitutes were treated particularly harshly, and given twenty-four lashes.[16]

Communications were restored as the railway linking Suez to Lydda was completed. The Jaffa–Jerusalem railway, which had been built by the French and destroyed by the Turks, was rebuilt (and the French compensated), and telegraph lines linked the major towns. In order to jump-start the economy, loans were advanced, backed by the Anglo-Egyptian Bank, to supply seed and stock to farmers. The administration distributed lorry-loads of wheat and soon had to augment supplies in Jerusalem, via the water conduit from Bethlehem, with tanks of water brought up by train. Proclamations were made calling on 'strong men willing to leave their houses and live in tents for 31 days . . . with food as wages', and those who responded were sent to build roads, repair the railways and plant trees.[17]

All forest lands outside private property were declared state property. The administration claimed the right to protect, control and manage forest lands. Unused land was to be used for this purpose. Wasteland was granted to private owners on condition they carried out afforestation. There were prohibitions on removing timber, burning or stripping off bark or leaves, burning lime or manufacturing charcoal (one of the fellahin's main sources of fuel, whether for heating or cooking), tar and pitch, and pasturing cattle on forest lands. Only dead and dry wood could be collected for firewood. Persons with rights in the forests were 'bound to assist' in putting out any fire. Special permits were needed to fell olive, carob or other fruit trees. A hundred and sixty thousand trees were eventually planted. Meanwhile, the British Army brought pinewood from Cyprus to stoke their stoves – unwittingly introducing to Palestine tree lice which were years later to destroy many of the pines the foresters had planted.[18]

The ill-treatment or overworking of domestic animals noted in many soldiers' memoirs, and which had added to the Yeomanry's reluctance to leave their horses behind, was punished. Infirmaries for sick animals were set up, a typically English contribution to the country. Stockpiling of food was prohibited and game was protected between 1 February and 15 July (as in England), during which time the partridges and gazelles remaining in the Galilee could not be hunted. And while localized acts of hostility led to collective punishment – the confiscation of up to one tenth of the livestock of a village – it was recommended that money should be taken, rather than cattle, 'as it was undesirable to further deplete the already scanty supply of cattle and livestock in the country'.[19] The government was also concerned to legislate for the proper treatment of livestock being transported across the country, whether by rail or road.

Jerusalem, which was to be the administrative centre of the country, was governed by Ronald Storrs, the Cambridge-educated son of a clergyman, whose colonial career had begun in Egypt under Lord Cromer. In June 1919, OETA moved to the old German headquarters, the Augusta Victoria Hospice between Mount Scopus and the Mount of Olives. German property was sequestered and catalogued, to the annoyance of the wives of British officers, who had pounced on any bedlinen and crockery the Germans left behind. Under OETA, the country was administered according to international law, which prohibited changes to Ottoman rule, so that Palestine remained divided into regions on the Turkish model. The Land Registry was closed and no transactions could take place, and Ottoman law continued to be the basis of the legal authorities and the courts – which, however, were reduced in number and reorganized.[20]

Despite the bans on change, the shape of a future British administration was emerging. From 1919, advisers for finance, law, trade and agriculture – and later for public works and health – were appointed. The military regime could not change the old Ottoman taxation system, but it substituted direct collection, by District Governors, for the tax farming of tithes.* Under OETA, Arabic replaced Turkish as the language of instruction in the schools, two boarding and training colleges were opened in Jerusalem for Arab teachers, and local educational committees set up in Turkish times were encouraged to meet, as municipal money was needed to help the schools function.

A number of magistrates courts were manned by local judges, Arab

---

* Under Ottoman rule, collection of taxes was performed by 'tax farmers' who took a cut of the revenue for themselves; sometimes tax was collected in kind – for instance, by taking a 'tithe' or a tenth of the produce.

and Jewish, most of whom had been trained in Constantinople; higher courts were presided over by British legal officers, and there was one Court of Appeal, with a British judge. The judicial system eventually established was headed by the Chief Justice, who was second only to the High Commissioner in rank. It was decentralized, as in Ceylon and Cyprus but not elsewhere in the colonies, with District Judges of the Assize courts moving around on circuit. Appeal could be made to the Supreme Court, which included both Arab and Jewish judges. It was a system, as a British jurist who visited Palestine remarked, 'only feasible where the population has attained to a certain standard of civilization, where there are well-organized communications, where there is a local Bar resident and practising in the district', and it was generally respected.[21] But in one important sense it alienated local people, reminding them that – Mandate or no Mandate – they were living in a British colony.

The business of the courts was carried on in English, with simultaneous translation into Arabic and Hebrew. Arabs and Jews who knew no English could therefore understand the gist of what was going on, if not the legal terms; but the judges could not assess their response directly. Under the military regime only one judge, the Turkish-trained Jewish lawyer Gad Frumkin, could understand all the languages used in the court, and a whole army of interpreters and clerks had to be mustered from among the local population. Edward Keith-Roach commented in his memoir: 'The courts in Palestine never won the approval or the heart of the people. Possibly the fundamental cause was that no British judge ever took the trouble to become competent in a local language, but invariably trusted to translators.' The Arabic and Hebrew renderings of new legal orders were often unintelligible.

Interpreters remained important throughout the Mandate: in the courts, for official correspondence and the answering of petitions (the colonial dialogue between rulers and ruled), and to decipher the message of the local newspapers. While formally there were three official languages in Palestine, few officials knew even rudimentary Arabic. Examinations were introduced in both Arabic and Hebrew for Mandatory officials, but they were voluntary – ignorance of local languages did not disqualify a candidate for service under the Mandate, since colonial turnover was more frequent here than, for instance, in India. The first three Chief Secretaries spoke Arabic, but after they left, very few senior officials were able to communicate with the Palestinian Arabs in their own language. Only one of seven High Commissioners, Sir Harold MacMichael, who arrived in 1938 from the Sudan, spoke Arabic. When Sir Charles Tegart was brought from India at the height of the Arab Revolt in 1937 to reorganize the police, he was shocked to learn that: 'Only two or three superior British police officers knew Arabic well, rather more passably, and the rest insufficiently or not at all. Unless an officer can talk well and freely to the people, he will make no friends and will learn nothing.'[22] While some Mandate officials knew Arabic from previous postings, few officials ever troubled to learn Hebrew. This was to prove a grave handicap to British Intelligence officers when, in 1946, after arresting most of the leadership of the Jewish community, they seized documents which they were unable to read. No Palestinian Jew would assist them, and the Colonial Office had to scour British universities for a translator.[23]

The military administration, headed by professional soldiers, was drawn at random from the ranks of the Army. It included, in Storrs's account, men from a wide variety of professions in civilian life: 'a cashier from a bank in Rangoon, an actor–manager, two assistants from Thomas Cook, a picture dealer, an army coach, a clown, a land valuer, a boatman from the Niger, a Glasgow distiller, an organist, an Alexandria cotton broker, an architect, a junior service London postal official, a taxi driver from Egypt, two schoolmasters and a missionary'. But this round-up – typical of Storrs's urbane commentary on his period of office – is misleading. The key officials who arrived with the Army, many of whom remained in their posts for many years under the civil administration, were men with high qualifications for the work to which they were assigned. In this sense they did not resemble many colonial Civil Servants later sent to Palestine in the ordinary course of duty. Storrs himself had served twelve years in Egypt and had come fresh from the War Cabinet Secretariat in London. The 'architect', Ernest Richmond, had worked on the restoration of ancient buildings in Cairo; a fluent Arabic speaker, he became assistant to the Chief Secretary in charge of political affairs in the first administration, and its main liaison officer with the Arabs. Eric Mills, a Cambridge mathematician, prepared most of the statistical surveys of the country and later became Director of Immigration. The heads of the Health and Agriculture Departments were, respectively, Colonel Heron, late of the public health administration of Egypt, and Edward Sawer, who had supervised experimental farms and handled forest conservation in Rhodesia, Natal and the Sudan, from the beginning of the century. All these men remained in Palestine for years and became deeply involved in the country's conflicts.

More typical of the colonial administrators of the time were two other men in key positions. Edward Keith-Roach, District Commissioner in both Jerusalem and Haifa, and Humphrey Bowman, the first head of the Department of Education, had both had their formative colonial experiences in the Sudan. Political service in the Sudan was second only, in colonial prestige, to the Indian Civil Service, and fully a third of its Civil Servants came from clergymen's families who had proprietary feelings about the Holy Land. Many were public schoolboys for whom team games and their honour code were central to their ideas of administration. Like most Mandate officials they expected Arabs and Jews to abide by British gentlemen's agreements. For instance, they provided 'sealed' armouries in beleaguered Jewish settlements and trusted the settlers never to open them except in situations of proven danger. The Zionist official who negotiated this agreement was a British Jew, Frederick Kisch, a Brigadier with the Royal Engineers, and a former public schoolboy.

Keith-Roach, the youngest son of a large clerical family from Gloucestershire, served first in India – as an alternative to a safe but boring job in banking. In Palestine he was Custodian of Enemy Property after the First World War and then, after an initial period in northern Palestine and a spell in the Colonial Office in London, District Commissioner of Jerusalem. Keith-Roach had spent a few years in the Sudan administering the large, semi-desert Eastern Area. Few crops could be grown, trade was still carried out by barter, communications were maintained by camel, and Keith-Roach became, in his own words, the King Solomon of the region, giving judgment on the basis of quotations from the Bible (which he had time to read through twice during his lonely evenings). After the signing of the Armistice he managed to get an introduction to OETA via Cairo. On his way up to Jerusalem in December 1919 he got out of the train to stretch his legs, breathed in the Judean air and 'made an instant resolve to stay in Palestine'. Bowman, educated at Eton and Oxford, had served under Cromer in Egypt, in the Sudan and in Iraq before arriving in Palestine. He was convinced that only a British education could educate Arabs and Jews to live together in amity, and deplored both Arab and Jewish brands of nationalism. Like Keith-Roach, and many others in the Colonial Service, he thought that speaking English would inculcate tolerance by osmosis. True to his British schooling, in which organizations like the Scouts were non-political and 'character forming', he failed to understand that both Arab and Jewish youth movements were bound to be politicized.[24]

The most unusual colonial officials of all were the British Jews, some of whom arrived as soldiers. Three became leading and contro-versial figures in the Mandate government: Storrs's 'London postal official', Albert Hyamson, who was also a scholar and was to become the chief immigration official of the country until 1934; Max Nurock, who, arriving in Palestine as part of a Zionist delegation in the OETA period, became a member of the Secretariat in Jerusalem; and Norman Bentwich, Senior Judicial Officer with OETA and later the Mandate's first Attorney-General, who resigned in 1932 – largely as a result of the hostility of his colleagues. All these men were utopian Zionists of the Balfour type, sympathizers with that small and powerless group of Palestine Jews which favoured a bi-national state in Palestine, territo-rial compromise with the Arabs. This did not prevent them from being attacked in the Arab press and, in the case of Nurock and Bentwich, shot at in public by Arab gunmen. In their work, they were scrupu-lously impartial, which earned them the bitter enmity of Palestine Jewry. Edwin Samuel, son of the first High Commissioner, became, unusually for a Jew, District Officer in an Arab area. Henry Kantrovich, a lawyer from the East End of London who acquired knowledge of the Ottoman land laws, was to help extricate the govern-ment from one of its most complex land disputes near the end of the Mandate – the Sultan Abdul Hamid case.* There were many other conscientious men of their kind, who often had to face the covert or overt anti-Semitism of many of their non-Jewish colleagues, and the dislike of Palestinian Jews who saw them as little better than traitors.

When British rule began, the Palestinian Arabs constituted about 90 per cent of the population. Most, including the vast majority of the

* See Chapter 2.

rural population, were Muslims, but in the towns the educated merchant and professional population, some intermarried with Turkish families, included many Christians, most of whom were Greek Orthodox, members of a Church which had maintained an uninter-rupted presence in Palestine over nearly two thousand years. Arab life in Palestine until the mid-nineteenth century had been semi-feudal, with local chieftains enjoying both judicial power and, as tax gather-ers, considerable independence of Ottoman control. Turkish reforms thereafter promoted the urban 'notables' from wealthy and educated families, many of whom attained administrative status under Ottoman rule, to positions of influence. As well as increasing Ottoman control, this enabled the notables to dominate both the urban and the rural scenes. Both the notables and the leaders of the Muslim clergy belonged to the great families who also owned large tracts of the countryside. A history of Ottoman service in what was administratively a province of Syria, family and clan loyalties, local patriotism, and, among the fellahin, the intense attachment to a particular plot of land, had made their political identity complex; but among the educated city dwellers in particular, a local Palestinian nationalism was growing. The southern desert areas were populated by nomadic Bedouin tribesmen who observed laws and customs of their own, and other Bedouin lived on the northern and eastern frontiers; each tribe had its own clearly defined territory – which often crossed the colonial frontiers.

Of all these groups, the Muslims resident in Jerusalem – which, because of its religious importance in Islam, rivalled Damascus as the centre of an independent district under Ottoman rule – were the most important. At the beginning of British rule, the Christian Arabs (pro-portionately the best-educated of the Palestine Arabs because of the proliferation of foreign mission schools and colleges) enjoyed consid-erable prominence as merchants, newspaper owners and theorists of Arab nationalism. But it was the notable Muslims who had the widest power base: their members were leaders of the clergy and controlled Muslim finances, while the Muslim sheikhs, who had retained much of their social status in the rural areas, were the natural leaders of the Palestinian Arabs in the smaller towns and the countryside. In the cities, and particularly in Jerusalem, the cultural institutions of the Palestinians included scholarly libraries in the possession of the notable families and a variety of newspapers that maintained a lively debate on contemporary issues, but whose circulation was limited. From the outset of British rule the administration sought support from among the notables, but exercised a close watch on the newspapers, which were subject to censorship. Those which expressed too energetic an opposition to British policy were periodically closed down.

The small Jewish minority comprised two distinct populations: the older was made up of the orthodox Ashkenazi and veteran Sefardi (western and eastern) communities which had lived since the early nineteenth century (and a few communities even earlier) in the four sacred cities – Jerusalem, Hebron, Safed and Tiberias. The strictly orthodox Ashkenazi Jews, who had lived for generations under the protection of one or other of the foreign consuls, and subsisted mainly on charity from abroad, lived almost exactly as they had done in European ghettos, sealed off from their Gentile environment. Initially, they appealed to the British for protection against the Zionists, and elicited some paternalist concern among the British, who regarded them as bullied by the godless 'Bolshevik' newcomers. The Sefardi Jews were far more independent of British patronage and better-attuned to life among the Arabs. The newer population, on the other hand, was composed of the settlers who had emigrated from Europe and imperial Russia from the 1880s onwards: some observant Jews, others secular Zionists. It was their townships which, to the soldiers, had looked like European villages. The more spartan outlying settlements, the collectives or kibbutzim which could be seen in the centre and the north, were known as the Jewish 'colonies'.

The Arab and Jewish communities to which Britain had made a dual commitment lived together yet apart at the beginning of the Mandate. In the cities Arab and Jewish merchants had commercial links – the Chamber of Commerce and the Masonic groups in the cities were to be among the few meeting places for the two communities. Arabs and Jews sometimes collaborated in running the 'mixed' towns (Jerusalem, Haifa, Tiberias, Safed and Jaffa), Arab and Jewish lawyers met in the courts, but often they lived in different towns or different quarters of the towns, and sent their children to different schools (apart from attendance by some poor Jews at the British mission schools, the only meeting place, the missions claimed, for all national groups – although very few Jewish children were ever sent there before the 1930s). Ashkenazi Jews rarely spoke Arabic. The British community sometimes employed both Arabs and Jews as servants. Keith-Roach, for instance, as Jerusalem District Commissioner, employed a Jewish cook, a Muslim butler and a Christian Arab houseboy.

In the countryside, the separation between Arab and Jew was even more marked, though the longer-established Jewish plantation and vineyard owners on the coastal plains employed many Arab fellahin, some of whom added their Jewish employers' names, as they had done with Turkish landlords, to their own. In the collectives in the last decades of the nineteenth century, when Jews from Eastern European towns were arduously teaching themselves to build and farm, the first paid guards – in a countryside still open to marauders – had been Circassian Muslims. (Later, when the Jews decided to handle self-defence on their own, they adopted the headdress of Bedouin or Circassian fighters.) According to Musa el Alami, one of the few Palestinian Arabs to maintain a political dialogue with the Jews throughout the Mandate, the mothers of Sefardi Jewish and Arab neighbours in the poorer districts of Jerusalem's walled Old City sometimes became foster-parents, one mother in case of need suckling the other's child.[25] But in times of political tension the orthodox Jews in their quarter inside the walls – like their relations in the ghettos of Eastern European towns in a rather different context – barricaded themselves into their homes, with kettles of boiling water ready to pour on Arab rioters who might go on the rampage after listening to anti-Jewish sermons in the mosques. While for most Jews liberation from the Turks and the Balfour Declaration heralded a golden age, the Ashkenazi orthodox were wary of the newer, Zionist immigrants, most of whom had abandoned orthodoxy. A few leading Sefardi Jews felt they had their own understanding with the Arabs which the Zionists were endangering; many orthodox Jews opposed Zionism outright, believing that in trying to rebuild a Jewish polity in the Holy Land the newcomers were usurping divine providence, and protested against the Zionists to their new rulers.

The combination of so many different subject communities in one small dependency was puzzling to the colonial Civil Servant. The fellahin and the Bedouin reminded them of the settled and nomadic peasantry of Africa and India. The Arabs of the towns aroused their instinctive dislike of the mercantile 'Levantine', as compared with the desert Arab. The professional Arab class aroused their suspicions of the 'Europeanized' colonial, and the culture of the Ottoman notables and Muslim clergy, with whom they had very little informal contact, was foreign to most of them. But in general, Mandate officials felt that with the Arabs they were on sure ground: they had ruled Arabs before. The Zionist Jews, with their competitive skills and political organization, and an efficient lobby in London, were quite outside the colonial experience. The Jews in Palestine who were Europeans resembled not in the least the white settlers in the highlands of Africa and Ceylon or the planters in Malaya with whom colonial officials were familiar. Different High Commissioners had very different attitudes to the Jews: Herbert Samuel, with his Anglo-Jewish upbringing and education, had little in common with his co-religionists from Eastern Europe – and underestimated the fierce nationalism of their leaders. After leaving Palestine he even tried to persuade them to accept minority status in a bi-national Palestine. The third High Commissioner, Chancellor, did not believe the Jews of Palestine would be loyal to Britain: '80 per cent of them were Poles and Russians, many atheists, socialists or communists'; and he expressed his sympathy with the Arabs openly in official meetings with their leaders.[26] The fourth High Commissioner, Sir Arthur Wauchope, who took a lively interest in Zionism in general and Jewish agriculture in particular, compared the kibbutzim with agricultural communes he had visited in Western Australia, and on one occasion even sent an invitation to Jewish farmers in Hebrew – a breach of Government House protocol (while the Jewish Hyamson refused to use Hebrew in his dealings with the Jewish authorities). Cunningham, the last High Commissioner, understood that the Jews he governed in the post-war period were living in the shadow of the Holocaust, and even tried to explain (unsuccessfully) to Arab leaders that every Jewish family in Palestine had lost relations under the Nazis. But their reproaches and demands exasperated him none the less.

The Balfour Declaration was not officially published in Palestine, nor was its existence publicly acknowledged by the administration, until February 1920 – an indication of the fluidity of the situation as much as of the recognition, by the military, that it was an incendiary document so far as the Arab population were concerned. It took the best part of two years for the Allied powers to assign the Palestine Mandate to Britain, and even longer for the League of Nations to endorse that decision – until July 1922.

In August 1919, the political adviser to OETA, Colonel Richard Meinertzhagen, argued that: 'The people of Palestine are not at present in a fit state to be told openly that the establishment of Zionism in Palestine is a policy to which HMG, America and France are committed.'[27] Meinerzhagen (the name was Danish, not Jewish) was the only pro-Zionist member of the military administration, but the generals who were in command agreed with him. This did not mean that the Arabs of Palestine were not aware of British policy or of the changed status of the Jews in Palestine. In March 1918, while the fighting continued, and while, pending international agreement, it was still unclear who would rule Palestine, a Zionist Commission, authorized by the Colonial Office, had arrived in Jerusalem. Its role was ostensibly to provide liaison between the military and the local Jewish population. The Jewish community was not solidly behind the Commission, which helped local Zionists to outmanoeuvre the rabbis and assume control of the Jewish communal organizations. In revenge, the orthodox Jews set up their own assembly, and petitioned the military authorities repeatedly, asking for separate representation. Their improbable spokesman in the British press was the eccentric Jacob de Haan, a Dutch lawyer, ex-socialist, ex-Zionist, born-again orthodox Jew, and homosexual. De Haan became one of the men most hated by the Zionist community for his scathing attacks on the godless Zionists in the *Daily Telegraph* from 1919 and in the 1920s in *The Times*. He was to be assassinated by two members of a Jewish militia, allegedly on the orders of the Zionist Labour movement, in 1924. The background of the killing has never been clear, but given the importance the Zionist movement attributed to its image in the British press, silencing de Haan may well have been a priority.

The Zionist Commission, meanwhile, acted as if the Declaration had already been implemented in Palestine. They asked the administration to make Hebrew an official language, like Arabic, and to appoint Jews to government jobs. These requests were granted, but not others: to appoint a Jewish mayor of Jerusalem and to appoint Jews as half the members of the town council, in accordance with the city's demographic balance. Meanwhile, the Commission began its practical work by paying subsidies to Jewish municipal police and clerks, railwaymen and telephonists, to bring their pay up to European standards.

For the Palestinian Arabs, the reception given to the Zionist Commission was ominous. Under Turkish rule very few Jews had attained administrative positions, and their status was that of a minority tolerated so long as they did not intervene in politics. But the members of the Zionist Commission, whether privileged English Jews, confident of their background, education and standing in their own country, or European Jews who had emancipated themselves from both religion and the ghetto, gave the impression that, under British protection, they were to introduce a new kind of Jewish minority into post-war Palestine, assertive and politically ambitious. Petitions and protests were submitted by the Arabs to the military administration. In November 1918, on the first anniversary of the Declaration, a parade and celebrations were held by the Zionist Commission in Jerusalem, a forthright demonstration of the new spirit of Jewish independence in Palestine. Arab community leaders, the heads of leading families, and the religious communities, all protested against Zionism and its adoption by Britain.

The military was inclined to sympathize with the Palestinian Arabs. They saw the Jewish newcomers as arrogant and provocative. But in dealing with Arab protests the British military administration soon realized that there was no single authority with which they could negotiate. Since the majority of the Arab population was Muslim, and the most important of the Muslim clergy came from the dominant families, and also given the special status of Jerusalem, the military decided to promote the local mufti (a religious title given to a respected jurist) to be the representative of all Muslim Arabs in Palestine as Grand Mufti. This title was a British invention.

OETA treated independently with Arab community leaders, suggesting alternatives to government policy, for as long as the exact form British rule was to take was still uncertain. They indicated their support of the Arab case with the greatest indiscretion. Among the anti-Zionist petitions was one from a new organization, the Muslim–Christian Association, formed in Jaffa and Jerusalem. OETA's second Chief Administrator, General Watson, believed that it was representative of 'moderate Arab opinion in the country', and that it should be heard. Later he was to assure this group – apparently without authorization – that although Britain would set up a 'National Home' for the Jews (a term whose meaning remained vague), it would give the Arabs of Palestine control of the governmental system. The third Chief Administrator, General Bols, together with Allenby, and Lord Milner at the War Office, recommended – unsuccessfully – that the British government issue a declaration sympathetic to Arab aspirations in Palestine and Iraq. Bols's Chief of Staff, Colonel Waters-Taylor, a professional soldier who had fought in the Boer War and in Nigeria, again acting on his own private initiative, made sure that the Palestinian Arabs knew of this.

However, in February 1920 the administration finally announced that it intended to carry out the provisions of the Balfour Declaration. There were immediate and widespread Arab demonstrations and protests. The Arab–Jewish conflict under British rule began on 4 April 1920 with the first violent anti-Jewish street riots by Palestinian Arabs, during the festival of Nebi Musa – the mass pilgrimage to the alleged tomb of Moses between Jerusalem and Jericho. Arab crowds attacked Jews in several parts of Palestine, in what became known as the 'Easter riots' by the British and were aimed equally against non-Muslim rulers and Jewish intruders.

During the nineteenth century, Ottoman rulers had encouraged the traditional Muslim spring festival to be timed as a counterpoint to the Easter pilgrimage to Jerusalem by Christian pilgrims, most of them from Tsarist Russia. This would have been a time of inter-ethnic tension even without the advent of Zionism. According to Meinertzhagen, who sent a furious protest to Curzon at the Foreign Office, Colonel Waters-Taylor had actually encouraged the instigators of the riots, who included Haj Amin el Husseini, and Aref el Aref (a scholar and, later, a Mandatory official), in order 'to show the unpopularity of Zionism'. Meinerzhagen resigned. Waters-Taylor was recalled, the organizers of the riots were exiled, and the first of many official enquiries on Palestine took place.

It was significant that a religious festival should have sparked conflict. That the festival was in memory of Moses – a forefather claimed by both Muslims and Jews – only increased the political significance of the pilgrimage. One of the chief elements in the still-embryonic Palestinian national movement was the centrality of Jerusalem and its

Muslim shrines. The British image of the Holy Land in anodyne terms, 'sacred to three religions', meant in practice that Jews and Muslims shared many religious and historical sites; but this, rather than forming a bond, was a source of potential confrontation. The Western (Wailing) Wall is in fact the retaining wall of the platform on which stand the Dome of the Rock and the El Aksa mosque. The Jews identified this platform as the site of Solomon's Temple, the Arabs venerated it as the Muslim Noble Sanctuary. The area at the foot of the Western Wall was contested territory. The Jews had long worshipped there only on Muslim sufferance, in a narrow alley packed with Arab traffic and, at times of tension, to a background of deliberate noisy interference. When, through Storrs, Weizmann offered to purchase the area and rehouse the occupants in 1919 – the first of many Zionist attempts to claim Jewish rights, though the Turks, too, had contemplated selling the site to the Jews – he was refused. Throughout the Mandate the Western Wall was to be the site of conflict and a headache for the administration.

Pilgrimages to the tombs of local saints and to sanctuaries made up an important part of the religious life of the Palestine Arabs, and the Nebi Musa pilgrimage attracted Muslims from all over the country, from the Galilee to Hebron in the south, in a celebration lasting a whole week. Stewart Perowne, secretary to the Anglican Bishop and later a teacher at the Arab Training College, saw the pilgrimage as a picturesque folk event, with peasant sword dancers, wrestlers, or 'morris dancers', the music provided by shepherds' flutes. The 1920 riots taught the new rulers that Nebi Musa was decidedly a political event. After 1920, the slogans chanted by the participants were supposed to be submitted in advance to the authorities, and the banners carried by the various delegations were scanned at a ceremony at the Jaffa Gate, presided over by the District Commissioner, rather like a secular priest blessing the proceedings. The dangers of such gatherings were to increase.

The veteran British residents of Palestine, members of the Anglican community, saw all the country's conflicts in terms of the ancient battles between the faiths of the Holy Land. The imminent defeat of Islam in the Holy Land stirred Bishop Rennie MacInnes, then head of the Anglican community in Cairo but soon to move to Jerusalem, to write to Allenby suggesting that the latter take official possession of every building erected originally as a Christian church but now used as a Mohammedan mosque. He put this forward not only 'in his ecclesiastical capacity' but from the political point of view. The British government, wrote the Bishop, 'in its desire to placate the Mohammedan races, sometimes adopted measures which have the opposite effect. The measure designed by the Western mind to show magnanimity and tolerance is regarded by the Eastern as a sign of weakness and fear.'[28] Canon Stacy Waddy, who ran St George's, the Anglican school, reported to the Jerusalem and the East Mission in 1918: 'We have taken over the control of a country whose inhabitants do not form a nation in any political or accepted sense: it is a country peopled not by a race or races but by religions.' Among British duties he stressed improving relations with the 'Separated Churches', bedevilled by 'mutual ignorance'.[29]

In taking on the Holy Land, Britain had inherited, in addition to its other responsibilities, that of governing the Christian communities, particularly in Jerusalem. The oldest-established Christian community was the Greek Orthodox, in which the priests were Greek and the laity Arab. The Protestant missionary groups, who had made a few Arab converts, had settled in the country only in the nineteenth century, and the Anglican Bishopric was established in Jerusalem in 1842. The Bishop in (not of) Jerusalem – whose diocese extended across the new frontiers – and the Anglican missionaries were now, for the first time, under Christian rule. St George's, with its cathedral, Bishop's Residence, and school, was housed in a complex outside the Old City walls. Designed on the model of New College, Oxford, St George's made few concessions to its Arab surroundings, though it was the élite school for Arab Protestants, run on the lines of a British public school, with houses and prefects to encourage team spirit and responsibility. The entire complex was to become, with the High Commissioner's Residence, a focus of British social life in Jerusalem. The churches in Jerusalem had always been competitive and fiercely jealous of hereditary privilege. Though the English bishops were relative newcomers, they too were to be drawn into the political conflicts of the country.

Relations between the Bishopric and the Jews of Jerusalem, always problematic, became more so with the arrival of the Zionists. The Church Missionary Society and London Mission to the Jews, with their Evangelical belief in the Christian significance of the Jewish Return (which was to precede the Second Coming), had attempted, unsuccessfully, during the last decades of the nineteenth century to convert the highly orthodox Jews of the old community, and had educated and treated many poorer Jews in their mission schools and hospitals. It was largely as a response to this Christian challenge that the Jews developed their own institutions, which were to grow with the national revival. Shortly after the end of the First World War, there was a vigorous campaign in the Jewish press against the mission schools and those Jewish parents who sent their children there, mostly poor Sefardi Jews – Moroccan, Persian and Yemenite – who were unable to pay the Zionist school fees.

Bishop MacInnes, like his successors, was deeply hostile to Zionism. He knew that the administration had received deputations from the orthodox Jews and he shared their apprehension of the 'Bolshevik' character of the Socialist Zionists from Eastern Europe. In December 1919 he requested an interview with Weizmann. After a brief expression of theological sympathy with the 'hopes of Jewry', the Bishop suggested that the Return, in his view, was a religious ideal, could not be a mass movement, and was surely not to be realized 'by political wirepulling', or by the Jews' 'claiming to rule Palestine or oust the other peoples living there'. Though Weizmann had his own problems with orthodox Jewry, he tried to explain the background to the press campaign, and made it clear why, in Palestine in particular, the Jews feared sending their children to Christian schools. The discussion ended on a sour note, with the Zionist leader reminding the Bishop of Christian persecution and Jewish fears about proselytizing Christians. 'Those who leave us are traitors,' he stated.[30] MacInnes continued to criticize the Zionists, and was rebuked by Churchill in 1921 for stating, in a circular letter, that: 'At a time when Palestine is so unhappily disturbed by the unjust and intolerable demands of the Zionists, it is good to see the missionary schools contributing something of great worth to the Holy Land in the levelling and uniting influence they bring to bear on all these young and opening minds'. The Archbishop of Canterbury cautiously defended MacInnes, but the main problem was twofold: the Bishop had to bear in mind not only his responsibility to his Arab parishioners and his relations with the Eastern Churches, but the fact that Anglican doctrine was still in thrall to the theological notion of the Return. So the unrepentant MacInnes told the Archbishop that while he agreed with the 'ideal of Zionism – lofty sincere and spiritual', he was critical of the Zionists who 'had rent Palestine from Dan to Beersheba . . . [who] did not care for the susceptibilities of the people [i.e. Arabs]', and 'seem to delight in doing things that will annoy'.[31]

The Mandate administration was as concerned as the Bishopric about religious tensions in Jerusalem. After fending off the first protests of orthodox Jews against the Zionists, it had to rule on the stubborn quarrels among the Christian sects. The first challenge to the administration as a newly established Christian power was from the Greek Orthodox Arab laity, which appealed to the new rulers to adjudicate in its differences with the Patriarchate. Unlike the Latin and Protestant clergy and missions, who had always taken on themselves the welfare and education of their flock, the Orthodox clergy, who owned valuable properties in Palestine, were accused of neglect. In contravention of late Ottoman law, they had also appointed a Greek Bishop in Nazareth who spoke not a word of Arabic. The Arab laity claimed that administration of properties had been wrongly vested in the Patriarchate; later they demanded increased powers through mixed councils of ecclesiastics and laymen, and the right to levy taxes for the building and maintenance of educational and social welfare institutions. They also wanted admission to the powerful Confraternity of the Holy Sepulchre.

Two Commissions of Enquiry were set up early in the Mandate, manned by British jurists with a knowledge of Greek ecclesiastical history, to report on these controversies. The Patriarch, Damianos, was not prepared to compromise, though some relief for the laity was extracted from the Greek Orthodox revenues. The second Commission concluded that despite a clear violation of Ottoman law, the government could not withdraw its recognition of the Patriarchate and had no real sanctions with which to back up the Commission's criticisms. The quarrels lasted until the very last weeks of the Mandate, when certain of the lay communities were threatening to cede from the Greeks entirely and go over to the Orthodox Church of Russia.

Despite their opposition to Zionism, the Anglicans in Jerusalem were reconsidering their relationship with the local Jews. Missionary work had reached only the very poor, sick and disadvantaged among the Jewish community. So in 1918 MacInnes made an unusual appointment, as his librarian, of an intellectual who was to carry on a dialogue with 'the better-educated and higher social classes of Jews'. It was characteristic of the new librarian, Canon Herbert Danby, that he immediately noted and deplored the absence of the Jewish Encyclopaedia in St George's library.

Danby, a Hebrew scholar and Anglican priest, sympathetic to the Zionist cultural revival and determined to build bridges between Christians and Jews in Jerusalem, saw that the conventional Anglican approach to the Jews of Palestine was self-defeating. Instead of working through the missions, therefore, Danby made his contacts with intellectual Jewish circles in Jerusalem through Jewish friends in England. He was soon able to claim, rather like a secret agent, that he had 'penetrated' the Jewish community in ways no Christian had before. Danby became secretary of the Palestine Oriental Society, which was packed with Jewish scholars, and formed the Jerusalem Musical Club – which was almost exclusively Jewish. Soon he found himself 'in the absurd position of editing the one English Jewish newspaper in Palestine, with circulation throughout the world'. Later, he became correspondent of both *The Times* and *Near East*, and head of the Palestine Association of Press Correspondents – 'the only Christian among swarms of journalists in Palestine'. Danby thought himself 'the only living Gentile' interested in Hebrew literature and scholarship; he was befriended by the founder of the Hebrew language revival, Eliezer Ben Yehuda, as 'a specimen to gloat over . . . the first Gentile to acquire the habit of speaking modern Hebrew'. He also helped the Jewish historian Josef Klausner write the first *Life of Jesus* by a Jew – in which Danby claimed that his own work on the gospels was incorporated – and co-operated on a standard translation into English of the Mishnah, the basic text of the Talmud. When Danby left Palestine in 1936 to become Regius Professor of Hebrew at Oxford, the Bishop commented that it would be difficult to replace him. In fact it proved impossible. Danby's sympathy for Zionism, which, he wrote, had created 'an admirable civilization in Palestine', was as rare in Anglican circles in England at this period as it was in Mandate society. In 1938 the Church of England's Council for Foreign Relations condemned the proposed partition of Palestine into Arab and Jewish states as against Christian interests, deplored political Zionism, and recommended that Britain retain Palestine indefinitely and put an end to Jewish immigration. Canon Danby was the only member of the Council to dissociate himself completely from the document.[32]

Despite Danby's efforts, relations between the Anglican community and the Zionist leadership remained chilly. Jewish attacks on the missions ceased, probably, as Danby commented in his reports home, because the missions' efforts at converting the Jews were so unsuccessful. A few Jewish intellectuals such as Dr Magnes, the President of the Hebrew University, continued to meet with MacInnes's successor, George Graham-Brown, to discuss Jewish–Arab understanding and the possibility of a bi-national state; but Anglican sympathies in Palestine remained firmly with the Arabs. In public Graham-Brown dutifully visited Jewish settlements and admired the pioneering farmers; in private he castigated the Zionist 'Bolsheviks' (Danby called this 'flippant rot') and deplored their political domination of the orthodox Jews.[33]

In England, meanwhile, the Anglican Church was reassessing its attitude to the theological problem of the Return of the Jews as part of a much wider response to challenges to Christian faith, from contemporary science, philosophy, and even psychoanalysis. In 1922, a group of leading Anglican theologians began assembling periodically to 'set out the true doctrine' and reconcile different schools of thought within the Church. One of its concerns was the interpretation of Old Testament prophecy and the identity of 'Israel of God' (the Church) and 'Israel after the Flesh' (the Jews). The Archbishops' Commission, as the group was called, was to publish its findings in 1937, just at the time when the Anglican Church was also having to determine its stand on the prospect of partition of Palestine, the Holy Land, between Arabs and Jews. The Commission's views on the very small point of God's 'promises to the Jews' was a total reversal of the previous, Evangelical, support for the literal Return of the Jews to Palestine – a subject on which there was now no disagreement, though Evangelical theologians were included in the group. In discussing 'the Church in scripture', the Commission concluded that:

> Phrases and terms which in the Old Testament denote or describe Israel in its ideal aspect as the people of God are in the New Testament carried over and applied to the Church as the new, redeemed Israel in which God's ideal

for His people is held to be actualized. Thus the Church is not only 'the Israel of God'; it is also the 'elect race'.

The report went on to state, in the sentence relevant to the Return: 'It is the affirmation of the New Testament that the ancient Israel – "Israel after the flesh" [in other words, Jewry, and, by implication, those who were now claiming their ancient birthright] – has forfeited its claim to the promises.' The Commission made no direct mention of the Return; it even recognized that its approach to the interpretation of the Old Testament would be 'uncongenial to many non-theologically minded enquirers'. But the key sentence was seized on eagerly by Graham-Brown, the Bishop in Jerusalem at that time, who quoted it both in letters to *The Times* (reprinted in Palestine) and in internal church correspondence, and by his successor, Weston Stewart. Stewart, in a letter to the Church's Council on Foreign Relations, understood the Commission's report as rejecting totally the previous Evangelical view that Zionist claims based on Old Testament history were valid. This was, he said, 'bad Christianity, whether or no it be good Judaism'.[34]

In its immediate post-war years, Mandate Palestine became a haven for the English Arts and Crafts movement, chiefly because of the patronage of Ronald Storrs, the first Governor of Jerusalem. Like so many British administrators, Storrs had more of a passion for Jerusalem than for its people – it was he who was to coin the saying: 'There is no promotion after Jerusalem.' But he was impatient with both Arab and Jewish nationalist rhetoric, and felt contempt for the warring Eastern Christian sects (he once physically stood between Greeks and Armenians when they tussled inside the Holy Sepulchre). Storrs was musical (he celebrated the final defeat of the German troops in Palestine by playing snatches of Italian and Wagnerian opera on his own Steinway) and he set up a music school in Jerusalem for both Arab and Jewish pupils. Neither the orthodox Jews nor the Muslim Arabs showed the slightest interest in classical music, and he finally handed the school over to European Jewish immigrants.

The architectural restoration of Jerusalem preoccupied Storrs above all else. Arabs and Jews alike, over the decades preceding the war, had introduced industrial building materials which clashed with the hand-chiselled stone of traditional Muslim masonry. In April 1918, barely five months after the occupation of Jerusalem, and while fighting against the Turks still continued, Storrs put up a public notice prohibiting the demolition, erection or alteration of any building without permission within a radius of 2,500 metres of the Damascus Gate. He forbade the use of stucco and corrugated iron within the walls of the Old City, in order to protect the 'respected tradition of stone vaulting'. The 'Pro Jerusalem Society' he founded was set up not only to preserve archaeological sites (a task later taken over by the Mandatory Department of Antiquities) but also for 'the encouragement in the district of Jerusalem of arts, handicrafts and industries in consonance with the general objects of the society'. These were:

> the protection of and addition to the amenities of Jerusalem and its district; the provision and maintenance of parks, gardens and open spaces in Jerusalem and its district; and the establishment in the district of public museums, libraries, art galleries, exhibitions, musical and dramatic centres and other institutions of a similar nature for the benefit of the Public.

With the exception of (private) libraries, all these were alien to all previous local tradition, Muslim, Christian or Jewish.

Western researchers had alerted the Turks to the value of archaeological remains in Palestine. When the British arrived in Jerusalem, they found that among Turkish abandoned property were crates of Palestinian antiquities ready for shipping to Istanbul. The revival of local artisans' skills was also wholly English in inspiration. The architect Ernest Richmond, a close friend of Storrs, late of the War Graves Commission in Cairo, oversaw the restoration of the Dome of the Rock, the shrine whose ceramic exterior was badly weatherbeaten, with the help of funds raised by Muslim clergy. Clifford Ashbee, whom Storrs brought to refurbish and restore historic Jerusalem, was a disciple of William Morris and the survivor of the now almost defunct Arts and Crafts movement in England. Storrs had found him teaching in post-war Cairo.[35]

Ashbee had lectured some years earlier at the School and Guild of Handicraft, which had opened in June 1888 in darkest East London, a trial-run for his real colonial experience. The working men of the East

End had been as apathetic towards his anti-industrial message as the middle-class, to whom he subsequently preached, were enthusiastic. Ashbee, himself of German–Jewish ancestry on his mother's side, and all the more critical of Eastern European Jews, had thought the Jewish immigrant population of Whitechapel deaf to the social philosophies of Morris. He was thus amazed, on visiting a Jewish settlement in Palestine, to be shown a 'Tumbeal' – a local Toynbee Hall (many of the pioneers were formidably well-read on social welfare issues in Europe). Ashbee expressed astonishment and pleasure that 'the Essex Hall boys had not given their lives in the Great War for nothing'. However, before accepting Storrs's invitation, Ashbee had talks with the Archbishop of Canterbury about 'the most efficacious way of getting British support and British funds for Palestine research in conjunction with the wealth of America, and as a counter to Zionism'. Of the Jews in Palestine as a whole, he wrote: 'These fellows are longing for a British Administration – being in a minority – but have no thought of the Arab, who is in many ways so much nicer than the Jew; not such a modernist, but so much more of a gentleman.'[36]

Under Ashbee, the Pro Jerusalem Society was to spring-clean that entire area of Jerusalem which lay within the sixteenth-century Ottoman walls. This included the restoration of the mosaics lying beneath the sixteenth-century ceramic skin of the Dome of the Rock shrine and the restoration of the seventeenth-century Suq el Qattanin, the Cotton Market, including the stalactite work over the lateral openings, which reminded Ashbee 'irresistibly' of Tudor vaulting. The first task was accomplished with the help of Armenian artisans, but the second proved beyond the Society's resources. The major achievement of the Society, however, was not restoration, but the removal of the debris, rubbish, and human and animal waste which had clogged up the approaches to the Citadel, the Turkish stronghold at the north-west corner of the Old City wall. The Society planted gardens and made a pedestrian walkway along the ancient ramparts, a promenade which, in Ashbee's vision, was to be 'the largest, perhaps the most perfect medieval enceinte in existence, rivalling Carcassonne, Chester and Nuremberg'. This was certainly a European vision, since Muslims (and many of the priests in the monasteries whose courtyards lay underneath the promenade) hated being overlooked.

The cleaning work was done using Muslim refugees from es Salt, the desert town in Transjordan, who had been quartered in the Citadel by the Turks, and their recruitment was described by Ashbee as 'so to speak, tidying up their own house'. Most of the labourers were young women with picks. Crêches were set up to look after their children, though the women often disappeared when their husbands returned from war or captivity. Convict labour was also used, and the men given a token payment 'to avoid resentment'. Money came from the various relief funds put at the disposal of the military government by well-wishers. The refugees also cleaned up the historic gates, which the local people had taken over from Turkish soldiers and turned to their own purposes. At St Stephen's (Lions) Gate a bath contractor had appropriated the whole of the top of the gate for baking dung cakes as fuel, and the Turkish guardhouse had been used as a public latrine.[37]

The local population, whether Jewish or Arab, did not always appreciate Ashbee's reforming zeal. The Jewish quarter was crowded and insanitary, with no open spaces or gardens. Pro Jerusalem planned a recreation area for children on ground reclaimed from a nearby site: 'one of the city's worst slums'. Though the work was financed from both Arab and Jewish sources, 'After the first work of planting, a series of nightly raids was made upon the garden, which was stripped of every tree, shrub or flower.' The work was suspended, Ashbee commenting that: 'The elementary duties of citizenship had not been learned.' He also wanted to preserve the overhanging wooden windows and balconies in his favourite street, the Bab el Selseleh or Street of the Chain. But since these belonged to the Muslim trust – the Waqf – and were going to cost more to retain and repair than to rebuild, the residents wanted to rebuild them flush with the wall. Ashbee objected, and the Pro Jerusalem Society paid for specific repairs to be done and the old balconies retained. The removal of the Turkish clock-tower at the Jaffa Gate, useful for the local people but an eyesore to Ashbee and his fellow aesthetes, also had to be carefully negotiated. Houses were numbered, for the first time in the history of the city, though this clashed with the orthodox Jewish belief that it brought ill luck – the children of Israel were not to be counted. But all this was less problematic than Ashbee's attempt to 'revive' local arts and crafts in the spirit of Chipping Campden.

Ashbee's chief ambition was to encourage the local crafts of weaving, tile-making and glass-blowing. Cheap imported textiles were on sale everywhere, and the petrol can, so much more durable than clay, had replaced local ceramics both for decoration, for storage, and even in building. As an English teacher remarked some years later:

> It is the universal container for water, oil or flour; it is cut up and made into cups, funnels or dustpans; a row of them along the edge of a balcony constitutes a garden, painted green and planted with straggling carnations, or rose bushes. Fitted with a hinged flap and a padlock it serves as the family strong-box. It is even flattened out and used as building material for sheds and outhouses.[38]

Though the stonemasons retained their traditions, many of the skills passed on from father to son were already beginning a long decline, but Ashbee believed he could halt this process in its tracks. The Armenian tile industry survived for a while. Experts were brought from Kutahia in Armenia to re-create the ceramic skin of the Dome of the Rock; they remarked that the kilns imported by Ashbee from the English potter William De Morgan had gone out of use locally in the sixteenth century. The weavers' idea never caught on, as the wares they produced could not compete with cheap, imported textiles, though the American Red Cross had provided looms for refugees to provide relief work. Ashbee hoped to convert the Cotton Market, whose main feature was currently a public latrine, to what he thought was its original purpose – a market for weavers. The beautiful wooden doors had been used for firewood; the Society remade them. A flour mill was removed to make room for the workshops, and a company named Jerusalem Looms was set up, with seventy workers. Muslim boys became 'indentured apprentices' – an idea based on the Samuel Montagu East London apprenticeship fund, under which many craftsmen were bound in the late 1890s. But within three years the entire venture had collapsed.

Glass-making still existed in Palestine, particularly in Hebron, though Ashbee believed that the decline of Palestinian glass 'reflected the influence of Western industrialism on Eastern craftsmanship'. Masses of debris remained from cheap, machine-made lamps and littered the Hebron shops. Glass-blowers had given up using their own 'good quartzy Hebron sand because it was cheaper to use the waste products of English factories, which had come as the ballast of ships'. So Pro Jerusalem made an effort 'to lift the old craft out of the industrial mire, to make things of real service, not merely knick-knacks for tourists, or the last degraded relics in coloured bangles and beads for poverty stricken peasants'. Arrangements were made for contracts with the glass-blowers. Old craftsmen were uncooperative, however. Ashbee complained that they kept the secrets of their art to themselves and did not even teach their sons the skills they regarded as unremunerative.[39]

Ashbee's clients were ultimately not the local people but his own colleagues. The first High Commissioner's Residence in the German Augusta Victoria Hospice was to be decorated almost entirely with the products of his craftsmen's labours. The boudoir of the High Commissioner's wife was hung with elegant, woven cloth, carpenters laboured on custom-made furniture, and the Hebron glass-blowers crafted giant chandeliers powered by electric light, showers of crystal which lit the Commissioner's dinner parties. Keith-Roach expressed reservations about Ashbee's campaign: 'Excellent philosophy, but terribly trying to live with, especially in the dining room where the six-foot-high back to the sideboard was carved by a craftsman whose last job had been to design and build an immense hearse.' Even in his work as a decorator, however, Ashbee was unable to meet deadlines; the Hebron glass-blowers could not understand the hurry and suspended their work to go off and get in the tomato crop. The peasantry continued to prefer their bangles, beads and petrol tins. The entire venture had been artificial, grafted on to local relief operations by administrators who were really preoccupied by cultural developments in England. There was also a colonial agenda underlying Pro Jerusalem, spelled out clearly by Ashbee: 'Work with the hands, the creative work, the work of the imagination applied to a man's personal labour, keeps men from empty political speculation. For every craftsmen we create, we create also a potential citizen; for every craftsman we waste, we fashion a discontented effendi.'[40]

So if Pro Jerusalem was an extraordinary campaign for a military administration to take upon itself, it also typified the spirit in which the first British administrators entered Palestine. Storrs was disconcerted that the Jews of Palestine, whether the orthodox sects with whom he felt uncomfortable or the Zionists whose propaganda tired him, should so little resemble the wealthy, cultivated Western Europeans who to him represented Jewry. Ashbee was taken aback that Arab craftsmen were so little impressed by his theories. Both men shared a dislike of Levantine townspeople, and a preference for the desert tribesmen and their rulers, with whom Storrs and his colleagues had dined in their tents and on whom the British government was to bestow the governments of Iraq and Transjordan. Storrs and Ashbee felt, like so many high officials of their time, that enlightened British patronage would protect the Arabs from Western industrialism, and the Jews from 'sectarianism', and would therefore enable them to settle their differences. Their successors in the Mandate Department of Education were to promote Arab crafts rather than encouraging technological development, even in the teeth of Arab opposition.*

Under Storrs's and Ashbee's influence, conservation took priority over development when town planning for Jerusalem was undertaken. William MacLean, the City Engineer of Alexandria, whom Allenby had brought to Palestine, had been commissioned by him to make a first modern Jerusalem plan, and both this and the New Delhi scheme of Edwin Lutyens influenced successors. MacLean's plan envisaged isolating the Old City entirely from the rest of Jerusalem by mapping out an area around the seventeenth-century walls in which building was to be restricted. Stone facing to all building in the city was to be obligatory. All this was approved. But the plan also included the development of the new city to the west of the old, and this part of the plan, entrusted to Ashbee to implement, was frozen for the remainder of the military regime. The concern with conservation and planning was to remain a priority with the Mandate during its first, hopeful years. The Town Planning Ordinance was the first item on the agenda of the Advisory Council, an *ad hoc* assembly of officials, Arabs and Jews: a sign that the belief that progress towards self-government was inevitable.[41]

The Zionists, meanwhile, were busy recruiting British planners who could help with what Ashbee had called their 'modernist' plans for Palestine. Chief among their recruits was the town planner and polymath Patrick Geddes, who had experimented with his ideas of civic

* See Chapter 4.

reconstruction in British India. Zionism appealed to the Scottish Protestant element in his education – particularly reading the Prophets. His plans also called for minimum expenditure, and hence should have been attractive to the Mandate. Geddes had written to the Anglo-Jewish writer Israel Zangwill in April 1918 on the 'cleansing and mending of old cities' and his fascination with hill cities and sacred sites, and Jerusalem looked like the perfect opportunity for realizing what he called 'the city of the global ideal'. At first Geddes's ideas appeared to fit both early Mandate ideas of conservation and Zionist ideas of expansion. From 1919 he accepted Zionist commissions to plan the Hebrew University on Mount Scopus and put forward proposals for the city of Jerusalem, as well as Jewish suburbs and settlements elsewhere in the country. The Zionists also brought the Anglo-Jewish artist David Bomberg to Jerusalem in 1923. Although he accepted the post of official artist to the Zionist Organization, Bomberg had no interest in painting Jewish cowsheds or factories, and it was Mandatory high officials who appreciated and bought his work. Although in England he had identified with the experimental avant-garde of the post-war era, Bomberg painted only representational works in Palestine, most of them landscapes of Jerusalem, where he preferred to depict Arab and Christian quarters, domes and church spires. This was not at all what his sponsors had had in mind.

Geddes was equally refractory, displeasing both his Zionist mentors and the first Mandatory administration. The Hebrew University, opened in 1925, was planned as a Jewish institution which would admit Arabs but where teaching would be in Hebrew. But Geddes's ideas of 'synthesis' meant more vigorous Jewish–Arab co-operation, and he did not like the idea of Hebrew as the only language of tuition. Only one part of his plan, including the university library, was eventually realized; the greater plan was rejected by the university founders as being 'too grandiose and impracticable'. It had at its centre a huge Dome of Synthesis, with arts and science buildings radiating out from it. His Jewish sponsors protested that domes were Roman, symbolizing Byzantium or Islam. Geddes's replanning of Jerusalem, sketched at the request of the Zionist Organization, also elicited protests from the Foreign Office as intervention within Mandate affairs. It included what he thought would be 'the most extensive Sacred Park in the world, including all the graveyards and tombs'.[42] Geddes redesigned the approach to the Wailing Wall, and was later to argue that, had his plans been adopted, Muslim–Jewish clashes at the site would have been avoided. Throughout the period of the Mandate, artists, planners and visionaries of all kinds continued to find inspiration, excitement and frustration in Palestine – as they had always done – and to embarrass and annoy its rulers.

The first High Commissioner, Sir Herbert Samuel, arrived off Jaffa in July 1920, wearing the white, gold-braided jacket and steel spiked helmet of a Colonial Governor. Despite this brave show, the odds were against him. As a Jew and avowed supporter of Zionism he was immediately suspect to the Arabs. He could scarcely live up to the euphoric expectations of the Jews. As an administrator with no colonial experience, and no knowledge of the Arab world, he was entering uncharted territory.

Herbert Samuel had entered the Cabinet (as Britain's first Jewish cabinet minister) in 1909, as Chancellor of the Duchy of Lancaster. In 1910 he was Postmaster-General. When appointed Home Secretary in 1916, during the period of his intensified activity for the Zionists, he was returning to a ministry he had served as Under-Secretary in December 1905. In 1916, when Lloyd George took office, he offered Samuel the chance of continuing as Home Secretary, but Samuel, loyal to Asquith, refused, in a gesture which effectively ended his career as a cabinet minister.

Samuel had read Disraeli's orientalist novel *Tancred* more than once between 1905 and 1920, the last time before going out as High Commissioner. Whether or not he shared Disraeli's vision of the Arab Near East as a playground for imperial adventurers, his Palestine appointment promised to resolve his ambivalent attitude to his fellow Jews. Samuel was uncomfortable with orthodox Judaism. He had been brought up in an observant, if assimilated, Anglo-Jewish family, and – although he attended synagogue from time to time (as a Christian politician might have been seen in church) – found in Zionism an outlet for his Jewish allegiances.[43] He seems to have believed that it would also redeem Jewish honour. In his cabinet memorandum he had written that Zionism promised that 'the sordid associations which have attached to the Jewish name will be sloughed off', and that 'the race had produced great men in Palestine, and would again'.

Samuel's Middle Eastern career began with an adventure in Transjordan – which he visited barely a month after taking office. In mid-1920, after Feisal lost control of Syria to the French, and was set up in power in Iraq by Britain, the east bank of the Jordan became no-man's-land. Fearing the expansion of French rule, sheikhs from the region came to visit Samuel in Jerusalem, appealing for British protection. In a letter to his wife, Samuel described them as: 'picturesque men, many of them in Bedouin dress, bearded and swarthy, clomping across my tiled floor with iron shod boots. They are an amiable and courteous people. I love them all.'[44] However, the Foreign Secretary, Lord Curzon, rejected Samuel's recommendation for direct British rule and instructed him to offer limited assistance, in the form of a few political officers, to the region, where they were to encourage self-government and organize public security. So on 20 August, with a handful of officers and soldiers, Samuel set off for es Salt, in the wild country across the Jordan. There was an exchange of courtesies, which on the sheikhs' side involved a massive 'fantasia' with 400 mounted Arabs letting off their rifles.[45] It must have been an intoxicating experience for the ex-cabinet minister and specialist in taxation reform and social welfare, most recently offered only the post of Controller of Disposal of Surplus Stores (Huts and Hutting Material section).

Samuel's adventure in Transjordan was only an interlude. In early 1921, control of Palestine passed from the Foreign Office to the Colonial Office, under the newly formed Middle East Department, and trying to reconcile the Palestinian Arabs to the Zionist presence was from now on to exercise all Samuel's skills in administration and arbitration. He had acted as economic and financial adviser to the government on the Zionist question, and was well aware of the disadvantages suffered by the Palestinian Arabs. From the outset, his policy was to try to boost Arab agriculture and education. During the first year of his administration he issued loans to farmers impoverished by the war, introduced tobacco crops, and opened sixty of a planned 300 new village schools before his budget ran out.[46] Samuel also recognized, as did many British officials after him, that Jewish financing and expertise were essential not only for the Jews but for the development of the country as a whole. Hence he supported granting concessions for the electricity network and Dead Sea minerals works to the highly qualified Jewish engineer and technical expert Pinchas

Rutenberg, despite some opposition in Britain to this Russian-born entrepreneur.

Until his appointment as High Commissioner, Samuel had expressed his belief that Palestine would eventually (in a private letter he mentioned a period of some fifty years) become a 'self-governing Commonwealth with an established Jewish majority'.[47] In office he was far more cautious. His immediate concern was to bring Arabs and Jews together in some kind of representative assembly. At the first meeting of the Advisory Council in late 1920, Samuel declared: 'It should be clearly understood that this is to be regarded only as a first step in the development of self-governing institutions.' After outlining the Mandatory's plans in banking, agriculture, health and education, and the restoration of a peacetime society – including an amnesty to political offenders – he introduced a new government department in charge of both immigration and labour. This linkage underlined the conception that Jewish immigration would only be allowed with reference to the 'capacity of the country to provide employment'. Samuel was confident that Jewish immigration would now spiral and Jewish investment would boost that capacity.[48]

But despite Weizmann's prediction to Balfour in 1918, of 'five million Jews' ready to move to Palestine, the Zionist movement was unable, during the years of Samuel's administration, to recruit more than a few thousand Jewish immigrants a year; Weizmann was unable to raise more than a fraction of the capital he had expected from 'world Jewry', thus limiting some of Samuel's more ambitious development plans. The Zionist Commission was unable to provide work for all those who did arrive in Palestine, so in the autumn of 1920 the government initiated a road-building scheme to employ the immigrants. Even the trickle of Jewish immigrants to Palestine, however, was sufficient to arouse Arab hostility, and to dash Samuel's optimism.

The underlying tension exploded in the anti-Jewish riots of May 1921. Two rival Jewish left-wing groups, Socialists and Communists, fell out in May Day demonstrations on the outskirts of the Arab quarters of Jaffa; the street brawl spread, Arabs armed with knives and clubs set on the demonstrators and pursued them into Jewish homes. Many Jews not involved in the demonstration, men and women alike, were killed and their homes looted. Eliezer Margolin, an officer who had served in the Jewish regiment during the war, rallied thirty-four recently demobilized Jewish soldiers, made his way into an army camp and handed out rifles which were used against the Arabs. When army detachments arrived, other Arabs were killed. The trouble spread: over an entire week of violence, almost a hundred Jews and Arabs were killed and over two hundred wounded in Jaffa and on the borders of Jewish towns elsewhere. Margolin was forced to resign and the Jewish soldiers were discharged from the Army.

After two days of rioting, Samuel suspended Jewish immigration and a few days later declared martial law. The following month he made a policy speech which qualified, in all important respects, his earlier support for political Zionism, redefining the Jewish National Home as something which had to be balanced, at all times, with British obligations to the Arabs of Palestine.[49] Race, it emerged, was not everything.

Though Samuel still encouraged Jewish settlement, other officials were voicing sympathy for Arab grievances and a distaste for the secular spirit and permissive culture of the pioneering Jews. Both Ernest Richmond, one of Samuel's political advisers, and Percy Bramley, head of the police, saw in the small Jewish Communist party the vanguard of a sinister Russian, anti-British and anti-Christian conspiracy. Captain William Brunton, one of the OETA officers who had accompanied Samuel to Transjordan, and now Political Intelligence Officer in Jaffa, witnessed part of the rioting and the way in which the Jewish defence was organized. He concluded in a report circulated to the Cabinet that Arab frustration at their political powerlessness, and Zionist provocations and contempt for local customs, were both responsible for the violence. These included the influence of the Zionist Commission, the use of Hebrew as an official language, and the 'immorality' of the Jews: men and women 'scantily clad' (Jewish pioneers, men and women alike, wore shorts) and walking around together. He deplored the presence of too many 'low-class' Jews, and said he thought all this offensive to both 'Muslim and Christian' feeling. Brunton interpreted the rioting as a sign of 'Arab determination to resist present British policy', and predicted that bloodshed and repression would be necessary, 'such as British public opinion and worldwide Christian and Muslim sentiment would not tolerate'. With his Transjordan experience in mind, he argued that it was inconsistent to give 'nomadic savages' in

Transjordan more independence than 'the comparatively educated or settled population in Palestine'.[50]

Samuel's policy after the riots was to set the tone for successive administrations, though none was to impose martial law so summarily. When violence broke out, stoppage or limitation of Jewish immigration became the corollary to the imposition of military control. Jewish immigration was adjusted to what the government declared at any given moment to be the 'economic absorptive capacity' of Palestine; and there was to be no more loose talk of a future Jewish commonwealth. Samuel continued his efforts to compensate the Arabs for the disadvantages imposed on them under the terms of the Mandate. That meant giving them some measure of self-rule. But – like the military administration which preceded him – his problem was to understand who, or what bodies, most faithfully represented post-Ottoman Palestine Arab society. Since he had so little knowledge of Arab countries, or of the power structure in the Ottoman world, he had to rely almost entirely on his advisers. The first Chief Secretary, Wyndham Deedes, sympathetic to Zionism, had been Chief Intelligence Officer with the army in Sinai and Palestine, military attaché in Constantinople, and Director of Public Security in Egypt. But the political secretary who handled liaison with the Arabs was the architect Ernest Richmond and, despite his lack of administrative experience, it was his view of who should represent the Palestinian Arabs, and through which body they should function, that was to be decisive.

Richmond had been appointed to the post of Assistant Chief Secretary (political) shortly after Samuel's arrival in Jerusalem. As there were at this time no senior Arab officials in Mandatory service (something which had aroused protest at the first Advisory Council meeting), Richmond swiftly assumed the role of chief mediator between Samuel and the Arab community. He submitted memoranda which implied expert knowledge not only of Palestine society but also of Islam and its legal system. Much financial power and legal authority were concentrated in the Muslim pious endowments (Waqfs) and the religious (Sharia) courts, reaching out into the smallest towns of the country, and the military had already made the position of Mufti, formerly a Muslim legal dignitary, that of *de facto* leader of the whole Muslim Arab community. The incumbent Mufti had died, and elections were held in April 1921 according to Ottoman precedent. This

was not a straightforward affair on lines familiar to a British administrator like Samuel, but involved much behind the scenes manoeuvering
between the leading Arab families: the el Husseinis and the equally
powerful Nashashibis. The winning contender, an elderly, well-
qualified man, was persuaded to withdraw, with Samuel accepting
Richmond's contention that the elections had been invalid (though
Deedes did not agree). The man appointed Mufti was Haj Amin el
Husseini, a young nationalist who had been condemned to ten years'
imprisonment for his part in the Nebi Musa riots of 1920. He had been
amnestied by Samuel, but was still blacklisted by the police as an agi-
tator. The appointment was never officially gazetted, the least of all
the irregularities in the situation and perhaps an indication of Samuel's
uneasiness at the procedure.[51]

Such king-making could have been seen as an interim measure, pla-
cating the most extreme opponents to British policy in order to win
hearts and minds in advance of the elections for a legislative assembly.
However, when elections were held later in the year they were boycotted by most of the Arab electors, who felt that participation would
amount to legitimizing Britain's policy towards the Jews. Samuel next
proposed the creation of an Arab Agency to balance the Jewish
Agency. But this, too, was turned down. Instead, a new body was
created, the Supreme Muslim Council, which was ostensibly to handle
Muslim religious affairs alone, but which, because of its control of all
Muslim monies and institutions, became a powerful political force
totally opposed to the Balfour Declaration and its consequences.[52]
Haj Amin el Husseini, the Grand Mufti, became its President. The
Colonial Office believed that honour had been satisfied all round and
that Samuel had reconciled Palestine's Muslims to the Mandatory
regime. The Supreme Muslim Council operated for only a few days out
of a room in the government offices on Mount Scopus and then transferred to the Noble Sanctuary, the Muslim heart of Jerusalem. It was
to become, in the words of a later Royal Commission, a third parallel
government within Palestine (the second being the Jewish Agency).
One of the first demonstrations of its independence and utter hostility to British rule came soon after with the ratification of the Mandate,
and the formal installation of Herbert Samuel as High Commissioner
– two years after he had actually taken office. Few Muslims were
present. The Mufti refused an invitation to attend.

Richmond's role was central. Those Arab notables who were in favour of at least a tactical accommodation with the Jews alleged that Richmond had encouraged the boycott of the elections, a view confirmed by a memorandum he wrote at the beginning of 1923, arguing that: 'no self-ruling bodies should be set up against the will of the population'. Richmond also proposed revising the Mandate to eliminate preferential treatment for the Jews, and the setting up of an 'impartial' administration. In this he was branding Samuel, who had done everything in his power to show himself a fair ruler, as biased in the Zionists' favour. The Arab leadership at this time believed that, but for Richmond's presence in the government, there would have been 'a policy of imprisonment and deportation' against the Arabs, though nothing in Samuel's record suggests this.[53]

In the short term, the policy of conciliation appeared to have paid off. The remainder of Samuel's term of office was characterized by civic quiet, though this was probably because of the slow pace of Jewish immigration. Richmond, however, was not content. His aim, it emerged, was to have single-handedly changed British policy on Palestine, ending support for the Jewish National Home completely. In 1924 he handed in his resignation, in the odd context of a refusal to attend a formal dinner given by Samuel. In his letter, he argued that the Zionist Commission, the Middle East Department of the Colonial Office and Samuel's administration were 'dominated and inspired by a spirit which I can only regard as evil'. His opposition to them was not merely political, he said, but moral and even religious (Richmond was a practising Catholic). He said that he had 'tried to alter the machine', but had completely failed and had to resign. Richmond left Palestine, but was to return in 1927 as Director of the Department of Antiquities. His appointment was the end of a long process during which various candidates were vetted and rejected, and his views, which were well known to the Colonial Office, were for some time an obstacle, until he gave an undertaking to take no part in local politics.[54]

Pending a plan to share decision-making with an elected assembly, the Mandate acquired a constitution of a sort, the Order in Council of 1922. This document placed power firmly in the hands of the High

Commissioner and a handful of British officials, who constituted the Executive Council. The Advisory Council, initially made up of British officials, Arabs and Jews, was soon an all-British committee, representing the different departments of the administration. Samuel's cautious endorsement of the National Home idea became the basis of the Churchill 1922 White Paper, which reaffirmed the British commitment to the Balfour Declaration. Transjordan – formerly included in the Mandate for Palestine – was now to be administered separately by a British Resident. It was also explicitly excluded from the area of Palestine designated as the Jewish National Home, a gesture which, in the view of the Colonial Office, would make good Britain's wartime pledges to the Arabs. Palestine, though an 'A' Mandate on paper, was now ruled like a 'C' Mandate conceived for more backward areas. It became, for all practical purposes, a British colony in the Middle East. High policy was decided in London, where in 1923 Samuel's voice was decisive in a cabinet discussion on the future of Palestine. Despite the misgivings of the War Office, it was decided that British imperial interests made the continuation of British rule in Palestine essential.

Mandate officials were by now uncomfortably aware of the incompatibility of their obligations to Arabs and Jews. Few had any sympathy with Jewish ambitions, but most believed that imperial interests demanded their presence in Palestine. Recording a conversation with Sir John Shuckburgh of the Colonial Office in 1923, Sydney Moody, who had been District Officer in Safed, in the Galilee, and was to remain in Palestine till the Second World War, believed that: 'If we could go on long enough with tact, patience and diplomacy, avoiding overt troubles, then time would bring a solution.' Moody saw his role as protecting a large minority of Jews, though their 'historical and sentimental arguments left him cold'. The Jews were the only people who were capable of rebuilding Palestine, he thought, because only they had the necessary money, enthusiasm and manpower, while the Arabs, 'if they are politic enough to make a deal with the Jews, have a chance of winning their independence'. None the less, Moody felt that the Jewish population, settled between Syria and Egypt, would prevent the establishment of a monolithic Arab bloc in the Near and Middle-East – and it was on this basis that Britain should encourage the National Home. At this stage of the Mandate, Moody suggested, 'purely administrative affairs such as agriculture, education, the system of taxation' could skirt controversial politics.[55]

But in Palestine, no affair was ever 'purely administrative'. Agriculture was connected with the land question, politically the most disputed area of all; education was to be inevitably politicized, with the schools as forcing houses for nationalism. Moody's most pervasive misconception, however (and not his alone) was the conviction that Muslim and Christian Arabs would never join forces. Moody thought the Christian Arabs, because they held many posts in government, wanted to keep up the hostility between Muslims and Jews, but that they would prefer a Jewish to a Muslim government if the British were to leave. They were not, he thought, as keen on independence as the Muslims. If not all officials would have agreed, few understood that religious differences among Arabs would ultimately be subordinated to a shared national goal.

The creation of the Supreme Muslim Council as a counterpart to the Jewish Agency (as it was seen by Samuel and the Colonial Office) allowed the officials in the first couple of administrations to believe that giving Muslim Arabs control over their religious affairs would satisfy their national aspirations. In Ottoman times, the classification of the minority populations as 'millets' or semi-autonomous religious groups had allowed the maximum freedom to different ethnic groups while retaining political power in the hands of the (Muslim) rulers. Under British rule, what began as a convenient adoption of Ottoman bureaucracy continued as a conceptual tool which allowed the administrators to minimize the real clash of nationalist ideals between Arabs and Jews for more than a decade. Defining Palestinians according to their religion identified all Jews as one national group, but did not allow for the growing rapprochement of Muslim and Christian Arabs. Until the 1930s it enabled British administrators to identify those elusive Arab 'civil and religious rights' to be protected under the Mandate as social custom and religion alone, and as far as possible to ignore the question of Arab self-determination and national feeling. But so far from stabilizing Palestine as a mixed society, it actually created new tensions.[56]

Classifying all citizens, in statistical surveys, as Muslim, Christian, Jewish and 'other' (mostly Druse) downgraded the Muslims, who were a majority in Palestine, to the status of a 'millet'. This system enabled the administration to perpetuate the non-recognition of the Arabs, as in the articles of the Mandate, as a group demanding national independence. But paradoxically, it helped the Mufti, Haj Amin el Husseini, and the Supreme Muslim Council to become the main focus of Arab nationalism in Palestine. Other organizations represented the Arabs – the Arab Executive between 1920 and 1934, made up of urban members of rival notable families from the propertied and professional class; and its successor, the Arab Higher Committee, headed initially by Haj Amin el Husseini and composed of leaders of Arab political groups. They never enjoyed the authority of the SMC.

The confessional division, when used as the basis for statistical information – in particular the periodic censuses – was controversial enough. In administrative terms it could lead to absurdity. When Samuel was trying to work out potential voting areas on a confessional basis by reference to the census of 1922, he wrote to the Colonial Office that in certain quarters of towns where the population was mixed, and where streets were not named, it was impossible to draw clear lines marking out differences, and if an entire quarter were declared to be one voting area, one religious group would probably receive all the votes. During the census of 1931, the Arab Census Committee (appointed, notwithstanding the classifications, to represent all Arabs) protested against the procedure, arguing that if the Jews were classified, to all intents and purposes, as a 'nation' rather than as religious group, so should the Arabs be – and not as Muslims or Christians. Although the census office argued that there was no 'Arab' nationality in Palestine, a question on ethnicity was added to the list, allowing those canvassed to identify themselves as 'Arabs', 'Jews' or 'other'. Migration statistics, from 1935 onwards, were classified under the headings 'Arabs' and 'Jews', conceding that the real divisions in Palestine were between nations, and not between religious denominations.[57]

Samuel believed that he was bound to afford equal opportunities to members of all the different communities in Palestine. He wanted as many Arabs and Jews as possible employed by the Mandate administration – but this only increased the conflict between them. There was no symmetry between the Arab and Jewish positions. Arabs in administration – in the absence of representative civil institutions – were (unofficial) representatives of their communities; the Jews, however divided their loyalties might be, were not, since the Jewish Agency – and, later, the Va'ad Leumi, an elected Jewish council – recognized as representing the Jews *vis-à-vis* the authorities. Jews and Christian Arabs were always over-represented because they were more highly educated. In making appointments the administration had to take account of the rival factions in Arab society (which related to family or political loyalties, more often than to religious belief) and also to balance Arab and Jewish appointments, with reference to the relative size of their two communities. The attempt at communal 'balance' was frustrated: Arabs could not be appointed to govern Jewish areas, or the reverse. There were few Arabs in senior positions in the Public Works Department, because there were so few trained Arab engineers. The most 'representative' Mandate service was that of the police, in which both Arabs and Jews worked under British heads; but this apparent harmony collapsed when there was conflict between Arabs and Jews. Nor was there proportionate representation in Mandate service. In the first, quietest decade of the Mandate, Jews constituted a quarter of the administration, though representing between 11 and 23 per cent of the population. As the Mandate progressed, and relations between Britain and the Jews became more strained, there were ever fewer Jews in high positions in government service. At the lower administrative level, the number of Arabs increased, while Jews were discouraged by the low pay. And despite fact that several Arabs had the requisite qualifications, none ever became head of a department.[58]

As Palestine became part of the colonial system, British officials were funnelled in from every part of the Empire. Though Palestine was not officially part of the Empire, there was, at Samuel's insistence, a Palestine Pavilion at the British Empire Exhibition of 1924 at Wembley, designed by Austen Harrison, the chief Mandate architect. Samuel had argued for a Palestine presence in order to encourage local industry, most of which, as the Arabs protested, was Jewish. Folk art was less controversial. A team of Jewish Yemenite jewellers worked in public in the pavilion, and Storrs, predictably, had dispatched Hebron glass and ceramic ware. Also on show, as the catalogue said, was 'a German bayonet which was beaten into a pruning hook by the Felaheen, and was found by the High Commissioner in the Jordan Valley, thus fulfil-ing the Biblical prophecy'.

Palestine as a vocation, for the score or so of extraordinary men who initiated British rule, now became Palestine as a way-station on a tour of duty, with the prospect of transfer always in mind. The provisional gov-ernment of 1917 had been framed on the model used by the British in Egypt, with a small legal and financial executive. Now it was adjusted to the Colonial Office model. As in Nigeria, Tanganyika and the Federated Malay States, the head of the Civil Service, who ranked second only to the Chief Justice, was known as the Chief Secretary. He was, like a Prime Minister, in daily touch with the High Commissioner (in the colonies more usually the Governor), and, unlike his superior, he was to be at the disposal of the public. Every complaint or petition landed on his desk. The Legal Secretary became the Attorney-General, and when it was nec-essary to supplement Ottoman law, not only English common law but colonial precedent was increasingly drawn on. This was particularly so when the suppression of dissidence, or rebellion, meant using draconian measures such as colonial rulers had used against rebels or terrorists in Bengal, Nepal or the Sudan. The chief difference was in the excessive centralization of Palestine, where no decision could be made without ref-erence to Jerusalem. A letter to the Chief Secretary from Richmond at the end of 1920 complained that: 'in this country District Governors appear to have too little authority in their own districts. Heads of depart-ments dictate to their officials what shall be done and what shall be left undone.' In the Sudan, he stressed, such officials were merely advisers to the District Governors, who decided on policy and got the department to provide the budget, or used their own authority – in assessing tithes, or building facilities, or getting a police escort for tax collection.[59] Keith-Roach described the Palestine District Commissioner as 'combin-ing . . . the functions of Lord-Lieutenant, of a county sheriff, town planner, Home Office official responsible for municipal and local coun-cils, policeman, county councillor, Inland Revenue officer, income-tax commissioner, assistant accountant-general, poor law guardian, justice of the peace, coroner and member of parliament'. But key officials could never act without endorsement from the central government.

Familiar colonial scenes were replayed in Palestine. Under the Samuel regime there were evenings of viceregal formality at

Government House, with guests lined up in the drawing-room before the heralded appearance of the High Commissioner, their names called out in turn before an official handshake. Guests were chosen carefully from the religious, professional and administrative élite of each community, though Muslims seldom attended. Mandate officials went straight from Sunday service at St George's Cathedral to cricket matches at the Jerusalem Sports Club. Samuel lectured on the poetry of Keats, and among the first amateur dramatics performances was *The Merchant of Venice*, with Storrs as Shylock and Ashbee as Antonio. Mandate wives competed at flower shows, held tea parties at which political conversation was taboo, and set up charitable institutions for needy people – but as elsewhere in the colonies, they seldom invited local people to their homes. The German Colony in Jerusalem, which before the war had housed the Templar German pietists, became the British residential quarter for all but those few officials who preferred to live among the Arabs and (occasionally) the Jews.

British sports were adapted to local conditions. The Sodom and Gomorrah Golfing Society drove off and putted on a nine-hole course on the gritty, salty banks of the Dead Sea. Brigadier Angus McNeill, who commanded the British Gendarmerie – the original Mandate police force – set up the Ramle Vale Hunt, in the coastal plain, where pink-coated officials, soldiers and senior policemen hunted jackals in the absence of foxes. Jackals' paws were severed as trophies and nailed to the wall in place of the fox's brush. There were race meetings and steeplechases over the terraces and rocks in the Judean hills. Shooting parties bagged partridges in Judea and wild boar in the Galilee. The British Gendarmerie boxed, and played a game called 'goffy' – like golf but using hockey sticks and a hand ball. These pleasures were not for the locals, who looked on bewildered. It was almost unheard-of for Jews or Arabs to apply for membership of the British Jerusalem Sports Club.[60]

The sun never set on the British officials' working day in Palestine, as the presence of three different ethnic groups or religions celebrating different days of rest and festivals meant that some of the local staff were always on holiday. There were four different calendars, celebrating different views of history. For Muslims and Jews the day started at sunset, for Christians at midnight. There were three days of rest weekly. Each of the three faiths had eight official days on which all the banks closed. Government offices were always open except on the King's Birthday, which was the only holiday all communities had in common. The Director of the Immigration Department maintained that as crises were always happening he had to be on duty twenty-four hours a day, since his juniors were so often absent. Another official commented with the dismal jocularity of so many colonial diarists: 'The authorities hope that the Palestine problem will be solved before anyone else accustomed to holidays on Monday or Thursday wants to come here.'[61]

There were very few venues where British officials could meet local Arabs and Jews on equal terms. One was the Palestine Oriental Society, over which Herbert Danby presided in the twenties. Founded by an American Assyriologist, Albert T. Clay, the POS brought together an international crew of British and French archaeologists, diplomats, professors and priests, Christians and Jews, and Palestinian Arabs, the most energetic of whom was Tewfik Canaan, a doctor and paediatrician who became secretary of the Society. Its official languages were English and French, and its journal was subscribed to by many top Mandate officials. The Society's field of enquiry was academic; apart from the archaeological, historical and linguistic discussions, it also encouraged the study of Palestinian folklore by Canaan and other Arab researchers. These were safely non-political pastimes, in which both Palestine Arabs and Jews could indulge the British appetite for ethnography and Bible studies.

Canaan lectured the Society on the development of Palestine demonology – the belief in spirits in running springs and living wells, the djinns from the lower world who traversed the waterways, the belief in good and bad planets, and the demons who took the shape of female temptresses – and examined ancient superstitions shared with the Greek Church. As a doctor, he also carried his own research into Palestinian rural health, and published findings on the superstitions and folk remedies which more often killed than cured. Elias Haddad wrote on the history of clan loyalties in Palestine, and noted that all the customs of the country had been transmitted orally, and not in writing; he also described peasant manners and discipline. Hana Stephan discussed 'Modern Palestinian parallels to the Song of Songs'; Omar el Barghuti (a 'young Muslim gentleman, son of a prominent sheikh in southern Palestine, who was intimately acquainted with the customs and practices of the Fellah and Bedouin') wrote on 'Judicial courts among the Bedouin of Palestine' and their punishments: capital punishment, blood money, banishment and indemnity. Canaan and Aref el Aref, a passionate Palestinian nationalist and also a Mandate official, were to publish the first anthropological studies along these lines. Their work was influenced by the European orientalists, particularly in their comparisons of Palestinian peasants to figures in the Bible.

The studies of the southern Bedouin were of practical interest to British officials. The nomadic Bedouin were from the outset governed according to separate criteria, with tribal courts which were given Mandatory sanction. These courts were set up to adjudicate in the Southern District, whose administrative centre was Beersheba. They were staffed by Bedouin sheikhs and had jurisdiction only over the tribes in this area. They were not bound by the formal rules of evidence and used tribal methods of cross-examination, including proof by ordeal, in which a red-hot iron was inserted in the suspect's mouth to ascertain whether or not he was telling the truth (the saliva of an innocent man was supposed to protect him). Mandate officials had to be familiar with these customs, which perhaps accounts for the presence of so many political and district officers among the Society's regular members.

Women in Mandate service, as elsewhere in the colonies, were confined to jobs in welfare and education. They came into particularly close contact with the Arab population, and insisted on criticizing British ill-treatment of the fellahin. Margaret Nixon, the Chief Welfare Officer, protested against the appalling conditions in the women's prison in Bethlehem, and was reprimanded when, during the Arab Revolt, she reported military harassment of the villagers. British women close to the Anglican missions also intervened in Mandate affairs. Frances Newton, who had lived in Palestine from the turn of the century, and was the only woman summoned to testify before the commissions investigating the land question in 1930, revealed that she had had unauthorized, random access to official documents and had taken it on herself to interpret British policy to the fellahin. Later, during the Arab Revolt, when critical of the behaviour of British troops, she was ordered out of Palestine by the High Commissioner. When she wished to return there during the war, the head of the garrison objected, since 'the arrival of new troops may result in incidents in Palestine of which people like Miss Newton could make capital'.[62]

There were also a number of single Englishwomen, not in government service, with ambitions to found a Christian sect or movement, do good works or spread communal understanding. Miss Lovell worked for the blind, and Miss Chapman helped the Arab deaf and dumb. Some broke away from the missions and worked on their own, and three such women became involved with the Eastern Churches: Emily Gertrude Butlin, Mary Alexander and Alice May Carey. Butlin, who had been with the Church Missionary Society before the First World War, settled in Jerash in Transjordan, working with village churches and Greek Orthodox believers among the Arab population. Alexander was a scholar and theologian, who did her own research into the Greek Orthodox Church. Carey began as an annoyance to the Bishop and, after a brief triumph, became a lifelong liability to the Anglican Mission.

Alice May Carey, a wealthy woman from Guernsey, first came to Jerusalem in 1922 to join the staff of Miss Warburton's High School as Matron, though it turned out that she knew nothing about children or health care. Her local vicar had described her as a 'woman of prayer', 'something of a mystic', and said that: 'she did not appear to pay the slightest importance to externals and . . . would work harmoniously with those whose outlook was different from hers'. After a year she was tactfully released from her job and moved to Ein Karem, the village which was the alleged birthplace of John the Baptist, to the west of Jerusalem, where there were a number of Greek and Russian Orthodox convents. A Dutchman transported her round the village in his mule cart and worked as her postman. She struck up a friendship with the Russian nuns and was soon enquiring of the Bishop whether as an Anglican she could celebrate communion at a Greek altar at the Orthodox church in the village – a question on which the Bishop referred her to the Archbishop of Canterbury.

Miss Carey purchased several acres of hilltop land with her own private capital, calling the place Ras er Rab, the Mountain of the Lord. She built several houses and a 'Byzantine shrine' on the site (with a 'white stone of peace' designed by Austen Harrison, the leading Mandate architect), where she promised that members of all three faiths would pray together. She tried to interest first the Anglo-Catholic congress in London, and then the local Assyrian Patriarch and his followers in the subject of inter-faith understanding. The Anglican Bishop would not commit himself to these 'wildcat schemes', and so things remained until the 1930s. Thomas Hodgkin, then secretary to the High Commissioner Arthur Wauchope, described her in his letters home:

> She lives in my village and is good to the villagers. I am sorry to say though that she firmly believes that the whole of the British Empire mandates, crown colonies, self-governing dominions and all are bound together by mystical and invisible chains . . . which run between them and the Royal Family. In her shrine, Christians, Muslims and Jews were supposed to meet and be reconciled, but didn't and weren't.

But Hodgkin had underestimated Miss Carey's determination and the fact that she was the owner of a valuable property. Using this as a bait, she was now to involve the Bishopric, the Jerusalem and the East Mission, and even the Archbishop of Canterbury in her plans for inter-faith brotherhood.[63]

Miss Carey told the Bishop that she wished to donate the entire hilltop site with the buildings to the Anglican Church as a centre of Christian philanthropic work among the villages. It was an offer which the Church, tempted by the prospect of having an order in the Holy Land to rival those of the Catholics and the Eastern Churches, could not refuse. After much consultation between the Bishopric, the Mission and the Archbishop, Miss Carey made out a deed of gift to the Mission, which was to hand over the property to the Sisters of the Love of God (Fairacres) from Oxford, a contemplative order to be accompanied by attendant priests. Ras er Rab, the Mountain of the Lord, was to be rechristened Fairacres, Ein Karem. But Miss Carey was not encouraged to live on the property, as she had intended, and work in the villages was not a priority. The idea of bringing Muslims and Jews together in prayer was quietly dropped.

The Arab Revolt of 1936–9, and then the Second World War, scotched the Anglican project. The road to Ein Karem from Jerusalem became too dangerous for newcomers to travel. The Sisters of the Love of God never set out for Palestine. Though for a while she ran the place as a hostel, Miss Carey's schemes had bankrupted her. The Mission, now landed with a worthless property, felt itself obliged to provide her with a 'stipendium' for the rest of her life. She was sent back to England, ailing, before the end of the Second World War, and lived on in mourning for her lost shrine for more than a decade. Later in the war, the houses on the hilltop were taken over by the Polish Red Cross as a nursing home for Polish army personnel, both men and women, stationed in Palestine. There were rumours that in the darkest days of the war the place became a human stud farm for the Poles in exile, where camp followers of the Polish detachments with the British Army gave birth. After the Israeli–Arab War, it was purchased from the Mission by the Israeli government and became, in quick succession, a rabbinical seminary, a mental home and an Israeli Intelligence centre. Ras er Rab, the Mountain of the Lord, Fairacres Ein Karem in the Mission correspondence, was locally known throughout the Mandate, and for some years after, as 'Miss Carey's'. Today, bristling with electronic masts, 'Miss Carey's' like so many other Mandate landmarks, is nameless.[64]

3

The Law Factory

DURING THE first ten years of British rule, nearly as many laws were passed in Palestine as in the British Parliament. In 1935, responding to a request from the Colonial Office for an updated list of Palestinian legislation as a supplement to 'Laws of the Colonies', the Chief Secretary said he was alarmed by the suggestion. 'Our legislation for the past ten years amounts to some fifteen hundred pages. The supplement for the ninth or tenth year might well be some thousand pages.'[1]

The Arab press referred derisively to the Mandate government as a 'law factory'. The first Attorney General, Norman Bentwich, claimed that there was a 'legalistic spirit which had spread among the people under British Administration, and made it necessary to have a legal text as the basis of any exercise of authority'.[2] The Mandate authorities tried to use the law books for a contradictory end: to perpetuate local traditions and at the same time to facilitate change. Herbert Samuel remarked in his final report (he borrowed the Bishop's copy of Lord Cromer's last report on Egypt as his model): 'The new wine of Western institutions could not be poured into the old bottles of Ottoman law.' But reconciling the two systems was a colossal task. In 1944, the Mandate's last Attorney-General, Leslie Gibson, noted despairingly that many legislative problems still remained unsolved which had accumulated over the whole period of the Mandate. The current priority was a new Bill dealing with Civil Wrongs, 'the drafting of which is a considerable undertaking involving a codification and adaptation to the conditions of Palestine of *one half of the common law of England as subsequently modified by numerous statutes*'. There were two other pressing problems: 'One is to overhaul the law relating to personal status with particular reference to marriage, divorce and adoption. Another is to try to reduce the chaotic conditions resulting from the Palestine Land Law into some kind of order.'[3]

The confused state of the personal and land laws to which Gibson referred was the inevitable result of the administration's belief that supplementing old legislation was better than introducing new. The law relating to personal status followed Ottoman practice in allowing the different confessional communities to control the private lives of their members according to their own religious traditions. But these traditions allowed for child marriage and other abuses of women and children, which often clashed with the provisions of Mandate criminal law.[4] Both Arab and Jewish women's organizations tried to persuade the Mandate government to raise the minimum age of marriage for girls – which was only 14 – but as Matiel Mogannam, a leading Palestinian Arab woman lawyer noted: 'The authorities are reluctant to deal with matters which may arouse any objection on the part of any religious authority.' Hence it was difficult for any women's organization in Palestine or Syria to obtain legislative sanction. Among the other anomalies dealt with in the Civil Wrongs Bill was the status of *diyet*: blood money. Payment of money to the family of the victim of murder or manslaughter, according to Muslim tradition, had been recognized under Ottoman law, and was accepted in the Bedouin tribal courts, whose autonomy, in certain matters, was recognized by the Mandate. But since, as an ordinary criminal court could award higher compensation in lieu of *diyet* and was not bound by Muslim religious laws, most applications were made to civil courts; some Jews even applied for 'blood money' in claims against Arabs. The Palestine Land Law preserved the categories of land holdings set out in the Ottoman land laws of 1858. In the historical and social context of Palestine, those laws had done nothing to protect the fellahin against exploitation by landlords and money-lenders. The landlords could sell the land from under them, and chronic insecurity tempted owner-cultivators as well to abandon their land for ready cash. But colonial precedent, the deep-seated reluctance to interfere with local tradition, meant that no fundamental reforms were ever introduced.

There was no uniform view among British legislators in Palestine about the introduction of specific English laws into the legal system beyond the instruction in the Order in Council of 1922 (the Mandate

Constitution) that, where there were gaps in the Ottoman system, English law could be referred to. This was common practice in the Empire. The place of British common law in the colonial legal structure had made it easy for officials to move from one part of the world to another, confident that the ground rules were the same. There were many variations. In colonies established by settlement, like the Bahamas, Barbados, and Bermuda, British common law prevailed with supplementary statutes added where necessary. Where a colony had been acquired by conquest, the Crown could choose: French law was respected in Mauritius and the Seychelles, Roman Dutch law in Ceylon and British Guiana, Spanish law in Trinidad. In Cyprus, Britain took over Turkish law, which consisted of Muslim religious law together with Turkish codes taken from European legal systems. (Turkish reformers, after the Young Turk Revolution, had modelled the Penal and Commercial Codes on French law.) 'One curious result of our scrupulous respect for the status quo', commented Sir Anton Bertram, who was brought to Palestine after serving as Chief Justice in Ceylon and Cyprus to rule on disputes within the Greek Orthodox Church, 'is that we preserve systems of law which have elsewhere become extinct.'[5] In Palestine, Britain froze Ottoman law as it had been at the conquest of Palestine – even while, in Turkey itself, Swiss law was the newest model.

Nowhere was the contrast of new and old legislation in Palestine clearer than in the two areas most bitterly disputed between Arabs and Jews: immigration and land. The Immigration Ordinances – which affected mainly the Jews – were worked out in close consultation with the Jewish Agency. The Land Ordinances – most of which were tailored to the predicament of the Arab fellahin – were superimposed on the existing Ottoman laws governing land tenure, in themselves so complex that only experts in the field had mastered them. They were often beyond the understanding of the District Commissioners and District Officers charged with their implementation. Successive Commissions of Enquiry into Palestine's problems all noted that, so far from respecting the laws, both Arabs and Jews contested, challenged, and repeatedly breached them. Frequently, they co-operated with one another in doing so.

Controlling immigration implied that Palestine's frontiers were recognized and that they could be effectively sealed. But the frontiers of

British Palestine did not correspond to anything in Palestine's past. They were new and, to the older inhabitants, artificial boundaries, designed primarily to show where British rule ended and French began. Palestine itself had been not one unit under Ottoman rule, but composed of several administrative areas, and Mandatory officials spent much of their time with maps and documents trying to locate the routes travellers might take to avoid frontier controls, or the exact borders of a piece of land whose ownership was uncertain.

Entry into Palestine was easy. To the north and east, the new frontiers led through the northern hills from the sea to the sources of the Jordan, and along the river bed of the Jordan valley to the southern desert, whose wastes provided the only real barrier to traffic. As Transjordan remained officially part of the Mandate, though governed separately and outside the area of Jewish settlement, the Immigration Ordinance allowed those resident in Transjordan to enter Palestine without passports. Residents of Syria and Lebanon were also free to enter Palestine if they had special border passes issued under the *Bon Voisinage* Agreement between Palestine and the (French mandated) Syrian government in 1926.[6] When the British port at Haifa came under construction in the 1930s, some ten thousand Arab workers from the Hauran in Syria streamed into Palestine each year after harvest-time was over. There was no accurate assessment of how many stayed behind.

There were innumerable routes through the hills, and fords across the Jordan – a trickle of a river which for most of the year could be easily crossed. Even had Mandate officials not had to check the entry of Jewish immigrants, they would have had their hands full with those residents of the region who were continually on the move and recognized no frontiers: pilgrims on their way to or from Mecca, shepherds, cattle merchants, Nejdian camel and sheep merchants travelling in caravans, salesmen and entertainers, former members of the Egyptian labour corps who, if they had entered before October 1920, had the right to work in Palestine, smugglers whose time-honoured routes ran through the Fertile Crescent, and nomadic Bedouin. The hot springs at El Hammeh, near the sources of the Jordan, attracted hundreds of visitors from within Palestine, Syria and Transjordan. In the milling crowds it was difficult to check how many were local residents, and as late as 1924 the immigration officials themselves were not even sure whether the springs were in Palestine or not (the point was disputed).[7]

Since the end of the war, all Bedouin tribesmen had been given identity cards according to the *Bon Voisinage* Agreement, indicating the number and kind of animals in their possession. Camels and goats had metal ribbons marked with an 'S' (Syria and Lebanon) or 'P' (Palestine) stapled into their right ears. However, the system failed to confine their owners to one area, and they forded the Jordan at need, just as they always had done, until the very end of the Mandate. 'They were supposed to leave their arms at the nearest police post after entering the country, just as we leave umbrellas on entering a picture gallery,' was the acid comment of one military observer.[8] On one occasion two Bedouin were found wandering with their rifles on a main road to the north of Jerusalem, thirty miles inside Palestine. They said they were looking for 'the nearest police station', and the magistrate accepted their plea. Another was caught in the act of wading across the Jordan with his rifle held up above his head. He did not know that the police were watching him on the Palestine side. In court, there were arguments as to whether the man had been on the Palestinian side of an imaginary line drawn in midstream or not. This, and the fact that he was looking for a cow, saved him from punishment.[9]

Arms smuggling went on continuously, and was virtually impossible to prevent. It was not illegal to carry arms in Transjordan, which had the longest frontier with Palestine – all along the Jordan valley. Although it was illegal to have arms without licence, at the beginning of the Arab Revolt in 1936 there were estimated to be about twelve thousand rifles hidden about the country.

There were a number of official entry checkpoints to the country: on the sea coast at Jaffa and Haifa, at Ras el Naqura where Palestine and Lebanon met, at Rosh Pina in the Galilee hills, on the Jordan at Samakh, and on the edge of the desert in Beersheba, Gaza and Kantara, near Suez. There were also two tiny airfields in the north which served British personnel. Some of the checkpoints were customs checks, not political boundaries, and even the customs lines excluded one large, swampy area in the Galilee (the Huleh), making it a perfect entry point for smugglers and sick animals. The initial control system was therefore impossibly complicated. At different points there was a customs check, an animal quarantine check, medical quarantine (there were periodic outbreaks of smallpox and bubonic plague in Palestine throughout the Mandate), plant inspection and, finally, passport control. Officers at the Samakh checkpoint in 1922 reported on the passage of Armenian refugees who had managed to get through to Tiberias on the Sea of Galilee, border inhabitants 'of the nomadic type', who brought chits or notes from their chieftains promising that they would return the way they came, and railway officials who had special permits to move into neighbouring countries and used them on occasion to transport their entire families.

For those who had no documents at the ready, no visa, card or chit, there were other ways into the country: mule tracks and trodden paths through every curl in the hills and valleys. Only local people knew where these led, and they soon learned there was a market for their expertise. Before long there was a steady supply of guides from Lebanon and Syria. The sea coast was no less permeable. Lists of passengers provided by the shipping companies in the twenties gave only names and nationalities; there was no check of passports and visas, making it likely that some ships' masters were involved in smuggling immigrants. The port officer of Haifa told the police in July 1925 that it was 'impossible, without the expenditure of a great deal of time and trouble, to be sure that no stowaways are present on any vessel coming from Constanza, Trieste, or other ports . . . on the line of travel used by the majority of Jewish passengers coming to Palestine'.[10] The hardier stowaways swung out of the lower windows of the ships on ropes to Arab boatmen waiting beneath and, in exchange for a silver watch or chain, were ferried to land beyond the checkpoints. In 1931 an exasperated District Superintendent of Police in Haifa, asked whether he knew about organized smuggling of immigrants in his (Northern) District, complained to the Commandant of Police and Prisons in Jerusalem: 'I have some one hundred and fifty miles of frontier, both land and sea. It is all open, and there is no difficulty securing illegal entry. Frontier posts are only for legals. I do not believe any organization exists as there is no need – anyone can enter the country.'[11]

Checking illegal entry from the north also needed the co-operation of the French authorities, who were reluctant to refuse admission to 'tourists' from Eastern Europe, and did not want to re-admit young people who passed through on their way into Palestine and were then deported. Though by 1933 the French were making it hard for such immigrants to obtain transit visas, in 1935 it was estimated that as many as three hundred 'pioneers' a month, bound for the northern Jewish settlements, were using this technique to get into Palestine. Once inside the settlements they were provided with Jewish trade union documents with their photographs, and – naturally – police questioning of the settlers never revealed their identity. An immigration official minuted a police report: 'There are literally hundreds of strangers who visit these colonies in a year and the mukhtars [kibbutz secretaries – Jews were given the same title as heads of Arab villages] are neither bound nor willing to give their names to the police.'

On the southern frontier, where all but the Bedouin boarded trains at Kantara on the Suez Canal to reach Palestine, there were problems with passengers on the overnight ride through Sinai. The sleeping-car attendants were not to be trusted, and 'pseudo tourists', with neither passports nor tickets, sometimes smuggled themselves into the darkened compartments. Control was difficult to reconcile with the comfort of genuine passengers, and access to the main part of the train meant knocking on the dining-car door, which warned the 'illegals'. When officials began checking inside the train, the manager of the Wagons Lits protested to the immigration officer at Kantara that: 'drastic measures would cause inconvenience to bona fide passengers. To awake passengers at Rafa at about 4.30 am [to check passports] would mean keeping them without sleep until Lydda, as only a few good travellers were able to sleep on trains after being disturbed.'[12]

Palestine had been recognized as a National Home for the Jews and therefore Britain was contracted to encourage Jewish immigration. This did not mean that the Zionist movement was able to bring large numbers of Jews into Palestine immediately after the First World War, or that it wanted to. In April and July 1919 the Zionist Executive issued directives stating that it would be disastrous to encourage mass emigration to Palestine at this stage.[13] There was no guarantee that there would be either work or housing for them, and the Zionists were anxious to recruit skilled, motivated immigrants who would help lay the foundations of a strong economy, and agricultural workers, trained

abroad for new settlements. The main constituency for Jewish immigration was Russia and Poland, where world war, revolution and then
war between the two countries, with the accompanying deportation
and persecution of Jews, had made penniless refugees of nearly a
quarter of a million. Less than 10 per cent of this number arrived in
Palestine, but they created problems for the immigration authorities
none the less.

In the chaos following the war, it was hard for refugees to find a
British representative who could issue immigration visas (none was
meanwhile accredited to Soviet Russia). Many Jews had no passports,
or other documents of identity, though the Foreign Office issued
instructions that temporary documents could be issued for all those
wanting to come to Palestine. Vetting was in the hands of the Zionist
offices scattered throughout Eastern Europe, and in two cities where
most of the refugees bound for Palestine congregated: Trieste and
Constantinople. Many Jews besieged the offices of British consuls and
of passport control officers elsewhere, who had the scantiest of
instructions and no way of assessing the immigrants' abilities.[14] Hence
many of the Jews entering Palestine at this stage were destitute or old,
and others – small shopkeepers, factory workers, or professionals –
could not hope to earn a living.

So in 1920 the Samuel administration decided on the first, simple
system of immigration control for Jews and, inevitably, the first
numerical quota: 16,500 heads of families and single people were to
be admitted (for whom the Zionist Organization was to be entirely
responsible during their first year in the country), and also an
unrestricted number of 'persons with the prospect of settling
independently'. But the Zionists were at this time unable to take full
advantage of the law; only 10,000 immigrants arrived under the quota,
and persons with independent means were rare. After the 1921 riots,
immigration was briefly suspended, and when it was renewed the
system was elaborated. Jewish immigrants now had to fit into one of
three categories: those with independent means, or 'capitalists'; those
with 'prospects of employment'; and those who were dependants of
persons already resident in Palestine. The first and last categories were
now to be approved by the Palestine government, and only the second,
'the labour schedule', was drawn up by the Zionist Organization.
Meanwhile, the Foreign Office began to issue tougher instructions. In

a circular letter to the chief centres of Jewish emigration in March 1922, they instructed consuls not to issue visas for dependents without reference to Jerusalem.[15]

In the summer of 1922, the Churchill White Paper, a document which incorporated many of Samuel's second thoughts on the National Home, recommended that Jewish immigration 'cannot be so great in volume as to exceed whatever may be the economic capacity of the country at the time to absorb new arrivals'. The head of Immigration commented later: 'No one seemed to be aware what this . . . meant and . . . no one either in Government, in London or Jerusalem, or in the Zionist Organization had any idea of how the flow was to be controlled or regulated.'[16] The instruction created endless disputes between the Department of Immigration and the Zionists as to its interpretation, since the former quoted the statistics of unemployment and the latter invoked the dynamics of development. 'Prospects of employment' depended on an infinite number of variables, so that the quotas for the 'labour schedule' were issued every six months.

The controversial issue of 'absorptive capacity' of the country at first related to the Palestine economy as a whole but rapidly came to mean the state of Jewish employment. Immediately after the beginning of the Mandate, there was a shortage of labour, so immigration officials put few obstacles in the way of the Zionist authorities. But soon it became clear that Jews expected higher pay than Arabs and that if they could not find work in the Jewish sector the Mandate would be responsible for their employment. The Zionist argument that Palestinian Arabs would profit from the development of the country by Jewish immigrants cut no ice with the Arabs and was received sceptically by British officials. But there were powerful objections to using the 'absorptive capacity' argument to check Jewish immigration: 'It should be remembered', wrote an immigration official to the Chief Secretary in 1922, 'that capital would not be made available for development if immigration were to cease.'[17] During the first post-war years Jewish support from abroad was inadequate for Zionist needs. But from 1929, with the broadening of the basis of the Jewish Agency to include leaders in the Diaspora, it was vital for the development of industry and the financing of separate services for the Jewish community. Treasury pressures on the Palestine administration to balance its budget meant that money from Jewish taxpayers helped keep the country solvent. So attempts by the Department of Immigration to keep out what it called the 'small shopkeeper and artisan class' – the majority of the applicants from Eastern and Central Europe – were unsuccessful.

As successive ordinances made Jewish immigration more complicated, so the stratagems to evade them multiplied. The records of the Immigration Department are a blow-by-blow account of a losing battle against Jews who were determined to get into Palestine, even if they could not get through the eye of the bureaucratic needle. Until 1934 it was also a one-man battle waged by Albert Hyamson, the (Jewish) head of the department during this time, against the Zionist establishment, which he argued aided and abetted evasion of the law.

Ironically enough, Hyamson had initially been an utopian Zionist of the Samuel type. An article he had written on the future of Palestine as early as 1914, together with Samuel's memorandum, had drawn Lloyd George's attention to Zionism. Hyamson, then working in the savings bank department of the British Post Office, was a scholar in his spare time (he was to write the classic work on the nineteenth-century British Consulate in Jerusalem). Later in the war he served in the Department of Information of the Foreign Office. From January 1921, under changing titles indicating the challenges of his office, he was variously in charge of the Departments of Immigration, Travel and Labour. In these capacities he helped draft and redraft the regulations on immigration in four successive administrations.

Catching 'illegals' entering Palestine was the job of the police. Hyamson was more concerned with the subterfuges employed by immigrants who sought to be included in the administrative categories. Pinpointing abuses of the system became an obsession with him; and he was as furious with what he saw as official indifference or permissiveness as with the desperate stratagems of the immigrants themselves, and what he saw as the 'sinister' connivance of the Zionist authorities. Hyamson accused the Jewish Agency of looking at Palestine not as a country that needed careful development and selective immigration, but as 'a land of refuge for unhappy Jews for as many of them as can get into it' (what he liked to call an 'El Dorado') – a view he clearly did not share.[18] His own declared aim was to keep old people, penniless refugees, 'Asiatic beggars' and other undesirables out of Palestine. When he functioned in the joint capacity of Controller both of Immigration and Labour, Hyamson – perpetually concerned with possible 'Bolshevik' influence in Palestine – was at odds with the Jewish trade union movement, which seldom answered his letters and asked him to write to them in Hebrew. He had earned their hostility early in the Mandate when he supported the Jewish owners of the Jaffa Bakeries against their employees, who had gone on strike for better sanitary and economic conditions. The unions took no stand, but Hyamson intervened on the bakers' side, complaining of union 'intimidation' which enabled them to sack the strikers.[19]

Not all Hyamson's colleagues shared his suspicions of the Zionist authorities. One of his memoranda was minuted, in a reference to the consultative role given to the Jewish Agency under the Mandate: 'The Zionist Organization did not set itself up as an imperium but had powers thrust upon it which we now realize should never have been assigned to it.'[20] The Agency could not be held responsible for fraud, the official added, any more than the Mandate administration was responsible for those officials who took bribes. And while his superiors praised Hyamson for his incorruptibility, Palestinian Jews loathed him for what they saw as his inhumanity.

The attempt to legislate for the control of immigration was problematic from the outset. The Mandatory authorities soon realized that demands for documentation and authorization were absurd, given the chaotic situation in post-war Europe. After the 1921 riots, when immigration was suspended, hundreds of immigrants with valid visas were turned back and immigration officials were sent to Trieste and Constantinople to try to help them. They learned that some Eastern European countries were using the Mandate's commitment to Jewish immigration to drive out Jews and refuse them re-entry, and that many Russian and Polish Jews were fleeing conscription. Although officials noted many Russian refugees and Bolsheviks among the crowds, they argued against Colonial Office proposals that only those with national passports should be admitted to Palestine. 'There would be no need for a control,' minuted H.M.V.C. Morris, the first Controller of Permits, 'because nothing would be left to be controlled.'[21] Many immigrants had escaped from Russia under false names, which also complicated things when they wanted to renounce their former nationality. No legal proceedings were taken against those who had travelled on other people's passports, or used other ruses to protect themselves.

Immigrants also wanted to adopt Hebrew names and discard the old completely, making it even more difficult for the Immigration Department to keep records. The Zionist Commission had suggested all Jews change their names when becoming citizens of Palestine, and consulted the Immigration Department as to the correct procedure. 'Why keep in memory the bitterness of the black exile in . . . your sweet country?' asked the Hebrew newspaper *Doar HaYom*, and English common law provided no help to the legislators: any man or woman could adopt a new name at any time, with the deed poll as the only evidence.[22] In Palestine, therefore, it became compulsory to refer to the Department of Immigration and explain the change, which it was hoped would enable Hyamson and his colleagues to trace those who had entered illegally.

In 1926 Hyamson, now head of Immigration, was sent on a tour of inspection of the Jewish immigration centres in Central and Eastern Europe, and he reported to the Colonial Secretary, Lord Lloyd, who dotted the report with exclamation marks, that he had come in contact with 'three million Jews burning to escape from their present homes'. Only Palestine was open to them, as in 1924 the United States, like Britain at the beginning of the century, had introduced strict restrictions on immigration.[23] Of the 34,000 Jews who had immigrated to Palestine by 1925, Hyamson estimated that 11,000 had either entered or remained secretly.[24] In his view, there were twice as many shops as 'necessary' in Tel Aviv and six times more than the 'necessary' number of doctors. Skilled workers, however, did not want to emigrate.

Hyamson's observations touched on the change in Jewish immigration patterns from Eastern Europe. In the mid-1920s many Polish Jews in this large community sought to emigrate because of increased taxation imposed by the (for the British, aptly named) Polish Finance Minister Grabbski. Some of these were wealthy people – the 'industrialists' whom Hyamson approved of, among them the founders of the important textile industry in Palestine – but most of these returned to Poland when the tax rules were relaxed. The mass were indeed economic refugees – the small shopkeepers and artisans – and they were far to outnumber both the veteran farming population and the pioneers who were prepared to extend the frontiers of Jewish settlement under tough conditions.

The pressures of anti-Semitism and economic need, rather than ideology, were now driving Jews to Palestine. This made careful planning impossible. During the 1920s the administration was called on several times to underwrite Jewish immigration by providing work for Jewish unemployed and, under the administration of Lord Plumer, the second High Commissioner, writing off the debts incurred by Tel Aviv, the fastest-growing Jewish town in Palestine. The early fears of the Zionist leadership that the Jewish economy simply could not support mass immigration were borne out in the years 1927–8, when more Jews left Palestine than arrived. At this stage the Zionists now called in, as advisers, British colonial administrators (something which was never to be repeated), and their reports indicate the mingled admiration and horror with which pukka colonial administrators regarded the slap-dash way in which the Jews were running their rural economy.

Sir John Campbell, formerly of the Indian Civil Service and an immigration and settlement expert, late vice-chairman of the post-war Greek Refugee Settlement Commission, was in 1927 invited to tour twenty-five Jewish agricultural settlements (kvutsot – the early kibbut-zim) and training farms, and was also able to compare them with the older Jewish plantations and with the co-operative settlements (mosh-avim). He reported that the lives of a heroic, self-sacrificing settler population were run by a leadership which put political gains before business management and economic principles. He found not a single colony on sound economic ground; the loans provided from funds raised abroad were never repaid, and no contracts were signed with the settlers. Expenditure always overran budgets, and Campbell thought the cost of settlement was up to 20 per cent more than neces-sary, with a loss factor of up to 40 per cent. Much of this was due to improvisation.

Campbell observed that money was advanced to buy cattle for settlements where none was needed, while the farmers had to sell crops immediately after the harvest at low prices, often with the aid of private loans at high interest in order not to lose the sowing season. In comparing the situation in post-war Greece and Palestine, Campbell found that Zionist expenditure was far higher. Greek settlers were experienced farmers, made do on whatever the Commission gave them and incurred no debts, whereas in the Jewish settlements expensive machinery was neglected and often discarded half-used; over-expenditure was encouraged, he concluded, for propaganda purposes. The Jewish National Fund, the Zionists' fund-raising arm, Campbell accused of running two budgets: one for publication, and one for work. Dependent on voluntary contributions and with no administrative tradition, it had exceeded its income for years.

Campbell had no doubt that it was excessive, unplanned immigration which was damaging the Zionist enterprise. His chief objection was that it left no time for 'organic growth'. 'It has to be remembered that the colonizing of the land and the settlement of Jews generally in Palestine is essentially an *artificial* movement,' he wrote, 'in the sense that it is admittedly not inspired by, or governed by, economic motives.' Unrestricted immigration was, in his view, 'criminal folly'.[25]

The spasmodic quality of Jewish immigration, and of Jewish investment, were to provide the British Treasury with further reasons to limit the Palestine budget. In 1933 Treasury officials argued, apropos of a guaranteed loan to the Palestine government:

> The revenues of Palestine were well maintained, but this satisfactory condition was due in part to the peculiar conditions which have the effect of causing a steady but abnormal influx of investment capital into the territory. The result was high customs returns, but these were unreliable. Hence it was unwise to burden the country either with increased expenditure on administrative and social services, or debts, including capita works which were 'not clearly and fully remunerative'.[26]

From 1927, under the Plumer administration, immigration categories were again reviewed and the resulting change in the law was a nice mixture of economic and humanitarian considerations. The financially independent or qualified class was extended to include professionals, skilled artisans and others with 'assured incomes', or who had 'a definite prospect of employment'. The Department of Immigration tried to check on applicants for the 'labour schedule', without much success. A new class was introduced, to include orphans

destined for institutions, 'persons of religious occupation whose maintenance was assured' (mainly rabbinical seminarists, who had always
had been supported by the charity of Jews outside Palestine), and students. The category of 'dependants' who had to be vouched for by
Palestine residents remained unchanged.[27]

Techniques of evading the immigration laws now became as
complex as the laws themselves. Those hoping to be classed as 'persons
of independent means' included many who borrowed money or
resorted to other stratagems; in one memorandum Hyamson quoted
the case of a barber who insured two combs and a pair of scissors for
five hundred pounds and then produced the policy as evidence of
'means'.[28] The labour schedules in the early years included Jews of all
ages, some over seventy described as 'working men and women'; a
mother of a family from Aden was found to be only five years older
than her 'children'. In the category of 'dependants', Hyamson's
bugbear was 'fictitious wives or fiancées' of Jews already in the
country. Under the Palestine Citizenship Order of 1925, any wife of a
Palestinian citizen became one herself, and could not be deported.
Eventually, the Mandate statisticians began to notice that the ratio of
recorded Jewish divorces to Jewish marriages was rising beyond the
'normal' and that 'professional husbands' were marrying and divor-
cing women, for a price.[29] Crossing borders illegally also, of course,
exposed the immigrants to exploitation. The Department of Welfare
reported having encountered, in the Bethlehem jail, five destitute
'respectable Jewesses' from Damascus, smuggled into Acre illegally by
a Syrian Jew who had taken their money and all their possessions,
saying they would be restored to them in Palestine.[30]

Hyamson's preoccupation with Jewish 'subterfuges' overshadowed
all the other, more usual duties of immigration officials in keeping out
criminals or 'undesirables'. These were usually smugglers (including
those who smuggled Jews), Arab labourers from the neighbouring
countries looking for work – who were repeatedly deported – and
suspected Communist agents. The most flamboyant undesirable was
Walter Schmerl, alias Graf Walter von Alkreuth, alias Otto Zarnakow,
alias Walter Uhlmerl, alias Boris Romanov, alias Comte de Ehrenreich,
etc., 'believed to be in Syria and making for Palestine'. With nine
aliases and five passports, he 'had a long record of convictions in
Germany for fraud and forgery, and was an escaped prisoner from

Novomesto in Czechoslovakia, where he was serving a sentence of 18 months for fraud and illegal possession of arms'.[31]

Bona fide Jewish immigrants from Russia found themselves trapped between the hostility of the Soviet regime and the Immigration Department's fear of Communist infiltration. The Russians refused exit permits to anyone of military age, but if they recommended a Jew for a visa the papers were vetted as 'protection against Bolshevik emissaries'. It was hard for many Russian Jews in the provinces to make their way to Moscow, where the British trade representative was empowered to issue visas, but the Immigration Department would not allow permits to be sent directly, as they could fall into the wrong hands. Collective visas were sometimes issued for 'pioneering youth' but not for ex-political prisoners, who had the most urgent reasons for leaving Russia. In 1924, two boatloads of Jews fleeing Russia, without visas, arrived and were admitted as 'emergencies' after the Zionist Executive intervened. When the same situation recurred in 1927 things were more complicated; by now the British *chargé d'affaires* in Moscow, who had been handling applications, had left because of an Anglo-Soviet crisis (the Zinoviev letter), and Hyamson opposed the entry of the Russians, arguing that: 'as the Zionist . . . Executive will refrain from guaranteeing no one, the question of merit cannot arise'. In November that year four young Jewish political prisoners in danger of exile to Siberia were refused visas by the Immigration Department pending reference to London; in the interim, their exit visas expired. The Jewish press in Palestine let fly. The liberal *HaAretz* asked whether Hyamson would have acted in this way towards any but Jewish prisoners, and the Labour party's *Davar* accused him of 'misusing the key to the gates of Palestine, which he had always used for the worse . . . his department is a symbol of wickedness'.[32]

The category of immigrants which, from 1924, spiralled completely out of control was that of 'travellers' – immigrants who entered on a three-months' tourist visa and remained for good. With increased prosperity in Palestine in the 1930s, the country began to attract not only Jews but non-Jewish fugitives from post-Depression Europe. In August 1933 Hyamson complained that Zionist propaganda was attracting young unemployed Germans, Austrians and Poles, all entering as 'travellers'.[33] They were also coming from farther afield. In October of that year the Immigration Department cabled the British Consul-General in Beirut: 'Understand there are some 200 Afghans in

Damascus with or without visas awaiting opportunities to settle in Palestine. Perhaps you can persuade High Commissioner to send them back to Afghanistan.'[34] Jewish immigrants masquerading as travellers were juggling 'bogus cheques, non existent banking accounts, dishonoured return tickets, borrowed capital, and adopted wives' – and telegraphic correspondence alone had increased six times in a few months. Ten thousand cases were awaiting attention. The Department of Immigration now estimated that there were twenty thousand illegal immigrants in Palestine. This was equivalent to 10 per cent of the official estimate of the Jewish population of 1933, and about 7 per cent of the total population increase of this community since the beginning of the Mandate.[35]

Despite Hyamson's dark hints about Zionist scheming behind illegal immigration, by the beginning of the 1930s it had become an embarrassment to the Jewish Agency, making it difficult to draw up labour schedules and/or to promise a certain number of immigration certificates to their offices abroad. Such planning was all the more difficult because the certificates were fought over between the different political groups in the Zionist movement. On the other hand, the way in which the 'illegals' disappeared into the Jewish landscape was used as evidence by the Jewish Agency, in their discussions with the administration, that the 'absorptive capacity' of the Jewish economy was infinite.

The uncertainty about Jewish numbers complicated Mandate allocation of funds to the Jewish communal authorities. The increase in the number of Jewish schoolchildren, raising the grant to Jewish education, was partly due to illegal immigration, for which the government did not see it should have to pay. Between 1931 and 1947 no census was taken, and one of the factors distorting the picture, despite annual revisions, was the presence of illegal immigrants. At this time it was found that the proportion of Jewish to Arab schoolchildren, according to Jewish requests for funds, was assessed at 33 per cent, rather than 28 per cent as official statistics suggested. Despite the doubts about the accuracy of statistics, the government agreed in November 1947 to pay the grant according to the revised assessment.

Applications for inclusion in the labour schedules were referred to the Immigration Department, which, in consultation with officials in other departments, was supposed to give an educated opinion about whether the candidates were really going to contribute to the country's economy. This was not a scientific process. It was clear that immigrants would often not find work in their own trade or profession, or might move to the country from the town, so that proposals of follow-up systems were impossible to implement. Jewish trade union (Histadrut) figures were regarded as inaccurate, and despite repeated statistical surveys the government had no exact breakdown of occupations. When in the early thirties applications started snowballing from the Jews of Central Europe, Hyamson and his colleagues tried to evaluate how many lingerie cutters, boot-tree makers, opticians, corsetieres, orthodontists and furriers among other Jewish trades, were 'needed' in Palestine. The Director of the Public Works Department argued in 1933 that too many engineers were applying: 'the local market is already overstocked in this direction'; an immigration official minuted an application, 'I do not think sausage making is a skilled trade', and the Director of Customs wrote to Hyamson: 'I am doubtful if there are any demands for umbrella makers in Palestine.'[36] Even the powerful Electricity Corporation, probably the single most important industrial concern in Palestine, to whom blank certificates were issued so that they could swiftly recruit the technicians they needed for the erection of turbines and maintenance of machinery, had trouble with the Immigration Department, which did not like exceptions to rules and demanded the return of unused certificates before more could be issued. 'The Electricity Corporation are merely asking for them because it suits their convenience to be able to bring in any person they require without reference to this section.'[37]

Men outnumbered women in the labour schedules, particularly on the new agricultural settlements, where women made up only 15 per cent of the population in the 1920s, and the Zionists were clamouring for a larger quota. Hyamson's middle-class, Anglo-Jewish upbringing meant that he was shocked at reports of Jewish women working in building and other manual jobs. He was in favour of reuniting husbands who had come to Palestine ahead of their women with wives and children, but thought it 'undesirable' for their moral welfare for girls and young women to be brought to Palestine unless they had friends and relatives to take care of them.[38] On the fate of young single women among the immigrants, Hyamson consulted Jewish women's organizations, the head of the Mandate Welfare Department, and Edward Sawer, the head of the Department of Agriculture. He asked Sawer what the proportion of the two sexes was 'in an ordinary [Arab] settlement'.[39]

Sawer's response was: 'As an ardent feminist I must urge that the ladies in any agricultural settlement be afforded an equality of opportunity. Experience of war showed that tractor ploughing, bull herding, or any other . . . work did not tax unduly the mental or physical capacity of our sisters.' Estates in England, he pointed out, had been efficiently run by women. In Africa – Sawer warmed to his subject – field work was done by the weaker vessels so that husbands could devote themselves to cares of state in contemplative calm, 'our real cosmic function'. He suggested that Hyamson take note of the advantages of polygamy in an under-populated country, and, as he understood that polygamy was not prohibited by Judaism, asked for Hyamson's views. 'As stock breeders we attach the greatest importance to eugenic principles, and would prefer to see the Immigration Department devote attention to selective mating rather than restrictive action – and breed strains of plough women, chauffeuses, dairy maids, etc., resistant to local climatic conditions.'[40]

By agreement with the Jewish Agency, British consular officials were supposed to give priority to young women with 'agricultural experience'. But they complained that 'robust young men or women really fit for agricultural work were not being chosen [by the Zionist offices]', but 'townbred dressmakers, etc., . . . obviously unfitted for any form of hard manual labour'.[41]

So Hyamson protested that 50 per cent of the women on the Zionist schedules 'appear to be of the seamstress and shop assistant classes and apparently unfitted equally in physique, in inclination and in upbringing for a peasant life'. The women's organizations, and Miss Nixon of the Mandate Welfare Department, explained to Hyamson that Jewish Eastern European girls preferred industrial work – in which they had experience – to the occupations, secretarial or domestic, which he thought suitable for young ladies. The Jewish women's organizations whom he consulted argued that there was no shortage of work for young women, but they deplored the girls' dislike for agricultural work – to which the organizations were ideologically committed – and their preference for becoming shop girls or factory workers. Using this information, Hyamson circularized all District Commissioners, asking them to examine very carefully applications from labourers and others for the admission of dependent relatives 'other than wives or young children', since the department was 'taking steps to limit all dependants of this kind'.[42]

The draconian interpretation of the immigration laws by Hyamson's department also made it hard for the pioneering farming settlements (whose altruism Campbell had praised in his report) to expand. Many had relatives in Europe whom they wanted to join them, and to whom, despite their poverty, they were sending funds. But crop failures, drought and pests towards the end of the 1920s meant that the settlers were still in debt in the early 1930s. In many cases, if the settlements had asked for financial help or relief works, their appeals to bring in dependants were dismissed. Only when Jewish organizations began to provide long-term loans to a number of northern settlements were additional dependants admitted, on the grounds that 'it was more economical to bring [relatives] to live in the village than to send funds abroad'.[43]

Every application, in every professional group, now had to be justified by proof that the Palestine economy would profit. The Tel Aviv opera group, under the musical direction of Mr Golinkin, late of the Petrograd Opera House, fell foul of the Department of Immigration when it was found that their general manager had brought in a number of 'suitable candidates' pretending to be opera singers, who had then gone off and found non-operatic work. The manager fled the country, leaving Golinkin to do his own recruiting. His request for a tenor was approved as 'bona fide and of an urgent nature' – tenors then, as always, being in short supply. Golinkin assured the Immigration Department that: 'the tremendous response to the performance of Johann Strauss's *Gipsy Baron* proved not only the Palestine public needed opera but that it is very easy to detract [sic] the public from the talkies and thus prevent the transfer of money out of the country'.[44]

The ultimate sanction against 'illegals' was imprisonment and deportation. The punishment for illegal entry to Palestine was two to three months' jail for the first offence and six months for the second – which, since many illegal immigrants tried again, was not unusual. But as the third High Commissioner, Sir John Chancellor, wrote to the Secretary of State for the Colonies in 1930: 'It is extremely difficult to find a man once he has entered Palestine, if he does not wish to be found, and even if he is found the difficulties in the way of deportation are often insuperable.'[45]

Deportation, which in the early twenties was used against some twenty immigrants a month, was used infrequently, as it was an expensive procedure. Hyamson was in favour of selected deportations, 'which has the advantage of advertising in the European centres concerned the inefficiency of deceit' – but when he wanted to do this systematically in the mid-twenties, the Chief Secretary's office refused to give a general authorization.[46] While District Officers and police officers were authorized in 1925 to order summary deportations, this seems to have been used against Egyptian labourers without passports, described as belonging to the 'vagabond and destitute classes'. Such people were very unlikely to find lawyers, launch appeals, or provide evidence of regular unemployment at the drop of a hat. Deportation was carried out within forty-eight hours or not at all.

In 1931 a census was to be taken, and the Jewish Agency argued with some logic that if a large number of Jewish immigrants had entered the country illegally, and their status was not legitimized, the census would be inaccurate. An amnesty was therefore issued allowing registration as citizens of all those who had entered the country illegally, to the end of that year.[47] But despite the amnesty, the 'illegals' kept on coming, and successive High Commissioners continued to reduce the numbers on the labour schedules by what they estimated were the current evasions. Although it was agreed that 'in flagrant cases' pseudo-travellers could be deported, Hyamson inveighed increasingly against the government's 'leniency'. In 1932, both the Levant Fair and the Maccabiah (the Jewish Olympic Games) brought thousands into the country as visitors, of whom many stayed on. As fast as the administration deducted 'illegals' from the numbers on its official lists, the 'illegals' legalized their presence by becoming nominated by the Jewish Agency for admission on the next batch of immigrants. Hyamson complained that, 'encouraged by the impunity which these people enjoy, the number [of illegal immigrants] is increasing'. He maintained that there were 'illegal' immigration centres in Damascus, Aden, Warsaw, Zagreb, Riga and Salonica. Friends in Palestine helped those without visas, and they were never deported. Orders for deportation were subsequently cancelled.[48]

New procedures were put into effect, complicating the old rules still further. The Departments of Police and of Immigration were to recommend deportation in select cases to be submitted to the Chief Secretary for confirmation. Some were 'requested to report for deportation', and naturally failed to turn up. The necessary speed was never observed. Illegal immigrants were not prosecuted unless it was decided *not* to deport them, since prosecution took time.

The Palestine government knew that deportation of Jews from the National Home which Britain was still contracted to support would be highlighted in the British press and perhaps questioned in Parliament. In a confidential dispatch to three District Commissioners and the head of the Palestine Police in early 1932, the Secretariat made it clear that no Jew found in Palestine without due permission, or having overstayed a visit, was to be deported without the prior approval of the High Commissioner himself. Another confidential dispatch from the Assistant Director of Immigration, R.D. Badcock, to the Assistant Superintendent of Police, showed what happened even when a deportation order was approved:

> You discover someone whom you recommend for deportation, you refer to CID and are in due course provided with the requisite order, CID sends Immigration a copy, in some cases the police get exclusion from the High Commissioner, . . . the passport is stamped instructing to refuse readmission. At this point the problems start. Individuals may obtain new passport and visa unless warnings are issued and the CID requests that all consuls are warned. If therefore you find that deportees are constantly returning to Palestine it is because the CID do not ask us to take specific action.

Badcock thought the courts should inflict heavy punishment on returning deportees, but 'in most cases you find that you might as well cry for the moon'.[49]

At the beginning of 1933, Hyamson's last year in Palestine, illegal immigration reached its peak. He again asked – unsuccessfully – for his own powers to be extended, arguing that the only way to enforce deportation rules was for him to have the authority of the countries from which the immigrants came to return them at any time within five years of landing. He wanted the Mandate to emulate the tough laws of the French mandated area, where the police could deport within four days, or Egypt, where anyone who had taken a course in Communism forfeited his nationality. Hyamson recommended, in addition to the existing regulations, that appeals be limited and only those with valid national passports be allowed to enter Palestine. He went on protesting that illegal immigrants threatened with deportation 'created vested interests' (found jobs); that Jewish employers gave them preferential treatment, in order to escape deportation; that unmarried women 'illegals' got married; that married women got pregnant; and that some immigrants arranged for themselves to be served with summonses to appear in court: all conditions which prevented the administration from expelling them.[50]

In June 1933, a CID report attested that of forty-seven prospective deportees, only one had actually been deported: most had either left of their own accord or could not be found. Further demoralization in the Department of Immigration followed when George Msarsa, of Arab–Armenian parentage, who had worked for the administration since the military regime, was convicted of passing dozens of fictitious applications for immigrant certificates for the enormous sum of £40,000.[51]

Hyamson returned to England in 1934. In 1937, together with Colonel S.F. Newcombe, of the British Army in Egypt before the First World War, and one of the founders of the Palestine Information Bureau in London in the 1930s, he co-authored a plan to settle the Arab–Jewish conflict. The Bishop in Jerusalem at this time, Graham-Brown, was one of the intermediaries concerned. Said to have the support of Arab leaders, and in particular Nuri Said, the Iraqi Foreign Minister, the plan envisaged freezing the Jewish population at under half the population of a sovereign Arab Palestine, with Jewish 'civil and religious rights' guaranteed – a kind of Balfour Declaration in reverse. The plan was no more successful than Hyamson's efforts to shape and limit Jewish immigration.[52]

With Hitler in power in Germany from 1933, the entire immigration picture was changing, as political, rather than economic, pressures built up behind a new Jewish exodus. Hyamson had been scarcely concerned with the impact of Zionism on the Arabs; he was preoccupied with the character of Jewish Palestine and his self-imposed task of fighting Eastern European Jewry. His successor, Eric Mills, the statistician and mathematician, believed that: 'The real trouble was that the Jews were not willing to gain the good will of the Arabs, and to allay their fears by agreeing to limit the extent of their infiltration and to reassure them that the Jews were not going to crowd them out.' In his conversations with Jewish Agency leaders in the 1930s Mills told them that he 'thought the Arabs would forgo the demand for limitation of immigration if the Jews would agree to build up a large industrial life in the country, leaving agricultural land to the Arabs'.[53] Although German Jews represented only about 20 per cent of the immigration of the thirties, they brought with them capital and business skills which now put the Jewish economy on a totally different footing. The transfer of Jewish capital from Germany, and the consequent development of Palestine during the 1930s, made it easier for the Jewish Agency to argue that increased immigration was in the country's economic interest.

The fourth High Commissioner, Sir Arthur Wauchope, who succeeded Chancellor in 1931, had been in Palestine for two years when the changes in Europe began to affect Palestine. Wauchope was torn between the desire to offer refuge to the persecuted and his duty to restrict immigration according to the law. On Hyamson's memoranda, he minuted that 'tourists' staying on after their legal limit would no longer be allowed to stay, and all illegal settlers would be turned out 'whenever the Government has the power to do so. The hardship of the individual must be ignored in order to check this illegal custom that has grown to such proportions as to damage the country and threatens to upset our whole system of immigration.'[54] But at the same time he was generous with certificates for German Jewry. Almost as soon as Hitler came to power, Wauchope doubled the number of 'capitalist' certificates and advanced 1000 'labour' certificates for distribution to German Jews under the age of 35. The British Consul in Berlin was provided with a quota of certificates to be granted to prospective immigrants in the first category without reference to Jerusalem; Wauchope promised that those already in the country would be given 'specially liberal treatment' to bring in parents or other near dependants, and expressed sympathy with Jews 'experiencing difficulty', as he put it, under Nazi rule.[55]

During Wauchope's period of office close on two hundred thousand Jews immigrated to Palestine, twice the number of those who came in during the entire previous period of the Mandate. Whereas Jewish immigration had rarely passed ten thousand a year, in 1934 more than forty thousand, and in 1935 more than sixty thousand arrived. Mills later responded quickly to messages from the consular offices in Berlin and Frankfurt after the pogrom of November 1938 (the '*Kristallnacht*'), issuing blank certificates to be taken up by those Jews who were only released from concentration camps if their admission to another country was guaranteed.

Though the question of 'economic absorptive capacity' was changing as the Jewish economy expanded, the political conflict between Arabs and Jews intensified with the unprecedented increase in Jewish immigration. The legal restrictions on Jewish immigration did nothing to placate Arab opposition. In December 1934, members of the Arab Executive, the self-elected leadership of the Palestinian Arab community, came to meet Wauchope to protest against the current land transfers and the increases in Jewish immigration over the previous two years. Wauchope's answer to the first complaint was, like those of his predecessors, that under conditions of prosperity there would be room for everyone. 'The Government was endeavouring to increase the productivity of the land, and he himself was devoting much of his time to improving methods of agriculture.'[56] But the Executive would not compromise over immigration:

> It had been argued that so large a total was justified by the economic absorptive capacity of the country, but whether that was so or not, the Arab Executive considered that this was not a proper sole criterion; the position for the Arabs was that their civil and religious rights, the protection of which was a Mandatory obligation, should be given first consideration. At the present rate of immigration, the Jews would outnumber the Arabs within a few years.

As the Colonial Office minuted: 'In other words, the Arab perception of civil and religious rights meant not being outnumbered.'[57] In fact, though the Jewish population of Palestine had reached 17 per cent of the total by 1931, by 1946 the Jews made up only 31 per cent and by 1947, just before the end of the Mandate, slightly less than one third of the population of Palestine.

Ships bearing Jewish refugees from Europe, with or without visas, began plying their traffic between the Baltic and Aegean ports and the beaches of Palestine immediately after the Nazi takeover. Between July 1934 and September 1939, forty-three ships bearing 15,000 refugees, organized by different political Jewish groups, made their way to Palestine. Some were intercepted. But it was not until after the Arab Revolt that there was a reversal of British policy towards Jewish immigration, the first since the Balfour Declaration. The White Paper of May 1939, which also imposed severe restrictions on the Jewish purchase of land, set a five-year limit to all Jewish immigration and made any further quotas dependent on Arab consent. Even before the outbreak of the Second World War, the administration finally countered Jewish desperation with brutality. The illegal ships and their owners and captains were fined, and the ships made liable to forfeiture; the immigrants were threatened with fines they could not pay, and imprisonment, and those who managed to reach Palestine were interned or deported to Mauritius or Cyprus. By the war, the Mandate administration, with the Navy behind it, was in direct confrontation with the Jews, who by now had a network of agents all over Europe, chartering ships. The Jewish underground helped the immigrants who evaded the patrols off the beaches and into towns and settlements. While Arabs crossing the frontiers were also deported, the immigration ordinances became irrelevant, overtaken by a series of Emergency Regulations which legitimized drastic action against the immigrants.[58] Force, not law, now decided who entered Palestine.*

The 'chaotic state of the land laws' deplored by Gibson in the last years of the Mandate was, once again, the result of efforts to square obligations to Jews and Arabs alike. Under Article 6 of the Mandate, Britain was obliged to encourage Jewish settlement, especially 'on state lands and lands not required for public purposes'. It was also pledged to promote the material and moral welfare of all sections of the population, which included protecting the interests of the Arab peasant farmers – the majority of the population. But the land laws (or ordinances) which the Mandate imposed on the old Ottoman system did little to

* For the later conflict over immigration, see Chapter 5.

change the conditions which led inevitably to the fellahin's dispossession. Ottoman rule favoured the interests of the landlords over that of the farmers. Palestine had a semi-feudal system of land ownership, archaic conditions of tenure, and farming methods which despoiled and exhausted the land – all of which had impoverished the fellahin.

Most Arab villages were in the central highlands and hilltops, wherever there was fertile soil. They were picturesque: made of grey limestone with stone terraces, surrounded by fruit gardens and orchards, though a closer look indicated that there was no sanitation; wastes were piled to one side of the village, not always downwind. Infant mortality – usually from dysentery – was high. Soap, though produced in Palestine from olive oil, was rarely available, and the peasants used breadcrumbs, wood ashes and a special clay to rub off dirt; but this was not enough to destroy the bugs. British officials who spent the night in the guest houses, or those of the wealthier peasants, might find their clothes infested by morning.[59]

The crops were rain-fed – olives, figs and almonds, grapes, vegetables and cereals. Palisades of prickly pear surrounded each village, the sign of the continuing fear of raiders, whose horses could not get through the spikey leaves. Bedouin raiding during the previous century had also meant that much good farming land in the valleys or plains had been abandoned. Much was unreclaimed marshland or covered by sand dunes, and was occupied by fellahin families who scratched a living from the depleted soil, grazed cattle or buffalo, or used the reeds to make baskets or mats. On lands owned by city landlords, the tenant farmers (for the most part illiterate) were bound by custom and by debt to the owners. The British tried for years to persuade the Bedouin tribes in the north to register their claim to a specific area of their traditional territory, and to settle there permanently.[60]

The peasants' lives alternated between sowing and harvest periods, when all village labour was enlisted, and interim periods when all farm work was suspended. In April and May the barley was harvested, in June, the wheat. In the hills, the fig and grape season was between July and September; in October, the olives were beaten off the trees, using long sticks. Entire families went out to the fields, or into the hills, to the orchards and vineyards, and camped out, in storage huts or under canopies of sticks and branches to protect them from the summer sun. The threshing floor, a flat rock on which the women used big sieves, was communally owned and exposed to wind, so that one of the commonest conditions the Mandate doctors had to treat was eye infections from seeds which had lodged in the peasants' eyes. The crop was weighed for taxation, the men filled the sacks with grain and the rest of the harvest was used in the village: stalks for the baskets, straw for building or fodder.

This looked like a self-sufficient economy; but every Mandate official charged with tax collecting soon discovered that most of the peasantry was in debt to money-lenders in the city, at astronomical interest rates.[61] The administration, heir to a tyrannical Ottoman regime, was seen as the enemy; when Edwin Samuel began his career as District Officer in the 1920s, he needed an escort of fourteen policemen on visits to the villages. Such officers acted both as tax collectors and local magistrates, trying peasants who carried firearms or cut down trees – not only for firewood, but because cutting a neighbour's trees down was one method of carrying on a feud. Blood feuds were settled by the equivalent of 333 gold napoleons, or £3 6s. 8d.[62]

The peasantry was not only at the mercy of the landlord and the taxman, and fluctuations in the price of wheat; their crops could be destroyed by natural disasters – drought being the most common, but also plagues of locusts and fieldmice, with which Mandate officials had to cope during the 1920s. There had been one devastating locust attack in 1915. In 1928, swarms stretching over an area of two to five kilometers, 200–600 metres deep, were sighted. The 'crawlers' moved forward inexorably, even stopping the trains because the wheels could not bite on to the rails. Once they became 'hoppers' they took to the air and devoured every growing plant, and the females landed and hatched out thousands of eggs. Ploughs, zinc sheeting, flame-throwers and poisoned bait were all used to check the invasion. As it was hard to destroy locusts on the wing, Sawer, the head of the Agriculture Department, decided to trap them when they landed to deposit their eggs. A small army of fellahin under British command dug trenches, drove the locusts into the ground, covered them with poison, ploughed them over and then collected the eggs by hand.[63]

In addition to such natural threats to their livelihood, the fellahin were not even sure of their formal title to the land they lived on. In 1925 it was estimated that three-quarters of the land in Palestine was held by unregistered title.[64] Even by the very end of the Mandate, titles to huge tracts in dispute were still not settled, for the existing Ottoman registration was unreliable. Under Turkish rule, ownership of land had rendered the owner liable not only to taxation but also to conscription, so sometimes it was registered under a pseudonym, or in the name of a notable who had promised the farmer protection against the state, the tax farmer, or the money-lender. Private transfers of land took place while the lands remained on the books of the Land Registry in the name of the original owner. Sometimes the area was deliberately minimized; sometimes its boundaries were described only in relation to local landmarks: a large rock, a ruined castle, a wall or other people's fields.

The Turkish reforms of 1858 had made it easy for the urban class to buy up much of the fertile land of Palestine, mostly in the coastal plain. In many cases they were now able to sell the land over the heads of their tenants. Tenancy agreements in Palestine, for that matter, often depended on custom and oral agreement. And as in the immigration question, the Bedouin were a law unto themselves. Each tribe had its own traditional grazing-ground, sometimes on peasants' land after harvest-time. In the large desert areas south of Beersheba, it was agreed that legal jurisdiction would be subject to tribal custom, and the Bedouin were not required to pay Land Registry fees – in the hope that they would legalize their holdings. But there were thousands more Bedouin in northern parts of the country, who often made claims to occupation or grazing rights which the British administration was inclined to respect.

As puzzling for the British administrators as the documents in the old registry was the system of classification of land under Ottoman law. The distinction between public and private property, between state land and individual holdings, was flexible and, had farming methods been more efficient, should have encouraged agricultural prosperity. There was land whose owners held it legally but which they could not sell without official consent. If it remained uncultivated for over three years, ownership reverted to the state. This included land which had been appropriated by the last Ottoman Sultan, Abdul Hamid, for his private use and profit. State land which had been neglected could, however, be claimed by individual farmers if they could prove that they were ploughing it anew, and paying taxes. Another category of state land was allotted to communities for grazing and woodcutting. Some land was endowed to Muslim religious or charitable institutions. There was unoccupied land – over half the area of Palestine – scrub and woodlands, to which no one had title. And there was land in collective village ownership, parcelled out in strips between the inhabitants and periodically redistributed: *mesh'a* land – a destructive custom which led to over-use and neglect. *Mesh'a* also complicated questions of tenure – in one village, Zeita in the Tulkarm district, there were no fewer than 906 claims to ownership – and title deeds could not be regarded as collateral when held in the name of the whole village. *Mesh'a* land was often mortgaged to private landlords, and individual parcels sold off to Jewish buyers.

The administration swiftly realized the inadequacy of the Turkish system of land registration. The ordnance maps of the whole country prepared by military engineers for the Palestine Exploration Fund in the nineteenth century were insufficiently detailed. General Bols initiated a further survey in 1920, using Turkish maps modified according to a system used in the Sudan. But surveying and land registration (land settlement) were at first separate activities, making efficient assessment, whether for taxation or endorsement of sales, impossible. Sir Ernest Dowson, an expert on cadastral affairs, previously of the British Financial Department in Egypt, was summoned to examine their co-ordination, and the more effective Torrens system, based on that used in Australia, was introduced from 1928. This involved judicial examination of every holding, and resulted in assessment not only of ownership but of the land's current and potential use. But eight important years had been wasted, and the pace of surveying varied according to political events. Surveying in the plains (where the Jews more often bought land) was swiftly accomplished. During the Arab Revolt, work went on slowly in the hilly areas (where the Arabs rarely sold land), with the surveyors often needing a police escort. The 1937 Royal (Peel) Commission – which recommended the partition of Palestine – reported that even after twelve enquiries, carried out over fifteen years, the Palestine government 'was unable to state with any degree of accuracy how much land they held either as State Domain or as waste land'.[65] By 1940, only 219 of over 800 villages had been settled. By contrast, with 700 surveyors working during the Second World War (an unprecedented period of prosperity and calm in the history of Palestine), another 473 villages were settled, with 102 pending.[66] Post-Second World War unrest, together with the chaos preceding the end of the Mandate, prevented the completion of the survey.

Where land settlement was incomplete, wrote the Jerusalem District Commissioner in 1937, the land ordinances the government introduced were used by trespassers, to blackmail registered owners.[67] Both parties offered evidence of ownership by ploughing land or fencing it, or putting it to some use. Once land had been properly surveyed, there were fewer disputes; some land holdings were rearranged to encourage more productive farming. But land settlement also often meant forced sales, when the owners could not pay their taxes. The Ottoman classification of land remained, even if not fully understood. Many local officials, as well as experts like Dowson, urged the abolition of the *mesh'a* system, in the interests of the fellahin. The Colonial Office, however, demurred. So the local mukhtars, or headmen, whose power rested on their authority to divide land periodically, had the last word; and with the power structure unchanged, District Officers found it difficult to persuade the fellahin that change would be to their advantage.[68]

The only way in which the Mandate could both have retained Ottoman practice, and reconciled its own obligations to Jews and Arabs, would have been through agricultural reform, enabling the fellahin to make far more intensive and profitable use of the land in their possession. This would have meant not only confirming their right to tenure, but also lowering the high taxation on agricultural produce, providing agricultural credit and loans, and introducing new methods of cultivation on a comprehensive pattern.

None of this happened. The pace of land settlement was made even slower by the submission of claims which often could not be proved. When endless disputes over ownership, between Arabs as well as Arabs and Jews, led to violence, more laws were introduced. A Land Disputes Possession Ordinance was introduced in 1932, enabling District Commissioners to take possession of land where a 'breach of peace' was likely to occur. Taxation was reduced, but pegged to the basis of an average price in previous years – shortly before a disastrous slump in agricultural prices in the late 1920s.[69] Agricultural loans were issued mainly before 1923, though their recipients were still struggling to repay them a decade and more later. And although the third and fourth High Commissioners, Chancellor and Wauchope, were notably sympathetic to the fellahin, new methods of farming were adopted in only eighteen of the eight hundred or so Palestinian villages.[70]

The natural disasters which periodically recurred in Palestine – droughts, floods and pests – caused less destruction than the way in which the land was farmed. Not only wartime deforestation, but also grazing by sheep and goats, and ploughing up and down the hillsides, rather than along contours – the corollary of the *mesh'a* strip system – had caused winter rains to wash topsoil down the gulleys and the destruction of much cultivable land. The improvement of life-expectancy and security under British rule made things worse rather than better. Health was improved, infant mortality shrank, without conscription more men remained in the villages and, under Wauchope, rural taxation was reduced as an incentive to farmers to produce more. But there were now more mouths to feed, and each village had to bring more land under cultivation to survive. Land became scarcer, steeper slopes were worked, scrub and forest was cleared to produce more farmland, but irrigation schemes were few, fertilizers were rarely used and the soil was not rested or replenished. Landlords made few profits, and as smallholders fell deeper into debt (with the interest taken by money-lenders rising to as much as 30 per cent), the temptation to sell became irresistible.

Near the end of the Mandate, a British agricultural expert, writing on the acceleration of soil erosion under British rule, castigated the administration and the farmers alike for not having introduced land reform or improved methods of soil cultivation. He included the Jewish settlers, 'despite their superior educational standards and access to information', in his condemnation of farming methods. 'The fact that after twenty-four years of settled government, regular trading, and fair conditions of taxation . . . erosion and loss of soil occurs at an accelerated rate is a very poor advertisement for the leadership and energy of all sections of the population.' Changes in farming practices, he argued, would profit the farmers and increase yield by as much as 30 per cent. He recommended the adoption of contour ploughing, intensive afforestation, the abolition of the *mesh'a* system, the control of grazing, the establishing of proper titles, the proper shaping of plots under land settlement, and the alteration of the existing Muslim laws of inheritance – something which had already been done in Iraq and Turkey. 'Is it beyond the powers of our leaders, administrative and agricultural officers, etc., to bring this about?'[71]

To an expert concerned only with the professional and technical aspects of land use, the remedies seemed obvious. Britain's experience in India and Africa, too, might have supplied precedents for coping with peasant indebtedness and agrarian reform. In the Punjab, careful assessment had resulted in the elimination of debts. The Egyptian government had given guarantees to mortgage companies to help repayment of loans by Egyptian cultivators. In the Sudan, a Land Settlement Law had compelled owners of small fragments of land to transfer their share to neighbouring owners, and when Norman Bentwich tabled the Palestine Land Settlement Ordinance in 1927 the Sudan law was his model, particularly in his efforts to modify the mesh'a system. But the Colonial Office felt that the substitution of larger for smaller individual holdings was 'of doubtful vision' and 'directed against the village communities of Southern Palestine'. 'I doubt', wrote Lord Lloyd, 'whether it is advisable in this manner to allow an undermining of tribal custom and traditions'; and Ormsby Gore thought such a move should be 'optional rather than compulsory' – which would have made it obviously unworkable.[72]

Ultimately the Palestine administration, with limited funds at its disposal, exercised all its legislative and administrative ingenuity on what it thought would control or defuse the political conflict between Arabs and Jews. When it did have disposable income (as in 1926, when revenue over expenditure amounted to over £6 million pounds, or in 1935, when the surplus was twice the yearly budget), the money was spent on police and prisons, not on bailing out the farmers. The land laws introduced from 1920 onwards were designed to prevent the dispossession of the Palestinian fellahin and to block mass movement to the towns – which, after the rise in life-expectancy, was the most significant demographic change in the Arab population. These laws had less connection with land reform than with the fear of the creation of a rebellious, landless, and possibly criminal, underclass, which the administration would then have to support and control.

The sale of Arab land to the Jews was regarded as the cause, rather than the result, of the legal powerlessness and impoverishment of the fellahin. In 1935, the Chief Secretary summed up land laws as follows:

The special policy which the Mandatory Power has undertaken to carry out in Palestine [i.e. the encouragement of Jewish settlement] makes land legislation a matter of politics and not of administration. At the same time, it has the advantage of securing that the views of all responsible bodies and persons concerning land legislation are carefully considered.[73]

So the administration was baffled by the fact that, despite all its best legislative efforts, the sale of land continued to Jews, both by Arab landowners – including many leading nationalists – and later by small-holders and fellahin, and the laws were regularly circumvented by both sides. The Palestine government, too, was frequently obliged to com-promise its own declared principles regarding the sale or lease of land, and even – when fellahin refused to take advantage of the new laws, holding out instead for monetary compensation – to become involved in their eviction.

The first and second Land Transfer ordinances of 1920 and 1921 tried to make land available to Jewish investors while protecting the Arab tenants. Other land ordinances of 1920 were aimed at regulating and demarcating state land, in an effort to prevent its cultivation without permission, and to register land that had been reclaimed. Under the Land Transfer laws, the administration was enabled to with-hold consent to land transfer unless the tenant in occupation retained sufficient land in the district or elsewhere for the maintenance of himself and his family. But very often, by the time the proposed trans-fer reached the Land Registry, there were no tenants left. The head of the Registry, J.N. Stubbs, later reported:

We . . . instructed the District Officer to report on the tenants. He would go out to the village, and in some cases he would find that the whole pop-ulation had already evacuated the village. They had taken certain sums of money and had gone, and we could not afford them any protection what-ever. In other cases it was found that a large percentage of the population had already gone before the transaction came to us, and we could not find out who the tenants were, they had no written contracts, and we did not know what compensation they were getting.[74]

As for state lands, the head of the Agriculture Department, Edward Sawer, reported in 1925 that Arab peasants had become experts at turning forest or wasteland into ploughed land overnight, in such a way as to convince officials the next morning that they had reclaimed it over a period of years.[75] Nor did the ordinances check speculation. They expressly forbade the purchase of land by foreigners; but such purchasers could register property in a Palestinian name. Another stipulation, that land could not be bought and sold within a year, could not be enforced, as agents could buy up title deeds and then sell the land in the original owner's name. Prices rose because of increased development and security under British rule, because of a worldwide rise in land prices, because Jewish buyers competed with one another, but also because Arab landlords and, later, smallholders, understood the Zionist thirst for land and raised prices accordingly. Jewish buyers often refused to accept land until it was free of tenants, and either included the price of their resettlement in the purchase price or were prepared to buy them out. The largest single sale of this kind was the marshy, but potential fertile, land in the Esdraelon valley belonging to the Sursock family of Beirut and sold in the mid-1920s. In all but one of the twenty-two villages in the area the tenant farmers accepted compensation and left.

The administration was not prepared to sell state land outright, as the Turks had sometimes done, but rather, to lease large tracts to the Jews under the terms of the Mandate. State land was often unreclaimed marshland, as in the coastal plain, or covered by sand dunes. The new laws obliged the administration to provide alternative land for the tenants, but in the case of the Athlit Kabbara zone near Haifa, this took so long that the Jews and the Arabs reached an arrangement: the Jews compensated the Arabs, providing them with land and cash, and the administration was obliged in return to allot the Jews free title to the land. In another case, in land covered by dunes, the opposition of Arabs whose claims were based on both ownership and grazing rights combined with doubts as to the legal status of the territory: no unanimous verdict was reached in the courts after nearly a decade of litigation.[76]

The government's principle of leasing, and not selling, state land was infringed in a different way in the Beisan land case, in the Jordan valley. Land previously belonging to the Sultan was sold to the tenant farmers – semi-nomads – in 1921 on condition that it was partitioned and settled after the survey was completed, and intensive cultivation undertaken; the only land allowed as *mesh'a* was grazing-land. But settlement of this potentially fertile area dragged on into the 1930s, and by then, though the payment period had been extended in 1928, the owners were selling off parts of their land as they could not meet the instalments. The original agreement, drawn up by Bentwich, the Attorney-General during the Samuel administration, was severely criticized in subsequent British Commissions of Enquiry. The agreement was made, said the critics, 'in order to provide the Arabs with a holding sufficient to maintain a decent standard of life, not to provide them with areas of land with which to speculate'.[77] The irony here was that the Samuel/Bentwich regime was continually accused of Zionist bias, though in the case of these lands its main aim had clearly been to conciliate Arab public opinion. Although much of the land was subsequently sold to Jewish buyers, Bentwich was never forgiven by the Zionist right wing for his role in the affair.

Under Lord Plumer, the second High Commissioner, the problem of displaced fellahin received official recognition. In 1929 the first in a series of 'Protection of Cultivators' ordinances was introduced. About 80 per cent of these 'cultivators', it has been calculated, were fellahin working their own land, and the remainder were agricultural tenants. The new laws delayed the handing over of the area, obliged the seller to pay monetary compensation to those dispossessed (thus legalizing the practice which had made land transfer unworkable) and established boards and commissions to decide disputes. But while the definition of tenants was constantly widened, Mandate legislation did not protect the fellahin smallholders, those who were selling part or all of their land in order to meet debts.[78] Moreover, it did nothing to secure for those dispossessed a sufficient area for the maintenance of their families. Statutory provision of such an area – what was called 'the lot viable' – was repeatedly discussed but never took place, partly because its 'viability' depended so greatly on whether or not it was intensively cultivated or, more important, irrigated.

Landlords and purchasers alike found ways round the legislation. Some landowners refused to renew leases to their customary tenants. Others raised the rent of land beyond the tenants' ability to pay. The owner of tenants in one large village, Shatta, let the lands to another landowner and, after the end of the lease, ejected the tenants – who were not protected under the law. Collusive mortgages were made and debts forfeited to get round the law.[79] Sometimes the landlord made an agreement with tenants not to collect part of the crop as rent, and paid the tenants' debts instead, so that they would leave. As litigation was expensive, it was inevitable that, if the case was won, those who paid the costs often took a share of the land. During the 1930s some lawyers who went in for financing land disputes would receive half the land in payment if they won the case.[80] The Waqf religious trust sometimes concluded a written agreement with the Arab plaintiffs, undertaking to finance the lawsuit and, in return, claiming the property as its own; the plaintiffs then became Waqf beneficiaries.

The Samuel administration had underestimated the willingness of Arabs to sell land to the Jews. The Plumer administration appears to have misinterpreted it as a sign that there was no fundamental enmity between the two peoples. This belief could have been encouraged by the fact that Arab politicians themselves did not make an issue of land sales until 1928, instead focusing their opposition to British rule on the Balfour Declaration and Jewish immigration. During the 1920s most of the sales had been by absentee landlords resident in Lebanon and Syria. But from 1928, it was local landowners, and later small cultivators, who sold most of the land to the Jews.[81] In public, the Arab Executive demanded an end to land transfers to Jewish purchasers, while in private several of its own members sold land themselves. The Arab press castigated the sellers while naming few landlords; those who came in for most criticism were the brokers. The most effective opponent of land sales, at the turn of the decade, was not an Arab but the new High Commissioner.

Sir John Chancellor, unlike his military predecessor and successors, was a seasoned colonial administrator. After service with the Royal Engineers in India and the Sudan, and as secretary of the Colonial Defence Committee, he had been Governor of Mauritius, then of Trinidad, and became the first Governor of Southern Rhodesia in 1925. Chancellor was now nearing retirement, and would have preferred the job of Under-Secretary at the Colonial Office; instead, he was sent to Palestine, after a very cursory briefing with the outgoing High Commissioner in February 1928. Plumer told him that Palestine was secure, unlike Transjordan, where 'it was necessary to reassure the Emir that he would be supported against the French, the Persians and Ibn Saud'. The plans for Haifa harbour were nearly ready, the Treasury was 'squeezing Palestine', while the Arabs would press for a legislative council. Plumer advised Chancellor that he should put off granting them this for as long as possible. Jewish–Arab relations, Plumer assured his successor, 'were not a cause for anxiety'.[82] At about this time, Stewart Perowne, one of the Mandate élite, recalled that at the end of a meeting of the Executive Council presided over by Plumer, a District Commissioner said: 'You've said nothing about the political situation.' Plumer dropped the monocle from his eye against his blue serge suit and said: 'Crosbie, there is no political situation, and don't you create one.'

The Zionist Organization, which monitored the character and views of each successive High Commissioner through its contacts in London, reported in early 1928 that Chancellor, though 'totally ignorant on Palestine', believed that the Western Wall should come under Jewish control, and wondered 'why no great Jewish philanthropist had not bought it yet'.[83] The Jews also hoped that since Chancellor had shown an educated interest, following his Rhodesian experience, in farming matters, he would approve their colonizing efforts. Later that year, after briefing Chancellor on Jewish development work in the north of the country, Frederick Kisch, the head of the Jewish Agency Political Department, noted that Chancellor had read the reports of Campbell and others on the new settlements, and was disappointed that 'more effective use was not made of Jewish investments'. Chancellor had enquired about the Huleh region, the swampy area some were recommending be drained for cultivation, asking 'whether meanwhile we [the Zionists] should not be quietly buying land in the neighbourhood, a remark which was characteristic of the general tone of his observations'.[84]

But by the end of the following year Chancellor had become convinced that it was necessary to restrict Jewish land purchase drastically, or even ban it altogether. He wanted an end to the collusion between Arabs and Jews in the sale of land, and he was worried about the effect of dispossession of fellahin on the social structure of the country. He became deeply involved in the Wadi Hawarith case, an important legal battle over the displacement of Arab tenants. And while this continued, the first serious outbreaks of Arab violence against Jews in eight years belied all Plumer's optimism.

In April 1929, the chief Zionist land-buying organization, the Jewish National Fund, bought a large area of land at Wadi Hawarith, between Haifa and Tel Aviv on the coastal plain. The vendors were members of a Palestinian Arab family some of whom lived in Jaffa. As often happened, they did not want their identity known, nor the price they were paid, so the land was sold at public auction; the sum the family received was more than three times that publicly announced. The JNF had also paid compensation to the 1,200 farmers, agricultural workers and shepherds – Bedouin and fellahin – and village officials nearby, in order to prevent trouble when it took possession. The Arabs were given notice to quit the land within a year. Though the administration challenged the validity of the sale, successive court judgments pronounced it legal, and ordered the eviction of the Wadi Hawarith Arabs, who also failed to qualify for tenancy privileges under the first Protection of Cultivators Ordinance (which had initially been introduced as a response to this very case). Chancellor did all he could to prevent their displacement. He had one portion of the area classed as state land; and through the Jewish Agency, the JNF was persuaded by Chancellor on three occasions to lease part of the land for an interim period to the administration – which then handed it over to the fellahin. Alternative land was offered the Wadi Hawarith Arabs in the Jordan valley, with transportation, fodder and plots planted in advance on irrigable land. All this was turned down. By intervening in the case, therefore, the High Commissioner himself had become involved in attempts to manipulate or circumvent the laws he himself had promoted, as well as taking on a paternalistic, rather than a legal, role.[85]

Chancellor was now convinced that the only way to protect the tenant population on land sold to the Jews was to stop such sales completely. In putting forward a proposed Transfer of Agricultural Land Bill, he wanted to prevent the sale of 'Arab land' to 'non-Arab', unless sanctioned by the High Commissioner himself; he made it clear that he would not approve such transfers.[86] He also invoked legislation restricting the sale of native land both in the Mandate for Tanganyika and in the Federated Malay States, and argued that it was the the government's duty in Palestine, too, to protect the farming population. But the Attorney-General, Norman Bentwich, opposed the Bill, pointing out that Chancellor's proposals contradicted the terms of the Mandate and its obligations to the Jews. He argued that much land which could be farmed was still uncultivated, and that the main problem was not Arab farmers but the grazing traditions of Bedouin tribesmen, which he thought could be dealt with in separate legislation. Tanganyika, as a 'B' Mandate, was no parallel, he suggested, and distinguishing between 'Arabs' and 'non-Arabs' was racial discrimination.

This was not simply a difference of opinion between a High Commissioner and his chief legal adviser – or even a hostile front against Bentwich, since the Solicitor-General, Drayton, backed Chancellor's views and others in the Chief Secretary's office agreed with the Attorney-General. It was the worst clash between any High Commissioner and Jewish Mandatory official. Bentwich's professional views were only, in Chancellor's eyes, a confirmation of his belief that no Jew really had British interests at heart. Chancellor accordingly told Bentwich that his Jewishness (which, for Plumer, had seemed a political advantage: 'invaluable as a Jew') disqualified him from his post – quite apart from his avowed Zionism. Bentwich protested, to no avail, that fellow Jews held high office in the Empire and that other non-Jewish officials had Zionist sympathies. The Colonial Office backed Chancellor. Bentwich was put on leave with pay, and then detained in London under the pretext of 'giving temporary assistance to the Legal Department of the Colonial Office'. He was then offered the post of Chief Justice in Cyprus, which he refused. Fortunately for the Colonial Office, Bentwich was offered a teaching post at the Hebrew University. But announcement of the post was held up by the opposition of a member of the University Board, who cited the Attorney-General's pro-Arab ruling in the Beisan lands case. When the administration urged haste, 'to give the appointment of a new Attorney-General a perfectly natural appearance', the President of the University, Judah Magnes, told Chancellor that, although favourable to Bentwich, they 'felt disinclined to let themselves be utilised merely as a means of extricating HMG from the difficulty'. After many months, the appointment was finally approved, though when Bentwich first appeared on the podium to speak on international law and peace there was uproar, with students shouting that he should 'go and teach peace to the Mufti'.[87]

Chancellor had wanted his term in Palestine to crown his colonial career – he was soon due for retirement. Everything conspired to frustrate him. On his first home leave, Palestine was shaken by the first serious outbreaks of violence in a decade. A quarrel over Jewish rights at the Wailing Wall in the autumn of 1928 led to Arab rioting and murders of Jews and – in restoring order – the killing of Arabs by British police and soldiers. The Palestine garrison which, 'squeezed' by the Treasury, Plumer had incautiously reduced, had to be hastily reinforced. The incident was exploited by the Mufti during a year of incitement, which culminated, in August 1929, in more bloodshed: the massacre of entire families within the Jewish community in Hebron and Safed by Arab rioters. Two Commissions of Enquiry were sent out over the period from London, and both re-examined the whole question of Arab–Jewish relations under British rule. While the first Commission recommended a complete overhaul of policy, on land as on other questions, the second gave a low estimate of the cultivable area of the country and declared that, apart from the existing Jewish land reserves, there was 'with the present methods of Arab cultivation no margin of land available for agricultural settlement by new immigrants'.[88]

Both Commissions had been deeply influenced by Chancellor's now strongly held views against the transfer of land. Lord Passfield, the Colonial Secretary, issued a White Paper in October 1930 incorporating his recommendations. For several months it appeared that land sales to the Jews were to be officially halted, and that Chancellor had succeeded in reversing one of the most important provisions of the Balfour Declaration. But the British government, under pressure from the Jewish Agency, was not yet prepared for such a radical change of policy. A letter from the British Prime Minister, Ramsay MacDonald, to Weizmann in February 1931 modified the White Paper in such a way as to forestall any ban on land transfers, instead returning to the principle of compensation, in either land or money, for those dispossessed (the Arabs dubbed this the Black Letter). Additional provisions helped those who (like the Bedouin in Wadi Hawarith) had grazed or watered animals, or cut wood or reeds on lands up for sale, for five years, and limited the landlords' ability to raise rent without government sanction. A new Department of Development was set up to examine the claims of 'landless cultivators' and to resettle them. But the category of the 'landless' was highly restrictive: it excluded those who had found employment elsewhere and those who had sold of their own free will, and included other conditions which disqualified most of the applicants. Fewer than seven hundred out of

more than three thousand applicants were accepted as eligible for resettlement. The disappointment of many fellahin who had believed that
they would be restored to their previous lands only increased their motivation to circumvent the laws.

The Mandate officials charged with implementing the land laws knew
the extent of the fellahin's debts. Some put forward proposals to alle-
viate their situation, from promoting co-operative societies (which,
though legalized in 1920, had never been introduced among the fellahin) to a scaling down of interest on debts by the courts. Most of the
suggestions were rejected out of hand. Morris Bailey, the Assistant
District Commissioner for Haifa, who had been in Palestine from the
days of the military government, criticized the government in 1933 for
not having actively encouraged co-operatives ten years earlier. He suggested that the government should repay creditors by bonds or notes
at a low rate, taking over the fellahin debts. His suggestions were
unconditionally rejected by the Treasury, whose spokesmen argued
that the ordinances for the protection of tenants were sufficient. 'Any
proposal to repudiate debts even though the fellah is virtually bankrupt without giving creditors the ordinary right of liquidation is . . .
commercially immoral', and taking responsibility for the collection of
debts was 'out of the question'.[89] In the early days of the Mandate a
few longterm loans had been made and farmers had mortgaged their
property to the government as security. When the time came to sell,
however, the debts sometimes exceeded the value of the land.[90]
Another proposal in the early thirties was to advance loans to Arab
landlords who agreed to employ landless farmers, but few landlords
co-operated and the suggestion was dropped.[91]

The Commissions set up in the mid-1930s to adjudicate between
tenants and owners gave Lewis Andrews, of the Development
Department, hope that 'the public was beginning to realize the advantage' of the revised ordinances. The new High Commissioner, Sir
Arthur Wauchope, instructed District Officers to inform the villagers
of their rights as soon as they heard of an impending sale. But many
thought the 'new law' gave them the right to any land they could
plough. Sometimes squatters claimed tenancy rights, in order to force
the Jewish owners to bribe them to move on. On one occasion a Jewish

company gave Andrews a verbal assurance that they would *not* tempt Arab tenants to evacuate land with advance compensation. Andrews lambasted those 'foolish tenants' who renounced their rights and had to be protected against themselves. 'It is impossible to legislate for fools, and cases of foolish tenants accepting cash in lieu of a subsistence area are bound to occur,' he noted.[92] His views were shared by Keith-Roach, who recalled:

> Most British officials thought that the Arabs had had a raw deal, but did not realize that the Arabs' future lay largely in the Arabs' own hands. They sympathized with the peasant who was quite content to sit under the shadow of his single tree and watch the Jews plant scores of new ones on land that had formerly belonged to Arabs.[93]

By the mid-thirties sympathy for the fellahin in the administration was waning. In 1935 the Commissioner of Lands, Albert Abramson, circulated all district officials, both Commissioners and District Officers, proposing that various 'village improvement schemes' encouraged and sometimes financed by Wauchope should also comprise mutual help schemes and grants which, together with land settlement and an Irrigation Ordinance now on the books, would reduce the fellahin's debts.[94] The responses, particularly those of the Arab District Officers, were critical of the fellahin. Nicola Saba, District Officer for the Jerusalem, Bethlehem and Jericho sub-districts in the south of the country, pointed out that fruit trees were being supplied at low rates and rural taxes had been reduced:

> Experience has shown that fellah in the hills has his eyes wide open to see where he can obtain a loan . . . once he gets it he lavishly spends it on unproductive schemes . . . he will never be able to repay . . . without pressure. The curse of the fellah is his laziness in changing from extensive to intensive cultivation.

Saba said each fellah had three months in the year to work on extra terracing but was not doing so: 'I do not believe in enforcing culture on any person.' Abdallah Kardus also thought that the seasonal pattern of the fellahin's life should change, and that instead of importing poultry, eggs and meat, the administration should encourage the farmers to produce them. The Jerusalem District Commissioner J. E. F.

Campbell, summing up all the responses, said that there was agreement that the fellahin should find work during the three winter months, and that giving or lending them money encouraged idleness: 'The fellah has come to think that every loan is a government grant.'[95]

All this did nothing, of course, to improve the condition of the land itself. Landlords were cautious about leasing and releasing land, in many places preferring to leave the land fallow rather than to run the risk of farmers claiming tenancy rights. They tended to let lands for less than a year and thus prevented the farmers cultivating winter crops, so that while wasteland was suddenly ploughed to claim rights, other, fertile land lay uncultivated in order to *prevent* claims from being put forward. Everyone went to court. The Royal (Peel) Commission of 1937 found that:

> The work [of land settlement] is impeded by a large number of fictitious and frivolous claims all of which have to be duly recorded, examined and decided. This procedure inevitably provokes and multiplies litigation, especially in a country where there has been a sudden and abnormal increase in land values. Whereas at first disputed claims were about 10 per cent of the total submitted to Settlement Officers, there is now reported 'a growing tendency to dispute every claim where there is a shadow of a case, and often where there is not'.[96]

In 1935 a *fatwa* was issued, signed by Haj Amin el Husseini and five other muftis, forbidding land sales to the Jews. Those who did so were branded as traitors, their burial in Muslim cemeteries prohibited, and they were to be exiled from Muslim society. The Mufti toured the country invoking the *fatwa*, the Arab press attacked the brokers, and a fund was set up by the Arab Executive to buy land earmarked for sale – though it had little success.[97] Yet sales of land went on, not all of them by impoverished farmers. Lewis Andrews named in his reports members of both the Arab Executive and the Supreme Muslim Council who had been involved, as agents or sellers, in the commerce.[98]

The Arab Revolt of 1936, an uprising against the British and the Jews alike, eventually caused such destruction and chaos throughout the countryside that it negated any progress towards agricultural reform that had been made. The question of the 'lot viable' for the landless was put aside and land settlement came to a halt in many areas of the country, as half the district courts were closed. Agricultural and horticultural stations, including an experimental fruit station paid for by Wauchope, were attacked by Arab rebels. The sole Arab agricultural college in Palestine was closed, and its entire herd of 33 cattle looted. Andrews himself was a target of rebel anger: shot dead on his way to church in Nazareth in 1937. His murder was the trigger for the deportation of much of the Arab leadership of Palestine, and the flight of the Mufti.

Yet even during the Revolt, sales went on, even if in secrecy. The Jewish National Fund ceased registering purchases, but it quietly acquired, between 1936 and 1940, most of its property in the Galilee and over half of that purchased in the Jordan valley. Moreover, where formerly land was bought chiefly in areas where Arab settlement was sparse, it was now bought for strategic reasons, staking a claim to Jewish control over the whole of western Palestine.[99]

It was not until the end of 1938 that the Revolt began to come under control. By this time, the British government was convinced that on the issues of both immigration and land, only stringent measures would placate Arab political opinion. In May 1939, when the White Paper was issued restricting Jewish immigration, the new High Commissioner, Sir Harold MacMichael, was given the power Chancellor had been denied: to limit land sales to the Jews. Thus in 1940, new Land Regulations were issued restricting further Jewish purchases to 5 per cent of the area of western Palestine – in towns and a small coastal area where Jews were already resident.

The regulations were only partially effective. Bedouin sheikhs sold the Jews large tracts of land in the Negev, the southern triangle between the plains and the desert. The methods varied; most often Arab land brokers made purchases at public auctions of land that had been collusively agreed on before hand. J. F. Stubbs of the Land Department, in conversation in 1939 with a member of the Agency, indignant at the new regulations, said that he could not see how sales by Arabs to Jews could be prevented: 'If a Jew purchased from an Arab outside the Land Registry, and if that Arab sold the same land to another Arab (and registered the sale), he would be able to get an order of eviction.'[100] He was right. Many years later, one of the main Jewish land purchasing agents explained:

We said to an Arab, we won't buy from you, transfer the land to the name of the Arab we give you. He took the money and transferred the land to the second Arab. How could that Arab transfer the land legally to us? You tell him, dear sir, it says here that you have had money from us, you took a loan from us. After that, we will sue you for the return of the loan. But you will not return the money; you are declared bankrupt, and so all your property registered in your name in any place is at our disposal, we can legally seize it, and this is what the White Paper [of 1939] forgot. He [the British legislator] forgot that, and through this loophole we bought a great deal of land.[101]

The suspicion arises that if the British legislator had 'forgotten', most British officials knew perfectly well what was going on but hoped that passing laws – even if they could not be implemented – would save both British and Arab face. British pretence that obligations towards the peasants were being fulfilled was matched by the Arab pretence that the sales were not taking place. This seems to have been the reason, too, why the previous legislation was never cancelled.

During the Second World War, there was another reason to question the usefulness of the Protection of Cultivators ordinances. Thousands of dunams (approximately four to the acre) of land which could have provided vegetables and cereals were wasted because the owners could not work it themselves but feared to let others do so lest they should claim the land as their own. By this time the Chief Justice, William FitzGerald – an Irishman – admitted, in correspondence with a leading Jewish lawyer, that the Protection of Cultivators ordinances were unsatisfactory, though 'the time was unpropitious' for their repeal. In internal correspondence the reason was made clearer: 'The main argument against total repeal seems to be the political agitation that would probably result on behalf of the 'landless Arab' and that this is a bad time to risk stirring up sleeping dogs.' Discussions for further amendments went on, but FitzGerald did not believe further tinkering would help:

I am convinced that if we are to solve satisfactorily the problem of the fellah cultivator in Palestine, far more drastic measures will be called for. My study of the files has convinced me that the problem is the old one that has caused revolutions in the various states of Europe during the past 200 years. It is the problem of the peasant's dawning consciousness of his right to the soil that he tills, as he breaks away from the state of feudalism. It is accentuated in Palestine as it was in Ireland by the incidence of absented [sic] landlordism.

In France, Russia and Ireland, Fitzgerald concluded, it had been realized that there was only one solution: 'The state must acquire the landed estates and parcel them out in smallholdings to the cultivator at a rent which will cover interest and capital, so that after a certain number of years the cultivator acquires the land in freehold.' In Palestine, though, all legislation had been 'at the panacea stage'. The problem should have been tackled at the early days of the administration, in which case: 'we would have avoided many of the political troubles that have retarded the progress of Palestine.'[102]

Those 'political troubles' gave the impression that the Jews were taking over much of the land of Palestine. In fact, over the entire period of the Mandate, they bought only a fraction. Of the territory which became Israel in 1948 only about 8.5 per cent was owned by Jews, of which 54 per cent was vested in the Jewish National Fund, largely in undeveloped and unpopulated areas as a base for rural development, the remainder being privately owned, mainly in and around the towns.[103]

Many of the land disputes took place not between Arabs and Jews, but between the government and landowners, between the fellahin themselves, or between fellahin and Bedouin tribes. The fellahin had not been slow to realize that unprofitable land could be turned into cash put down by the Jews. They also knew that the government had money for compensation. They trespassed on land the government had expropriated for the purpose of afforestation or agricultural stations, claiming it had been theirs 'from time immemorial', and tried to raise the compensation figure by pretending that their land was fertile. Some planted wild olive suckers, others cleared away shrubs to plant cereals which had no chance of growing, and even went to the lengths of cutting down trees the government planted.[104] Sometimes both Arabs and Jews made common cause against the government.[105] Often the courts had to rule on disputes between fellahin and Bedouin, both of whom claimed ownership of rocky wasteland on which nothing had ever been grown, but where Bedouin goats had customarily grazed. In one Jordan valley village, the fellahin brought two civil cases in 1930 against nomads for 'encroachment'. The local District Officer argued that the nomads, 'as tenants of the crown', represented the government, 'if only as its humble dependant'. These 'unlettered nomads', he argued, might have 'in all simplicity' laid claim to lands not theirs. But until this was proved, they were entitled to the same consideration by the government 'as was accorded to the enterprises of Sir Francis Drake by his Queen'. On the other hand, he went on: 'Cunning and sagatious [sic] persons' might have taken advantage of the Bedouin to enrich themselves at his expense, armed 'with every artifice of litigation'.[106] The case went on for five years and no compromise was reached. Only the lawyers profited. No villager was too unsophisticated to have heard of the money to be made out of the British land laws – and this included two Bedouin tribes, though one had long been sedentary. The Ed-Duyuk Arabs of Jericho brought their animals to graze on Deir Dibwan land near Ramallah when it was not under cultivation, and the Dibwans went down to the Judean desert with tents and flocks, to a spot where in winter some sparse greenery sprouted in a patch of land allegedly in Duyuk territory. This arrangement had gone on amicably until land settlement began in 1936. At first the boundaries were amended, but this pleased neither side, and after an order prohibiting trespass was issued, the Duyuk tore the Dibwans' tents, cut their ropes, and shot at some of the villagers. When the Duyuk built some mud brick houses on the land, the Dibwans attacked them and demolished their encampment. The court found that the land belonged to neither party, was used as pasture land by both, and that the real reason for the fight was that both the Duyuk and the Dibwan were trying to sell it to an unnamed buyer.[107]

The most complex, extensive and hard-fought land case of all, which continued for more than a decade and nearly involved the British government in a financial and political catastrophe, had nothing whatever to do with the conflict between Arabs and Jews. It began with one of the usual tussles over the ownership of land in the obscure village of Muharraqa, in the Gaza district. The villagers, who had long cultivated the land, claimed it as their own. Officially, the land was still registered in the name of the last absolute ruler of Palestine before the Young Turk Revolution, the Sultan Abdul Hamid. Such land had long been regarded as government property – as, for instance, the land in the Beisan case – and the Settlement Officer assumed likewise. Since all Turkish state land in Palestine had been ceded to the government of Palestine under the Treaty of Lausanne in 1923, he registered the land as government property, but allowed the fellahin hereditary rights of cultivation in a portion. The government appealed against this decision, and the Land Court, which decided on such matters, ruled against the fellahin.

Astute lawyers, meanwhile, had spotted a technical error in the proceedings. The Sultan, by an Ottoman act of state (or *iradeh*) shortly before his deposition in 1908, had transferred all his private holdings to the Turkish state. However, not all the details of this particular transfer had been checked when the alteration in the Land Registry was made in 1932. Hence the procedure by which the land had been declared the property of the Palestine government was technically faulty.

In any ordinary case, this would not have caused trouble. The Ottoman Land Registry had been so badly kept, so full of false claims and evasions of the law, that where ordinary mortals were concerned, a certificate in the Turkish Land Registry alone was not considered sufficient evidence of ownership. But lawyers challenging the government's right to the land were acting for an exceptional team of plaintiffs: the three widows of the deposed Sultan Abdul Hamid, resident now in Canada with their four sons and five daughters. One of the Sultan's sons, Prince Selim, filed the original petition claiming ownership of the Muharraqa lands in 1934. After his death, the Prince's three widows, and their sons, swelled the list of plaintiffs. Six widows were now in the field.

What was at stake was not just possession of the land in a village near Gaza. The despotic Sultan Abdul Hamid had during his long reign commandeered fully one seventh of the land area of Palestine, and his former property there was valued at one hundred million pounds sterling. What was decided regarding the Muharraqa lands in the Palestine Land Court was going to constitute a legal precedent affecting not only stretches of country all over Palestine, but all other land in the Middle East which had been under the Sultan's rule. If they lost, the plaintiffs were planning to take their case to the International Court of Justice at the Hague.

The dispute, while simple in its general outline, was complicated by the small print of Ottoman law. In essence, the plaintiffs argued that the lands were private property, of which they were the rightful heirs. The defendants – the Mandate government – maintained that the lands had been acquired by despotic practices, and that for this reason the Sultan had been judged unworthy to retain them as his own. The Turkish government, it was argued, had not confiscated private land, but had taken over state land which had been illegally acquired. But this was enormously difficult to prove. The lawyers for the plaintiffs quibbled over every detail in Ottoman law, and on the eve of the Second World War the case was taken to the Privy Court of St James, the appellant court for Palestine. A retrial was ordered on technicalities. By the time this happened essential documents were found to be out of reach in the Archives Nationales in Paris, which had come under Nazi occupation. The vital Acts of State themselves were in Istanbul, but the Foreign Office was nervous about the possible reaction of the Turkish government to the affair, and it took years for them to agree to approach the Turks directly. By agreement by both sides, litigation between the six widows and the Mandate government was postponed to the post-war period.[108]

When dealing with the Palestine landowners, or the impoverished fellahin, the administration had repeatedly had been tripped up by its ignorance of the Ottoman Land Code. In the Muharraqa case this became a nightmare. Successive Attorney-Generals who handled the case had to do so in close consultation, at all stages, with the British government.

By 1946 the Attorney-General was a newcomer to Palestine, Leslie Gibson. Gibson had served in the Malayan Civil Service, and as Attorney-General in Trinidad. He now found himself in what he modestly called 'one of the most absorbing [cases] with which he had ever had to deal'. Neither he, nor any of his British colleagues, possessed the requisite knowledge to refute the plaintiffs' claims. They did not know whether at the time of the Young Turk Revolution Gaza was or was not part of the independent administrative area of Jerusalem – a vital point in the case. They did not know how precisely the property of a Turkish Sultan descended on his death, and whether his successors (the Turkish government) or his heirs (according to Muslim law) should inherit it. They did not know the exact power of the *iradeh* at the time of the Turkish Empire, or what formalities had been required for it to be considered legally binding.

On the first point, Gibson and his Solicitor-General, Sir Michael Hogan, sought help from Jewish lawyers, both inside the administration and in the Jewish land purchasing organizations, who had long experience of arguing land cases within the framework of Ottoman law. (The plaintiffs' lawyers, too, were all Jews.) Gibson also sought expert help from Ruhi Bey Abd'el Hadi, once an Ottoman functionary and at one time Assistant Secretary in Jerusalem – the highest appointment ever made to a Palestinian Arab under the Mandate. Ibrahim Pasha Hashim of the Arab Bank of Amman was asked for his opinion on the other questions, but his reply was indecisive. The legislative powers of the *iradeh*, he said, needed a 'treatise' to expound them. Gibson realized that he needed not only further expert advice but above all, true and authorized copies of the documents in the Turkish archives. He therefore took matters into his own hands and, accompanied by Ruhi Bey Abd'el Hadi, flew by night to Ankara, where he shuttled between the British Embassy and the Turkish Foreign Ministry. The diary he kept 'as a record' rivals that of William Boot. He discovered that the Regent of Iraq was also in town, and that:

> Iraq was very worried, because, although they had passed a law confiscating the Sultan's property, they felt that there was now a danger of the matter being taken up before the International Court. If they lost the case, Iraq might be virtually bankrupt because of the fact of the Mosul Oil Field (which the plaintiffs were also likely to claim).[109]

Gibson refused to be tripped up by Turkish government bureaucracy (the release of any state document had to be authorized by the Prime Minister), by the jealousy of the young First Secretary at the British Embassy (who felt he was being bypassed), or by the manoeuvres of the plaintiffs' lawyers, who had also been canvassing learned opinion in Turkey. He found that other potential heirs, who knew nothing of the proceedings in Palestine, were lining up in the wings. The Turkish Foreign Ministry maintained that the idea of suing the Palestine government had come from the former Jewish dentist to Sultan Abdul Hamid – a shady figure who also pursued Gibson, urging him to come to terms with the heirs. Other 'mysterious callers' tried to sell him useless information. The Sultan's widows were carrying on parallel proceedings against the Turkish government. When Gibson motored up the Bosphorus to the country home of a learned professor of Ottoman law, he discovered that he had already given the Turkish government an opinion which was against the Mandate case on every point.

However, with Ruhi Bey Abd'el Hadi to help him check and authenticate the documents, as well as help from Perkins of the Legal Department of the British Embassy, Gibson succeeded in obtaining copies of most of the documents he needed, chief among them the *iradehs*, and arranging for others to be forwarded. As he said, the case involved millions of pounds sterling's worth of property in Palestine alone, and he had obtained, 'by any means possible the best and fullest evidence'. Also, it might have been added, at bargain price. Perkins received £59 for his expenses and the Turkish–Jewish lawyer through whom he worked, £131.

Gibson's tenacity was rewarded. A few weeks later, in January 1946, the Land Court in Jerusalem ruled against the plaintiffs, basing its arguments mainly on the documents Gibson had secured. In Turkey, in June, the Court of Cassation gave judgment in favour of the heirs, totally ignoring the *iradehs*. But when the plaintiffs went to the Palestine Court of Appeal, in March 1947, it unanimously confirmed the Land Court's ruling.

In March 1948, only eight weeks before the end of the Mandate, yet another appeal was pending before the Privy Council in London. In view of the international importance of the case, the documents were sent to London, with the successor states to have access. But Gibson, already packing his bags, declared that the Palestine government 'did not wish to take any part in the appeals since the government is not interested in the result'. In a memorandum to the Chief Secretary, the Attorney-General noted that the record of the case was only sent off on 6 March, and would surely not reach London before 15 May, when the Mandate would terminate, as 'in view of its great bulk, it was sent by surface mail'.[110]

4

Patching up Palestine

WHEN THE British arrived in Palestine, the 'average' fellah was expected to live only thirty-five years – a statistic resulting in the main from the very high rate of infant mortality. Almost the entire rural Arab population was illiterate. By the end of the Mandate, the rural Arab could expect to live another fifteen years, the Arab population had doubled and a majority of village boys were attending school, though most for only four to six years. A massive public health offensive had brought Palestine's endemic diseases under control – most important among them malaria, but also the eye disease trachoma, which led to blindness and which, at the beginning of the Mandate, affected three-quarters of Arab and over a third of Jewish children.[1] Infectious diseases which had regularly killed thousands, including smallpox and typhoid, were now prevented by innoculation or located and treated before they could spread – with the exception of tuberculosis, for which there were hospitals only in the Jewish sector.

Nevertheless, both the subject peoples had grievances. Arab leaders, mayors and villagers complained of the lack of local clinics and schools, and looked enviously at the superior facilities of the Jews, subsidized from abroad and partly financed by self-taxation; Jewish organizations protested that government grants-in-aid to their health and school systems, allotted according to their numbers in the population, were inadequate, given their proportionately greater contribution in taxation.[2]

The Departments of Health and Education struggled to stretch a thin financial blanket over a constantly expanding population, and the results embarrassed both the administration and the Colonial Office.

The last Director of the Health Department, H.M.O. Lester, found only the 'skeleton of a fine service' when he arrived in 1946, though he had heard it was 'the only real Health Service in the Colonial Empire'. He observed that, because of the 'scandalously low' salaries, most government doctors also ran private practices, and that bribery was widespread at the municipal level.[3] The Education Department, too was criticized for leaving so many illiterate. The Royal Commission of 1937 thought more money could have been found for education at the expense of 'public works of the not vitally urgent kind'. In 1942 a Colonial Office advisory subcommittee on education reported of the Arab rural sector that: 'at no time since the Occupation [i.e. 1917] has the provision of school places satisfied the popular demand'. It noted that by the 1930s the school population had doubled and there was dangerous overcrowding, but there was no budget for extra school buildings, the estimated cost per pupil being 'immoderately low and only obtained by overworking the teachers and impossibly large classes'.[4] The share of the annual budget devoted to health and education never rose beyond 7 per cent of total government expenditure, and was often only half that sum. The budgetary priority was always security, which meant that the public – particularly in rural areas – profited only incidentally from government investment: for instance, the new roads which allowed some towns and villages better access to hospitals. Towards the end of the Mandate, government expenditure on police and prisons was five times the budget for education.

Report after report stressed that poverty, ignorance and the lack of sanitation were mainly responsible for the high rate of mortality and grip of infectious disease on the country. However, the hygiene lessons prescribed for schools were bizarre, given that in most cases they preceded the installation of running water and drains. ('Importance of washing eyes often and keeping them free of flies and discharge. Importance of being free from flies, lice and mosquitos . . . danger of spitting on the ground . . . open windows in bedroom.') Still, discontent with progress under the Mandate was also a result of the administration's success in promoting public health, and awareness of preventive care, in a formerly neglected population. The rise in life-expectancy and the drop in infant mortality led to chronic overcrowding in the schools and unprecedented demands for admission to hospital, even from the peasantry (which, at the beginning of the Mandate, had had more faith in folk remedies than in foreign doctors). Improved conditions led to greater expectations – and inevitably, to bitterness when these were not satisfied. Since medical checks were carried out mainly in the schools, those villages without schools were often without proper health care – and fellahin girls were seldom sent to school. Surveys carried out during the Second World War (a period of prosperity in Palestine) revealed that the urban poor, both Arab and Jewish, suffered from poor sanitation and inadequate nutrition.[5] Conditions were worst in the shanty towns in the ports of Haifa and Jaffa, where Arab labourers from the over-populated villages found work in the ports and the new industries. Here the petrol cans shed by the oil industry which had changed the Middle East, beaten thin and nailed together, provided tens of thousands with their only shelter.

The administration's decision to invest in security and public works meant that health and education were starved for funds. Fortunately, Mandate doctors could count on help from the missions and religious charities of Palestine. Jewish institutions in particular contributed significantly to the control of malaria and other infectious diseases in all communities. The older Jewish hospitals which dated from the previous century, financed by European Jewish philanthropists, had been set up not only to improve health but to prevent Jews accepting help from the missionaries. They suffered initially from a lack of funds – the Wallach Hospital in Jerusalem was discovered in 1918 to be functioning without a resident pharmacist – but the situation changed completely after the First World War and the arrival of the Zionists. The sophisticated Jewish medical facilities set up primarily for the Jewish population in some respects benefited the population as a whole. The Hadassah Medical Association, an American–Jewish organization, founded hospitals and a chain of mother-and-child clinics which were open to Jews and Arabs alike; another Jewish relief organization, the American Joint Distribution Committee, contributed a substantial sum to the British health authorities – with no strings attached – to be used in the battle against malaria from 1919: a Malarial Research Unit was established from this money. Hadassah treated all schoolchildren in eye clinics, and fielded rural doctors under the guidance of an ophthalmologist, so that by the mid-1930s the incidence of trachoma in Jewish children had been reduced by two-thirds. Jewish settlers cleared some of the worst malarial-ridden areas on the lands purchased by the Zionists; and those Arabs employed in Jewish enterprises who were also members of an Arab union affiliated to the Histadrut (the Jewish labour federation) could benefit from its health insurance scheme.

Mission hospitals and schools took up the Mandate shortfall as well – though they were not eligible for the grants-in-aid which the Health Department distributed to local and community institutions. The St John Eye Hospital in Jerusalem, founded in 1882 (which traced its history to the Knights Hospitaller), and its clinics, like the Jewish institutions, dealt with trachoma and the other eye diseases which afflicted so many in the rural population. There was no government eye hospital. But it was a problem for the administration that both Jewish and mission health facilities were inaccessible to so many Arabs. Christian institutions, located near sites of biblical significance, were – apart from Jerusalem and Nazareth – generally distant from Muslim population centres. A notable exception was St Luke's Hospital in Hebron, a diehard Muslim town with an orthodox Jewish minority. A Christian mission in Hebron clearly had no future whatever, and for this reason the hospital founded in 1893 by the Mildmay Mission in the place of a German mission was transferred eight years later to the United Free Church of Scotland, which – rapidly discouraged – handed the torch to the Anglican Church Missionary Society. The CMS was obliged to close the hospital in 1928 for lack of both funds and personnel; by 1921 it maintained only one 'blind evangelist' among the Muslims, and though the Bishop in Jerusalem later appointed 'a catechist and a bible woman to follow patients home', things did not improve. The following year, that of the Western Wall riots and their sequel, was marked by a massacre of Jews by Hebron Muslims, and when the hospital reopened a few days later, a picket of soldiers had to be mounted for its protection. When the Mission nurses returned, they distributed milk and clothes to the destitute Jews. One of the nurses commented that: 'As the Jews have now their own doctor and nurse we do not need to do so much for them. . . . Mixing the two races is difficult in a clinic, owing to the bad feeling. Out of my babies registered only 2 have been Jews and the rest Moslems.' Despite objections from the Mission headquarters in England, the Scottish Dr Paterson carried on in what he termed the 'most exacting district in Palestine' with two Arab Christian doctors; his successor Dr Forster served the area throughout the Arab Revolt, when most British officials had left the town, and the hospital continued functioning up to 1947.[6]

The Mandate administration was never able to provide health care and education for the Arab population to compare with the services the Jews provided for themselves. There was no compulsory education law. The Jewish community and its supporters abroad financed and ran their own health services and schools at a cost far beyond the Mandatory pocket. While this meant that more taxpayers' money was available for Arab schools and government doctors, and for public health schemes, the contrast between health care in the two sectors was glaring. In 1935, when the Jewish population of Palestine had grown to roughly 28 per cent of the total, the maintenance budget of the various Jewish health authorities was more than twice that of the expenditure of the Department of Health. Hadassah and, later, a Jewish co-operative health insurance system in Palestine, Kupath Holim, supported well-equipped Jewish hospitals, where a bed in the last years of the Mandate cost three times that in a government hospital. Most Jewish women preferred to give birth in hospital, compared with only 2 per cent of Muslims, and by 1946 hospital admissions of Jews were twice as high as that of Muslims, though the Jewish population was by now roughly half that of the Arab.[7]

While at the beginning of the Mandate there were only five Arab doctors practising in the countryside, a decade later the Jewish population could call on a huge reservoir of doctors, for the most part refugees from Germany, since the professional immigration from Central Europe during the 1930s raised the ratio of doctors to patients in the Jewish community to the highest in the world: one to every 300 patients. The Jewish community taxed its members to maintain an educational system from kindergarten through eight years of elementary school for almost all its children, while the government could not afford schooling for even half that period for more than a third of Palestine Arabs. In the Arab towns, the Welfare Departments tried to involve the municipalities in financing and running hospitals and welfare centres, or at least contributing a share of building and maintenance costs for clinics and schools. The villagers were expected to build schools or extra classrooms themselves on the Dotheboys Hall principle, and sometimes to pay the teachers into the bargain; but even so, only about a third of all Arab villages had schools. The Mandate Departments of Health and Education were also saddled, with little help from voluntary organizations, with responsibility for relief works and the care of severely ill mental health patients from all communities.[8]

Neither in health nor in education – the two most important services for the general population – was the administration able to integrate the several communities. Forming a 'composite state', 'getting Jews, Christians and Muslims to work together and develop a common Palestinian consciousness' – those pious hopes often voiced by the Colonial Office – clashed with Article 15 of the Mandate, which stated that 'each community had the right to maintain its own schools for the education of its own members in its own language'. From the comfortable distance of Whitehall, the Colonial Office and some philo-Semitic Members of Parliament believed that Jews and Arabs would best communicate with one another through the medium of English – preferably in higher education. At a meeting with Plumer and Amery in 1928, a pro-Zionist MP, Josiah Wedgwood, expressed the shared belief that even the Eastern European Jews could be brought round to British ways of thinking: 'Teach them English; then they will read and think English.' Although in government hospitals, mission hospitals and schools some Jews and Arabs did sometimes share facilities, and occasionally work together, institutionally speaking it was only in prisons and mental hospitals that Arabs and Jews shared (often appalling) Mandate facilities on equal terms.

Those who ran the Health Department built up their service almost from scratch, and left Palestine a much healthier place than they found it. The Education Department left the Palestinian Arabs deeply angry that their constant demands for more schools and better technical education were never met. The officials in charge had little sympathy for local cultures – always excepting what they considered to be traditional arts and crafts: they patronized the Arabs and were often hostile to the Jews. And their educational ideology (though they would hotly have rejected such a term) was never accepted.

The Turkish administration's idea of public health was rudimentary: quarantine for pilgrims going to and from the Holy Land, Muslims passing through Palestine on the Haj, via Egypt, on the way to Mecca by way of Suez and the Red Sea – and isolation for the worst cases of infection. Under British rule, it was the safety of Egypt which was paramount. Up to 1921 pilgrims who were not Egyptian were not permitted to proceed through Egypt except on special ships. For Palestine pilgrims, the administration had no money to charter ships, but in that year a 'quarantine escort' was arranged, and from 1930 free pratique to all pilgrims if they could prove they were in good health. Permission to travel on Egyptian ships, for Palestine subjects, was however an 'act of grace', and in 1933 an agreement between the Palestine and Egyptian governments ensured that all Palestine Muslims were checked before entry into Egypt: they needed not only to carry certificates of vaccination against cholera and smallpox but a pilgrim's booklet with their photograph and thumbprint, and a return ticket.[9]

This did something to check outbreaks of smallpox and locate cases of bubonic plague, which recurred periodically, carried by rats, in the port cities of the Levant. Yet not only the living, but also the dead, were continually on the move to and from Palestine: Jews who had died abroad leaving instructions that they were to be buried in the holy soil of the land, Arabs from the surrounding countries whose families wished them to be buried in their native countries. With a more efficient investigation of local crimes, and since the British had introduced coroners' courts into Palestine, there were frequent requests for exhumations of bodies – one more health hazard for the department to deal with.[10]

The Turks had done nothing to check malaria, Palestine's main endemic disease. The only preventive treatment for malaria, which could kill but more often recurred sporadically, debilitating those infected, was quinine – which was expensive. Malaria was partly responsible for the neglected state of so much of the country. The Jordan valley, a fertile, marshy area, had been deserted by the peasants fleeing the disease. Devastating epidemics occurred in the early Mandate period, like that which hit Beit Jibrin in the Hebron district in 1920, where one sixth of the population died within three months. In some areas in the south, malaria was so prevalent that crops were left unharvested for want of men and women strong enough to bring them in. Fifty per cent of the children in the Jewish settlements in the early Mandate period had enlarged spleens, the indicator of chronic malaria. The disease was under-reported, since so many suffered from recurrent, undiagnosed 'fever'.

The campaign against the anopheles, malaria-carrying mosquito, which had been begun by the Army continued under Colonel George Heron, the head of the Health Department, who had arrived with the Army in Palestine from Egypt. 'A diversity of problems added interest to the campaign,' he commented when he came to write up the anti-malaria war. Surveys established where the mosquitos bred and what species were responsible. The Anti-Malarial Ordinance of 1922 gave the government power to make property owners responsible for drain-ing and cleaning malarial swamps and streams. Medical Officers examined the blood and palpated the spleens of thousands of school-children, and of many adults. A complete survey of towns, villages, and swampy areas was carried out during the first few years of British rule by British Medical Officers, the Malaria Survey financed by the Rockefeller Foundation, and the Jewish Malaria Research Unit which funded work in Jewish settlements until 1931. Jewish land-purchasing and development companies drained suspect areas on the land they bought. The Department of Health's campaign began in the towns, the most densely populated area, in an attempt to stop the constant epidemics. In Jerusalem alone, where water was kept in more than seven thousand cisterns, the cesspits, tubs, wells and barrels were recorded and numbered. Work gangs trained by the department spread every water surface with a special oil which asphyxiated the larvae. Heron reported that the effect on malaria was 'almost electrical'; in Jerusalem, deaths from the disease were eliminated in six years – most in the very first year of operations.[11]

In the countryside, the problems were more complex; to oil every pool or stream was impossible. Mechanical methods – diverting streams, ditching and channelling – were supplemented by chemical controls, and the application of larvicides during the mosquito breed-ing seasons. All this demanded both expertise and a small army of labourers. The Health Department could provide only supervisors and technical staff, and the main source of manpower had to be the people of Palestine themselves. In the Jewish 'colonies' the settlers did the work; in Arab villages, 'voluntary labour', or – more accurately – 'forced labour'. At the same time, the Health Department supplied free treatment in villages unvisited by doctors, and intensive treatment was given to the nomadic Bedouin, who were not only heavily infected themselves but often created fresh sources of malaria by the unsupervised damming of streams to water their animals. Both malarial control and treatment were interrupted during the 1936–9 Arab Revolt, when communications with the villages broke down almost completely, and malaria levels again rose among the fellahin. In 1938 the Senior Medical Officer in the coastal plain had to ask for an armed escort even for the Arab engineer responsible for anti-malarial work, Nafi Khatib, on his rounds.

Growing industrialization – most of it carried out by Jewish firms – did not automatically do away with malaria. Some development projects, like the canalization of water near Haifa, the creation of salt pans in Athlit, and the mineral industry set up at the southern end of the Dead Sea, themselves caused the destruction of the larvae. Others, like the raising and lowering of water levels, for hydro-electric purposes, of the Sea (actually a lake) of Galilee created new breeding grounds. The migration of the fellahin in search of work to shanty towns of coastal cities, where there was no sanitation, led to fresh outbreaks of the disease. In the mid-1930s, a group of twenty-one Jewish landowners who had purchased small estates on the north shore of the lake (including Lady Reading, wife of the ex-Viceroy of India, who had the largest holding) delayed repairs to the last remaining focus for mosquito breeding in the Tiberias area while they were absent abroad or disputed the bills they received.[12] By the 1940s, the Health Department found that while it could control the public water supply, the increased irrigation of the growing citrus industry in the coastal plain, run by both Arabs and Jews, made proper supervision much more difficult. Dr William Bigger, a Senior Medical Officer who had been in Palestine since OETA times and was an expert on malaria, warned in 1943 that no government inspector could 'immediately discover every broken or leaking pipe or tap in an area of thousands of dunams, and it is this problem which has given us more trouble than any other in past seasons'. For him, the rapidly multiplying irrigation cisterns, fish ponds and channels were less signs of agricultural progress than 'artificial forms of nuisance'.[13]

In the last decade of the Mandate the villagers, while now recognizing the causes of malaria, were less willing than in the past to work as an unpaid labour force. Fellahin and Jewish settlement labour had put in 30,000 days' work in 1934 alone, Heron attested: 'for the most part willingly given, and recourse to administrative pressure or final legal measures is happily seldom required'[14] – though there were disputes inside the villages as to who should do the work. But by 1944 things had changed. Palestine was now a British army base, and the Health Department had been forced – unwillingly – to share its malarial work with army units in the countryside. The Army caused the Department of Health 'severe embarrassment' with the villagers. Some army detachments raised 'press gangs' to clear out swampland, others were accused of 'extravagance' (having paid for drainage work), and on one occasion their lack of expertise provoked an epidemic. With increasing taxation of the rural population, and a rise in the cost of labour, there was growing dissatisfaction with existing policy, and the villagers demanded that the Department of Health pay part of the cost of drainage work.

'Malarial work' was imposed unequally on different sections of the population. Outside the large properties and development areas, it was the villagers who were expected to do all the work in natural streams and seepage areas elsewhere, and Bigger was sympathetic to their complaints. He suggested that the government should bear the entire cost of drainage and maintenance in the open countryside, since the fellahin very often had to clean up not only water on their own holdings but also public streams, which did not benefit the owners. Malaria was a danger to grazers and holiday-makers downstream as well as the landowners – a matter of national health like typhoid or smallpox. Fellahin harvesting their crops were often ordered to carry out temporary drainage work. In the process, they contracted malaria and then carried the illness back to the villages in healthy areas. The subsequent epidemics cost the government more than a better-organized system would have involved. Bigger thought that paid labour, using machinery, would effect permanent canalization of long wadis in place of the previous, stop-gap measures and the use of forced labour. The Senior Medical Officer in Haifa, Dr John MacQueen, concurred, terming it 'distasteful' to force villagers and settlers to turn out in gangs to clean up streams and wadis from which they derived no visible benefit. The government had to acquiesce; at the end of 1945 draft estimates for the following year included the additional expenditure involved in the change of policy.[15]

Though the Health Department had malaria under control within only a few years, it took decades to eradicate it completely. Surveys, drainage and treatment of suspect areas had to be repeated annually, and in one huge marsh area – the Huleh basin in the north – and in the Jordan valley, malaria remained a threat to public health until well after the Mandate period.

Sanitation and inoculation prevented the spread of other endemic and infectious diseases. Smallpox and cholera were brought under control in the 1920s by vaccination and quarantine, though typhoid still accounted for much illness in 1933, with the mortality rate twice as high among Arabs, though its actual incidence was higher among Jews. Jewish immigrants were in general far more prone to the enteric diseases in the 1920s to which Arab adults appeared to have developed a certain natural immunity, though gastro-enteritis was the chief cause of infant mortality in both communities.

Preventive measures against disease made some headway in Jerusalem with the introduction, by British sanitary engineers, of modern drains and latrines. In the port towns of Jaffa and Haifa, Turkish sewers were handy refuges for rats, – presaging disaster. British planners had not been much concerned with the disposal of human wastes until raw sewage actually landed on their doorsteps. This happened to Ashbee in 1922 when a new drainage system, financed by the Zionist Commission in the orthodox Jewish area of Mea Shearim, overflowed into Wadi Joz, where he lived. As late as 1932 the Medical Officer in Bethlehem and Beit Jala wrote to his senior in Jerusalem about the sewage problems which had preoccupied him for a decade: 'I would like to know if government is really interested in this subject and whether they intend to do something.'[16] Builders in Palestine did not provide latrines, nor – when they were forced to do so by law – did they see to their maintenance.

Chlorinated water and pasteurized milk were introduced in the towns but enforcing hygiene in the villages was difficult. The mukhtars were supposed to report on births, deaths, non-vaccinated persons, rapid feverish diseases ending in death, the arrival of strangers, and the pollution of water, as well as infectious diseases, but this turned out to be beyond their abilities. Registers were often not kept, or unreliable;

the mukhtars tended to register births but to conceal deaths. Arab infant mortality in particular was underestimated by 30 to 40 per cent during the first decade of the Mandate. Applications for marriage certificates often stated incorrectly that brides had reached the legal age for marriage, and searching for birth dates in incomplete registers was frustrating. The government ultimately made its own assessments by relating all available statistics to the 1922 census.

The lists of public health 'requirements' for the villages indicate why diseases spread so rapidly. They included: keeping wells and springs clean, rather than washing clothes, fruit and animals in them; finding an alternative to the village street as the place to slaughter animals, to cut hair, to use as latrines, or for spreading manure; and placing public latrines and cemeteries downwind and well away from drinking water.[17] As the doctors at St John's stressed frequently, epidemic conjunctivitis was a social problem and, like trachoma, could not be brought under control 'until an elementary knowledge of hygiene is brought into every home'. It was not enough to perform eye surgery and send the patient home. Many peasants' eyes were lost each year from post-operative sepsis before the sulphonamide and penicillin drugs appeared in the 1940s.[18]

Failure to install proper sanitation in the port towns repeatedly involved the Mandate government in disaster. Bubonic plague, transmitted by rats and fleas, recurred in the poorer, Arab districts in Jaffa and Haifa throughout the Mandate. The outbreak in Jaffa in 1926 took three years to stamp out entirely. Shacks were pulled down, rat-catchers sent out like hunters, traps set, and buildings in suspect areas 'rat-proofed' – by concrete flooring and the destruction of double roofs. Lower floors were reinforced with metal, ventilator skylights screened with wire-netting, and rainpipes installed to discharge water to gulleys with gratings, to trap the rats. But the new sewers constructed in the 1930s in Haifa bypassed the shanty towns, and the city slaughterhouses and markets also teemed with vermin.[19]

On 5 May 1941, the management of Haifa port circularized the government departments with the news that plague rats had been discovered there.[20] MacQueen and Heron warned the Chief Secretary that the whole of Haifa was threatened.[21] Every temporary structure in the port was torn down in the effort to confine the infection to one area. But on 17 July the first human case occurred in a nearby slum.

Later that month there was a second case, a third in August, and a boy visiting Haifa from Jerusalem died suddenly in the French mission hospital and was buried before the doctors realized the probable cause of his death. Infected rats were found outside the port. MacQueen noted in August 1941: 'The sanitary survey necessitated by the presence of the plague in Haifa has shown that an enormous amount of work is required to improve the sanitary conditions in the poorer part of Haifa.'[22]

It was too late for mere 'improvement'. MacQueen decided on a campaign of wholesale destruction of slum areas. Thousands of huts were torn down and market areas, Arab and Jewish, were destroyed. An isolation compound was set up at the government hospital as MacQueen feared the appearance of pneumonic plague, invariably fatal. By October there had been nine human cases – but there was no epidemic and, as yet, no fatalities; then, 'a sudden death occuring virtually in the street' in January 1942.[23] Hundreds more families were evacuated to camps, food and clothing were burned, and 800,000 square metres of surface treated, as holes were blocked, cemented and plastered, and the old Turkish sewers of Haifa made rat-proof. With Haifa an important British naval base, every possible emergency power was invoked to contain the disease. Ships' captains hesitated to anchor off the city. In Olivia Manning's 'Levant Trilogy' reference is made to a Polish soldier serving with the British Army who has contracted the plague in Haifa and is hospitalized in Alexandria, and the fear of local diseases runs through the entire book.

The Palestinian Arab newspaper *Falastin*, which had earlier attacked the demolition of Arab property, suddenly began praising government action. Inevitably, some rats got through the cordon, and cases of human plague were identified in Acre and in Shefa Amr, an Arab town in western Galilee – the fifteenth in thirteen months. In November 1942 a young girl from Jaffa died of the plague in the Tel Aviv municipal hospital, indicating that the danger had moved south. After a renewed offensive in Jaffa, the plague seemed to recede – only to recur far more frighteningly in 1944.[24] Between 22 June and 19 September, twenty-nine people in Haifa were infected, eleven of whom died. Dramatic posters in red and black, swiftly recognizable even to those who could not read, were pasted up in the port towns, ordering people to tear down temporary structures, burn rubbish, repair their drains and report all rats, alive or dead. The Chief Secretary appealed to the Crown Agents for the Colonies to send Palestine supplies of DDT, but none was available in the entire Middle East. By November 1944 there had been seventy cases of plague, and twenty deaths – the worst outbreak of the Mandate; 50,000 people were inoculated. The government's unwillingness to spend more on sewage and sanitation had backfired: whereas the entire campaign of 1926–9 had cost the government £1,000, £13,000 was spent by the government on plague control in 1944 alone.

By mid-1947 the supplies of DDT – used to kill the flea vectors which were transmitting the disease – had arrived in Palestine, in time to check the last major outbreak of the plague in the country which began in July that year when the Health Department believed it faced a 'formidable epidemic'. The rat hunt was on again, pilgrims – on the move again in the post-war period – were quarantined for 26 days, and the spraying began. This time the Army and all the local authorities were mobilized for a wholesale attack on fleas and rats. People in the ports were daily intercepted on the streets and dusted with DDT, and houses were sprayed with solutions of DDT in paraffin. Emergency powers were invoked to carry out house-to-house inspection and examinations of those suspected of infection; thousands were inoculated. Goods trains leaving Haifa were sprayed and rat-proof covered wagons used for trains leaving for Egypt. By the end of the year the department claimed that the human epidemic seemed to have been arrested by the DDT campaign, no new cases having occurred since September. Fifteen people were infected in this year, three of them in Afula, a Jewish town in the Jezreel valley, where a grain sack containing a rat was detected; one person had died. Neighbours' quarrels multiplied in Tel Aviv as fears grew of suspect rubbish and vermin. The Health Department was bombarded with letters from a Mrs Renee Zilka, who thought she had spotted rats in the nearby cowsheds belonging to a Mr Belinkoff.[25]

Other sicknesses were linked not only with sanitation but with rural hazards and peasant tradition. Rabies was endemic to Palestine, with an initial mortality-rate of 7.5 per cent, the most dangerous source of infection being jackal bites. A report by Bernard Walker of the Jerusalem and the East Mission in Hebron in 1938 listed not only the usual enteric and respiratory diseases but also rheumatic fever

139

(endemic to the hill regions of Palestine), which can lead to heart disease, in children and adolescents. Walker had spent two years in Yemen, where the climate was similar, and had encountered no such problem; the cause in Palestine, he thought, was the fellahin's habit of sleeping in the vineyards during grape harvesting.[26] The winnowing of grain, after harvesting, was another health hazard. Because so often flying seeds set up infections in the villagers' eyes, the Health Department tried unsuccessfully to prevent the siting of threshing floors inside the villages. A clause in the Public Health Ordinance referred to these sites as 'public nuisances', and officials tried to persuade the villagers to locate the floors outside the villages. But local feuds made them fear for the safety of their crops. In Anebta village, in the Tulkarm sub-district, the villagers leased an alternative site, under pressure from the administration, but never used it.[27] During the Arab Revolt, when insurrection and local clan feuds were hopelessly entangled, the doctors at St Luke's in Hebron had to patch up stab wounds, fractured ribs and skulls, and festering gunshot wounds.

The Hebron sub-district was the centre of tens of villages, in an area notorious for its poverty. Here many women and children were diagnosed as suffering from hereditary syphilis, and health checks in the schools revealed many boys to be infected. A special clinic was opened in nearby Beit Jibrin after the local Medical Officer complained, in November 1927, that: 'the only available place for treatment was the mosque, where prayers are continually held . . . I find it difficult to examine women in such a public place'.[28] But few Muslim women would agree to be examined by men, and Heron also reported that he had no budget for the treatment of venereal diseases. The first serious and detailed report on venereal disease – widespread in both the Arab and Jewish communities – was written by Miss Nixon, the Mandate Welfare Inspector, and Mrs Neville of the Jerusalem and the East Mission in 1933, half-way through the Mandate, noting the need for 'public enlightenment' on the 'personal and racial effects of the illness' – that is, eventual sterility. But teachers in government schools had no training in biology, no missionary school taught general physiology, and advice was eventually provided only in ante-natal clinics staffed by women. Only the Jewish schools taught these subjects and gave lessons on sexual hygiene.[29]

From the mid-1920s the fellahin began to attend the hospital out-patient departments, but pregnant women and infants were not among them. The lack of mother and child care, of midwives and of doctors' attendance at difficult births was clearly the reason for the very high rate of infant mortality, which in 1925 was 200 per 1,000 among Muslim Arabs and 131 among Jews – chiefly in the poorer, veteran population in the cities. Dr Tewfik Canaan, a Palestinian paediatrician, carried out his own private survey in 1925 among the Arab villages he visited, noting that of some two thousand pregnancies, a fifth ended in abortions or stillbirths, and nearly half the new-born died within a short time. Though those babies who survived acquired remarkable immunity, and – to Canaan – surprisingly few women died of puerperal fever, infections spread fast in the dark, damp village houses where nursing mothers and the new-born spent most of their time. Despite Palestine's brilliant sunshine, Mandate doctors diagnosed peasant mothers and infants as suffering from rickets caused by 'insufficient sunlight'. Canaan himself thought many deaths were due to 'overfeeding and swaddling the new-born'. He reported that those doctors who did visit the villages found it impossible to stop the peasants administering their own remedies: cauterizing the babies' stomachs with red hot nails, cupping and bleeding, and putting a necklace of pomegranates on children suffering from diarrhoea.[30]

Edward Keith-Roach maintained that the most important contribution made by the Mandate to the rural Arabs was 'the abolition of the birthing stool'. The pioneers were the Quakers, who set up four experimental centres in the villages in the Ramallah district, north of Jerusalem, in 1926.[31] The nurses lived in the villages and carried out simple ante-natal checks, ophthalmic therapy and school nursing. The first Mandate training centre for Arab midwives was associated with the Princess Mary Maternity wards at the government hospital in Jerusalem, but beds in the maternity centre in Jerusalem were too expensive for most of the Arab mothers, and it was closed in 1927. The Muslim midwives' training committee only sent one trainee and was not willing to pay for a staff nurse, though the Arab women's movement in Palestine tried to encourage families to allow their daughters to go in for nursing.[32] The system eventually adopted by the government was for all midwives in the Arab sector to be trained, under government supervision, by British nurses recruited through the Colonial Service, who had worked in India, Uganda, Mesopotamia and British Guiana. They trained a generation of new Arab midwives throughout Palestine, attended pregnant women both at their homes and in the centre, inspected and licensed the existing midwives (who were often illiterate, but who were given special courses and licensed to practise), as well as supervising ante-natal and infant welfare work. In contrast to most British officials in Palestine, these nurses, who gave their first lectures and instructions in English, were expected to study Arabic, and to pass the government's Primary Arabic Examination within one year.[33] This may well have contributed to their success. By the end of the decade there were government ante-natal clinics all over the country, difficult cases were sent to hospital, infant mortality had fallen by 25 per cent, and the superintendent of the maternity services in Hebron reported that women were being taught 'to do away with harmful quackery and charm treatment and rid themselves of the prejudices against trained attendance and hospitals'.[34] Arab midwives were trained in the hospitals, where the very poor and destitute gave birth. Gynaecological clinics, too, were restricted to the very poor – all others had to consult private doctors. Fellahin women were now coming regularly to ante-natal clinics and infant welfare centres all over the country, and close touch was maintained through Medical Officers and nurses. No infant deaths at all were reported in Jerusalem in 1929, an astonishing statistic. In villages nearby, the only deaths were of infants whose mothers had not kept up visits to the centre. The Health Department made sure that no one who could afford a private doctor exploited the clinics.[35]

Though the midwifery campaign was a success, the infant welfare centres suffered from restricted government budgets, which would not stretch further than the payment of doctors and nurses. There was a chronic shortage of basic equipment; in the Jerusalem centre, in 1929, there were not even scales for weighing the babies. Buildings for clinics and accommodation of staff had to be provided by the towns and villages. The government grant in aid to the municipalities covered most expenses but MacQueen – then Heron's deputy, fumed at the reluctance of the wealthier Arab towns to contribute. In December 1929, he noted: 'If the [Bethlehem] municipality cannot raise the balance I suggest that the centre should close down. There is plenty of money in Bethlehem.' He thought Bet Jalah, another predominantly Christian town, should pay a third of the cost.[36] In Jerusalem, the wife of the Director of Education, Mrs Bowman (who was to die a tragically early death of a viral infection a short time later), volunteered to pay the rent of the infant welfare centre in the Bab el Selseleh, in the Muslim quarter of the Old City, for the first year, but as the local people did not want to contribute, she continued supporting the centre for another two years before the department decided to foot the bill itself.[37] In 1935, Miss Rogers, the chief superintendent of the midwives, raised £20 from an Arab welfare centre committee in Jerusalem for a playground for the toddlers who accompanied their mothers, noting: 'the children from two to five years of age are cast adrift to fend for themselves, they roam the suk, dirty and often ill, the way being paved for life-long bad habits and disease'.[38]

Hospital accommodation in Palestine was always inadequate. The beds in government hospitals were designated first and foremost for the accommodation of government officers and employees, and members of the police. Local people were only admitted if suffering from a dangerous or highly infectious disease, or as mental patients – when beds were available – or to maternity wards if they were difficult cases. What this meant was that most of the sick either had to pay private doctors or to knock on the doors of the charities. The Army had its own facilities, and there was some provision for accident victims and the very poor. Jewish hospitals provided just over a third of available beds, mission hospitals just under a third, and government hospitals the rest.[39] Most of these were in improvised buildings, and only the Haifa Hospital – a Mandate showpiece – had proper wards, laboratories and equipment. From 1925 the municipalities contributed a share in financing the upkeep of Mandate hospitals; when this was more than half the cost, as in Jaffa, Gaza and Nablus, the mayors headed the local hospital committees.[40] Later, villagers who had built their own clinics had also to share maintenance costs. In many of the smaller towns, clinics were staffed by nurses only, so that the sick had to travel to find doctors. During the Arab Revolt the roads which had made access to doctors and hospitals easier became almost impassable to patients and doctors alike. In August 1938 bombs were thrown at the Gaza Government Hospital.[41] In Beersheba, an area inhabited by nomadic Arabs, the police had withdrawn and left only a gendarmerie force of 150

Bedouin. The District Office and all its files had been burned, like the officials' houses. Sir Gawain Bell, who was sent to the southern area in 1938, six months after being posted to Palestine from the Sudan, noted in his diary that 'the nomads had cut off their noses to spite their faces' by destroying all the dispensaries, smashing the medicine bottles and burning down the veterinary posts.[42]

The shortage of hospital beds worsened with the onset of the Second World War, when Italian and German hospitals – run by enemy aliens – closed down. In Haifa, home to a large Arab population, only the government hospital was open to Arabs – the Jewish hospital was too overcrowded – and even surgical emergencies were barely accommodated. At the end of British rule, with so many officials wounded in crossfire or terrorism, the British demand for hospital beds added to the pressure. There was a chronic shortage of drugs and dressings, and doctors in government hospitals had to tell patients to buy their own supplies from pharmacies outside. Most of the police were treated like out-patients, and put on the long waiting-list for beds, though they were supposed to have priority. But the idea of putting up even a small police hospital had to be shelved because, with the wartime economic boom in Palestine, wage rates had risen so far as to make the costs of construction five times what they had been pre-war.[43]

The Colonial Office was concerned, however, with Palestine's appearance. Despite the problems with funding, both hospitals supported by charities and those the government constructed were able to commission some of the leading architects of Palestine; Hadassah Hospital on Mount Scopus, which opened in 1939, was designed by Erich Mendelssohn (whom Heron also chose to design the government hospital in Haifa), and Clifford Holliday planned an extension to the St John's Eye Hospital in Jerusalem. Dr Strathearn, its Director, had told Holliday that the many rural Arab patients who patronized the hospital were 'in the habit of sleeping in khans', and so instead of planning modern ward facilities for them, Holliday designed khan-type rooms, with a low, tiled platform where they could put their bedding. When, at the end of the Mandate, with bombs being thrown daily and chaos threatening, the construction of a long-overdue, second government mental hospital was contemplated, what preoccupied Whitehall was that: 'any buildings newly erected [in Palestine] are liable to be discussed in cultivated circles not only in Palestine but throughout the world'; so 'it was important to get the best man'.[44]

One of the first acts of the Mandate Health Department had been to establish the country's first mental hospital, in Bethlehem. As Keith-Roach put it: 'It was considered no longer appropriate for the insane to live chained to the walls of an isolated orthodox convent near Bethlehem, in the hopes that the sanctity of the surroundings would restore their minds.'[45] Arab villagers sequestered their mentally sick or handicapped, which may be the reason why Mandate statisticians maintained that the incidence of mental sickness among Jews was more than ten times higher than among the Arabs, and in 1926 the Department of Health suggested that prospective immigrants be checked for their mental stability.[46]

In a 1928 report to the Colonial Office, Lord Plumer noted that: 'In Palestine, although among the indigenous population the prevalence of insanity is less than in Europe, a rate of insanity corresponding to the European standard is found in Jewish immigrants.'[47] The Jewish pioneers, said an early Mandate report, were particularly prone to mental illness because they had severed ties with their families back in Eastern Europe, where they had often suffered starvation, persecution and forced military conscription. But Zionist fund-raisers, who claimed they were creating a new, psychologically healthier, Jewish society, were unsuccessful in eliciting help for the mentally sick. The Zionist Organization was neither prepared to provide its own mental hospital, even with government subvention, nor to repatriate mentally disturbed immigrants, as the Chancellor administration requested.[48]

The Bethlehem Government Mental Hospital was always over-crowded, with a long waiting-list, and the pressures on the staff great. Heron and his team had managed to train a number of Christian Arab girls and were trying to attract girls from Muslim families as well when a serious setback took place. The first Matron of the Bethlehem Hospital, Miss Whitaker, had a furious row with a Muslim nurse and locked her into an isolation cell reserved for maniacal patients. Whitaker was dismissed from her post. She appealed to high officials and to the Overseas Nurses Association in an effort to reverse the decision; but when she failed, she became distraught – 'utterly insane', according to Heron – and was herself referred as a patient to a mental hospital near Beirut. Although she had no pension (the Nursing Pension Ordinance had not yet been passed), the cost of her hospitalization was paid out of Mandate funds. Heron commented that though the department had tried to present the nursing profession as a respected and respectable one: 'The incident at the Bethlehem Mental Hospital is known throughout the hospitals of the country and has already severely shaken the confidence of the Palestinian nurses of the service in the attitude of the British members of the Department of Health.'[49]

Unlike the rest of Palestine's sick – apart, perhaps, from the country's lepers, who sometimes exhibited their deformities as beggars, urban Arab mentally ill were visible and audible. Many of them wandered the streets without having the chance of any form of treatment, or lived, according to a 1931 report, 'under conditions which . . . frequently, through ignorance and fear, do not fall short of cruelty': 'treated' by sheikhs or magicians, chained to walls, put on a diet of bread and water, or whipped to drive out 'demons'. The Mandate authorities were constantly preoccupied with getting violent, frightening psychotics off the streets and into some kind of seclusion – which meant, in practice, that many of them were imprisoned. While the Zionist Executive in Palestine repeatedly applied to the Department of Health to construct a new mental hospital (never built), 'lunatic' Jews and Arabs were treated together in the existing government institutions, and sometimes, for lack of hospital beds, 'accommodated' in jail. There were only two prisons in the country – in Acre and Jerusalem – and their conditions were described as medieval, with up to forty prisoners in a cell, a bread-and-water diet, and dangerous prisoners often kept in chains.

In the 1920s there was only one Jewish mental hospital in Jerusalem, the Ezrath Nashim Hospital for women, which crammed in twice as many patients as its legal capacity allowed. Consequently Jewish mental patients (particularly the elderly) were often treated together with Arabs in government hospitals – in 1926 one third of the beds in the government mental hospital in Bethlehem were occupied by Jews. Sometimes they were placed in Christian institutions such as the St Vincent Hospice in Jerusalem. When some 'harmless old ladies' were transferred from Ezrath Nashim, the Department of Health was

1. The Jerusalem cenotaph today

2. The surrender of Jerusalem, 9 December 1917. The British sergeants
with the mayor of Jerusalem and his 'white flag' party

3. General Allenby

4. Colonel Ronald Storrs, Military Governor of Jerusalem, 1917-20, with local workmen, April 1918

5. Sir Herbert Samuel (*centre*), first High Commissioner, with
T.E. Lawrence (*second from left*) and Arab leaders at Amman
in April 1921, just prior to the first serious riots in Jaffa

6. A meeting at Government House (Augusta Victoria hospice), 1922, showing Sir Herbert Samuel with, among others, Fakri Nashashibi, St John Philby, Wyndham Deedes and Lord Allenby: Norman Bentwich is in the middle row, behind the High Commissioner and his wife

7. British show of force, Jerusalem, August 1929

8. Sir John Chancellor inspecting the Arab Boy Scouts, Ramla, 1931

9. Humphrey Bowman, first head of the Department of Education,
in his capacity as Scoutmaster, with Arab schoolboys

10. Sir Arthur Wauchope (carrying stick) with, to the right,
Stewart Perowne and Edward Keith-Roach at the opening of
Haifa Harbour, October 1933

11. A British army pastime: the donkey race 'Grand National'
during the Second World War

12. The Right Reverend George Francis Graham-Brown

13. The Peel Commission, 1936

14. The Arab Higher Committee. Front row, second from left, is Haj Amin el Husseini, Mufti of Jerusalem and President of the committee

15. Ruhi Bey Abd'el Hadi, the highest Arab British Mandate official, 1937

16. Sir Arthur Wauchope with his ADC outside Government House, Jerusalem, 1937

17. 'Destruction to property in Jaffa during the Arab revolt'
(clearly the result of British army demolitions)

18. A derailed train on the sabotaged railway

19. A British army convoy ambushed on the Jenin Road, 1936, at the beginning of the Arab Revolt

20. British guardsmen in windows of houses bridging the Via Dolorosa in Jerusalem during a search of the Old City during the winter of 1938/9

21. Sir Harold MacMichael, relaxing with his pipe

22. The King David Hotel after the bomb attack
by Jewish terrorists, July 1946

23. Jewish illegal immigrants on the British troopship
Empire Rival awaiting landing craft to take them
to Cyprus, August 1946

24. Lieutenant-General Sir Alan Cunningham,
last High Commissioner of Palestine, on arrival
at Lydda airfield, November 1945

requested to provide lower beds for them, oilsheets, and a mattress, as 'they liked sitting on the floor and the stones were cold'. Private mental hospitals, usually run by Jews, multiplied: a member of the distinguished Arab el Khalidi family was admitted to Ezrath Nashim, and late in the Mandate the Supreme Muslim Council appealed to the Health Department to hospitalize the daughter of a sheikh who maintained he was being ruined by the high fees paid to a private Jewish institution in Haifa.[50]

In the early years of the Mandate there was only one bed in mental hospitals for every 10,000 inhabitants of Palestine – proportionately half the number available in Egypt and a tenth of what was offered in London. Plumer expropriated a German orphanage in Bethlehem to serve as a second mental hospital and converted the unused wing of the Central Prison at Acre into a ward for the criminally insane. There they remained even when, during the Arab Revolt, the execution sheds where both criminals and rebels were hanged was situated next door. In 1942, the dearth of mental hospitals still troubled the High Commissioner, Sir Harold MacMichael, who felt that the situation 'reflected badly on Government'.[51] At that time, only 157 patients of the 1,500 estimated as needing care were actually hospitalized. When Heron visited another private Jewish mental hospital in a Tel Aviv suburb in 1942, he found that the isolation rooms were 'beyond description . . . not fit to use for animals', the means of looking after maniacal patients 'scandalous and brutal'. He did not blame the staff entirely, as the hospital was under-funded, the Tel Aviv municipality having cut off financial help. The High Commissioner, however, praised the owners for 'keeping dangerous and even homicidal lunatics off the streets'.[52] In the last year of British rule, the High Commissioner's Arab milkman told Major Chichester at Government House in Jerusalem that a cousin of his was 'dangerously insane' and begged the Major to get him admitted to the Bethlehem Hospital. Although agreeing to have the man examined, Dr MacQueen wrote to Chichester: 'As you are probably aware, there is a great shortage of beds for mental cases in Palestine, and only the more dangerous cases can be admitted, if we are to do anything about treating those who can be cured.' Prisons only released the mentally sick when the British left Palestine. When the Mandate was about to end, the criminal lunatic wing in Acre, which had housed both Arab and Jewish patients, released them separately into their own communities, the last and final act in the separation of the two populations under the Mandate.[53]

Relations between the Department of Health, the Jewish medical authorities and Arab doctors were problematic, though there was more co-operation between Jews and Arabs in the health field than in any other context in Palestine. Jewish and Arab nurses worked together until shortly before the end of the Mandate, when government hospitals were handed over either to Arab or Jewish personnel, though there was little social contact after work. But Jewish doctors found it hard to find work in the Health Department.

At the beginning of the Mandate, when the Zionist Organization wanted to find places for Jewish doctors in government service, Heron demurred – his ostensible reason being that most of them knew neither Arabic nor English, which 'put them out of court'. 'Much friction' was reported, with Dr Eder of the Zionist Commission complaining to the High Commissioner, Samuel, that the best doctors were almost inevitably refused; despite the great number of Jewish doctors, there were only seven Jews among the thirty-five employed by the department. Heron argued that Jewish physicians wanted better pay than his department could afford – though the Jewish Agency denied this. In June 1921, during a typhoid epidemic in Jerusalem, a Zionist organization placed its laboratory at Heron's disposal for the analysis of specimens; but according to Eder, Heron was 'jealous of Jewish organizations', and preferred to send the specimens all the way to the government laboratory in Haifa.[54] Despite the excessive number of Jewish doctors in the 1930s, many of whom had to find work as building labourers, they were rarely employed in government service. While in 1930 the department employed six Jews, compared with fifty-three Arabs – most of them Christians – by the 1940s there was only one assistant Senior Jewish Medical Officer in government service, and all other Jewish staff were technicians.[55]

However, it was the Jewish health insurance service, Kupath Holim, which made the only proposal during the Mandate to organize the health services in the country on an inter-ethnic basis. Because of the economic crisis which overtook Jewish Palestine in the early 1920s, when Jewish unemployment was running at about 30 per cent, the working population was unable to pay its health insurance rates, and Kupath Holim was on the verge of bankruptcy. Their best option seemed to be to appeal for government support within a new, country-wide health insurance scheme.

Kupath Holim proposed that all salaried workers, Jewish and Arab, should be obliged by law to join a sick fund – with Arab funds to be created on the Jewish model – and pay a health tax to the government, to be paralleled by government and by employers' contributions: an idea modelled on a 1911 British scheme for lower-income groups. But the Jewish Labour Federation leaders deferred discussion on the proposal for three years, fearing that the scheme would diminish its control of Kupath Holim – a major source of political power. Only pressure from the International Labour Organisation in Geneva, which in 1927 decided to implement obligatory health insurance laws in member states, forced the Federation into action. In January 1930, the proposal was submitted to Chancellor, now in his last year as High Commissioner. It was rejected for budgetary reasons almost immediately, despite efforts by the Jewish Labour movement to have the issue raised in Parliament by the British Labour party, then in office. Whether because of the Zionist leadership's lack of enthusiasm, or the reluctance of the Mandate to introduce expensive social legislation, the plan failed.[56] But the Department of Health had been attracted by the idea, and in 1936 it was with a Jewish doctor's help that MacQueen launched what he called the 'germ of an insurance scheme' which he hoped would change the whole health care situation in Arab rural areas.

Dr Meyer, of the little Jewish town of Zichron Ya'akov, between Haifa and Tel Aviv, worked in a government clinic in Arara village, 15 kilometers away. He had been chosen by the villagers, 'following unsuccessful efforts to secure an Arab doctor from Haifa who would undertake the task'. The government subsidized Meyer for the cost of his travel by car and the medicines he handed out free – for malaria, eye and venereal diseases. A male nurse gave eye treatment, and paupers got free consultations, while other villagers paid a small fee for examinations and for other medicines. The villagers had provided a building for the clinic, and the arrangement was financially elastic. The clinic in Arara also served four or five villages in the surrounding area. At the end of 1938, at the height of the Arab Revolt, when the administration was forced to introduce relief schemes throughout the countryside, the head of health services in the north, Dr MacQueen, repeated his proposal, believing his experiment was flexible. He was supported by Arab doctors, who, he said, 'would accept the same subsidy even if today it did not more than cover their expenses'. In 'lean years', MacQueen proposed that the scale of fees could be reduced and subsidy increased, though larger villages would need less government help. The scheme, he argued, was simple, inexpensive, and a step in the direction of early preventive treatment; it would be:

> a real bargain for Government; indeed, from the purely money point of view, almost a shameless one. From the health aspect it confers benefits which cannot be measured against the cost. At present neither I nor my doctors are getting out to the villages. This would provide me with an excellent means of keeping my fingers on the pulse of my rural communities. If epidemic disease really gets a firm hold before we know about it, Government will be required to spend more like half a million than fifty thousand [his estimated cost of the scheme] to deal with it.

With an average of three doctors per sub-district, MacQueen thought he could extend a large measure of relief across the country. But there was no response from the government.[57] In 1945, encouraged by the inauguration of the British National Health Service, he revived his proposal, comparing the situation in Palestine with that in England, where MacQueen thought twenty-five doctors were needed for every 50,000 people. In Jenin, a Palestinian Arab town of this size, he pointed out, there were four. Heron backed MacQueen's suggestion, but – perhaps because it smacked too much of real social reform for the colonial service – it was never adopted by the Palestine government.[58]

By the 1940s there was only one doctor for 20,000 people in the Hebron district, the Beisan district of the Jordan valley, and in Gaza – districts populated only by Arabs. By contrast, there was one for 14,000 in the Tulkarm district, near the Jewish town of Netanya, one for 2,000 in Ramle in the coastal plain, close to many Jewish settlements, and one for 1,500 in the Nazareth area, near the Jewish hospitals at Afula and the Emek – where many Arabs came for treatment.[59]

Arabs who could afford to pay for treatment often preferred to consult Jewish doctors and specialists, and by the 1940s this had come to be much resented by Arab physicians. In 1945 Drs Canaan and Dajani, on behalf of the Palestine Arab Medical Association, wrote to the Chief Secretary requesting more thorough sanitation schemes and medical help, especially in the villages, and a sanatorium for tuberculosis patients. They also wanted a couple of young Arab doctors sent yearly to British universities for specialized training, as the Arab population needed a 'backbone of specialists'. They complained bitterly about Jewish physicians monopolizing the profession, and objected to the increase of licenses issued to Jews by the government. The Jews 'had tried and succeeded in upsetting the normal proportion of Arab doctors to population' (which Canaan and Dajani estimated at one to 3,500) by drawing away a great number of their clients:

> Such a change is detrimental to the income of the Arab physician, as (1) the Arab population as the whole is poorer than the Jewish one; (2) it does not seek the help of the doctors as often as the others; and (3) practically no Jew will come to an Arab physician for treatment following the fundamental Jewish principle, viz: Jewish work only for Jewish workers; non-Jewish work for all.

The yearly number of Jews licensed to practise, they complained, was greater than that awarded Arabs – 'the original inhabitants of the country' – though the Arabs were twice as numerous as Jews. If this went on, they concluded, the next generation of Arab doctors would be unable to make a living.[60]

The Departments of Health and Education were largely responsible (as social welfare was bracketed with education and linked with health) for relief projects. Here government help was given not on a proportional basis (as in health and education in general) but where the need arose, and expenditure was similar for Arabs and Jews. At the beginning of 1939, the Army having finally put down the Arab Revolt, the administration had to cope with a devastated countryside. The Army had commandeered men from the villages for road work and repairs, artisans dared not leave the towns for fear of arrest and imprisonment, the citrus crop, on which so many depended, had failed, and Heron reported many cases of destitution and famine among the fellahin.[61] In June 1939 social workers in the administration complained that military restrictions on traffic, and the fact that so many Arabs were still in jail, was 'strangling the economic life of the country'. Later that year Jewish leaders also appealed to the government for relief for Jews in the cities: 5–6,000 families were alleged to be destitute, as much money had been diverted from Palestine on the eve of war to help the Jews of Poland; with the outbreak of war, Jewish funds from abroad diminished further.[62]

The government at first wanted to restrict relief grants to cases of outright starvation in the large towns, but in the view of those colonial officials who had experience of Asian famines, few people in Palestine appeared to be actually starving. The doctors who were asked to assess the extent of 'destitution' among both Jews and Arabs and produce an 'average' found it hard to decide on a definition which would fit both communities. The poorer Jews in the cities were often worse off, they concluded, than the Arabs in the countryside. The fellahin could revert to subsistence crops, while the Jews were over-dependent on the citrus industry. The overall success of the Jewish economy in the thirties had disguised pockets of appalling poverty, particularly among immigrants from Arab countries in the towns. In the Mahane Yehuda quarter of Jerusalem, for instance, nearly half the Yemenite population was assessed as destitute, with families of ten with no wage earner living in one room.[63] Among Arab Palestinians, while there were no voluntary schemes like those of the Jews, communal self-help, based on local traditions, had increased in the villages during the Revolt. In the towns there were hostels and homes for children at risk, many of them run by the women in the Palestinian middle class who, since 1929, had taken part in the Arab national movement.

In Tel Aviv and Jaffa, where Jews and Arabs were close neighbours, the Senior Medical Officer, V. L. Ferguson, found poverty and hunger in the slums of both towns in the first winter of the Second World War. Because of the long strike which had begun the Arab Revolt, Jews had developed their own alternative in the new Tel Aviv port for lighter traffic, and no longer used the old port of Jaffa – on which the Arabs' commercial life in the town had depended. In Tel Aviv, in the poorer Jewish industrial areas there was 'a whole host of shoddy, ill-run, ill-maintained factories . . . which were continually going bankrupt and changing hands'. The thirties' boom had ended with the war, and penniless immigrants had added to the unemployed.[64] The Deputy Director of the Health Services, George Stuart, who visited all the poor quarters of the larger towns, found Arabs in Jaffa living in cellars but with full larders, having sold off their furniture to buy food, while in Tel Aviv there were a number of immigrant families 'who had crossed the borderline between starvation and near starvation' and had no household goods to sell. He blamed this on the higher cost of living in the Jewish town, and 'the easily recognizable difficulty of a largely occidental population trying to exist on the customary meagre rations of the oriental'. But he added: 'It is almost axiomatic to assert that Jews will never starve, and in the light of my present experience I would reiterate that no distressed family visited could not be paralleled or even outmatched, in poverty, hunger and dirt, by many inhabitants of the east-end of most large English and Scottish towns.'[65]

Despite the need for relief measures in the towns, the Second World War was for Palestine a time of political truce and economic prosperity. With Palestine a major military base, there was ample employment, the restoration of calm encouraged agriculture; and with few imports, the peasant farmers and fishermen found they could, for the first time, name their price. A British nutritionist asked to come up with an optimal 'average' diet for Palestine found that there was no such thing. Statistics were unreliable, though 'Palestine is a land of committees, not of milk and honey'. Though the government introduced rationing according to a points system, and food control, these were largely ignored. The fishermen caught thousands of tons, but 'were quite prepared to sit down and not catch any fish if they feel they are being discommoded in any way'.[66] Consignments of food were sold to Palestinian merchants in Egypt and came into the country at three times their value. There was a glut of food for what was by British standards an undernourished population, which ate everything and anything that came to hand. Only the farmers ate the barley and millet grown in the country, though there was a shortage of cereals. Camel meat was smuggled into Palestine, and the government imported buffaloes from Iraq for protein. Salted herring, previously only a Jewish dish, was imported from Turkey and became popular in Arab villages. The Polish army units under British command in Palestine devoured almost the entire egg production of Gaza, so that egg powder had to be hastily imported for the British. The milk supply was at the mercy of the farmers after the rationing system failed. Mandate dieticians deplored the eating habits of all the communities, criticizing even babies' consumption of breast-milk. Arab mothers breast-fed babies too long – for two years – they said, Jewish mothers not long enough.[67] They complained that the Jewish population ate too many fats and sugars, that the Arab farmers sold too much and ate too little, that neither community knew how to cook (by British standards) and that the black market in food, which flourished with the support of both communities, was 'scandalous'.[68]

A year before the end of the Mandate, the Chief Secretary called a press conference on the distribution of funds by the Department of Social Welfare among Arabs and Jews in response to complaints in the Arab press. He announced that there was no fixed ratio of expenditure between the communities, and no formula for its distribution. The statistics he gave showed that grants to institutions in both communities were roughly equal, though if government institutions serving mainly the Arabs were taken into account, the Arabs received slightly more. Each side, however, continued to complain that the Mandate government deliberately favoured the other. At the war's end, the Colonial Secretary, Arthur Creech Jones, wanted to set up a social welfare advisory committee; but representatives of the Arab and Jewish sides would not agree as to its constitution, the Jews insisting, as usual, on 'parity' as strongly as the Arabs opposed it.[69]

When Humphrey Bowman, Director of the Education Department from the period of the military administration onwards, first visited the government school in Hebron in December 1924, he was pleased to find that each class had its own teacher, with 'a healthy spirit of friendly rivalry between masters and classes' – reminding him, no doubt, of the 'house' system of the British public school. The 'technical instruction' – carpentry, book-binding and broom-making – was of the simple kind he approved, and he suggested (Dotheboys Hall again) that the school's desks, which were falling apart, could be replaced by the pupils in carpentry class. On his next visit, in April 1926, he was less enthusiastic; there had been one pupils' strike (the 'ringleaders' were expelled) and more were pending, the new headmaster was keeping the cash from sales of books and brooms in his own house, instead of in a separate bank account, and the boys were wearing their overcoats in the (unheated) classrooms instead of braving the cold. Apparently unaware that Muslim literary and religious traditions converged, and that there was an accepted style of declaiming texts, Bowman complained that: 'Boys still tend to recite by shouting in a mechanical way.'[70]

Throughout the Mandate, the public school and Oxbridge graduates who ran the Education Department judged the behaviour and potential of their Arab protégés by English middle-class standards; and in their eyes, few of the schoolchildren in their care merited the benefits of secondary and higher education. They opposed all attempts by Arab officials and teachers to decentralize educational policy. They were affronted by the involvement of the schoolchildren of Palestine, whether Arab or Jewish, in politics. They deplored all 'ideologies', and attempted to impose public-school ideas like 'team spirit' and 'character building' on the Arabs in their charge. Town schools and village schools were run according to different criteria and different curricula, indicating the British desire to keep villagers down on the farm. Colonial experience had taught the Colonial Office, the officials in the Education Department of the Mandate and the missionaries that peasants educated beyond mere literacy left the countryside for the cities, where, on the margins of society and often unemployed, they might be recruited to nationalist movements. Stacy Waddy, the principal of St George's, the chief Anglican Mission school, wrote in 1922: 'All education at present does harm here, because the immediate result of getting it is that the young men turn up their nose at life on the land and in the villages. We MUST [emphasis in the original] counteract this. Palestine needs educated and public-spirited landlords.' Like the heads of the Education Department, Waddy favoured 'practical agricultural demonstration', sports, and scouting as antidotes to nationalism.[71] Bowman, summing up Mandate education in the 1920s, stressed: 'the danger of giving too literary a bias to village education . . . tempting the village boy to the town where he may become unemployed and unemployable'. And when the second High Commissioner, Lord Plumer, wanted to decentralize education for financial reasons, which would have given more autonomy to local officials, an official in the Colonial Office referred to 'horrid examples of the dangers of literary education turning out large numbers of unemployable clerks' in India, Egypt and West Africa.[72]

Education was 'voluntary', as the government could not afford to finance a universal scheme, and segregated, to conform with Article 15 of the Mandate on cultural autonomy. The Education Department, like the Health Department, had under its nominal control a patchwork of institutions serving the various communities: Muslim, Jewish, and Christian. The Education Department ran government schools in the Arab Muslim sector. Jewish and Christian schools received grants in aid, on a proportionate basis, from the government, and were subject to periodic visits by department inspectors. There were school-leaving matriculation examinations in the three official languages, set by educational experts drawn from all the communities. Private elementary Muslim and Jewish schools ignored the Mandate syllabuses and taught according to a traditional curriculum. The few Mandate secondary schools were situated in the towns; two, the Arab College in Jerusalem and, later, a girls' secondary school in Ramallah, were intended for the training of a cadre of elementary school teachers – initially together with secondary studies, later in a further course. Jews financed their system from communal taxes and fees levied on the parents, Christians had the fee-paying church or mission schools.

Matiel Mogannam, the Palestinian women's movement leader, argued in 1937 that the mission schools, which taught in several different languages, had a 'disintegrative effect' on the Arabs and prevented their pupils from developing a national consciousness.[73] Only the mission schools accepted children from all communities, though Jewish parents who sent their children to such schools came under attack, and, by the thirties, the children too were often ostracized. From the 1930s, with the growth of Palestinian Arab nationalism, private 'national' schools appeared, most of them in Jerusalem and Jaffa, both centres of political action. The Hebrew University, a Jewish institution funded largely from the Diaspora and founded in 1925 in the presence of Lord Balfour, was nominally open to all communities, but the fact that all teaching was in Hebrew meant that only a handful of Arabs ever attended it. A privileged Arab minority, Muslim or Christian, sons and sometimes daughters of the 'notable' class, went abroad for higher education. From the early 1930s, selected graduates of the government secondary system were awarded scholarships in

British universities and technical colleges on the understanding that they would then accept work inside the colonial system; but there was no opportunity for higher education for Arabs in Palestine itself.

In the Mandate schools in the towns, children studied for six years, in the villages for three or four, but even by the end of the Mandate about half the 800 Arab villages had no schools at all. In the towns English and some science were taught in the last two classes; in the villages, apart from religion and the three Rs, only rudimentary history and geography. All schools tried to encourage some kind of practical farming or market gardening. After the Samuel administration ended, no serious effort was made to provide education for all. The Mandatory obligation to provide equal opportunities for Muslim and Christian Arabs alike, let alone for both Arabs and Jews, was never realized – and not only for budgetary reasons. Two of the three Directors of Education – Humphrey Bowman and his successor Jerome Farrell – dominated the scene for most of the Mandate period, and it was their beliefs and preferences which counted.

Bowman, the old Etonian, old Sudan hand, and Director of Education in Iraq before his arrival in Palestine, believed he had 'sympathy and understanding' for the Arabs, while thinking them a 'lazy and unenterprising people' who needed prodding and disciplining, preferably on the sports field or in the scout camp. Even though he recognized their nationalist feelings, he believed their ambitions could be accommodated within the framework of colonial rule, while at the same time maintaining the semi-feudal structure of Arab Palestine unchanged.

The language of instruction in Ottoman times had been Turkish. In keeping with Article 15 of the Mandate, elementary studies were in Arabic. But Bowman, entirely on his own initiative, decided that the language of instruction in government secondary schools was also to be Arabic. English was used in other British colonies and in the mission schools which many Christian Arabs attended. Bowman defended this anomaly before the Royal Commission of 1937 'on educational grounds',[74] as did Stewart Perowne, who taught at the Arab College in Jerusalem, the leading government secondary school. Perowne noted in a memoir: 'Teaching in Arabic was denounced as "colonizing" by the so-called [Arab] "national" organizations whose own schools, where they had any, taught their secondary classes through the medium of English.'[75] One such school was at Bir Zeit, the first venture of its kind in Palestine – a Christian Arab foundation, connected neither with the government nor with any missionary society, built up and directed by Miss Nabiha Naser, which educated both Christians and Muslims. The original co-educational plan proved unsuited to Muslims, but in the higher classes a solitary boy might find himself in class of girls, or vice versa. Children came from all over Palestine, and the staff were all Arab, most with degrees from the American University in Beirut; the head, Wadia Tarazi, was a graduate of Brynmawr.[76]

Bowman's decision, which so puzzled the Royal Commission, was of a pattern with his stated aim before the Commission of developing an 'agricultural bias' to education and 'to stop the drift to purely clerical or urban life'.[77] At this stage in Palestine's development, insisting on the use of Arabic even in secondary schools meant a paternalist acceptance of nationalism – which Bowman agreed was absorbed by Arab children 'with their mothers' milk' – while limiting their access to higher education and technological skills, since a working knowledge of English was essential at this stage for admission to colleges in England or the American universities in Cairo or Beirut.

Jerome Farrell was a less paternal figure. An Irish Catholic and classical scholar, whom Bowman believed to be 'too good for the job he holds', Farrell was contemptuous of the Arabs, and his hostility to the Zionist Socialists, and to Jews in general, intensified over the years – even though he professed sympathy for the veteran religious and oriental Jews of Palestine. While Bowman encouraged technical studies for the Arabs, after 1936 Farrell made it clear that he would not finance any Arab secondary education outside the main towns, on pseudo-scientific grounds. In February 1941 he sent a remarkable circular to all District Commissioners, Assistant District Commissioners and District Inspectors of Education on the subject. In this memorandum he set out 'a statement of practical policy' which he said should be used to reject, out of hand, all the 'impossible demands' for the opening of secondary classes in small town and village schools. Academic secondary schooling had to be severely limited, 'since the maximum percentage of those capable of a high standard of achievement in this branch is very small . . . fixed by nature . . . and cannot be increased by education'. Admission to vocational schools was limited by financial considerations: 'and may be conditioned by the necessity of keeping adolescents under public control in the absence of a satisfactory home life'. It was to be clearly understood that: 'there was no immediate prospect of money becoming available for the establishment of new secondary classes of either type'. Farrell calculated that no more than one in thirty pupils admitted to school was 'so endowed by nature as to merit the expenditure of public money on his secondary education'. Department funds were thus to be spent on increasing accommodation in existing schools, and providing boys' hostels for those from towns and villages who merited admission.[78]

Policies such as these brought Farrell into confrontations with Arab teachers. In 1944 Rafiq Bey Tamimi of Lydda, a Sorbonne graduate and ex-headmaster of the Jaffa secondary school, complained that there were only two complete Arab government secondary schools in the country, with only one or two classes available to most of those who wanted to continue studying (generally financed by the Arabs themselves), and that the education budget comprised around a fortieth of the whole Palestine budget. Farrell replied that not all could profit by a university education. He minuted Tamimi's letter to the effect that it 'implied the belief that secondary schools and universities can be produced out of a silk hat or be created by rubbing a lamp or ring'.[79]

But there were British officials outside the Education Department who sympathized with the Arab villagers' demand for better education. The Assistant District Commissioner in Tulkarm, commenting on a 1946 request for a secondary school to serve fifteen villages, wrote:

For some time I have been strongly impressed by the demand for education on the part of the fellahin. It is particularly tragic to see this urge being frustrated and this very frustration leading to western condemnation of the people as backward. . . . The townships have better prospects, but towns don't accept boys from the village. What is required is the creation of a complete secondary school in each district dedicated to the service of the fellahin.[80]

But with men like Bowman and Farrell in control, there was little hope of this happening.

Had Arab officials ever managed to challenge British control of their education, things might have been different. Together, Bowman and Farrell blocked the progress in their department of the most intellectually gifted Arab ever to enter Palestine government service, George Antonius. Ironically – given the belief of both men that a British education was superior to all other and the model for all colonial education – Antonius was himself the product of the colonial system, and dogged by the ambivalence of his position throughout his career.

George Antonius was a Greek Orthodox Christian, educated in Victoria College, Alexandria (an expatriate British public school) and King's College, Cambridge, where he graduated brilliantly in the mechanical sciences tripos. At school, his headmaster had told him that with a British university degree he would be the equal of any Englishman. He was to be sadly disappointed. Antonius served during the First World War as Deputy Press Censor in Alexandria, at the same time working on an Arabic technical lexicon. His connections with British Intelligence were manifold, and he helped the British government negotiate the frontiers of half a dozen new states, though he regarded the entire Near East as one Arab geo-political unit. But his attempts to rise in the Mandate administration were rebuffed. OETA accepted his application for a job but – as he was a foreigner – not the commissioned rank that should have gone with it. This was only the first of many snubs.

Under the Samuel administration Antonius was appointed Inspector of Arab Education, and after a year, Samuel chose him as second to Bowman, with tenure; in 1924 he was made Assistant Director of the Education Department, with Farrell serving under him, though there were Muslim protests. Meanwhile, as a member of the Local Government Commission set up by Samuel, he drafted its recommendation that the Department of Education should devolve some power in educational matters to locally elected Arab bodies. Though the idea was backed by Samuel, it was opposed by both Bowman and Farrell (though neither was a member of the Commission). Bowman argued that while 'in Europe the virtues of honesty of truth, of straight and honourable dealing, etc.', were taught in the home as well as at school, 'in Palestine, as in most Oriental countries, the inculcation of such virtues is left by the parent for the most part to the teacher', and that British officials would be 'false to [their] trust' if power over the teachers were handed over to local bodies. Farrell's argument was that the local population was immature and required 'the general development of character, sense of duty and local unity' – which could only take place in British-run schools – before it could achieve self-government. The Commission's final recommendations on education, though considerably modified, were ultimately shelved by Plumer.[81]

In 1927 the Palestine government sent Antonius on two important diplomatic missions to the Hejaz and Egypt, the first as adviser to Sir Gilbert Clayton, head of British Intelligence in Egypt and the second as mediator between the Colonial Secretary, Lord Lloyd, and the Egyptian government. On his return, Antonius discovered that Bowman had promoted Farrell over his head to become Bowman's deputy – in line for the directorship of the Education Department when Bowman retired. Antonius was transferred to the Secretariat, where he remained only two years before resigning from government service, arguing that his treatment had been 'morally indefensible'. He went on to play an important role as eloquent spokesman for Arab delegations to Whitehall, as well as writing *The Arab Awakening*, an effective statement of Arab nationalism in the Middle East, first published in 1938.[82]

Despite the divisive educational system – a compromise between the legacy of Turkish rule, Article 15 of the Mandate, and British colonial precedent – both the Colonial Office and the administration encouraged any private initiative which they thought might bring Arabs and Jews together, supposedly creating the elusive 'Palestinian' identity. In 1922 a British Jew of Iraqi origin, Sir Ellis Kadoorie, left a sizeable bequest for the education of Jews and Arabs in 'Palestine or Mesopotamia'. Samuel, then High Commissioner, and Bowman initially supported the project, visualizing a school on public-school lines, with English as the language of instruction, modelled on the Gordon school at Khartoum in the Sudan, where Bowman himself had taught. But Samuel was rapidly discouraged by the Jewish leadership, whose priority was 'to unite the various elements of Diaspora Jewry by using the Hebrew language'. Moreover, while the Jews wanted another secondary school, the Arabs were pressing for a technical agricultural college on the model of the Jewish Technion in Haifa, which was turning out a cadre of highly qualified architects and engineers. Consequently, in 1925, two separate schools for agricultural studies were set up in different parts of the country, though the Colonial Office lamented: 'HMG will lose a tremendous opportunity to try and get Arab and Jew to work together in one school and learn to understand one another as children, an opportunity which may never come again.' As they emerged, the two schools exemplified the divisions between the two communities. The Jewish Kadoorie school, in the Galilee, was from the late 1930s also an élite military centre – where Yitzhak Rabin, Israel's future Chief of Staff and Prime Minister, among others, received his training. The Arab Kadoorie school in Tulkarm supplied the Arab villages with about fifteen teachers a year, while the remaining fifty-five sought to enter government service. When this trend became apparent, the principal of the school sent all further applicants a letter stating that the school was intended to help students improve their own lands or those of their families, not to help them get clerical jobs. The Tulkarm school was ill-fated: in 1936, during the Arab Revolt, rebels sacked the school and removed its herd of 30 cows. Like so many Arab schools, it was occupied by the British Army between 1936 and 1945.[83]

If the aim of government education in Palestine was to enable the Arabs to acquire better agricultural and technical, rather than 'literary' skills, this was precisely what the Education Department failed to encourage. The Tulkarm Kadoorie school (run by the Department of Agriculture) remained the only source of trained Arab agricultural instructors. They taught grafting, pruning, bee-keeping and simple soil science, from the sole Arabic textbook, in 'school gardens' provided by the villagers. But this happened in fewer than half the village schools, many of which were personally financed by the fourth High Commissioner, Arthur Wauchope (a keen gardener). Despite the pleas of the Village Congress, a group of Arab rural leaders who, in November 1929, asked for more agricultural and technical training, little was done. At Dura, near Hebron, again with Wauchope's encouragement, teachers revived the local traditions of terracing and dry-walling, and new types of fruit trees were introduced. But the administration rejected any attempt to put Arab farming on a scientific basis on a parallel to the Jewish sector. In 1935 the mayor of Gaza and a company of notables including Ahmad Hilmi Pasha, one of the executives of the Arab Agricultural Bank and the Arab Bank, wrote to the head of the Department of Agriculture and Forests, Dawe, asking for government support for a second agricultural school at Gaza, to include laboratories, a dairy industry and the teaching of improved means of growing cereals and fruit trees. Dawe and Wauchope were inclined to consider the proposal seriously, both because of the success of the Dura school and because Hilmi and others were prepared to make financial contributions, though other officials were sceptical. But Farrell, now acting-Director of Education and shortly to succeed Bowman, insisted that one Arab Kadoorie school was enough to provide a suitable education for 'sons of larger landowners, junior employees of the Agriculture Department . . . and teachers in general schools with an agricultural bias' – those Arabs favoured by the British administration. Otherwise only 'severely practical', 'lower vocational schools' were to be encouraged. The proposal was rejected.[84]

Arab technical education was even more seriously neglected. In 1945 the acting-District Commissioner in the Lydda district, R. H. Greig, wrote an irate letter to the Chief Secretary complaining that with the large programme of public works and post-war reconstruction in view, he had looked in vain all over Palestine to find an (Arab) candidate for the post of Municipal Engineer in Jaffa and was now trying in Egypt: 'This situation provides an outstanding example of the serious lack of qualified Arab engineers and technicians in this country.' There were no contractors in Jaffa, he added, who could be entrusted with the laying of drains or repairing of streets, or competent carpenters, plumbers and electricians. This revealed 'a serious fault in the educational system of the country . . . after twenty-five years of British administration', especially if the aim was to equalize the standard of living of Arabs and Jews. The Public Works Department, as Greig anticipated, concurred. Farrell indignantly rejected the charge: he blamed lack of funds, an absence of 'popular demand', the unrest of the previous nine years, and British military occupation, from the Arab Revolt through the war years, of many workshops and the one government trade school, established in Haifa bay in 1935.[85]

There was another reason why the Mandate administration failed to train Arab engineers and technicians, and this was the continuing influence of the traditionalist, Arts and Crafts colonial ethos familiar in Palestine from the time of Storrs and Ashbee. The supervisor of Arab technical education, W. A. Stewart, came to Palestine in 1930 from the Cairo School of Arts and Crafts where he had designed forging courses for wrought-iron work. His chief interest was in local handicrafts: weaving, the sheet copper work done in Nazareth and, for women, traditional embroidery. When graduates of school courses in such crafts wanted to open new industries, however, they found that the government would not support them; in Bethlehem, in 1935, students abandoned the weaving sections for this reason.[86] Like his colleagues, Stewart assumed that 'industrial training' for Palestinian fellahin meant enabling them to manufacture their own ploughs, hoes, locks, window frames and household utensils (supplied meanwhile from Lebanon and Syria) during their 'free time' between seasons of sowing and harvesting. The report Stewart wrote in 1946 summing up his career in Palestine ended with a manifesto urging the encouragement of local handicrafts. 'Palestine stands now on the brink,' he wrote. 'It would seem that the present industrial system of Europe and America is doomed to collapse through its own internal rottenness', . . . 'the time for large foreign export business is over', and the industrialization of Palestine would result in 'a large class of unemployed'. The development of industry in Palestine, he therefore concluded, 'should be related through the development of its crafts to the country's primal activity, agriculture'.[87]

Welfare legislation was also affected by the government's hostility to social change and reform. In 1930 the administration had opposed Jewish proposals for health insurance for the salaried worker for financial reasons. In 1938 a proposal was made to ban the employment of Arab children under the age of 13 and reduce the hours of work for all children – the Industrial Employment of Women and Children Ordinance of 1936. The Mandate administration itself employed many under-age Arab children as messengers, both in government departments and in the Post Office, and the Attorney-General pointed out uncomfortably that the Palestine government was 'deviating from accepted international conventions' designed by the ILO in Geneva. But as with the Jewish proposal for health insurance six years earlier, the Mandate administration opposed the social legislation which would have brought it in line with ILO directives.

Farrell opposed the Bill for two years. He thought preventing young children working would only be desirable if they were otherwise in school, in 'superior home surroundings' or 'playing in a park or the country. . . . In Palestine the Arab child would not enjoy these advantages. There are school places available for less than 50 per cent of the applicants aged 7 to 8 and even fewer for children aged 12 to 13.' According to Farrell, 'it was preferable that [the child] should be in decent employment in the Suq than roaming the Suq without healthy occupation and without means of support', especially as in the employment of children, Arab labour competed favourably with the Jews.[88]

A. L. Tibawi, the Christian Arab educationist who was inspector for the Southern District of Palestine thought it 'unclear for what future the government educational system was designed to educate children, Palestinian, Arab, or British Dominion'.[89] The history syllabus in government schools indicated what Tibawi called 'an attempt to harmonize local and Western culture'. The Arab schoolchildren began their history lessons with potted biographies of thirty-two of the 'principal characters in ancient Arab history'. Later they tackled medieval history, 'dealt with' Khammurabi, Nebuchadnezzar, Cyrus, Socrates, Alexander the Great, Herod, King Alfred and Charlemagne, Edward I of England, Muhammed the Conqueror, and Joan of Arc. In modern history they learned about Columbus, Drake, Cromwell and the struggle between King and Parliament, Watt and Stephenson and their steam-engines, Wilberforce and the abolition of slavery in British dominions, Napoleon, Nelson, and Gordon of Sudan. There followed the stone age in the Nile valley, Sumerian civilization, and the Egyptian, Assyrian and Hittite empires, 'with special reference to Palestine'. A tour of Arab history ranged from the Semites and the rise of Islam, to the decay of the Caliphate, life in the Ottoman Empire and, finally, 'The Turkish Constitution and its failure' and the results of the Great War. After studying the revival of arts and learning in the Renaissance, kings and parliaments in Europe in the last year of school, the children were introduced to 'the history of society and its institutions', from primitive man and his family (including that of their own Arab villages and the Indian caste system), to the Greek and Roman city states, constitutional government and republics. Finally, after revising all they had learned on the Turkish system in Syria and Palestine, they concluded their history studies with 'the present administration in Palestine' – the colonial hiccup after this enormous meal of history. There were no Arabic textbooks in neighbouring countries which mentioned Palestine, and no budget to have new ones written, so most of the syllabus was in the form of lectures which the pupils were supposed to reproduce, as best they could, in examinations.[90]

The rationale behind this programme was outlined by Stewart Perowne, who had arrived in Palestine as secretary to Bishop MacInnes and remained until 1934 a dominant figure in the Arab Training College, in Jerusalem, the most important secondary school in Palestine:

> It is certainly interesting to see the difference that the application of English methods does make. One naturally has qualms about forcing English ideas and institutions upon these people but there is no doubt that if you are going to do it at all, it is best to go the whole hog. . . . The people here are not Arabs, nor do they have anything in common with the 'mystic east' with the sole exception of their great dislike to any kind of work. They are simply Arabic-speaking Levantines, a type which may speak Greek or Turkish or Arabic, but is much more in sympathy with the West than with the East. Those people who are loudest in their cries of 'Palestine for the Palestinians' and so on, are always the ones who have assimilated most of Western ideas. . . . Boys find Arabic poets dull, love Shakespere [sic]. In giving them an English education . . . one is not really denationalising them, because for the most part they have not the remotest idea of what their nationality implies; they have no traditions, and they are likely to find . . . more akin to their aspirations in Nelson & Cromwell than in Salah ed Din and Suleiman the Magnificent.

Perowne could see no career open to talented Arab pupils but in the colonial service. There was no future for them in 'this little apology of a country. The agricultural basis of society is inadequate, and its only alternative, an industrial one, is impossible.'[91]

The curriculum of the few government secondary schools in the towns was accordingly modelled on British precedents; even Latin was introduced into the syllabus of the three leading secondary schools in Jerusalem in 1939, evoking protests and a strike organized by the Arab teachers. But English literature was understood in ways that Perowne may not have anticipated. Helen Wilson taught in the 'national school' in Bir Zeit at the height of the Arab Revolt, where boys and girls, Muslims and Christians, were all united against British rule. She recorded that when she read Milton's *Aeropagitica* with her class, a Muslim boy asked why there was no freedom of the press in Palestine. As for Shakespeare, *Hamlet* did indeed touch familiar chords: the duty of revenge; the destructive dependence of Ophelia on her father (the daughter of the mukhtar of Bir Zeit, Wilson noted in her diary, could 'hold her own intellectually with the best'); and the young man who had been to Beirut University, rather than Wittenberg, and had come home to protest against the backward social customs in his village. When a matriculation examination set the question: 'If you had the power what would you do for the improvement of your town or village?', the answers were: up-to-date agriculture, a hospital, ventilated houses, a night school for illiterates, and a school library. No one mentioned arts and crafts.[92]

The attempt to impose British standards on Arab children failed most miserably in the case of the scouting movement. The first training camp of the Palestine branch of the Baden-Powell Scouts was set up by Bowman, as County Commissioner for Palestine, in 1922. But from 1928 the Arab Scouts became increasingly politicized, marching in processions organized by nationalist movements like the Istiqlal party, or parading with Islamic, anti-imperialist slogans at the Nebi Musa and other religious festivals, the 'Scouts' (many of them adult men) carrying staves and daggers. In the town of Tulkarm and the nearby village of al Tayyiba, local Scouts troops set up their own fighting units. They played an active part in the Arab Revolt, and from then on the police appealed to the government to disband them. This was impossible because of the potential embarrassment for the Baden-Powell movement as a whole, but Mandate scouting was discredited. When Bowman left Palestine in 1937, no one could be found to take over. His temporary successor stated:

This is no country for any youth movement which includes the wearing of uniform and a resemblance, however remote, to military formations. Even in England the movement is not free from jingoism; in this country it is a focus for nationalism and so far from drawing the two races together it is being used to accentuate racial differences.[93]

Stuart MacLaren, the Jerusalem District Commissioner, declined the job of Chief Scout on the grounds of his 'very strong antipathy' to the movement, whose 'subversive propaganda' he had judged 'one of the main causes of the riots in 1929', and the task was dumped in the lap of the High Commissioner. By 1938, the head of the Palestine CID reported that the Scout movement had become 'almost entirely political'. The Jewish Scout movement, meanwhile, which was not affiliated to the Baden-Powell organization, and enrolled boys and girls alike, was equally nationalistic, if better behaved, and – characteristically – had no ties with the British; only girls from the pro-British Evelina de Rothschild private school in Jerusalem joined the Girl Guides. But the pretence that education, and sporting activities organized through the schools, could be kept apart from politics was maintained by the Department of Education throughout the Mandate.[94]

The Palestine matriculation examination opened the doors of the outside world to graduates of all the secondary schools in the country who chose to enter, with both Jewish and Arab scholars among the examiners. But those examination questions which related to Palestine sometimes seemed more suited to the colonial setter than the local sitter. A geography exam in 1946 stated: '"Geographical conditions control the mode of man's life"; Discuss this statement with reference to the following: a pygmy in Central Africa, a mixed farmer in Palestine, an office worker in London.' And in the compulsory general history paper, for that year, the only question that bore any relationship to Palestine was: 'Describe the part played by England in the Near Eastern questions during the nineteenth century.'

Though the Education Department had dismissed Arab ambitions so cursorily at school level, the Colonial Office and the administration wanted to set up a British university which would provide education for those Palestinians who met their standards and Farrell's criterion of natural selection, and would, at the same time, rival the American universities in Cairo and Beirut. As early as 1922, when the plans for a Jewish university were still on paper, Storrs and Bishop MacInnes proposed an English university in Jerusalem, to incorporate both a Hebrew and an Arabic department. Storrs invited leading Jewish scholars to join, and two – David Yellin, and Eliezer Ben Yehuda, the pioneer of spoken Hebrew – accepted. But under pressure from the Zionist Executive, they withdrew. The planned English university was seen by the Jews as a bid to introduce what the historian Klausner called 'an alien culture' into the city's academe, and to pre-empt the status of the Hebrew University of Jerusalem.[95] The Royal Commission of 1937 revived the idea of a British university, 'open to all English-speaking students in the Near and Middle East, which would not compete . . . but co-operate with the Hebrew University', which would send its post-graduate students there. Such an institution, the Commission thought, would do something to correct the effect of the separate Palestinian school systems, which, it had concluded, were 'definitely widening the gulf between the races'. As late as 1944–5, the Education Department was still discussing setting up an Institute of Higher Studies in Jerusalem, where 'a percentage of the key men of the future would [acquire] a British bias and background'; but the Colonial Office, while admitting the need for Arab higher education, thought it unclear whom the Institute would serve, and was apprehensive of Jewish objections.[96]

Only the Anglican schools, outside the public education system, and hence not affected by the terms of Article 15, realized the utopian British ideal of 'integration' for children from every community. Most subjects were taught in English (a policy for which the Anglicans were criticized by the Department of Education), but there were also classes in Hebrew and Arabic. As government provision for secondary education was so meagre, British rule was a boost to the mission secondary schools, though the mission schools in general declined in influence during the Mandate, and Bishop Graham-Brown's attempt to elicit a grant from the Colonial Office in 1934 was turned down.

The oldest Anglican institution, the English College of the Church Missionary Society, was, according to its founders' manifesto: 'intended to benefit all classes of the people of Palestine. To this end the Principal will as far as possible aim to maintain an equal balance between the number of Jews, Christians and Moslems resident in its walls at any one time.' But the Anglican schools were not equally representative of Arabs and Jews, or of Christians and Muslims: most pupils were drawn from the well-off, urban, Greek Orthodox, Arab minority, with a small number of Jews and even fewer Muslims.[97]

The schools were set up to instil Christian values, and instruction was given in both Old and New Testaments – enough to deter even those Jewish parents prepared to risk condemnation for sending their children to 'conversionist' institutions; most Muslims stayed away for national reasons. Nevertheless, St George's School in Jerusalem educated many sons of the Palestinian Arab élite, while the chief educational contribution of the Anglican schools was probably to women's education. The Jerusalem Girls' College, which claimed to have more than twenty nationalities represented by its pupils, had graduates serving in most of the Mandate departments, and sent others to the universities of the Middle East and Europe.[98]

Among the girls, in particular, friendships grew up between Arabs and Jews, and the 'old girls' magazines show that a real attempt was made to carry on a dialogue between the different communities, at least until 1936. Whether the teachers were equally well disposed to all seems dubious. Espie Emery, teacher and later headmistress at the Haifa High School for girls, where Jewish pupils accounted for 10 per cent of the school, wrote: 'It is a very good proportion to have, as the Jews are much the most pushing, and if there are very many of them they lower the tone of the whole school.' Miss Emery in her letters also blamed Weizmann for the problems of the Arabs, wished him dead, and explained her sympathy for those Arab rebels who had been, in her view, forced into violence, by comparing them to the British suffragettes.[99]

During the Arab Revolt, when most of the Arab schools in the Mandate system went on repeated and prolonged strikes, very few pupils in the Anglican schools were intimidated into staying away. In Haifa, where Arab–Jewish relations were closer than anywhere in Palestine, the pressures were considerable, both because of militant Islamic elements in the Revolt and the determination of nationalist Arabs to boycott Jewish enterprises such as the Electric Corporation: Miss Emery wrote:

> The Arabs and Jews have had a very trying summer, bombs and rumours and fear everywhere. We represent something peaceful and friendly and it gives them confidence again. . . . What is trying the Christian Arabs very much is that the bandits keep issuing orders which no Arab dares to

disobey. Men must wear kaffiehs and ladies and girls a mandil – a light chiffon veil over the hair. No Arab may use electric light; no Arab may play the gramophone or listen to wireless except to the news. . . . Most [pupils] were vexed about the electric light ban, as nobody possesses any [oil] lamps!

Jewish mothers of girls in school were worried that hats identified their daughters and exposed them to attack; only Arab girls wore veils.[100]

Relations between the Department of Education and the Jewish educational authorities were strained throughout the Mandate. Nothing could have been further from British colonial experience than the school system run by the Zionist leadership, under which 65 per cent of Jewish children studied (the others attended religious orthodox or private schools). This system was organized along political rather than educational lines, in three main 'trends': General (usually right wing), Mizrachi (religious Zionist), and Labour. All competed to enrol children of new immigrants, and argued over the distribution of funds. The generally permissive atmosphere in the schools, the familiarity (children addressed their teachers by their first names) and the constant intervention of parents: all these were strange and displeasing to Bowman, who deplored the lack of discipline. Farrell was more hostile to the exclusion of the religious orthodox from the Zionist system, noting that the poorer oriental Jews among them remained at the bottom of the educational ladder. Much of the Zionist curriculum was dedicated to Jewish and Hebrew culture, with many hours of Bible as history, geography and literature. While some Evangelical Protestants might have supported an equally literal reading of the Bible, the Catholic Farrell did not; he saw all this as 'racial and national exaltation'. Under the Plumer administration he wrote to Amery, suggesting that the government introduce in Jewish schools 'ideas based on British ideals of education and conduct'.[101] Nor could British public-school graduates approve a system in which organized games were not an important part of school life, while after school hours most children over the age of 10 were recruited into political youth movements.

While the Department of Education fielded inspectors in all the country's schools, it could decide policy and curricula only in the Arab sector. The main cause of dispute was how far the government should support the Zionist system financially. The Jewish leadership argued constantly that the substantial Jewish contribution to taxation, and in general to the development of Palestine, placed the government under an obligation to subsidize Jewish welfare on a par with expenditure on the Arabs, given that the Jewish system was largely self-supporting. Farrell, summing up the dispute towards the end of the Mandate, argued that this claim rested on the tacit assumption that the Jews were entitled to universal education, whether or not it could be granted to Arabs, and to a longer period of primary education than Arabs could afford. The system worked out was a compromise.

Until 1927, the government gave the Jewish Agency only small annual grants for education. From that year until 1932, when the Agency turned over responsibility for education to the Jewish National Council (Va'ad Leumi), it received a block grant proportional to the Jewish population. The Mandatory now recognized the Zionist schools as a 'public' educational system, and the block grant was calculated according to the number of Jewish schoolchildren aged 5–15. This did not satisfy the Va'ad Leumi, which also wanted a per capita allowance parallel to that expended on the Arabs. Nor did it satisfy the Education Department, which objected to annual updates as the Jewish school population grew – with many of the children having entered outside the legal immigration quotas. Farrell thought that salaries paid to Jewish teachers should have been deducted from the grant. The Government Treasurer also insisted that the Va'ad Leumi budgets should be available to the government for its approval, and that it should detail its expenditure on education in audited accounts furnished to the High Commissioner.[102]

This rarely happened, if only because of the chronically uncertain state of Zionist finances, the political pressures under which the administrators laboured, the constantly increasing Jewish school population (which at the end of the Mandate was ten times its original strength), and, above all, because the Jewish teachers were organized in a powerful trade union. Education officials remonstrated periodically with the Jewish leadership that they had no control over the way government grants were spent. But in any disagreement, the Zionist leadership had only to threaten to hand over financial responsibility for their schools to the Mandate government to put an end to the discussion. In 1931 the political secretary of the Jewish Agency, Chaim Arlosoroff, told the Chief Secretary that the Agency was considering withdrawing its financial support from the (Jewish) educational system altogether. There was a tendency 'to devote as much of Zionist funds as possible to constructive economic undertakings while placing responsibility for the social services, as far as possible, on local Jewish communities and the Palestine government'. Two years later the message was clearer: the Jewish leadership warned Wauchope that: 'The Jewish Agency would turn over the whole system to the government, which would end up with the poorer schools, and the government would fail to get money from parents.'[103]

Those threats worked, and the trouble continued. The Va'ad Leumi's education administration was always in debt; budgets were not produced on time and items were often unapproved; teachers' salaries were paid late, which resulted in strikes for which the Va'ad was unable to discipline the teachers; money earmarked for the religious schools was not handed over, and the Va'ad procrastinated over the department's demand for more technical and agricultural classes. At the end of the thirties the government refused to increase the block grant, as requested for three successive years, hoping thereby to coerce the Va'ad into submission. Some of the desired reforms were introduced, but the carrot and stick policy continued. The Jewish leadership continued to insist that the government was favouring the Arab sector at Jewish expense, and the Mandate government to demand that the Jewish leadership should run education 'on a strictly economic basis'. But the Zionists operated according to a different principle – that of constant improvisation – and the government, in retaliation, delayed the updating of grants.

Farrell, who dominated policy until 1946, thought the Jewish system over-ambitious and impossible to maintain financially, while the Jewish leadership insisted that all Jewish children were to receive an education, from kindergarten onwards, seeing this as the most important tool in welding together immigrants from so many different countries and backgrounds. However, the first Zionist budgetary priority was that of economic development, and the funds left over for welfare were sparse. The kibbutzim and moshavim (co-operative settlements) provided free education. Elsewhere, the Agency had at first contributed most of the cost, gradually handing over responsibility for kindergartens to the municipalities in Jewish towns, then introducing tuition fees and taxes levied on the whole community. But by the 1930s even this did not ensure adequate funds to pay the teachers.

In a memorandum written in 1932, Farrell reported that the Jewish teachers were working for a pittance (less than that paid to Arab teachers in government schools), but that they were then charging overtime for piece-work, a method 'incompatible with pensionable service and injurious to the prestige and morale of teachers'. The formal scale of salaries did not decide what the teachers actually paid, 'and in all probability can never be fully paid unless the ideal of universal education is abandoned'.[104] A year later, he complained that: 'The Jewish educational authorities will give no return for Government money once spent. The quid pro quo must be exacted in advance, and no reliance can be placed upon promises to deliver. . . . No reforms can be effected without opposition from the teachers'; nevertheless, the teachers continued to set the tone. For six years, Farrell lamented that the principal British and Jewish officers of the Education Department had been 'pouring water into Danaids jars'.[105]

Reports by the Jewish inspectors in the department indicated that Jewish school administration during the years of peak immigration was indeed chaotic. At the beginning of the school year 1933–4 one of the department's Jewish schools' inspectors, Avinoam Yellin, reported that many Va'ad Leumi schools had not opened because of uncertainty regarding funds. In others, the timetable was not fixed, or only one or two teachers had turned up on time. Even in Tel Aviv, the most prosperous Jewish town, where the municipality itself supported education, there were classrooms designed for forty pupils crammed with more than twice that number, and many parents refused to send their children to school. There was no official list of maintained schools and teachers, no real pension scheme, and dismissing an incompetent or redundant teacher meant risking bringing the entire union out on strike. The syllabus was updated only by issuing circulars.[106] Another Jewish inspector in Mandate service, the orientalist S. D. Goitein, found in 1938 that in Jerusalem, Jewish schools were continually shunting classes from the poorer schools to those where the parents were better able to pay fees, and closing the others down. Although on paper all Jewish children were reported as receiving eight years of schooling, only two of the six General trend elementary schools in Jerusalem in that year actually had eight functioning classes. Goitein also reported that at the beginning of the 1939 school year, in the prestigious Tahkemoni School in Jerusalem, parents had fallen behind in payment of fees and most of the pupils in two classes had to be sent home as a consequence.[107]

In the war years relations between the Va'ad Leumi and the Education Department reached an impasse. During 1940–1 Farrell proposed that Jewish teachers' terms of service be brought into line with those of government officers (the Va'ad Leumi had agreed, but was unable to impose this change in the face of opposition by the teachers' union); that the elementary curriculum be diversified, particularly towards vocational training; that more attention be paid to the teaching of English; and that government assistance be provided equally to all Jewish schools (including the religious) – a proviso reflecting Farrell's resentment of the dominance of Jewish Labour, 'the party' in education. While the Va'ad was not opposed to reforms, only unable to impose them, the real issue was how far British authority in Palestine could be brought to bear on Jewish affairs. A disgruntled report forwarded to the Colonial Office by the High Commissioner, MacMichael, with the comment, 'Under which king, Bezonian?', came back minuted by the Colonial Secretary Stanley: 'Under which king indeed'. H. S. Scott, an authority on English education consulted by the Colonial Office, commented: 'From the beginning, a different system was adopted in Jewish and in Arab schools. If the purpose of the Mandatory was to establish a composite state, one would have thought that unity of treatment in education should have been adopted from the beginning'; while a Colonial Office official minuted the report plaintively: 'I doubt whether any Department of Education in Palestine could have succeeded in running a unified system covering both Arabs and Jews, however hard it tried.'[108]

Farrell's dislike for the Socialists, who controlled so much of the Jewish education system of Palestine and the teachers in their schools, was now unconcealed. Every meeting became a confrontation. Farrell complained that the teachers:

apparently claimed cost of living allowances as public officers but their
conduct was not that of public officers; they submitted to the authority of
neither the local education authorities, nor the Va'ad Leumi, nor the
government. The behaviour of the officials of the teachers association
would, in Russia, have ensured their immediate liquidation.[109]

In his last year of office, 1945–6, Farrell insisted that no grant would
be paid until the budget was approved, and the Va'ad refused to submit
one. It was only after the intervention of the Chief Secretary, Sir John
Shaw, 'to dispose finally of this tiresome controversy', that Farrell
agreed to pay the grant and arrears, grudgingly advising the government 'to overlook to some extent the seditious attitude' of the Jewish
administrators.[110]

It was inevitable that, in this atmosphere, yet another Palestine
Commission should have been set up, this time producing the McNair
Report on Jewish education in Palestine – or rather, on its awkward
conjunction with British rule. That the government contemplated
actually taking Jewish education away from the Va'ad Leumi is
implicit in the Report's recommendation that it should remain in
Jewish hands 'if that can be achieved consistently with efficiency and
economy'. The Commission found that the absence of a Jewish education code on standards, qualifications for teachers, salaries and
pensions was 'one of the gravest defects of the Jewish school system'.
This system, they argued, was over-politicized, with no mechanism for
checks and balances, and no adequate overall authority or planning.
Everything that diverged from British norms was criticized: the intervention of parents in school affairs, the one-session school day, the fact
that nearly 40 per cent of the cost of Jewish elementary education and
almost all the cost of secondary education was borne by the parents,
rather than by all taxpayers; and, of course, the recruitment of schoolchildren to political youth movements, which the Commission called
'the submission of children of a tender age . . . to the exciting and
disturbing influences' of politics. The Report was a last attempt to
reconcile British responsibilities for the two communities. The
Commission found that compulsory education and integration of the
Arab and Jewish system would have been preferable to the inequities
of a situation in which only a third of Arab children aged between 5
and 15 received any education whatsoever. They recommended that

English 'unite' Jews and Arabs in higher education.[111] Against all the evidence, the Mandatory continued to dream of a docile, colonial Palestine in which Jews and Arabs were going to sink their differences in an Anglicized environment.

The McNair Report was far too anodyne for Farrell, whose innate anti-Semitism had been rendered virulent both by his trials in the administration and, possibly, by the fact that in the post-war period all British officials were now the potential targets of Jewish terrorists. In his final recommendations on Mandate education, and in observations on the McNair Report, also presented to the Anglo-American Commission of Enquiry in 1946, he made his personal views on Jewry all too clear.

At the end of 1945 Farrell wrote a lengthy memorandum giving the reasons why he thought that, in order to run education fairly in the post-war period, heavier taxes should be imposed, the grant in aid to the Va'ad Leumi should be withdrawn altogether, and an adequate subsidy be found, from imperial resources, for Arab education. The memorandum rejected all Jewish claims to higher educational expenditures from the general Mandate revenues. Most of the Jews of Palestine, Farrell wrote, belonged to that section of Jewry which had 'by no special merit of their own, become partially assimilated to Western civilisation in the nineteenth century'. It was true that the Jews of Palestine contributed more to the revenues, but their education system was vitiated by their 'intellectual pride and political intolerance', and their hostility to religious and oriental Jews. Their public schools had developed 'an exaggerated and exclusive rationalism largely divorced from the Jewish religion – little understood by most Englishmen'. 'It is now alleged, not without some colour of truth, that the ideological resemblance between Zionism and Nazism is becoming more marked. This is a cause of uneasiness to all who are concerned with the moral aspect of the war aims of Great Britain and the US.' Few Zionists had had the moral courage to condemn civil bloodshed. Britain, Farrell insisted, 'should not be incouraging independent Jewish education at all', and it followed that: 'Any administrative changes in the Jewish education system should be such as would tend to check the progressive debauching of young minds with Nazi ideas.'[112]

Farrell developed his pseudo-historical argument against the Jews in his comments on the McNair Report, written a year later on the eve of his departure from Palestine. Here he argued that the 'vigorous racial and national propaganda' in Jewish schools was inspired by the desire 'to eradicate the liberal education absorbed by Jews in Western Europe and the United States', that it produced terrorism, and was 'education for murder'. He castigated what he called the 'immoral and hypocritical attitude of Zionist leaders (Poles, Russians and other Easterners)', who were 'identical with Nazis, Russian Communists and fanatical Muslims'. Blaming the Colonial Office for its indifference, he said that the McNair Report had recommended eliminating nationalism from schools but recommended that nationalists should control education. Nor had it emphasized the faults in the Jewish educational system.

'There is no common moral and theological ground upon which politically organised Jewry and a Christian civilisation can stand together in harmony,' wrote Farrell:

> The inhuman mass-selfishness of concentrated Jewry, transmitting by a blind instinct all the marks of rational design, and perpetuated throughout millennia, is a phenomenon so far as I know without parallel in history. In neither Palestine nor Nazi Germany have the moderates exhibited power or courage, and the future of Palestine or even world Jewry, unless controlled by international force, will lie with a few older extremists who encourage savagery natural in young animals.

Farrell claimed that the government schools had restrained Arab national feeling (his colleague Bowman had stressed that all Arab teachers were fervent nationalists). However: 'Judaism is now a neotheism which leads to that racial self-worship which Albert Rosenberg [sic] borrowed from the Jews for Nordic ends.' A Gestapo would be needed, Farrell concluded, since 'the Zionists enjoy a great advantage in evil . . . over the Arabs'.

Thus the head of the Education Department of the Palestine government, a year after the end of the Holocaust. Farrell's comments were minuted, in the Colonial Office: 'a long and valuable note by Farrell', Joy Ferguson wrote; 'an extremely fair-minded analysis of the Report'.[113]

5

Iron Gloves

In Palestine our difficulties are much greater than in other subject states, as the thinking classes definitely accuse us of promoting an unjust policy, of taking sides, and moreover, in order to carry out this unpopular policy we have had to employ large numbers of Englishmen in every post, thus depriving the native of the country of almost all power. It is a fallacy to think the Oriental content with high wages and no power. If the Indian, in whose country we have made untold improvements, would throw off European control were it possible, how much sooner would the Arab of Palestine do so. . . . Whatever the aims of Zionism, it is clear that old methods of government are no longer adequate. Nationalism is a very real thing, which cannot be neglected nor abolished. . . . We have either to hand over much power or rule by force.

Colonel Peake, Resident in Amman, writing to
Chancellor after the 1929 riots.[1]

The riots and killings of 1921 and 1929 were eclipsed in the Mandate's second decade by the Arab Revolt, a widespread rebellion which began with a strike of Arab tradesmen and workers in April 1936 and soon grew into total insurrection. Towards the end of 1938 the government had lost control of large areas of the country, the roads were dangerous, the railways under constant sabotage, and even the walled city of Jerusalem was – for some weeks – impossible for a British official to enter. After much hesitation, the government handed extraordinary powers to the military, enabling it to crush the Revolt well before the outbreak of the Second World War. A period of truce followed. But once the war ended, it was the turn of frustrated Jewish nationalists, furious at immigration cuts and land purchase restrictions, to resort to violence. After two years of further attrition, Britain admitted that it could no longer make the choice Peake had thought inevitable; it was neither able to delegate power, nor to continue to rule by force.

After the First World War, keeping order in Palestine looked like the familiar imperial task of controlling tribal marauders who did not recognize colonial frontiers and rounding up the rural bandits, some of them highwaymen who demanded ransom, who had long made local travel dangerous. With the aid of the Air Force (which had already been used for a similar purpose in the Sudan), this seemed a job for a British cavalry regiment and a mounted police force. The first head of police under the military regime, Lieutenant-Colonel Percy Bramley, had been Deputy Inspector in the police in India, fighting brigands near the Nepalese border, and his men were mostly ex-soldiers. At the beginning of the Mandate he was replaced by Brigadier Angus McNeill, an Irishman who reorganized the local police after the riots of May 1921, adding two new defence units: a Palestinian gendarmerie (a semi-military mobile unit) made up chiefly of equal numbers of Jews and Arabs under British command, and a wholly British auxiliary force.

Despite the troubles of 1921, the administration saw the main role of the gendarmerie as stopping arms smuggling and raids from across the border, and it was thus ill prepared for keeping the roads safe or protecting isolated Jewish settlements. There was no modern road across the coastal plain, or linking the coast with Jerusalem; policy was to encourage the use of the government-owned railway lines, rather than to spend money on road-building. The existing roads led through the hilly spine of the country, where their twists and turns made ambushes easy for Arab attackers, who could take refuge in familiar villages or caves. Most of the Jewish settlements beyond the coastal plain were planted in a zigzag fashion across the northern part of the country, and many were reached by tracks almost impassable in winter. After 1921, at the request of the Jewish Agency, the Jewish settlers were equipped with rifles locked in sealed armouries, to be used only in response to attacks by marauders from across the northern frontier and, later, from neighbouring villages. These armouries were set up in the greatest secrecy, without official correspondence, and the rifles were overhauled and lubricated every three months by British police officers. In 1926 (with Jewish immigration apparently in decline, and the interior of the country peaceful), the British Cavalry Regiment was withdrawn, the gendarmeries disbanded, and the TransJordan Frontier Force (TJFF) was established – an Arab unit raised across the river under British command. The police also began to withdraw the sealed armouries.[2] Consequently, in the autumn of 1929, the riots at the Wailing Wall in Jerusalem, the killing and looting in the suburbs, and wholesale massacres of Jews in the Jewish quarters of Hebron and Safed, found the Jews almost defenceless and took the administration completely by surprise. In the Galilee, Edwin Bryant, a resourceful police chief, provided the settlements with Verrey lights with which they could signal distress to police stations miles away. But in Jerusalem, the civil administration could not give orders to the armoured car unit in the vicinity to fire on the rioters, and had to wait until the RAF Group Commander arrived from Amman to co-ordinate the response with the police. When Arab policemen hesitated to fire into the mob, it was left to individual British policemen and even civilians to respond. Raymond Cafferata a veteran of the First World War and of the gendarmerie, single-handedly and armed only with a revolver, checked a Hebron mob made up mainly of Arabs from the surrounding villages (some Hebron Arabs sheltered Jewish neighbours) but was unable to prevent the murder of fifty-nine Jews and the destruction of synagogues and seminaries. Police Commander Faraday took similar action in Safed; while a party of students from an Oxford college tried to defend Jews in Jerusalem. Two battalions were hastily summoned from Egypt to reinforce the garrison.[3]

The police were reorganized, this time by C. H. Dowbiggin, called in from Ceylon and described by the Colonial Secretary, Ormsby Gore, as 'the star police turn of the British Empire'. Yet there was still no riot drill, and no specific training for police summoned to deal with violent demonstrations. In October 1933 in Jaffa, the District Commissioner, army officers and others stood on the balcony of the local government building as a crowd protesting against Jewish immigration harangued them and threw stones and bottles at them. For some time the police dithered, according to C. H. Imray, one of a large contingent drafted to maintain order which was deployed across the main square. He described the use of firepower as 'hesitant', after a baton charge with horses proved useless – the horses panicked. Imray cut his way out of danger using his police shield: 'all very violent and primitive', he complained. It was only after Faraday (together with Cafferata) was injured by flying stones that two 'controlled volleys' dispersed the crowd, killing some of the demonstrators. As a result of this incident, a Palestine Police riot drill was finally drawn up. Imray thought the hesitation was 'post-Amritsar' – a reference to the notorious slaughter of Indian demonstrators by British troops in 1919.[4]

After 1929 the Jews of Haifa, which was a mixed town, demanded a separate Jewish police force, similar to that in Tel Aviv – a wholly Jewish town. Dowbiggin increased the police force, reinforced the cavalry and restored the sealed armouries. He was well aware of the nationalist and religious forces which had set off the disturbances. Yet, like the Colonial Office and the administration in general, he still insisted on the 'composite state' idea. He wanted the Jewish and Arab police to share barracks, for all Jewish policemen to learn Arabic, the language of the majority, and thought that: 'the Palestine force must be made as homogeneous as possible in spirit, though not in race, and the members of the Force must try to sink their individuality as Jews or Arabs in a common feeling of pride in the Force to which they belong'.[5] It took the Arab Revolt to reveal this as a fantasy.

The High Commissioner who tried first to delegate power and ended up ruling by force was Sir Arthur Wauchope, who had just begun a two-year extension of his five-year term in office when the first signs of rebellion appeared. Wauchope was a career soldier, three times wounded in the First World War; some thought his head injuries accounted for his eccentric temper. He came to Palestine in 1931 straight from Northern Ireland, where he had commanded the local British forces. It was said that he wanted 'not only to command the Brigade but also every battalion, company and platoon in it . . . the terror of the junior officer and the despair of the battalion commanders'. In just the same way he insisted in intervening personally in the work of every department of the Palestine administration – Agriculture, Education, Health and Public Works included; Edwin Samuel said that he inspected even the village latrines. Keith-Roach complained that he overrode his experts, turning proceedings at legislative council meetings into a farce. His private secretary, Ralph

Poston, remembered that he hated paperwork and would not read files, preferring to interrogate his subordinates. According to his second Chief Secretary, William Battershill, Wauchope regarded the Executive and Advisory Council meetings he was bound to attend as 'so much flummery', and 'mesmerized public servants' into doing his will. He knew nothing of public administration:

> Government House seemed to be littered with little blocks of paper with a pencil attached. These were used solely by the High Commissioner and were to take his thoughts and ideas on any subject that might occur to him at any hour of the day. . . . Half the administration didn't know what the other half was up to. No despatch was ever put up in draft, but sent up ready for the High Commissioner's signature.

Battershill often signed these drafts in Wauchope's place, 'for High Commissioner on tour', even when he was actually in Government House at the time. 'The Colonial Office never found out,' wrote Battershill in a private memoir.[6]

The first High Commissioner to inhabit Austen Harrison's newly constructed Government House, Wauchope, who was well read and liked music, gave dinner parties almost every evening, with an elderly widowed lady (he was a bachelor) playing hostess and rationing the hot water allowed to house guests. At state evenings, chamber music was played in the minstrels' gallery, and when Wauchope gave a hunt ball in Lent, his hounds walked about the ballroom. Poston, a countryman, had to kit himself out with two trunkloads of new clothes, tails, top hat, evening dress tailcoat, and a white waistcoat with brass buttons, 'a sort of a cross between a hunt ball and a club waiter', which Wauchope decreed as Government House staff dress. Wauchope disliked motoring, preferring to fly in RAF biplanes, sitting in a deck chair, while Poston, with a signals officer, followed in a second plane, and luggage or a picnic was carried in a third. They were met by a Rolls-Royce at Haifa, and usually made for Wauchope's weekend camp, near the ruins of a Crusader castle; when on leave he went shooting in Inverness-shire.[7] He was on one of these hunting sprees when the Arab Revolt began to get out of hand.

Despite Wauchope's chaotic methods, during his first five years in office Palestine prospered economically, chiefly because of the big influx of Jewish capital as Jews fled Europe. Public works multiplied, and the Haifa harbour – a strategic necessity – was built and completed in 1936, even though in global terms this was a period of economic recession. Wauchope had a flair for farming and tree planting, and planted olive trees, taken without their roots from other regions of Palestine, in the garden of Government House – where, despite the neglect of the grounds, they still survive. He personally backed a number of experimental farming projects and dipped deep into his substantial private fortune to support Arab farmers. However, according to Keith-Roach, by remitting rural taxation in many Arab areas as part of his personal policy of assisting Arab agriculture, 'the whole structure of government was undermined, and eventually we were unable to collect any rural taxes worth mentioning'.[8]

Though Wauchope's rudeness to subordinates was legendary, he maintained a courteous, diplomatic dialogue with both leading Arabs and Jews. He understood the background to the 1929 riots, and was apprehensive above all of 'raising the religious cry' among the Muslims. He believed that he could avert inter-communal violence by conciliating the religious leadership, and insisted that the Mufti, Haj Amin el Husseini, whom the Army and many officials saw as public enemy number one, was really a moderate, without whose restraining influence Arab violence would be more widespread. In August 1931 he persuaded the British government not to ban the Islamic congress which the Mufti was organizing. The Supreme Muslim Council was deep in debt, and dependent largely on government advances and bank overdrafts. Though Wauchope admitted later that 'no individual official knows exactly how the administrative part of the Sharia works, or how the Waqf funds are actually disbursed', he never insisted on strict accounting, or used the government's financial power (for instance) to prevent political incitement from the pulpit of mosques, which was officially deemed 'undesirable'. Instead, he continued to bail out the Mufti. Battershill 'found that there was an office order that letters from the Mufti were to be answered on the day of receipt and that replies were to be sent to him by hand'. Wauchope was also accessible at all times to a number of the Zionist leaders, including Weizmann and Chaim Arlosoroff, the head of the Political Department of the Jewish Agency until his murder in 1936. No High Commissioner became so intimately involved with the Zionist leadership, repeatedly taking them into his confidence in a way he never did the Arab leaders, and telling them in advance of many of his plans for maintaining order.[9]

For several years preceding the Arab Revolt Wauchope had tried to design a legislative council acceptable to both Arabs and Jews. He had little chance of success, if only because of the contradictory policies of the British government. While the Passfield White Paper of October 1930 had pledged 'a measure of self government . . . without further delay' to the Arabs, the Prime Minister, Ramsay MacDonald, had personally assured the Zionist leadership in 1931 that he supported the principle of parity. Wauchope wanted proportional representation, but the Zionists refused to accept minority status in the council. Arlosoroff argued that the Jews deserved parity because they were by now a majority in the larger towns, because they owned half the citrus industry, the hinterland of Haifa harbour, the control of the Electricity Corporation and the Dead Sea mineral concessions, and because they contributed 40 per cent of public revenue. Weizmann justified parity in conversation with Wauchope more briefly: 'One Jew as a unit of efficiency was at least equal to two Arabs.'[10]

In their talks with Wauchope over a period of several years, Weizmann and his colleagues continually reminded him of the fundamental claims of Zionism. In discussing relative Jewish and Arab claims to government assistance, Arlorosoff (who lectured Wauchope mercilessly on Jewish history and anti-Semitism) insisted that the distress of the fellahin in Palestine should be compared not with the 'relatively comfortable standard in the Jewish settlements' but with the plight of the Jews in Russia, Romania, Poland and even in Germany and America. In 1932 Wauchope resisted this argument, responding that 'if the Palestine government were faced with the alternative to provide either for a mass of poverty-stricken people in the country or for persecuted people abroad, it would have to consider the task at home first'.[11] Three years later, in 1935, with the Nazis in power in Germany, David Ben Gurion told Wauchope that the matter of the legislative council had to be regarded 'from the point of view of the Jewish people as a whole, and not just the Jewish population of Palestine'. As evidence of the Jewish need for Palestine he cited German and Polish persecution of the Jews, the failure to find homes elsewhere for Jewish refugees, and the capacity of the Jewish economy in Palestine to take them in. This time Wauchope asserted only that, although it was 'perfectly honourable' for the Zionist leadership to argue that they were not bound by Passfield's pledge to the Arabs, he himself had to respect it. The various safeguards he promised the Jews – while he intended to reduce the number of British officials in the legislative body, as proposed in 1922 by Samuel – included the right of the High Commissioner to dissolve the council out of hand, and a 'general warning' to the Arabs that he would abolish it altogether if no progress was made. But even this failed to mollify its Jewish opponents. Moshe Shertok of the Agency read him a lesson in government, pointing out that Wauchope's plans were not colonial practice.[12]

Knowing so little of colonial administration, Wauchope recognized none the less that he was being outmanoeuvred during contacts between the Cabinet, the Colonial Office and the Zionist leaders who commuted to and from London. These contacts were anything but secret. Shortly before the beginning of the Arab Revolt, Weizmann – invited in advance of a formal lunch – reported to Wauchope on his most recent visits to London. He told the High Commissioner that the Colonial Secretary was disliked, that the British Cabinet 'lacked co-ordination', and that the Colonial Office would shortly be informing Wauchope of 'the opening up of Transjordan for Jewish settlement and the granting of extra certificates for German refugees'. Weizmann added that when the Secretary of State, J. H. Thomas, had suggested worriedly that an Arab uprising in Palestine was possible, Weizmann had brushed him aside, saying that the Colonial Secretary 'shouldn't frighten him with such bogeys'. Some days later a Supreme Arab Strike Committee was formed which threatened to paralyse the country, demanding that Jewish immigration be halted, land purchases ended, and self-government begun. Weizmann immediately telephoned Wauchope from London to tell him that he was going to see the Prime Minister to report fully on Palestine affairs, and would recommend that the Strike Committee should be disbanded. The astounded Wauchope protested and, after he put the phone down, told Ralph Poston: 'The thing is I have never met the PM and I don't suppose I ever shall. Weizmann can go in there when he wants to.'[13]

Meanwhile there were mutinous rumblings in the administration. While some fumed at Wauchope's reluctance to get tougher with the Arab leaders, others advised the Arabs on how best to defend their position, asking their conditions for ending the strike, and encouraging them to stick together. All this was leaked to the Jewish Agency, which promptly reported to Wauchope that high officials of the Mandate were acting behind his back. Thomas Hodgkin, who had succeeded Poston as Wauchope's private secretary, was outraged by British policy, which he saw as the suppression of a movement of national liberation, resigned his position and wrote an article in a British Labour journal attacking the Mandate government's treatment of the Palestine Arabs.[14] (Hodgkin was later to become one of the staunchest intellectual backers of African independence.) But one young renegade did not trouble the High Commissioner. Wauchope's really powerful opponent was the Chief Justice, Sir Michael McDonnell, who now consistently undermined Wauchope's authority.

The strike was intended to encompass all Arab officials in government service, as well as the tradesmen and key transport workers. Wauchope approved Emergency Regulations enlarging his powers, and informed the Arab Higher Committee that legal action was being taken against those who had called on government officials to strike. The Chief Secretary, Hathorn-Hall, warned Arab officials that strikers would sacrifice their pension rights, and asked McDonnell to circularize this warning among the judges. Wauchope also appealed personally to McDonnell for his support. In the event, the Arab officials did not join the strike, but the Chief Justice would not comply. He had already objected that in sanctioning the emergency measures, Wauchope had not consulted him but had appointed a number of government officials to act as special magistrates. He now indicated his sympathy with the Arabs' demands by informing both Wauchope and the Colonial Secretary – in a personal letter – that a spontaneous Arab uprising could be prevented only by stopping Jewish immigration altogether. Four days later Wauchope requested McDonnell's removal, complaining that his Chief Justice had 'weakened the authority of Government and retarded the restoration of peace'.[15]

All this was confined to Colonial Office dispatches, but suddenly McDonnell brought his conflict with Wauchope into the public and political domain. Arab anger with the administration had already erupted into violence. Snipers in houses bordering the approach to Jaffa port were hindering its functioning, and in June Wauchope authorized the demolition of 250 houses, cutting a wide swathe through the town. The new Emergency Regulations, citing the Defence

Order in Council of 1931, indeed empowered the High Commissioner to take such action. In a meeting of the Mandate Defence Committee, Hathorn Hall and other decided that the demolition would be described as a 'town planning procedure' and posters offering compensation to property owners were put up in Jaffa. The stratagem was typical of Wauchope's continuing efforts to use legal rather than military measures to enforce order. It nevertheless backfired.

A householder whose property had been damaged challenged the government's action in an appeal to the High Court, and in hearing the case in the High Court in July – after the Colonial Office had asked for his resignation – McDonnell made the following comment:

> The petitioner has done a public service in exposing a singularly disingenuous lack of moral courage. It would have been more creditable, instead of endeavouring to throw dust in people's eyes by professing to be inspired with aesthetic or other quasi-philanthropic motives, if those responsible had said frankly that it was primarily for defensive purposes.

The Arab Higher Committee promptly had this broadside printed and distributed as a pamphlet in thousands of copies. It was circulated to the British Cabinet and McDonnell was offered the post of Chief Justice in the Straits Settlements.[16]

But McDonnell refused to go quietly, complaining angrily that Wauchope had tampered wilfully with the laws of Palestine. He made so much fuss over the financial terms of his retirement that the Foreign Office had to recommend that the Palestine government 'buy out Sir Michael McDonnell on his own terms'. In order to pay the very high pension McDonnell demanded on the basis of his twenty-five-year colonial service, and differences between the scales in West Africa and Palestine, a new law had to be passed (the Sir Michael McDonnell Pension Ordinance of 1936) so that he could be paid out of Palestine revenues. Chancellor's Attorney-General, Bentwich, had been sacked for his Zionist sympathies. Now McDonnell, sacked for his Arab sympathies, quoted the Bentwich precedent in pressing for more favourable pension terms, and the Colonial Office had no option – with the High Commissioner and the Chief Justice publicly at loggerheads – but to agree to his conditions.

In a final, furious letter, McDonnell, who had only with difficulty been restrained from publishing the whole correspondence in the British press, said that Wauchope's desire for his retirement had been based on the fact that: 'in the conscientious administration of justice I was compelled to expose in one case the duplicity and in another [a collective punishment case in Gaza] the incompetence of the executive of Palestine'. The Colonial Office commented ruefully: 'Although politics are strictly speaking no concern of his, it would be difficult to contend that an experienced senior member of the judiciary should be debarred from expressing his views to the head of the government under which he is serving on such serious issues as are here involved.'[17]

From this point onwards, the legal system of Palestine became harnessed to repression, as successive Emergency Regulations led to summary justice and the curtailment of civil rights, while collective punishment was used with increasing frequency. The roles of the Army and the police became increasingly confused: the Army was called in to deal with the armed bands against which the police were ineffective. The first administration had intended, in creating a multi-ethnic gendarmerie, that Arabs and Jews should co-operate in the internal security and defence of the country; but while Arab and Jewish police alike knew the terrain and the people, their loyalties were to their own communities, and the Army therefore took over many of the duties of the police. Before the Revolt, the army garrison had consisted of no more than a cavalry regiment, an RAF squadron in Amman and two companies of armoured cars under RAF supervision (Plumer's over-optimistic legacy to Chancellor in 1928). Over the next decade it had continually to be reinforced. During the first two years of the Revolt, successive heads of the military garrison – Air Commodore Peirse; then, as authority was transferred from the Air Ministry to the War Office, Lieutenant-General Dill and Major-General Wavell – all wanted a free hand in putting down the Revolt and urged the introduction of martial law.

But Wauchope was intensely reluctant to use force and argued initially against each tactic proposed by the military, from the use of tear gas to bombing villages suspected of sheltering rebels. Among the first, ineffectual measures taken – after a wave of stabbings of Jews by Arabs – was a ban on the manufacture of swords, knives or daggers, which prohibited any 'blade ending in sharp point and not primarily designed for use in profession, craft or business or for domestic use'. Anyone selling or wearing a dagger was liable to imprisonment, fine, or both (though blades measuring less than ten centimetres and without springs were legitimate). A Gaza lawyer protested that a number of men, mostly elderly, whose traditional living it was (celebrated in local verse) to produce daggers and swords, were put out of work.[18]

While the strike continued, armed rebels attacked both the Jews and the Mandatory. Between May and October 1936 the police recorded a rate of one Jew killed every two or three days in Jerusalem. Tens of British soldiers and policemen of all sections of the force died before the British government, in September 1936, decided to take tougher measures. Until this moment, intervention of the British Cabinet in Palestine troubles had been minimal: notably, the appointment of the Shaw Commission into the causes of the 1929 disturbances and the issuing of the Passfield White Paper in 1930. At the formal opening of the Iraq Petroleum Company's pipeline in Haifa in 1935, Lord Tanner, Under-Secretary at the Foreign Office, had told Ralph Poston: 'Young man, you should understand that Palestine is not even on the Cabinet map.'[19] But from the Revolt onwards, Palestine policy became part of general government strategy and subject to cabinet decisions. Even though the strike ended (the result of inter-Arab diplomacy), the garrison was doubled, the military command changed, and a Royal Commission was sent out to Palestine under the chairmanship of Lord Peel to examine Arab and Jewish grievances and produce recommendations. The military, meanwhile, marked time. They were critical of Wauchope's desire to wait until the findings of Commission were over, since they believed the Mufti and the Arab Higher Committee were behind the apparently random violence.

One soldier's view of the situation was that of Lieutenant-General Lawrence Carr, who arrived in October 1936 in Jaffa from England to command an infantry brigade. In letters home he wrote that Wauchope 'took no notice of the Army'. Carr regarded the local police as 'second class'; the Arabs defended Arab areas and Jews their own, with no co-operation between them. Disarming the population would mean declaring martial law, but in Carr's view this was unnecessary as he found the rebels badly armed, with antiquated rifles and old British and Turkish wartime ammunition that had been hoarded for twenty years or dug out of old trenches – most of it needing to be recapped. Carr found Wauchope a 'charming little man & delightful host, but I couldn't help feeling that he looks on the population of this country as if they were all Black Watch – all "his people"'. Carr's view of Wauchope is supported by a phrase in one of the High Commissioner's dispatches: the military might take unpopular measures but he himself was to remain a 'kind father' to the population. Carr's Palestine service dragged on while the Peel Commission held its hearings; once they were over, in the summer of 1937, the rebellion became more widespread and – with newer arms pouring into the country from the Arab states – better equipped.

The actual turning point between concilation and force was the murder of Lewis Andrews, the British official who had monitored land deals between Jews and Arabs for years, outside the church in Nazareth in September 1937. He was the first high Mandate official to lose his life. Wauchope was grouse-shooting in Scotland and Battershill acted in his place. As he wrote later: 'I had done what no "acting" person ought to do. I had changed the policy of the permanent holder of the post. It was Sir Arthur's policy to try to get security more by appeals to reason than appeals to force. I had perforce to change all that after Andrews' death.' The Arab Higher Committee was declared illegal, its leaders arrested and deported, and the Mufti was dismissed as President of the Supreme Muslim Council and went into hiding in the area of the Noble Sanctuary in Jerusalem, where he knew the police would not follow him. Battershill noted in his diary that it was 'impossible to guard all exits, as it would pin down too many police. If he makes a determined effort in disguise I think his attempt is bound to be successful.' This was precisely what happened a few days later, when Haj Amin escaped disguised as a Bedouin. Wauchope was a broken man. He told Battershill that he had asked to retire, 'overworked and tired and 63', though 'it means the end of so much I had hoped and worked for'. There are many indications that he was near a mental breakdown; it was hard to persuade him to leave the beautiful grounds of Government House.[20]

Wauchope was succeeded by Sir Harold MacMichael, formerly Governor of the Sudan, a competent colonial administrator who preferred reading thrillers to literary evenings and who had no problems with the Army. Military courts were introduced, empowered to hand down death sentences against which no appeal was allowed. But despite this measure, and curfews which the police were scarcely able to enforce, the murders of Jews by Arabs continued, while attacks on army patrols, arson and sabotage of roads and railways began. The Army for some time responded by demolishing the houses of the culprits – actions for which, unlike the civil authorities, they were not obliged to pay compensation. In October 1937, Carr wrote:

> This afternoon I went [to Lydda] and watched . . . houses being blown up by the R[oyal] E[ngineers]; there is a curfew on Lydda, but as the police have not sufficient strength to enforce it, a company of the Wilts[hires] is doing so. About 80 male inhabitants in the lockup. Telephone lines cut. Troops stuck in trains. The Arabs getting bolder with their sabotage. Railway lines tampered with nightly, telegraph lines cut and sniping. This morning two companies of the 60th had to go out to demolish houses in Qala and Rantis which had been identified as belonging to Arabs who had taken part in the train derailment. I went to Qala and saw to it that the RE put in enough explosive to not only demolish the culprits' houses but also all those adjoining it. In all I had eight houses obliterated. I shall go to Jerusalem tomorrow once more to plead for more energetic measures. . . . My battalions are out almost daily assisting the police by surrounding villages, blowing up known culprits' houses, etc. I generally go with one of them.

And in November:

> Tomorrow at dawn I am joining the North Staffordshires who are going to help shake up Beit Mahsir. 5 Jews killed working at stone quarry near Abu Ghosh [a village on the road to Jerusalem]. Sent armoured cars and 2 companies. Police had put 2 tracker dogs. Wavell arrived shortly afterwards. Police dog tracked murderers to Yalu. On foot chased Arab escaping from village.[21]

By the time Wauchope left, the Peel Commission had reached its conclusions. It recommended that Palestine was to be divided by partition into Arab and Jewish states. While the British government debated the recommendations, British police and troops intensified their campaign against the hill bands.

As early as 1930, Chancellor's administration had begun to suspect that those rural Arabs they formerly dismissed as mere bandits and highway robbers might be politically organized, and their attacks – whether on Jews or British officials – carefully planned. Their leaders, usually local sheikhs, could rely on a base in the villages. One of the first signs of this was the appearance in the Galilee of the Green Hand Gang (self-named – green was the Muslim colour), which, in October of 1930, fired salvoes into the Jewish quarter of Safed with long-range weapons. Police and troops returned the fire, captured some of the hideouts, and sentenced three of the group to death; but their supporters threatened to attack the more isolated Jewish settlements if the sentence was carried out. It took over three months for the police, the Army and reinforcements from the TJFF combing hills and wadis, with the RAF flying reconnaissance missions, to flush out a group of only twenty-five men, who recruited other followers at need from the villages where they received food and shelter. Police Intelligence believed that the group were supported by the Young Men's Muslim Association under the patronage of the Mufti. Chancellor told Passfield that such bands might be organized by 'disaffected politicians' in Palestine and Transjordan, and that the Green Hand Gang was a test scheme launched to see how such groups might operate. In the spring of 1930 most of the band was caught and its leader Ahmed Tafish fled, but its ability to challenge both the police and the troops had encouraged others.[22] In the Galilee there was Sheikh Izzedin al Qassem, a charismatic Islamic Syrian leader who continued to inspire Palestinian fundamentalists decades after his death. Al Qassem was killed in a shoot-out in November 1935, but his followers were believed to have assassinated Lewis Andrews. Later, in the central Jenin district, the chief rebel was Sheikh Farhan, of whom one of his British pursuers, Bernard Fergusson, a Brigade Intelligence Officer in the north and a cousin of Wauchope's, wrote: 'One might suggest as a remote parallel an English suffragan Bishop forming a small resistance movement and ravaging the Thames Valley from the Chilterns.'[23] In August 1936, Farhan and other local leaders came under the command of an Iraqi army officer, Fawzi el Kaukji, who for several months defied the British Army from the hills around Nablus. Keith-Roach, then District Commissioner in Galilee, claimed that he was ordered to 'engineer his escape to Jordan'. Farhan was ultimately found hiding in an empty cistern in a village and arrested, tried and executed within three days; another famous outlaw, Abu Jildeh (identified in police handouts as having a scar on his chin and very small teeth), who terrorized the north, was caught when the police put one of his relatives in front of the café where they had trapped him, so that he could not shoot his way out; in the Hebron district Sheikh Aissa Battat got through a siege mounted by police and Army and was eventually killed as the result of a plot involving a local Arab official and one of Battat's followers.[24]

Insurrection had begun with attacks on Jews in the main towns, and was countered by a police force backed up by the Army. With the spread of the Revolt to the countryside, once the local leaders had strengthened their hold on the villages, it was guerrilla warfare, with the Army unable to lure the bands into open battle, even after the death of so many of their chiefs. The dispersal of the Arab Higher Committee and the flight of the Mufti did not alter the fact that the Revolt had acquired a popular base.

The British soldiers brought in to help the police round up these bands knew little or nothing of Palestine politics; they were often hastily summoned detachments from other colonies, who fought a miniature war in the hills, 'bandit hunting' or 'oozling' ('oozabarts', their name for Arab rebels, was the corruption of an Arabic word) in the style of previous campaigns in the North-West Frontier province, Bengal, or the Sudan. The roles of Army and the police were no longer separate, and British administrators, too, were roped in as policemen.

Sir Gawain Bell was recruited by Sir Harold MacMichael, Wauchope's successor, in the summer of 1938 from Sudan service, on a two-year contract to Palestine; he observed that the civil administration had lost control of the countryside, where only the Army now functioned. No taxes were collected, the rebels meted out their own justice, and the Jews remained 'cooped up in their colonies'. All a District Commissioner could do, by this time, was to act as liaison officer between the population and the Army. Bell found this 'exciting and adventurous' except when he had to assist the police in tracking down rebels. 'The combing of a village entailed all the men and boys being collected and lined up. There would then be a search for wanted men. This meant that these people would be obliged to file slowly past a police armoured car in which a government informer was concealed.' Bell thought the system 'open to abuse' and 'unsporting', though he added, there was 'fair play and a sense of humour on both sides'. After eight months in the Galilee Gawain Bell was sent to the southern desert, where the rebels had destroyed every trace of British rule: police posts, wireless communications and dispensaries alike. His mission was to restore them and where possible to round up rebel bands, and for this purpose he was made Deputy Superintendent of Police.[25]

In the spring of 1938 Sir John Hackett commanded half a squadron which set out every fortnight from Beisan on cordon and search missions on Arab ponies. They carried nothing but barley in feed bags and lived off the countryside. This, he insisted, was not taking advantage of the Arabs (whose economy, by this period of the Revolt, was in near collapse). 'They liked giving hospitality. . . . It was a perfectly splendid war for a young Cavalry subaltern and I don't think even when I was at New College I was happier than fighting a subalterns' war.' Hackett insisted that he and the rebels understood one another and had the same 'sporting' attitude to the conflict. His particular adversary was Abdul Rahim, the commander of a rebel band in the Nablus Jenin area, to whom he sent a message to say that he

> considered it beneath the dignity of a British regimental officer to be shot at by a bare arsed Arab with a bent bundook using bad ammunition and if he cared to send a musketry contingent to my camp I'd give them some instruction. He answered courteously that his best shots were rather busy just now. Abdul Rahim was killed by his own men a few weeks later.[26]

Such facetious exchanges between enemies, according to Bell, had been common during the Boer War.

The Jews had long been on the defensive, almost entirely reliant on British protection. From March 1921, when the Hagana – the Jewish militia – was formed and began acquiring arms, it was geared to protecting the settlements and the Jewish quarters of towns. The Mandate government, accused frequently of failing to protect Jews against Arab attacks, turned a blind eye to the formation of this (officially illegal) organization, while placing restrictions on the Jewish police. In October 1935, however, a particularly large consignment of arms was intercepted in Jaffa, and the administration wanted the Jewish Agency to disavow its involvement and support the government in bringing the culprits to book. But Shertok, arguing from experience, pointed out that despite the Agency's confidence in the government, much of the Jewish population could be wiped out before the British could bring in extra forces.[27] Jewish Agency leaders had continually pressed Battershill to form a force of British and Jewish police, trained and armed by the government, but he held off, feeling that stationing Jews in Arab areas would mean trouble. However, in July 1936, with the Revolt in full swing, the Jewish supernumerary police force was formed, more than three thousand strong with over two thousand reservists. Initially they were armed with rifles, but they knew where the Jewish arms caches were, and in March 1937 they were finally permitted to operate officially outside their settlement perimeters in 'hot pursuit' of marauders from nearby villages.[28]

There was no camaraderie between the British troops in Palestine and the Jewish settlers. Gawain Bell summed up the feelings not only of the garrison but of the British officials providing liaison: 'We knew that in all these settlements they were busy training their men and their women in the creation of an underground army, and clandestinely acquiring supplies of arms.' Bell preferred the hospitality of the Arabs:

> With smiling protestations of loyalty on one side and equally hypocritical expressions of confidence on the other, we would depart before mid afternoon. An evening ambush on the road home, to which our host might just conceivably be privy, was always a possibility. I admired but found it very difficult to like the Jews. . . . I liked and sympathized with the Arabs but in general had less admiration for them. . . . The soldiers instinctively felt a preference for the wild men who sniped at them from the hillsides to the seemingly friendly Jewish settlers who over-keenly entertained them with food and beer. The cause for which the Arabs were fighting was, to us, understandable and just, [though] their methods and the means they employed, particularly against unarmed and innocent Jews and frequently against their own people, were often barbaric and inexcusable.[29]

Collective punishment was used routinely against the Arab rebels. The measure was almost as old as the Mandate itself, with the first such measure proposed after the Jaffa riots of May 1921. At that time the Jewish judge Gad Frumkin, posted in Jaffa, had volunteered to help the Arab police investigating the killing of Jews in the town and looting of their property. But both Arab and Jewish witnesses were afraid to come forward, and the Chief Justice, Sir Thomas Haycraft, felt it unsuitable that Frumkin, an Appeal Court judge, should take part in criminal investigations. On his return to Jerusalem Frumkin told the then Attorney-General, Bentwich, that 'nationalist' crimes could not be solved in the ordinary way, and if the criminals could not be brought to justice and the looted property returned, it was essential to impose collective punishment, to put responsibility for the material damage on the entire community from which the thieves had come. Frumkin's proposal was that peace-keeping be the responsibility of the heads of village communities, with collective fines imposed for theft and looting.

But Bentwich hesitated to draft what was clearly punitive legislation which would apply to the Arabs alone. The first Collective Responsibility Ordinance was imposed on certain 'tribal' areas and districts in 1924 by Samuel's administration, and for a period of one year only. It was then renewed for another year, and when the Collective Punishment Ordinance was redrafted in 1925, it was explained as a measure adopted to control feuds which erupted periodically between villages, not to check violence by one subject people against another. When Lord Plumer wanted to extend the ordinance to municipal areas, the Colonial Secretary Lord Lloyd argued that 'the powers granted by this ordinance are most exceptional' and were to be used only in specific parts of the country (as was the case in some British colonies in Africa). Its extension to the towns, he said, 'could not fail to lend colour to any criticism that the reason why we have to resort to such special legislation is that our policy is so much detested that the Arabs cannot otherwise be made to acquiesce in our rule'.[30] The ordinance remained in effect throughout the Mandate. It was frequently amended, and was indeed used in early 1930s mainly to control village feuds. It was common practice, when one village quarrelled with another, for one clan to cut down or burn the rival clan's trees and slash their crops before harvesting, so the 1926 ordinance was designed chiefly to stop what was called 'agrarian crime'. Clans also sometimes poisoned their rivals' cattle, putting arsenic in dried figs fed to the cows. In 1935 the ordinance was amended to make it unnecessary to prove that the crime was committed in the area of the village or tribe. Hugh Foot, then District Commissioner in Samaria, later remembered putting an end to tree cutting as his greatest achievement.

The ordinance enabled Foot to go in as soon as the police notified him, sit in the village as a magistrate, assess the damage, impose a collective fine on the clan responsible and collect it immediately. The money was then given to the owner of the trees, so that the clan could see that their money was going to their enemy. Foot recalled: 'The practice ceased, but the difficulty remained that in one or two cases, people cut down their own trees.'[31] Any villager who had failed to report 'agrarian crime', connived at the escape of the culprit, or suppressed material evidence, was judged as severely as the culprit himself. On the occasions when one clan killed a member of another but concealed the offender, the whole clan was sometimes fined. The ordinance was also used against the Bedouin tribes who smuggled arms across the southern frontiers. During the Arab Revolt, when it was necessary to quarter police in the village, the cost was borne by all the assessable inhabitants.

From the outset of the Revolt, collective punishment united the civil and military authorities in improvised actions against rebellious villages, the one fining the villagers in accordance with the Collective Punishment Ordinance, while the other demolished their houses under the Emergency Regulations. The complications of this policy are clear from the case of Indur in the Jezreel valley in 1936. Indur villagers were suspected of ambushing a military patrol, killing two soldiers and wounding three. A police dog followed the track to Indur, but the villagers denied all complicity. They also refused to identify a dead villager found at the scene of the ambush, whom officials knew to be a servant of Rafi Bey el Fahoum, a village notable who was a member of the Palestine General Agricultural Council and an expert on organic manure. When a cursory search of the village turned up an explosive fuse and amunition in two houses, these and that of the el Fahoum family were declared forfeit and demolished, the entire village was fined heavily, and Rafi Bey was imprisoned. The villagers were ordered to repair damage they were suspected of causing both to the electric cable track and to the oil pipeline – thereby working off part of the fine. But the el Fahoum family demanded compensation, and the damage was duly assessed. Knowing nothing of the incident, the Agricultural Council continued to circularize Rafi Bey on professional issues. He wrote to them from prison: 'How much I would that the authorities would expend effort and take interest in the fate of the miserable Arab creatures of this country as much as one tenth the effort and interest taken for organic manure!', and offered his resignation. His brother, a Nazareth notable, complained that the family had not only lost its possessions but that the government had 'condemned to starvation' thirty fellahin families who worked for them. The Agriculture Department queried Rafi Bey's imprisonment, and the local District Commissioner who had ordered the demolitions, Kenneth Blackburne, replied:

> I was unable to believe that Rafi Bey was ignorant of the fact that villagers of Indur were shooting at the military patrols. Rafi Bey had previously received every consideration from local Government officials and has had every opportunity of giving Government confidential information of what was happening in the small village of Indur.

In other words, he had earned punishment for not having turned informer. And Keith-Roach replied to a protest from Rafi Bey's brother in Nazareth: 'If his brother is really responsible for the thirty families, why did he not prevent them from blowing up the pipeline?' None the less, Rafi Bey was released after a couple of months and Keith-Roach recommended that his membership of the council should not be cancelled, 'in view of the return of more normal conditions and of the political nature of Rafi Bey's connection with disturbances'. Indur – a village noted for its pugnacity from Ottoman times – continued to be involved in attacks on local police posts, and was implicated in the murder of a British constable the following year. The only evidence was a revolver found in a nearby cave, but the demolitions continued.[32]

Collective punishment existed in most British colonies, but in most places it needed the approval of the Colonial Secretary; however, the autocratic powers enjoyed by the Palestine High Commissioner made this unnecessary. The Chief Justice during the Arab Revolt, Sir Harry Trusted – Attorney-General in Cyprus before arriving in Palestine in 1932 – was uneasy about the use of collective punishment and though he had approved it to deal with the 'tree cutting menace', he argued that it was 'contrary to the ordinary principles of British administration of justice and should be pursued with extreme care'. The Attorney-General, William FitzGerald, was less ambivalent; he maintained that 'collective punishments and ordinances in most of the

British Colonies have achieved that desideratum of British law and administration, peace and ordered Government, with the least possible amount [sic] of repressive measures'. Fitzgerald said that he did not regard the fines collected as revenue in the proper sense of the term, but rather as 'special contributions' over and above taxes. Admitting that many of those paying were perfectly innocent, he thought the community concerned should subsequently have a special claim on the money. The Arabs recognized these hesitations, and towards the end of the Mandate began challenging the legitimacy of the measure in the courts. So the final amendment to the ordinance, in 1944, followed the Kenya and Uganda ordinances in providing that orders for such fines should be final and not to be contended by suit or otherwise. Wherever possible, the Prevention of Crimes Ordinance – which included similar collective fines – was invoked instead.[33]

The Palestine government had to resort to collective punishment largely because of its failure, through four administrations, to encourage local autonomy at the village level and to recognize the changes taking place in Arab rural society. British officials continued to insist, on the one hand, that tradition dominated the village, and was to be respected; on the other, they refused any real power to the mukhtars and clan leaders, which hastened the decay of the system. Legislation in 1934 increasing the powers of municipal corporations and local councils in the towns was not extended to the villages; in contrast with the towns, neither the village elders nor the mukhtars (appointed till then by the administration in accordance with Ottoman law) had any legal powers. The mukhtar was a convenient local foreman when administrators wanted to assemble a work force, or get a school built; but he had no real authority. During the Revolt he was also expected to be an informer. The job did not attract educated men, and the lack of clear guidelines meant that often a village was dominated by one family which did not represent the community. This also meant that the villagers had no efficient channel of communication to the administration, and that their requests for schools, or improved health facilities, took the form of rather pathetic petitions and appeals, in which they often complained about the mukhtars or the elders who nominally represented them. Only during the Second World War was legal status given to village committees appointed by District Commissioners, and that for one purpose: the distribution of food. It was not until near the end of the Mandate that a report of the first Committee on Village Administration and Responsibility resulted in a very cautious, hesitant allocation of limited powers to the villagers under the Village Administration Ordinance of 1944. 'Enlightened villages' (mostly Christian) were given priority. Even at this late stage, the proposed ordinance was intended – though not designed – to apply to Arab villages and Jewish settlements alike: a general law for a complex situation. Predictably it was attacked by the Jewish organizations running the settlements, which had profited from total independence from government supervision.[34]

Thus, during the Arab Revolt, short of declaring collective responsibility and imposing collective punishment, the government had no real hold on the villages. The decline in the authority of the elders meant that they sided with the rebels as often as with the government, and also led to the uncontrolled clan feuding and revenge killings into which the Revolt degenerated in its later stages.

The government's willingness to act rapidly against a whole community when Jews were killed was initially more hesitant than its response to 'agrarian crime'. Like Judge Frumkin in 1921, Jewish leaders argued that if the government failed to act when crimes could not be pinned on the actual perpetrators, the Arabs would assume that there was official sympathy for violence. After the 1929 riots, the political secretary of the Agency, Brigadier Kisch, told Chancellor that the Agency thought 'future security would in a considerable measure depend on the strict and effective enforcement of collective punishment,' (of the Arabs, that is). He complained that: 'No collective fines had been promulgated in reference to Hebron [i.e. the massacre] or Safed or Motza [a Jerusalem suburb where an entire Jewish family had been killed by its Arab neighbours]; even where sentences had been promulgated there was little attempt to collect the fines. The Arabs thought the Government was not serious.' Chancellor replied that he himself was very serious indeed, but had left it to the District Commissioners to decide when the fines were to be collected – the general idea was to do so 'when the first taxes were due'.[35]

By the 1930s Jewish settlements known to harbour Hagana militants were also appearing on the schedules appended to the Collective

Punishment Ordinance. But the administration hardly ever invoked the ordinance against the Jews, and, when it did, the Jewish Agency was outraged. Jewish retaliation against Arab attacks began in the summer of 1936. In August, two Jewish nurses in a government hospital in Jaffa were murdered, and the Hagana threw a bomb into a market in Jaffa, killing several Arabs. Later that month, four Jews were killed by Arabs in Haifa, and Hagana members shot a group of fellahin from Tireh village (from which the killers had allegedly come), killing a woman and wounding two men. A collective fine was imposed on the Jewish Ahuza district in Haifa, and Moshe Shertok, for the Agency, complained bitterly to Wauchope at this 'humiliation': 'Whatever might have happened in an isolated case, the Jews were the attacked community in Palestine and the Arabs were the attackers. The imposition of a fine upon a Jewish settlement was to stain Jewish reputation and to make it appear as equally guilty with the Arabs.' Wauchope promptly assured Shertok that it would not actually be levied unless the crime was repeated.[36] During the Arab Revolt, the Army was using the Jews both for intelligence purposes and in preventive raids on rebel strongholds, and had no interest in antagonizing them.

Contacts between Jewish and RAF Intelligence began in 1937. Arab documents detailing the identity and plans of the rebels captured during British raids were handed over to the Hagana, while the Jewish Agency, which had its own Arab informers, provided information on the internal discussions of the Arab Executive and Arab Higher Committee. Intelligence reports were passed on by Reuven Zaslani, a member of the Jewish Agency delegated for this specific task, about rebel bands, their composition, location and arms, and their connections with Arab politicians – information which had been gathered by Arab-speaking Jews. Jews were enrolled by British units in the summer of 1938 with the arrival of the maverick Colonel Orde Wingate and his creation of the Special Night Squads, British-led units trained in night fighting and surprise attacks which had a double purpose: to attack Arab irregulars and to defend the pipeline from Iraq. For the first time, Jews acquired the skills – night fighting, and surprise attacks – to carry the conflict into the Arab villages. Wingate, with his sympathy for

Zionism, his literal reading of the Bible and his quasi-chiliastic belief in the Return of the Jews, was in some ways an anachronism, though he had none of the conversionist aims of his Evangelical predecessors. Only James Patterson, who had led the 'Judeans' into battle during the Palestine campaign of the First World War, had matched his sense of mission in training Jews as fighting men.

However, too much can be made of Wingate's eccentricity and the extent to which his pro-Zionism was humoured by the Palestine High Command. The Jewish settlements became the headquarters of Wingate's squads because the Jews provided reliable information on the Arab bands' movements, and could guarantee security in operational planning and execution – all of which would have been difficult for units operating from bases employing Arab clerks and runners. Wingate himself was on intimate terms with the Zionist leaders, many of whom were as puzzled by the man as were his compatriots. But little real intimacy developed between the Jews and Wingate's officers, who spent several months billeted with the Jews and accompanying them on night raids. Young men working off testosterone in the Palestine variation of the North-West Frontier, whose interest in politics was so minimal that they could scarcely have named their own cabinet ministers, were unlikely either to sympathize with the intense ideological motivation of the Jewish settlers or to fail to be put off by their austere life-style. Not surprisingly, one of the young British members of the Night Squads, Robert King-Clark, whose hobby was racing cars and who went off to court an Italian beauty during his leave, had the view that: 'The Arabs' manners, tolerance, good humour and haphazard way of life had a greater appeal to most than the sharper, more intense and dedicated life style of the Jews, whether the Colonist of the kibbutz or orthodox of the town.'[37]

While Jewish confidence in their own defensive capacities was given a boost under Wingate's influence, neither subalterns' wars nor collective punishment had any real impact on the Revolt, which continued unabated through the spring of 1938. The rebels crossed and re-crossed the frontiers and paraded triumphantly in Damascus. British officials had become desperate at their lack of security: they could now be shot at or kidnapped on the roads, or ambushed in their offices.

Hugh Foot, District Commissioner in Nazareth, could not turn his back on a visitor or pick up a map without keeping his revolver in his hand.[38] Senior officials were escorted everywhere by detectives, could observe no fixed schedule and, from the autumn of 1937, preferred to travel by plane rather than risk their lives by road. Battershill recalled that the Civil Service 'went on with their daily work in conditions of personal hazard which had probably never before been equalled in any British dependency'.[39] Military courts took the overflow from the civilian courts, and death penalties were handed down for those carrying arms or ammunition. The rebels commandeered supplies and reinforcements from the villagers; they raided banks in the towns; they set up rival courts, with clerks working on typewriters stolen from British offices, and handed down penalties and sometimes death sentences against those who resisted them, mimicking British procedures. Miss Wilson, the English teacher in the 'national' Bir Zeit school near Ramallah, was conscious of 'being on both sides' – offered a lift down to the main road by armed rebels in the village, 'then on the main road accepting a lift into Jerusalem with British troops who would give a month's pay for the chance of a shot at those same rebels'. She sat in on one rebel court and watched the judge producing news sheets on typewriters and duplicators, aimed at publicizing the alternative rebel regime. In the Galilee, the 16th Infantry Brigade, in the course of several actions, succeeded in capturing 'a rebel headquarters complete with its banner and documents; and a court of justice with wig, warders and witnesses'.[40]

Arab towns were also in the rebels' power. The Assistant District Commissioner in the Southern District, Ivan Lloyd Philips, reported that Jaffa was 'completely and effectively terrorized', the mayor having gone on sick leave and other municipal leaders having been driven away by assassination attempts. The District Commissioner, R. H. E. Crosbie, who had been in Palestine from the beginning of the Mandate, noted that in the Ramle division: 'The wealthy Arab landowners have long ago fled abroad to escape the blackmail of the rebels and groves are being neglected. The rebels themselves have little interest in the citrus industry, and in an attempt to ruin the Jews will have no hesitation in ruining the Arabs also.' Ramle town was unlit at night, since (Jewish-owned) electricity was boycotted and all petrol lamps had long since been broken by hooligans. The rebels executed those who defied them and carried out their own rough justice, in the absence of the police: 'The prompt execution of petty robbers and others and the disposal of their bodies in public places does not fail to excite terror and admiration.'[41] The Bir Zeit villagers were even more unprotected: a rebel leader, Ibrahim, seized the village, forced the villagers to barricade or destroy all approaches, and commandeered their flocks of sheep.

From June 1937 detachments of troops were supported by air attacks on villages. From the beginning of 1938 air power was used in accordance with a War Office anti-rebel technique first tried out in Iraq. There, RAF Intelligence Officers were instructed to familiarize themselves with the area and get to know the tribal leaders. If this failed, suspected hideouts were bombed from air. If this, too, failed, people were told to evacuate villages and reduce them to rubble. Finally they bombed to kill. In Palestine, when Intelligence Officers had located a suspect site, the main body of troops would go to the village, and meet the mukhtar, with the police and the District Commissioner present. The inhabitants were assembled in the village square, and soldiers, with Arabic-speaking police, would search each house. If arms were found, the house was blown up straight away. The arms were usually concealed under the floor, or in grain in the outhouses, under straw. Later, they were hidden under rocks well out of the villages. 'Light bombs' were used against armed bands, but were forbidden within a thousand yards of towns or villages. Even heavier bombs, however, failed to explode arms hidden under rocks, and eventually the RAF was requested to demolish suspect houses from the air, as punitive measures 'after due warning and evacuation'. Villages where rebels sheltered repeatedly were bombed.[42] Colonel Harold Bredin, who served in the Galilee at that time, alleged later than Arab villagers told him that 'we enjoyed it very much, but . . . it was very unfair of you to use aeroplanes, we thought that was rather off-side'.[43]

Off-side or not, the air offensive did not succeed in eradicating the rebels. Lieutenant-General R.H. Haining took over command from Dill from the spring of 1938, with General O'Connor and General Montgomery in support. In May 1938 Haining and MacMichael decided on a change in the methods of dealing with hostile bands. Haining reported that they were no longer offering battle voluntarily and he considered that large military concentrations were producing increasingly smaller results. Short periods of occupation by the Army invited retribution on the villagers by the rebels, who were requisitioning supplies and press-ganging recruits. Accordingly, Haining ordered the prolonged occupation of villages in the Galilee and Samaria, with the object of denying bases to the bands, supporting the loyalists, covering road building and reintroducing civil control. Sir Charles Tegart, a police chief who had fought terror in Bengal and had been brought to Palestine at the end of 1937, now provided liaison between the police command and the Army. Initially Tegart had been asked to take command of the police, but he preferred to offer his recommendations after a tour of the country. He travelled by road (despite an abortive ambush on his car, in which an aide was killed), and took part in missions. When the British archaeologist J. L. Starkey was brutally murdered near Hebron in January 1938, with half his head cut away, Tegart himself, with Keith-Roach, ran behind police dogs following the scent of the murderers for over twenty kilometres. But the trail stopped at a dry wall in an Arab village, where they found only a revolver.[44]

Tegart was immediately struck by the contrast between the widespread powers of the Palestine Police, described in a high-level report as a body 'whose size and composition are not comparable with any other force in the colonial service', and its failings.[45] By May 1938 he had recommended replacing the burnt-out rural stations and posts, which had been abandoned, by seventy massive concrete forts, constructed at every main crossroads and vantage point in Palestine – which still lour over the countryside. Tegart wanted an electrified fence to be put up along the vulnerable northern frontier to check the constant passage of rebels, the use of police dogs (from South Africa) to hunt them down, and, above all, closer contact with the villages. He was scathing about the lack of fluent Arabic among the British police, their indecisiveness (he noted in his diary that 'Intelligence is difficult to collect by an officer who comes one day with a notebook and next with a Lewis gun') and their vulnerability. He insisted that the police wear khaki, not the blue 'bobby' uniforms which were visible miles away, and that the blue police buses in which they travelled be camouflaged. His main proposals were based on his Indian experience: he wanted tough local recruits, even if illiterate, who knew the area, not educated Arab policemen who were easily bullied; mobile patrols like those which functioned on the North-West Frontier province; and

trained 'watchers', like Indian scouts, who would funnel information
for payment. Villages were to be classified 'good' and 'bad' in a register, according to their alliances. Tegart strongly endorsed collective
punishment, but he wanted it balanced with rewards for those villages
which offered co-operation: 'In India [at least in the Punjab] the remis-
sion of the revenue of a whole village has been found to be greatly
appreciated and to have a most stimulating effect.' Schools, he
thought, could also be built as a reward. Most of his recommendations
were approved.[46] 'Tegart's fence' was erected, by a Jewish construction
firm, along the north-eastern frontier from the Sea of Galilee to Rosh
Pinna on the Palestine–Lebanon frontier and patrolled by the Army
after fellahin tried to pull it down; it often cut across their lands.

Haining noted the

> rapid deterioration, amounting almost to disintegration, of the Arab
> section of the Palestine police . . . who were faced with their duty to the
> government on one hand and their personal position in the future, should
> an Arab state materialise, on the other hand. The majority of these men
> were armed, or were in charge of arms, and they became little more than
> an easy source of supply for rifles and ammunition to the rebels. They were
> neither trained nor organised for prolonged resistance to attack, and the
> police stations with their stores of arms became merely a bait to the
> enemy.[47]

In July 1938 – the month during which the Jews began to retaliate
with terror of their own – a bomb exploded on a bus driven by a Jew
through the Arab quarter of Haifa. An angry crowd gathered and
stoned passing Jewish cars. An Anglo-Jewish businessman, Philip
Tobias, on his way home from his Haifa bay factory, was dragged from
his car and stabbed to death. A Jewish policeman grabbed the killer
and handed him over to Hashem Effendi, an Arab inspector who was
the highest-ranking policeman on the scene. But the man never arrived
at the police station and Hashem denied having taken him into
custody. It was one of many indications that the Arab and Jewish
police could no longer work together.[48]

The fate of the Arab police was both a problem of manpower and a
political issue. Their dismissal effectively halved the police force. If the
Arabs were to be dismissed more British personnel had to be recruited,
and the fact that the British police and the Jewish supernumeraries

were now working together was known to be resented by the Arabs.
Tegart and Haining therefore concluded that the Arab police could not
be dismissed *en masse*, but those whose contracts had elapsed were not
re-employed, and as many as possible were transferred to clerical jobs.
By 1939 all Arab police had been disarmed. Their place was taken by
Jews and ex-servicemen, but not all the latter relished the job. At the
end of 1938 the Inspector-General of Police proposed to the Chief
Secretary that the Attorney-General re-enact the Police Ordinance of
1921 to try in camera, in a specially constituted court of discipline,
'men who had committed a serious offence against discipline with the
sole object of incurring dismissal and repatriation which, apart from
a fine up to fourteen days' pay, is the heaviest punishment I can inflict',
as he was anxious to avoid trials in open courts.[49]

It took time for the new, tougher policy to have an effect. In Gaza and
Beersheba, R. E. H. Crosbie, the veteran local District Commissioner,
reported in August that economic life in the south was paralysed and
that, after an attack on Gaza, the British police had withdrawn, after the
wireless station, quarantine station and post office had all been burned
down. No railway stations now remained in this district.[50] In Hebron,
Dr Forster, a Briton who ran the local mission hospital, recorded in his
diary in summer 1938 that there was a new rebel commander in the area,
'Mansur', whose rule 'was just and equitable', and that he had popular
support. Mansur's 'private army' had grown from 3–400 to 2000 men by
local recruiting. No Mandate government department was functioning
in Hebron apart from the Health Department and the police. Post was
brought out to Jerusalem by a military convoy, and all phone communications had been cut. The law courts were closed, Forestry, Public
Works Departments and Land Registry officials had been withdrawn,
and only five British policemen remained. 'To give an Arab policeman a
rifle today is simply to present it to Mansur.' Taxes went uncollected,
and the only courts martial were those staged by the rebels. According
to Forster, only one quarter of Hebron, where the troops and British
police were billeted, remained under Mandate rule.[51] Later, the capture
of rebel documents revealed that 'Mansur' was the *nom de guerre* of
Abd'el Khader el Husseini (a cousin of the Mufti), who, after having
served as a senior officer in the Land Settlement division of the Mandate
administration, joined the rebels and was recognized as the leader of the
Jerusalem–Hebron district. El Husseini was to become one of the most

effective military leaders of the Palestinians in their later struggle against the Jews, and his leadership was so important that his death in battle in 1948, after the British withdrawal, led to the Arab loss of control of the Jerusalem road.[52]

The methods the rebels used against the British were also becoming more sophisticated: E. T. Cosgrove of the CID reported that, while 'people had previously thought that the bang alone caused damage and used sugar and potassium chloride or blasting powder in cans, bottles or bags, now skill was employed in constructing bombs using high explosives'.[53] Communications were in rebel hands. Taxis with false floors were used to carry rifles and ammunition. The trains – which ran through or close to rebel-controlled villages – were regularly derailed or sabotaged, despite their armour plating. Police or soldiers rode on trolleys on the railway line, 'looking for a spread in the rails, or a pin with a blue bead placed on it for luck, marking the striker of a buried shell'. This 'made their eyes go queer', and they had to keep just the right distance ahead of the train, in case it should run into them or rebels should spread or lift the rail between trolley and train. 'Once, hidden beside a damaged piece of line, were found, neatly laid out, all complete to nuts and screws, the things required to mend it. The platelayers were Arabs, and there were many retired platelayers living near the railway. Jewish labour cost too much for the Palestine railways, which do not pay.' In 1938, thirteen railwaymen were killed on duty and 123 injured.[54]

In Jerusalem itself, the centre of Mandate government, no European was safe inside the walls of the Old City. Even Arab shopkeepers were at risk: looting and arson went unimpeded. Inside the Noble Sanctuary, the mosque area of the Temple Mount, where the Mufti and subsequently others had taken shelter, the police had been driven out. Captured rebel documents scanned by the CID showed that the Sanctuary was the scene of killings, bomb-throwing, and rebel courts martial: what a British official called 'the violation by the Moslems of their own sanctuary'. No police were stationed there. Although British officials dared not enter the precincts, the rebels could come and go; most of the gates were open, and searches were ineffective.

At the beginning of September 1938, MacMichael wrote to the Secretary of State for the Colonies: 'The position is deteriorating rapidly and has reached a stage at which rebel leaders are more feared and respected than we are. The movement is definitely a national one, though financed partly by blackmail levied on a large scale in the country.' The High Commissioner recognized the Revolt as 'an attempt to achieve the complete reversal of government policy regarding partition and Jewish immigration'. The officials in Palestine were pessimistic because of the strain imposed on them, the knowledge that Arab officials and police all had a foot in both camps, the fact that the Commission set up to discuss partition was unlikely to produce results, and the fear that the British government continued to accept Haj Amin (the Mufti), in exile in Damascus, as representative of the Palestinians. As to the rural population, MacMichael realized that they were caught between the armed rebels and the Mandate authorities. He wrote that it was a tragedy that 'however much the villagers may groan under the bandits, they will not turn to us for two reasons: (a) because they fear being swamped by the Jews and (b) because we are not in a position to protect them.'[55]

Finally, in October 1938, Sir Edmund Ironside, the head of the British General Staff, arrived in Palestine to review the military situation and approved the dispatch of another whole division, which turned the scales against the rebels. With British military power so overwhelming, the Revolt began to crumble. The death penalty was now applied not only to those convicted of murder but also to rebels carrying arms, and sometimes for arson alone. Haining reported that many Arabs were willing to give information for payment, though he realized 'the ease with which personal or family feuds could be paid off this way'. Passes were now needed for any Palestinian Arab to travel outside his own town or village. Sir Alec Kirkbride, then a District Commissioner in the north, felt that

> having battles didn't do any good, even when you won them. They're regarded as being rather sporting events and stimulated recruitments among the Arabs. . . . My own practice in Galilee was not to encourage frightfulness on the part of the troops but to make everything awkward for people who were not co-operating with the government, if they wanted a pass to go anywhere it was very difficult to get the pass. I found that no taxes had been collected for years, and so when there was a case of sabotage instead of imposing a fine, I sent for the villagers concerned and said you've got to pay so much in arrears of tax, they'd . . . [argue] they didn't do it, and

I said what are you talking about, I didn't say you did. You do owe this money to the government don't you? and they had to admit that they did and eventually it stopped it.[56]

Once the danger to the pipeline was averted, the Night Squads were disbanded and Wingate transferred. But the Jews he had trained became the heads of the newly established intelligence service of the Hagana, Shai. The Hagana, using German immigrants, also infiltrated the Nazi-controlled German Intelligence networks in Palestine, and passed the information on to British Intelligence. For this reason, despite misgivings, the Army and the police rarely seized the caches of arms they knew the Hagana was amassing.

On the railway, twenty-five of the armoured railcars travelling the railway track were equipped with a pony truck on a long extension, which preceded the train for the detection and harmless explosion of mines. They had a flat sheet built over a single axle on which hostages taken from the villages near the railway line were made to sit.[57] The night curfew became permanent. A police post was established on the Sanctuary in Jerusalem and all but two gates were closed, with the others carefully guarded. Any public event which might lead to a demonstration was supervised. Only ceremonies within the area of the Noble Sanctuary and at Nebi Musa itself (a deserted spot, off the road to the Dead Sea) were permitted, and there were no processions and banners to be seen in the streets of Jerusalem. Such banners had to be taken to or from the traditional sites of celebration, 'privately wrapped in a packet'.[58] Death sentences rose between August and October 1938, the critical period of the Revolt, to a record thirty, of which only six were commuted. Within a mere three months, by the end of 1938, Haining was able to report that the whole country was in the hands of the Army and 'co-operation' of many of the rebel leaders had been obtained, while the others had fled the country. Haining expressed the hope that police and medical, educational and agricultural officers would now return, with military patrols, in their tours of various areas, and 'regain contact with the fellah that had been almost completely lost'.[59]

It was during the last, bitterest, period of the Revolt that some of the old Palestine hands, both within the administration and outside it, began to protest against the brutality which accompanied the suppression of the Revolt – Kirkbride's 'frightfulness on the part of the troops'. As early as 1936, the government Welfare Officer, Miss Nixon, had complained to the Chief Secretary about soldiers who had beaten villagers, destroyed food and clothing and taken money and jewellery from villages in Acre and the central plain. She herself alleged she had seen Bedouin tents 'ground up' under British 'tanks' (probably armoured cars). She was reprimanded and told that it was 'not her business to make these investigations', though she was also discouraged from resigning.[60]

Most of the protests came from the Anglican clergy, which acted throughout the Revolt as a self-appointed civil rights organization, and particularly the Bishop, Graham-Brown. The Archdeacon of St George's wrote to the Chief Secretary, saying that: 'From every side complaints are reaching me daily of the unnecessary and quite indiscriminate roughness displayed by the British police in their handling of the native, and particularly the Arab, population.'[61] He detailed 'wanton and unnecessary violence when searching houses' and the 'duffing up' of suspects (Douglas Duff was a police officer known for his toughness). After a Jewish bomb throwing in Haifa the chaplain of St Luke's church sent the Bishop an eye-witness account of the savage beating of a Jewish suspect at the central police station. The Army investigated charges of theft and looting where it could, but the Deputy Superintendent of Police, Wainwright, admitted that allowing soldiers to help in searches for arms could cause trouble, and that he would stop this, as 'there is very little hope of tracing culprits later'.[62]

'Indiscriminate roughness' paled beside its sequel, as the murder of police and army officers during 1938 was avenged promptly by razing the village responsible to the ground. Bishop Graham-Brown, writing to the Chief Secretary in April 1938, now described military and police action as 'terrorism for which the Government is morally responsible'. Christian Arab families had complained that their houses and stores of food were destroyed simply because they lived near a house where supernumerary police had been murdered by rebels, or where bomb outrages had taken place. After the murder of a British RAF Squadron Leader near the village of Ijzim, fifty houses were looted and destroyed by the Army, and an Arab was shot in the back and killed while 'attempting to escape' a search.[63]

The worst incidents took place in the Hebron district in May 1938, and were reported by Dr Forster, of St Luke's Hospital. In Halhul village, between Jerusalem and Hebron, on a scorching day, soldiers rounded up a group of men during a search for arms and kept them standing without water for hours. Eight men died of exposure; one was let down into a well when, in order to get a drink, he said there was a rifle there. When pulled up he was beaten with rifle butts, and, to save himself, cut the cord and drowned. Archdeacon Stewart, who was to succeed Graham-Brown as Bishop, was told that there had been 'regrettable errors of judgment deeply deplored' by the Army.[64] Other complaints by Dr Forster about army looting were investigated by the Army. Forster himself was ambushed and held for an hour until he was recognized as the doctor who often treated rebel wounded, though he noted that he did not like 'saving men for the rope'. Forster recorded his view that 'the rebels fight fairly and chivalrously and rule with kindness. The British kill the innocent, when no other enemy is near, and loot and rob the poor and destitute.'[65]

A. T. O. Lees, the Assistant District Commissioner in Hebron who, unlike most government officials, had remained in the town, submitted a report to the government in August 1938 detailing acts of vandalism, arson, looting and murder by the police forces sent in to reimpose order. In one incident four Arabs were killed and four wounded, including several old men. Lees, who was also the town coroner and so had the opportunity of investigating every killing in the area, wrote of 'acts of wanton and reckless barbarity perpetrated by English members of the military and/or police force against the local people, including a boy of 15 who was first beaten and then shot'. Lees alleged that one reason was that the victims had ignored the curfew, which many had not heard of. When the government school was attacked by rebels, Lees arranged for the damage to be repaired by Hebron townspeople in compensation, to prevent a collective fine being levied. It was Lees, too, later that year, who reported that a prisoner was shot and killed while handcuffed, by a British plainclothes policeman in Jaffa, though the accused argued in court that he was firing at an escaping prisoner. The policeman eventually served only an eighteen-month sentence, the defence counsel having argued that it was a tribute to British justice that policemen were put on trial at all in the atmosphere of the Revolt. Lees, in a confidential report to the local District

Commissioner, which also noted the beating of old men, wrote: 'I feel it is my duty as an Englishman and servant of the Crown of twenty years' standing to place before a higher authority information in my possession regarding acts which can only impair and tarnish the prestige of this government in particular and Englishmen in general.'[66]

During that summer the Essex Regiment took revenge for an attack on a patrol on a village between Acre and Nazareth, Kawkab Abu Haija. They burned half the threshing floors and destroyed the entire village, reported Dr Bathgate of the Edinburgh Medical Mission in Nazareth. When Bishop Graham-Brown once more protested to the High Commissioner, MacMichael responded that 'the village had a consistently bad record'. The drastic action 'merited and indeed necessitated by the circumstances' had had 'an extremely salutary effect. . . . Though no doubt hardship was suffered by individuals, the corporate guilt of the village rendered it, I fear, inevitable.'[67] In the village of Kfar Yasif, in early 1939, a British army truck on a new road ran over a land mine, which exploded, killing one soldier and wounding others. According to Eric F. Bishop, an Anglican minister, the surviving soldiers went on the rampage, torching seventy houses. Nine Arabs were killed as the soldiers sprayed the road with machine-gun fire.[68] Keith-Roach wrote that General Montgomery's troops 'ran amok' in the village of Bassa.

Some accounts of the brutality filtered through to the National Council for Civil Liberties in London, and the Howard League for Penal Reform. The occasional question was asked in Parliament, but the incidents were generally dismissed as unfounded allegations, fabricated by Nazi agents in Palestine. There was, however, sufficient disquiet to bring a group of young people, who called themselves the Peace Army, out to Palestine to investigate. Hugh Bingham and Margaret Pope were questioning Arabs when Bingham was shot dead by an Arab terrorist in Jerusalem in January 1939.[69] Each of the three rival British generals provided selected reporters with his version, though as Major-General Bredin, of Wingate's subordinates, recalled: 'At that time you didn't have to bother much about foreign opinion . . . In 1938 Montgomery sent for the press in Haifa, and told them he didn't want them any more. The reporters from Jerusalem thus had no stories about Northern Palestine.'[70]

Probably more numerous than the victims of these actions were those innocent people who were not directly involved with the rebels but who none the less suffered from the suppression of the Revolt. Dr Bigger, who had always sympathized with the Arab predicament, complained in a letter to Heron that although government roads had provided some work for the fellahin, conditions in the towns were worse:

> In Jenin, for instance, where the spectacular character of the demolitions has attracted a disproportionate amount of charity, only about six mothers are considered to require assistance. . . . It should, I think, be very strongly represented to the government that a great deal of the present distress is easily preventable. I have, for instance, this morning received a complaint from a Nablus woman whose husband was taken by the military over a fortnight ago for road work and has been kept imprisoned ever since. It is alleged that he is paid for his work, but meanwhile his family of ten persons is starving and he is only one of many. If it is essential that press gang methods should be employed by the army I suggest that enquiries as to the welfare of dependents should always be made. There is a considerable number of poor artisans whose work normally lies in the village. These are almost all out of work, not because there is no work but because they dare not leave the town for fear of arrest and imprisonment by the military.[71]

By the spring of 1939, the Arab Revolt was over. The British government, concluding that Arab grievances should now be addressed, issued a document which was to turn the Jewish population of Palestine, in its turn, against British rule: the White Paper of May 1939, which set unprecedented limits on immigration and on land sales to the Jews. But with the outbreak of war in September of that year, the Jewish leadership decided that, despite its opposition to the White Paper, it would provide what assistance it could to the British war effort. The British Cabinet decided in February 1940 not to impound Hagana arms. Both Britain and the Jews of Palestine feared a possible German offensive in the Middle East. For Britain, this threatened the Mandate in Palestine. For the Jews, it threatened annihilation.

There followed an extraordinary episode during which, for a short but important period, the British Army provided money, arms and training for a group of Jewish volunteers who were to become the nucleus of the future Israeli Army – the Palmach, or commando section of the Hagana. This was an undercover operation, handled by the Special Operations Executive (SOE) the dare-devil commando unit invented by Winston Churchill, which enjoyed almost total independence of the military bureaucracy.

Following the fall of France, with Syria under Vichy French rule from June 1940, the Chief of the SOE in Cairo, Lieutenant-Colonel Sir John Pollock, laid plans for sabotage operations on roads and railways, and for Intelligence forays into Syria. The SOE representative in Jerusalem, Greatrex, planned to set up a network of agents, targets and arms dumps in Palestine, independently of the Army. The Jewish Agency had suggested that Jews take part in sabotage activities in the area and collect trading information for the Ministry of Economic Warfare (the government department to which the SOE was answerable) and offered to place Hagana agents at the disposal of the British secret services in both German-occupied and neutral territory. The SOE was convinced that 'they could be extraordinarily useful from this point of view as their connections are widespread and their organisation and intelligence service very efficient'. For sabotage in the region surrounding Palestine, wrote the head of the newly established SOE branch in Jerusalem, there was no organized minority available other than the Jews, who had offered forty men for training who spoke many languages and had great technical ability: 'No better human material could exist for our purpose; these are honourable fanatics who will stick at nothing, physically and mentally tough, highly disciplined and used to guerrilla warfare.' Wherever possible the Jews were expected to 'make their own arrangements,' 'and even manufacture some of their own ammunition'.[72]

In September 1940, SOE chiefs in London met Moshe Shertok and other Jewish Agency leaders who proposed undertaking espionage work in Syria via Jewish contacts, and suggested that British officers train Jewish saboteurs and establish arms dumps for their use. The SOE rejected the first suggestion, as British policy was to win over the Arabs to support the Free French by promising post-war independence – and involving the Jews was not going to make this easier. The second and third proposals were approved in principle.[73]

But even at this early stage, there were problems with the civil and military authorities. The SOE knew that they were negotiating with the very men who had previously planned illegal Jewish immigration, and that dealing with them meant 'bypassing normal official channels'. Pollock wrote from Cairo in November that he wanted to train about a hundred men, heavily armed, as an attacking force: 'a small irregular band of toughs based in Palestine'.[74] For over a year Hagana members trained in a secret camp on Mount Carmel were sent into action only outside Palestine. A course in amphibious landings and sabotage was provided over the following winter in Tel Aviv, and thirty Hagana men were involved in a plan to sabotage the Vichy oil refineries in Tripoli. Twenty-three of them set sail under a British officer, Major Anthony Palmer, but were lost at sea. A company of Hagana men, under Moshe Dayan, was enrolled before the British invasion of Syria in June 1941, charged with reconnaissance, and Dayan himself lost an eye in a firefight with the Vichy forces. A number of Hagana recruits, among them women, were parachuted into the Balkans in an effort to link up with Jewish resistance groups in Nazi-occupied territory. Many of them were captured and put to death.[75] Despite this display of bravery, the Palmach – the crack Hagana unit created in May 1941 – was desperately short of arms and funds. The offer of help by the Jewish Agency had been primarily a morale-raising exercise for the Jews, as the Palmach did not even have personal weapons for its own men. So what happened next was an unexpected boost for Jewish fighting capacities.

Up to the end of 1941, despite the SOE's ideas, the British Army hesitated to extend British training in sabotage techniques to more than a handful of Jews, or to allow them to operate in Palestine. But in early 1942 the Japanese overran the Malay Peninsula, and the Colonial Office sent all colonial governors and the SOE requests to prepare plans for the defence of British territories. German armies were advancing in North Africa and threatened British control of Egypt and Palestine. In February 1942, therefore, an SOE plan, known as the Palestine Scheme, was put to MacMichael and to the military (the 9th Army and Palestine military headquarters) and approved. The Scheme involved training a picked force of Jewish volunteers for sabotage work behind the German lines in the event of an enemy invasion of the country. They were to blow up bridges, lay mines and attack German transport routes, and also report, via clandestine wireless stations, on enemy movements. Initially, MacMichael approved only the training of 180 men, but the scheme snowballed and, by June, 153 instructors and leaders and 250 volunteers were scheduled to be trained in the use of explosives and other sabotage equipment ('toys' in SOE jargon).[76] Yet even within the SOE there were misgivings. One SOE officer wrote: 'The Friends [Jews] scheme is developing to enormous proportions and we are evidently committing ourselves very deeply.'[77] He was also sceptical about the usefulness of Jews in 'post-occupational' (i.e. German-held) Palestine, as they would be marked men in what was basically planned as a suicide mission. That summer, however, the situation looked desperate, with Palestine almost totally unprepared for a German invasion judged to be only three weeks distant. There were only four British wireless telegraph sets in the country, working off the main electricity supply. The SOE waited for financial sanction to train more men and for permission to operate an experimental battery set, made locally by a Tel Aviv Jew. Between June and October 1942 officers of the Royal Engineers trained 160 Hagana men in sabotage and wireless operations in a special camp set up in Mishmar HaEmek kibbutz in the northern Esdraelon valley, and several tons of explosives were hidden in caches under army supervision.

The Palestine Scheme was terminated abruptly, however, as soon as these recruits had been trained. The Jewish Agency was informed that no further training should take place, the CID was brought into the picture, and orders were issued for all the equipment and explosives issued to the Hagana to be collected. 'The experience of the Palestine Scheme', wrote the London Controller of the SOE in a memorandum, 'showed that the Palestine Jews, if used in anything approaching large numbers, were unable to identify solely with the war effort but continued to try to promote their own parochial nationalist aspirations at the expense of services required of them.'[78] And another memorandum regarding those already trained said: 'We count on the Jewish Agency to assist us in ensuring that these men [the trainees] will not engage in any unauthorised activities, which particularly includes the training of any other Jews.'[79]

But the Scheme had been cut short not by a breach of understanding by the Jews but because of the indiscretion of an SOE Commanding Officer, Major General B. T. Wilson. Initially it was charged that Wilson had 'failed to instruct his deputy in Jerusalem in the method of financial control . . .' and had expended money 'deposited for post-occupational purposes, against instructions', though the

Jewish Agency and the Army were supposed to have paid jointly for the training. Later, and by chance, it was revealed that, unknown to his superiors or to army security, Wilson had issued quantities of explosives to the Hagana and 'allowed bodies of Jews to form individual camps for training in weapons and explosives at various points in Palestine'. Wilson was dismissed. The SOE post-mortem on the affair described him regretfully as: 'a most lovable person with the heart of a lion, the vigorous energy of a flea, but [whose] sense of security was no more than that of an ostrich'.[80]

With Montgomery's victory at El Alamein, the threat of German invasion receded. Thereafter, though the Palestine Scheme had been ended, it was obviously impossible to collect all the arms which Wilson had distributed. MacMichael and General McConnell, now in charge of the Palestine garrison, were uneasily aware that those Hagana men already trained would train others in the use of explosives, and that illegitimate Hagana activity would expand. At the end of 1942, five men and a woman were caught by the police in Tel Aviv undergoing training as wireless operators, and though Jewish Agency leaders claimed that they had been training for undercover work in Syria, the SOE argued that they had no knowledge of their activities. The British had become 'the junior partner' in the Palestine Scheme, was the rueful conclusion to the internal SOE report: 'we have been suckers'.[81] The camp at Mishmar HaEmek was dismantled, but in March 1943, after fruitless protests by Jewish leaders against the recall of some of their weapons, a Hagana platoon from Kibbutz Yagur succeeded in getting into the SOE training school on Mount Carmel and stealing some three hundred rifles and machine guns – a demonstration of independence which put paid to relations between the Jewish Agency and the SOE.[82]

However, more than twenty-seven thousand Palestine Jews volunteered for service in the British Army in 1942 and in 1944, as the result of a decision taken by the British Cabinet, were allowed to function as a separate unit – the Jewish Brigade – which took part in the final stages of the war in Europe. Seven thousand Palestine Arabs also joined up.[83] The importance of British army service for the Jews who fought the Arabs for control of Palestine in 1948 was immeasurable. The Hagana was originally a militia, composed of pioneering settlers with (left wing) political affiliations, and not organized like a regular army or paramilitary force, though by the beginning of the Second World War it had paid officers and a Chief of Staff. It operated out of fixed localities, either for the defence of settlements or in sporadic attacks on suspected marauders – as in the Special Night Squads. Communications relied mainly on runners and carrier pigeons, and the Verrey lights which enabled one settlement to signal to another. The Hagana turned for support and services to the civilian population, and had no field kitchens or mobile sanitary equipment. Despite the stockpiling of arms, it had no real experience in regular warfare, and no real hierarchy or formal discipline. There was no clearly defined boundary between political and military leaders and their respective responsibilities. Therefore the experience of belonging to a highly organized, modern army, fighting in an all-out war, was an education.

From the British viewpoint, the risks of training core members of the increasingly dissident Jewish population had been obvious, but were thought to have been countered by two measures. The Brigade was to be used in Europe against the Germans and not sent to the Far East (the Jewish Agency was informed of this, clearly a reassurance to the Jews that they would be fighting their real enemy). The Jewish Agency was, however, not informed of the second step – that the Brigade group was not to serve in Palestine or to be sent there for disbandment or demobilization.[84] By April 1946, when it was decided to accelerate the release of Palestinian Jews, the Palestine government accepted responsibility for those recruits known to be illegal immigrants. However, disbanding the Brigade in Europe was still a risk, as its members were known to be involved in the illegal immigration campaign. Jewish soldiers had made contact in the Displaced Persons Camps with Holocaust survivors, whose fate was their prime concern.

It was apparent to the British soldiers searching for arms in Jewish settlements immediately after the war that the expertise acquired by Jewish soldiers in the British Army had improved their ability to fight in Palestine. Major-General John Cowtan of the Royal Engineers parachute unit, an ex-prisoner-of-war and saboteur in Italy, noted that Jewish Brigade veterans now knew how to mine railway lines and plant bombs. In August 1945, during searches in the Jewish settlements Ruhama and Dorot in the Negev, known to be Hagana bases, the two parachute battalions and Cowtan's squadron arrived before dawn, cordoned off the settlements, and caught a man in a vineyard with a

British radio set – an indication that, despite precautions, the settlements had been forewarned. When mine detectors failed to uncover
caches, dogs were brought in, on one occasion detecting a water tank
over four foot deep, loaded with arms and explosives. While Cowtan
understood why the Jews were hoarding arms – 'we'd have done the
same' – most soldiers felt that the Jews were 'ungrateful' for British
protection, and had no sympathy for their national aims.[85] The 6th
Airborne Division parachutists, with their red berets, were offended by
the song all the Jewish children sang mockingly as they passed by,
deriding the 'red poppies with the black hearts'. Sir Richard Gale, the
head of Intelligence operations, summed up the feelings of the Army
towards the settlers: 'There was a hardiness about the men and women
that was almost repellent . . . they resented the Mandate, forgetting
that it was Mandate which had made their existence in Palestine
possible – grim determined people working in the soil, training in
secret with their arms, sullen and resentful – they lacked kindliness of
heart.'[86] The wartime truce between Britain and the Jews of Palestine
was over.

From the early years of the war, illegal immigrants from Nazi Europe
had been interned or sent to other British possessions in neutral zones.
After the war, those who were captured while landing or – a far smaller
number – when they were found living in Palestine, were bundled or
dragged back on to British battleships and taken to Mauritius, Cyprus
and elsewhere. An effort was even made (as in the notorious case of the
'Exodus') to send them back to Germany. Those who carried out this
policy – naval and army officers – later defended their actions in several
ways; Rear-Admiral James Munn argued that in blockading and
boarding the ships – floating slums with no sanitary facilities which
could be 'smelled downwind' – no personal feelings were involved: he
was simply doing his job. Major Malcolm Gray, in charge of the
'Exodus' operation, saw the Hagana organizers (as the SOE had seen
the soldiers) as 'dedicated fanatics' who were using the suffering of the
people crammed into the ships to further their own political ends. But
ordinary sailors such as John Moore found the task distasteful and
remembered later that there were no volunteers for the boarding
parties, which were made up of an officer, a signalman, and twelve

ratings. The immigrant ships were overloaded, with superstructures built on the upper-decks, and could steam no faster more than 2–3 knots, making them easy prey for British battleships. The sailors went swimming while waiting for the ships to enter the three-mile territorial limit off the Palestine shore. Boarding them risked capsizing them. All the British eye-witness descriptions refer to the pathetic resistance put up by the refugees, who hurled bricks and bottles of urine at the sailors, while so many women tried to stab at the sailors with hat pins and knives that the men took to wearing football pads over their genitals. Some of the smaller boats avoided detection. The Hagana sent armed parties down to the beaches to guide them into shallow harbours at night, and often by the time the Army and the police appeared, the immigrants had disappeared into neighbouring settlements. Colonel Waddy, a British Colonel responsible for tracking down 'illegals', maintained that he could identify immigrants by their filthy clothes and the pallor from having spent weeks squeezed into the hold of a boat; but many were successfully hidden.[87] Forty thousand illegal immigrants succeeded in entering Palestine during the last three years of British rule; but between August 1946 and December 1947 over fifty-one thousand passengers on thirty-five ships were intercepted and interned in Cyprus.

The prevalent view in government circles in post-war London and Jerusalem was that the Zionist movement was knowingly sacrificing to their political ambitions the refugees in the camps in Europe, who by themselves would not have made for Palestine. The Army in Palestine also saw the immigrants as pawns in a propaganda game. The head of the garrison, Major General D'Arcy, gave the following instructions to the troops after an incident in the Jewish settlement of Bet Oren in October 1945, when women settlers with sticks, covered by men carrying machine-guns, attacked the police – who retreated:

In rounding up illegal immigrants it should be remembered that the immigrants themselves are for the most part innocent and unarmed people. Their entry into this country, whether by sea or overland, will however be covered by armed Hagana or Palmach formations. The Jewish Agency's object will be to arrange matters so that the immigrants are involved with a clash with the police or troops from whom the immigrants will be 'rescued' by the Hagana or the Palmach. In dealing with parties of immigrants the police should, therefore, be used to the maximum extent and a strong reserve of troops employed to deal with the Hagana . . . force.[88]

Meanwhile, the deportation of the refugees lost Britain international support, particularly in America. An Anglo-American Committee of Enquiry set up to examine the problem of the Jews in the Displaced Persons Camps in Europe recommended in April 1946 that 100,000 refugees be admitted immediately to Palestine – a proposal taken up by the Jewish Agency but rejected by the British government. Zionist political lobbying was now increasingly aimed not at the British Parliament, but at the United States. This new orientation meant the eclipse of the ageing Anglophile Chaim Weizmann and the rise of the dynamic and militant Labour leader, David Ben Gurion. It was in a New York hotel, the Biltmore, in 1942, that Ben Gurion had for the first time announced the explicit intention of the Jews in Palestine to set up a state – a challenge hurled at the British government.

Colonial precedent, so often invoked in administering Palestine, proved irrelevant once violence became widespread. The Arab countries surrounding Palestine supported the Arab uprising; later, the Jewish militias (some trained by the British) turned against the government. In the United States, after the war, Zionists and their sympathizers mounted a highly effective propaganda campaign, accusing Britain of reneging on its promises to the Jews and hounding the survivors of the Holocaust. Mandate officials found themselves without guidelines. Sir Henry Gurney, the last Chief Secretary, reflected that 'no colonial administration had ever been confronted with a situation in which the people in its charge . . . had all looked to sources outside the country for money, arms, and political support and direction'.[89] D'Arcy tried to cope with the challenge of the Jewish militias. He complained: 'An opposition government in almost open defiance of British rule controls an illegal army of 80,000 to 100,000 equipped with modern arms and trained on modern lines; I can find no precedent and little help in our long history of imperial policing.'[90]

During the last year of the war, a new threat to the Mandate appeared: Jewish terror. Until 1944, although there were Jewish extremists who challenged the authority of the Jewish Agency, the administration had been able to live with – and make use of – the Hagana. But rival militias had been set up by right-wing Jewish political groups, who now called for open rebellion against their British rulers and targeted the Arabs and the British alike. The Jewish Agency had no control of these militias, chief among them the Irgun (an abbreviated version of the Hebrew for the National Military Organization) and the breakaway Stern Gang (headed by Abraham Stern but in Hebrew called the Israel Freedom Fighters). From the time of the Arab Revolt, the Irgun had rejected the Jewish Agency's policy of restraint, carried out indiscriminate revenge bombings and killed Arabs. Now they raided RAF airfields, stole arms from military bases, killed British soldiers, and kidnapped British officers whom they held as hostages, hoping that death sentences on their own men would be commuted. The violence escalated steadily. In November 1944 the Stern Gang turned to political assassination; the murder of Lord Moyne, the new British Minister-Resident in Cairo, was an act which endangered even Churchill's support of the Zionists. The Jewish Agency denounced the murder and subsequently provided the CID with information which led to the arrest of several hundred Irgun leaders. But relations between the Mandate government and the Jews had soured. In April 1946 the Irgun killed seven guards in an army car-park in Tel Aviv and stole their guns. In June the first kidnapping took place. Irgun men hustled five British soldiers out of a Tel Aviv officers' club at gunpoint, and later, when death sentences on Irgun men were commuted, left them chloroformed in wooden boxes in the street. The officers came to and broke out, while passers by ignored them completely.[91]

During the summer of 1946, Agency and Irgun leaders co-ordinated their strategy for several weeks, and the Palmach – which had earlier launched raids on coastguard stations in an attempt to damage the blockade – briefly cut Palestine off from the surrounding states by destroying road and rail bridges around the country. In retaliation, the Mandate government sealed off the Jewish Agency buildings and arrested 3,000 Jews, among them most of the Zionist Executive. Many were arrested when troops entered those labour settlements known to be Palmach strongholds, where they encountered no armed opposition but some 'passive resistance'.[92] Significantly, the only settlement where an arms search took place was in Yagur – where that last raid on the

SOE base had been staged. Lieutenant-General Sir Evelyn Barker, who led the search, reported: 'Great ingenuity has been used in siting and constructing the caches, such as false backs to cupboards, window sills which pull out leaving a recess below, "coffins" let into the floor of the nursery over a veranda, circular concrete or metal containers let into the ground underneath footbridges.' The soldiers who carried out the search used mine detectors to locate a manhole in a tiled floor beneath which the main cache was sited:

> The Cheshires who carried out the roundup of the people at this settlement had the devil of a time with women trying to hold on to the men to prevent them being taken away, and refusing to obey any orders. After collecting them all into the main dining hall they had to use tear gas in order to get them out again on to the vehicles. The heavy oil projectors were very useful also in this.

Barker expected hostile reactions, 'and of course reports of looting and maltreatment of detainees'.[93] From this period onwards, all soldiers leaving the settlements were frisked to make sure that there was no basis for subsequent accusations of looting – frequently levelled in the propaganda war.

The alliance between the Hagana and the Irgun lasted only a month. In July 1946 the Irgun, on its own initiative, dynamited the British administrative offices in a wing of the King David Hotel in Jerusalem, killing ninety-one people, Arabs, Jews, and many British officials. The Jewish Agency condemned the action outright and broke off relations with the terrorists. Searching for the Irgun men responsible, the Army imposed a curfew on Tel Aviv for thirty-six hours. Five arms dumps were found, one in the basement of a central synagogue. The King David atrocity, in which many Mandate officials lost friends and colleagues, deepened the now-open hostility between the British and the Jews. Though the Jewish Agency condemned the Irgun's worst acts of terror, and still on occasion shopped its members to the CID, its desire and ability to curb them by now depended on its sense of the political risks involved in doing so.[94]

While the Jewish community in Palestine was already preparing for the inevitable battle with the Arabs, training a citizens' army and acquiring what arms it could, a United Nations team (UNSCOP) was sent to make enquiries and recommendations on the eventual partition of the country. The British post-war Labour government, despite its earlier declared sympathies for Zionism, was now far more concerned with relations with the Arab states in the Middle East and their oil resources. With the future of Palestine now an international issue, the Mandate government was reduced to impotence.

After the departure of MacMichael in 1944, the Mandate was briefly in the hands of Lord Gort – a stopgap appointment – and finally, of Sir Alan Cunningham, the last High Commissioner of Palestine. During this period, the post-war Labour government in Britain cast about for a device which would enable Britain to bypass the partition idea and remain on in Palestine. Because there were so few non-Jewish experts the government could consult, they recalled a key figure (yet one publicly little known) from Cyprus to advise on policy. This was Sir Douglas Harris, from 1936 Special Commissioner in Palestine and involved for years as adviser on a wide variety of policy issues. Harris, soon due to retire to East Africa, was brought to London at some expense (because of his wife's illness he insisted on staying at the Savoy) and only against his better judgement. He preferred Cyprus, he wrote, where 'one does not feel that one is ploughing sand' as he did 'when embarking on any constructive effort in Palestine'. Harris proposed the negotiation of a new Mandate, 'to get rid of some of the present difficulties and ambiguities', as he termed it, and clearly aimed at winning Arab support for Britain in the Middle East.[95] Cunningham was annoyed at being thus bypassed, but was equally critical of the terms of the Mandate. One of his first dispatches to the Colonial Secretary, Sir Oliver Stanley, was yet another protest, by the man on the spot, against the impossible brief he had been given; he thought the letter important enough to have it duplicated and sent to ministers at British embassies and legations throughout the Middle East. Britain, he thought, should have been franker about its own main interests ('an attitude of altruism is unconvincing to the Semitic races'); the present situation was 'the logical outcome of the dubiety with which the ulterior intentions of the Balfour Declaration were already shrouded and of the permutations and uncertainties of policy which have followed'. Cunningham thought that unlimited Jewish immigration would not only be disastrous to imperial interests, but to the Jews themselves, as it would provoke ever-growing Arab enmity. While in favour of the partition of Palestine, he saw it as the 'deferred penalty of vacillation'. Partition, Cunningham thought, with the optimism of the newcomer, would prove an opportunity for well-planned reconstruction of the country, in which Britain could play a benevolent part. Palestine should remain within the Empire. It was not surprising, given these views, that he and Weizmann became friends during the last two years of the Mandate, though it was a friendship which, on Cunningham's advice, was kept private, lest it damage Weizmann's standing among the Jews.[96]

The last High Commissioner was well aware of the tragedy of the Holocaust and its traumatic effect on the Jewish community in Palestine. He tried to separate the humanitarian from the political issues in Palestine, believing that the Jews would be satisfied if survivors and their families in the country were reunited. To that end, in December 1945, he asked whether there were statistics as to how many Jews remaining in Europe had relations in Palestine, something even the Jews could not have answered at that point.[97] Like Peake twenty years earlier, Cunningham recognized that direct rule was no longer possible without the use of force, but he underestimated – as Peake had not done – the force of nationalism (believing that once the Jews had their own state, immigration would diminish) and the sense of betrayal by the British now felt by both Arabs and Jews. Soon after his arrival in Palestine, Cunningham had noted the absence of Palestinians in the administration, the problem of Arab education, the need for irrigation to develop agriculture. These were to have been his priorities. Instead, his term of office was one of deadlock, rebellion and repression. In the autumn of 1946, the Palestinian leader Jamal Bey el Husseini told Cunningham that the Palestinian Arabs opposed partition, would never accept 'an alien element . . . which would destroy our continuity with the Arab world', and complained that the Jewish rebels were not treated with the same severity as the Arabs in the 1930s. Two months later, after the mass arrest of the Jewish leadership, Eliezer Kaplan of the Jewish Agency told Cunningham that the Jews had lost all confidence in the British. Cunningham, exasperated, asked Kaplan whether the Jews 'wanted the British and Jews looking at each other like angry dogs'. Kaplan replied acidly that he did not, but ultimately 'life in Palestine was for the Jews a future, for the British only a duty'.[98]

Cunningham's administration shared responsibility for maintaining law and order with an increasingly depleted and weary military force. In January 1947 General Barker was asked by Cairo headquarters for suggestions for a reduction of forces in the area, since the tasks of the British Army in Palestine were 'not properly the function of the soldier at all'.[99] In February 1947, the violence inside Palestine, the knowledge that Britain was condemned for its treatment of Holocaust survivors, and Britain's own post-war troubles – with food and fuel shortages persisting throughout a hard winter – led the British government to announce that it was handing over the Palestine problem to the United Nations. Britain had lost both the will and the ability to rule by force.

The armed forces in Palestine failed to eradicate Jewish terror for two main reasons. The first was the almost total lack of Intelligence. The dual military and administrative presence, and the need for liaison between the two, meant that throughout the administration 'Shulamit of the switchboard' and her Jewish colleagues were often forewarned and forearmed about British plans. 'Operation Agatha' – the crack-down on Palmach and Jewish Agency leaders – was planned like a wartime campaign, with all instructions in code, and a total blackout of the civilian telephone system. But an earlier contingency plan, 'Broadside', had been passed to the Hagana, enabling some of its leaders to go into hiding. The Hagana sometimes provided the government with information about the Irgun but tolerated no treachery within its own ranks; on separate occasions in 1940 seven informers were executed.[100]

The Army never brought full military force to bear on the Jewish population. In August 1946 a British officer reported to General Stockwell, the commander of the 6th Airborne Division during the final phase of the Mandate, that Tel Aviv was by now beyond British control, and that the only way of managing the situation would be 'to cordon the city and starve it out or . . . to go in with all guns roaring'.[101] Tel Aviv was indeed cordoned off during special searches but the Army never contemplated a major offensive against the Jews. In December 1946 the Middle East High Command concluded:

There was unlikely to be an early settlement in this problem and partition appeared the only possible solution. General Barker (C in C Palestine) had the situation well in hand. He had sufficient troops to carry out his role, provided there was no Arab rising. The principal point at issue was to ensure that the Jews realised that the Army was not at present being employed as an instrument of policy.[102]

Though no quarter was given to terrorists, neither the administration nor the Army wanted a confrontation with the majority of the Jewish population.

The most extensive 'cordon and search' operation in Jewish areas took place after the Irgun kidnapped a British judge, Ralph Windham, and one of his assistants from his court-room in Tel Aviv in March 1947, after one of their leaders, Dov Gruner, was arrested. Windham was released after thirty-six hours but under 'Operation Elephant' martial law was imposed for a fortnight on three Jewish towns – Tel Aviv, Petach Tikva and Ramat Gan – while a curfew paralysed business and confined 300,000 people to their homes. Troops blocked roads and searched from house to house for Irgun members and their arms. All non-essential British civilians were evacuated from the area and essential officials were put into cantonments. Only basic foodstuffs were distributed. But Major-General Richard Gale, who commanded the operation, kept the building trade and the port labourers working, out of concern for the effect of a stoppage on Palestine banking, credit and contracts, while the local Hebrew press was allowed to continue functioning, and there was no repetition of Montgomery's censorship of the foreign press. Throughout the period both the administration and the Army were aware that public opinion, particularly in the United States, was sympathetic to the Jewish cause, that all army actions were scrutinized and that questions would be asked in Parliament.

There were few executions of Jewish terrorists (Gruner was one, Stern shot on the run), whether for this reason or for fear of revenge kidnappings by the Irgun. But conditions of imprisonment in the overcrowded Palestine jails – the only Mandate facility shared by both Arab and Jews – and the flogging of Jewish captives caused more confrontations. Flogging, which was the punishment for all general crimes of violence, under Mandate law, from 1928, had been condemned by both Arab and Jewish judges as uncivilized. The flogging of Jewish terrorists in 1946 caused an uproar both in the Jewish Agency and in London. Late that year, when three Jewish terrorists were hanged, the Irgun seized a group of British soldiers and stripped and flogged them in revenge. Soon after, when Cunningham summoned members of the Jewish Council to protest against Jewish terrorism, they argued that flogging was intensifying hatred of the British. Cunningham said that he 'could not understand why people got so upset about this'. He himself as a boy had frequently been caned at school, and 'one shouldn't take these things so seriously'.[103]

Cunningham's meetings with Arabs and Jews were unproductive. His appeals to the Arabs to understand the humanitarian side of the Jewish problem were met by demands for stronger measures against the Jews and the complete stoppage of immigration. When he pleaded with the Agency leaders to control Jewish terror, they argued that they could not give away compatriots, and that if they did, it would lead to civil war among the Jews and the possible assassination of the moderate leadership. The Agency only promised Cunningham its co-operation after the Irgun atrocity of July 1947, when, as a reprisal for the execution of three of its members, it hanged two captured British sergeants and booby-trapped the site. The murder enraged not only the British in Palestine but public opinion in England, with consequent popular backing for the government's decision to abandon the Mandate.

Throughout 1947 the Army continued to search Jewish towns and settlements for 'offensive' arms, sometimes by dynamiting houses where they had been found. Major-General Richard Clutterbuck took part in searches in which the Irish Guards and the Royal Engineers joined forces with the Palestine Police. Skilled building tradesmen were best at the job, able to identify dead-end plumbing and false floors where weapons were concealed. But the finds were not impressive. In six weeks Clutterbuck's unit picked up seventy men but only a hundred weapons.[104]

Jewish terrorists had assumed many disguises to carry out their bomb outrages, and the constant toll on British nerves led not only to brutality but to farce. Near the Ezrath Nashim Mental Hospital for women, which was evacuated, the Irish Guards detonated a suspect building and accidentally blew a huge hole in the hospital. The Guards were left with three truckloads of Jewish female mental patients on their hands and nowhere to put them. In Haifa, the 6th Airborne Division shared headquarters with the Holy Carmelite order. An alert was raised when a large black taxi drove through the compound perimeter and four people dressed as nuns got out. In the back of the taxi, parked under the windows of General Staff offices, was a ticking grandfather clock. In the course of a rapid investigation the Guards discovered that the nuns were carrying no sub-machine-guns under their cloaks, and that the clock was genuine. The subsequent report commented:

> It appears to be extremely difficult to frame any regulations concerning access to Divisional Headquarters which will satisfy all parties living in the building. If the regulations are strict enough to ensure the reasonable security of the Divisional Staff, the monks bring down holy wrath upon the heads of the unfortunate sentries who have hindered their worshippers, visitors and colleagues, while the alternative compromise allows nuns in large black taxis to bring ticking boxes into the headquarters.[105]

On 29 November 1947, the United Nations debated the UNSCOP recommendations and voted to partition Palestine by thirty-three votes to thirteen, with ten abstentions – Britain among them. Implicit in the partition resolution was the creation of a Jewish state in Palestine, with borders marked out by the UN. Immediately, Palestine Arab militias, swelled by irregular Arab detachments from across the borders, attacked Jews throughout the country, the Hagana adopted what Ben Gurion termed 'aggressive defence', hitting at suspected centres of Arab operations, the Irgun continued to kill Arabs and British alike, and the Jewish Agency prepared to take over the administration of the country. Until the evacuation of the very last British troops from Palestine in June 1948 – a month after the formal end of the Mandate – Arab and Jewish militias continued a fight rapidly developing into fullscale war.

The chief concern of the British government was its relations with the Arab states in the Middle East; it had already given up on British rule in Palestine as a lost cause. What happened during the last few months of British rule was scrutinized, and criticized, in Britain, from this viewpoint. The civil and military administration in Palestine had different worries: their own prestige and safety, and the remaining obligations of the Mandate government to the people still under British rule. As throughout the Mandate, British policy directives clashed with the dilemmas of the civil administration. And despite reluctance to become involved in the fighting, British army forces were drawn, indirectly and directly, into battles in the Galilee, in Haifa and in Jaffa.

In January 1948 Cunningham cabled the Secretary of State with a statement of policy. He was aware that the Mandate government was being blamed for the breakdown of law and order in the country, and therefore explained that his main aim was 'to allow both sides to defend themselves'. With the withdrawal of British and Arab police from Tel Aviv and its suburbs, Jewish areas were now under their own protection. Liaison had been set up between the Hagana and the police in Jerusalem and Haifa. There were to be no further arms searches apart from those of caches suspected of being used in attacks – since Jewish units were trying to improve their positions by attacking British army posts.[106] The final combined operation between the military and civilian authorities was the withdrawal of all the civil administration to cordoned-off areas where they could be protected by the military until their evacuation. This was done by pronouncing statutory martial law – the ultimate negation of the Mandate – for two weeks in March.

Cunningham was determined to remain in Jerusalem, the seat of British power, until the very end of the Mandate. Now more than ever the policy was 'holding the ring': trying to ensure what in British eyes could be a fair fight between Arabs and Jews, but at the same time keeping the sides apart until the British withdrawal. After both Arab and Jewish fighters attacked one another's quarters, Cunningham tried to persuade Jews to realign in the west and the Arabs in the east of the city – and was rebuffed. Jewish arms were impounded and curfews imposed on the Arabs. An attempt to set up, under British auspices, an Arab defence force parallel to the Hagana also failed. Both sides continued to jostle for strategic advantages in the city and resented any British interference with their plans.[107]

In February 1948 British internal army directives were cautious:

Both sides in Palestine are preparing for the time when the British leave the country. They have considerable quantities of arms. Moreover, when the time comes, they will need them; even if only for a sincere attempt to maintain law and order in and between their respective states. Indiscriminate searches for arms will nearly always find them, but will achieve little other than embittered relations on all sides.

Only arms used 'offensively' or 'likely to be misused' were to be confiscated, there were to be no 'indiscriminate' searches, and 'reasonable measures for defence' were not to be interfered with.[108]

These very neutral directives were difficult to enforce by British soldiers targeted by both Jews and Arabs, and often much resented. The morale of the British troops in Palestine troubled the High Command, and was to do so even after the withdrawal from Palestine because of its implications for soldiers elsewhere in the crumbling Empire. Stockwell, Commander of the 6th Airborne Division until April 1948, asserted later that the troops' morale had been high because of their belief in their 'moral ascendancy' over the warring Arabs and Jews, the example given by their officers, and the good conditions they enjoyed. But by 1948 the average age of the recruits was 20; they had not seen active service in the war, and they knew nothing of the rights and wrongs of the Arab–Jewish conflict. As for their officers: Lieutenant-Colonel P. G. F. Young of the Oxford and Buckinghamshire Light Infantry reported that the troops were looking for action, and that it was 'the spice of danger' in killing Arabs and Jews and being ambushed by them that made their service worthwhile. Another officer thought the soldiers had developed a 'barbed wire complex'. Lieutenant-General G. H. A. MacMillan, who had taken over from Barker as head of the garrison in 1947, reported that several infantry brigades finally had the 'satisfaction', in the last stage of the Mandate, of going into action against both the Hagana and the Irgun, who were now co-ordinating military activities. Lieutenant-Colonel John Hackett, who had made his own sporting rules while fighting the Arab rebels in the Galilee, resented the fact that, as he put it: 'three thousand third-class Jewish lunatics could incarcerate and render impotent the flower of the British Army'. The chief lesson of Palestine, in his view, was that: 'Allowing people to carry arms for their own protection is an admittance [sic] that the Government cannot protect them, and faith is at once lost in the security forces.' Lieutenant-Colonel M. F. Scott reported that the soldiers' morale was boosted when they saw action, but that they were bored with guard duties and unsatisfied with their accommodation, facilities and food.[109] While some British soldiers smuggled or sold arms to the Jews and Arabs alike, deserters staged their own outrages: one, a car bomb which exploded in Jerusalem in February 1948 and killed fifty-two Jewish civilians.

As throughout the Mandate period, going from one Jewish settlement to another meant travelling along roads bordered by hostile villages. During the inter-communal fighting in February, March and April 1948, the Hagana organized convoys – usually in armoured cars – which carried military and civilian personnel, arms, supplies and medicines. Convoys which had 'official' status, whether Arab or Jewish, could expect help in areas still manned by British troops; but the Jews preferred to rely on the Hagana, though British soldiers were repeatedly blamed for failing to deflect Arab attacks. One such was that on the convoy sent from the mainly Jewish western part of Jerusalem on 15 April to the Hadassah Hospital – Hebrew University campus, a Jewish enclave on the eastern side, surrounded by Arab territory. (A week earlier the Stern Gang had carried out the notorious massacre of Arab villagers – contemporary estimates assess the number killed as 245 – at Deir Yassin, an Arab village to the west of the city, and so the tension between Arabs and Jews throughout Jerusalem was at its highest.) The Jewish convoy of armoured buses was ambushed as it passed by heavy firing from Arab houses, and a large crowd of Arabs waited for the trapped Jews to leave the burning buses. Colonel Jack Churchill, of an infantry brigade stationed nearby, tried to persuade the passengers to transfer to an armoured personnel carrier and a Palestine Police armoured car he had brought to the site. According to his subsequent testimony, Churchill radioed for artillery support but was refused by brigade headquarters, though he had insisted that he needed two 25 pounder field-guns to shell the houses and stop the firing. A desperate shouted dialogue between Churchill and the passengers followed. Churchill could not promise safety while they crossed the few feet between the buses and his armoured cars, but he believed they would be secure once under his command. The passengers refused, preferring to await the arrival of Hagana forces. 'The Jews were over-confident and endangered themselves, Churchill later recalled. Seventy-eight Jewish doctors, nurses and patients were killed as the attack continued. Only eight of the twenty-eight survivors emerged without wounds.[110]

The commanders of the garrison were concerned above all with an orderly retreat (or 'regrouping' prior to embarkation) of its forces in the north of the country. This sometimes meant blocking the movement of those Arab forces – both local and from outside – which might disrupt the British lines of communication. Moreover, the military assessment was increasingly that Hagana forces were the better organized, and hence the stronger element in the combat, who could be relied on to impose order in areas under their control – something which would help a British withdrawal.[111]

A parallel concern was the protection of civilians on both sides at any given moment in the fighting. British forces repeatedly offered safe conduct out of the field of fire to Jews and Arabs. As these offers were generally accepted only by the Arabs, it was British army forces which played a major part in the evacuation (or flight) of the Arabs of northern Palestine. Both the strategic clearing of an escape route and the help offered to Arabs leaving Palestine led to Arab accusations that the British had conspired with the Jews against them. Similarly, the British attempt to organize Arab defence and the continuing seizure of Jewish 'offensive' arms convinced the Jews that the British were aligned with the Arabs.

This involvement in an embryonic war, while they were in the process of a withdrawal, put the remaining, outnumbered British forces between the contending militias. Throughout February and March, fifty-five members of the Irish Guards tried to keep between three and four thousand armed Arabs and a thousand Hagana men from a battle over the Galilee town of Safed. Their Commander, Lieutenant-Colonel Eugster, who had taken over from a Middlesex Regiment under Colonel Hackett, the veteran of the 'subalterns' wars' of the Revolt, tried to persuade the Jews not to 'antagonize' the Arabs, and then believed he had persuaded the Arabs to 'guarantee' the safety of the Safed Jewish minority. However, 'wild and unruly' Arab reinforcements used the Irish Guards as a shield from behind which to launch an attack on Jewish positions. After complaining that the Arabs had 'broken their word and let him down', Eugster decided to pull out in order to protect his men. The Jews refused British offers to evacuate their civilian population from the town. At the beginning of April, after Arab forces had cut off the Jewish quarter of Tiberias and blocked communications between the upper Galilee and Jewish settlements elsewhere, the Hagana cut the Arab quarter of the city in two. The British forces nearby offered the Arab civilians in the city safe conduct westwards – which was accepted.[112]

The departments of the civil administration had begun to fray by the end of 1947, but the 'dual obligation' idea survived even the approach of partition. Both Arabs and Jews wanted the central services handed over to them, while Cunningham continued to insist that they belonged to 'the country as a whole' and could not be dominated by any one community. Even before the UN vote, Ben Gurion had approached Cunningham to discuss the handing-over of communications, the status of the Holy Places, the water supply and the fate of the two thousand 'lunatic prisoners' – Arabs and Jews – who continued to trouble all sides as they had throughout the Mandate: a jail break from Acre after terrorists blew holes in the walls had freed the mental patients there as well. Ben Gurion also wanted the Jewish supernumerary police reinforced and provided with arms as a counterweight to the British trained and led Arab Legion, which, even during the Mandate, staged operations against the Jews inside Palestine; but Cunningham responded angrily that the request was 'fantastic' in view of the ongoing terror offensive.[113] After the UN vote, Ben Gurion requested microfilmed copies of the Land Registration records for Jewish areas, supplies of fuel and control of a radio station, and promised that the Hagana would not interfere with British communications.[114] At the same time, Dr Khalidi, for the Arabs, protested at the 'shameful dismemberment' of Palestine by the United Nations, and told Cunningham that there would be no co-operation with its representatives. He also protested that British armoured cars had been decorated with Jewish flags. Cunningham told him that the soldiers were 'very young men anxious to be friends with everyone', and that whenever the UN arrived he would do everything he could to 'hold the ring' between the UN officials, the Jews and the Arabs.[115]

Even as law and order disintegrated in Palestine, officials in various departments functioned as if there were to be an orderly, peacetime handing over of the country's administration. By February 1948 the country's roads were in chaos, postal services had ended and the railways were – once more – halted by damage to the tracks. Yet the Land Registry records had been photographed and preserved, the work of a dedicated official in the Lands Department.[116] Until late in 1947 Mandate lawyers were formulating the exact powers of the Bedouin tribal courts in the south, before deciding to leave the final question to the 'successor state or states'. In March 1948 the Legal Department was still at work putting the finishing touches to a Bill governing the fate of the Rockefeller Museum; Robert Hamilton, its Director and previously head of the Department of Antiquities, noted that: 'As we are not allowed to "recognise" the successor states of Palestine we have to introduce ingenious dodges into the Bill, for enabling them to be represented in due course.' Even as law-making went on, outside in the streets of Jerusalem, as Hamilton himself noted:

> The streets are dead for many hours of the day; shops with their fronts walled up (Spinneys) [the Mandate department store]; others just blown up and ruinous . . . fellows with rifles and sten guns strolling about the place or checking traffic; bursts of airgun fire and no one paying attention unless in the actual 'target area'; a strange and curiously dramatic spectacle – the prelude, I suppose, to a bloody civil war.

Hamilton, a good family man with a professional affection for the decadent medieval Muslim ruler whose palace he had excavated at Jericho, wrote to his wife: 'It would be good fun to live in the Qasr, and rule the Museum and grounds as an autonomous enclave amidst the crumbling landscape of Palestinian dissolution.'[117]

Throughout the Mandate it had been a Legal Department obsession to put an end to pin-tables in hotels and other public places in the Holy Land – a losing battle, since in English common law no games (except perhaps cock fighting) were prohibited. The Mandate continued to wage war on gambling to the bitter end: even as the Army evacuated Safed and Tiberias, another rapidly composed ordinance on the very eve of withdrawal aimed at preventing the setting up of a lido or any dance-floor in the neighbourhood of the Sea of Galilee.[118]

Three months before the Mandate was due to end, and despite civil war, grants were still being made to approved schools, homes for orphans and the handicapped, and the Palestine General Council of Social Services, which was semi-official, was still functioning, with Arab and Jewish secretaries. In a report sent in one of Cunningham's last dispatches, it was described as a 'useful media of communication between members of different communities, and . . . several public spirited members of the British community not employees of the government would do useful liaison work after the administration left'.[119]

But the illusion that this could happen was rapidly shattered. This was particularly obvious where the health authorities were concerned. Plans to continue supporting the government hospitals after the end of the Mandate failed. These hospitals, which until the end of 1947 had employed both Jews and Arabs, had to release Jewish personnel after a Jewish nurse was murdered in the Jaffa government hospital. The Haifa and Jaffa hospitals, both staffed by Arabs and Jews, had to be 'written off' when stores and equipment were looted during the war, and according to Lester, the last head of the Department of Health: 'The collapse of Arab resistance in the mixed areas ruined the plans made for carrying on hospitals after the end of the Mandate.' Both Jewish and Arab doctors in shared facilities were killed by Arab terrorists: Dr Lehrs, the Jewish Medical Superintendent of the Bet Sefafa Infectious Diseases Hospital, and Dr Malouf, the Superintendent of the Bethlehem Government Mental Hospital. The Bet Sefafa Hospital, in an area of crossfire, was handed over to the Arab Medical Association, and the Jaffa Hospital, in a Jewish area, to the Jews.[120]

Though by April most of the Mandate departments were no longer functioning (and despite what had happened to the hospitals), until near the end of the month the Health Department maintained other services. The government even provided funds to subsidize three months' maintenance of the Bethlehem Mental Hospital after the end of the Mandate. Medical stores and equipment were divided between all the Palestine institutions. But in Haifa and Jaffa the hospitals were looted. The last head of the Department of Health, Lester, concluded:

One felt a feeling of relief at leaving Palestine with a whole skin, a feeling of disappointment at the collapse of a fine service, and a feeling of shame at leaving the Arab hospital staff in Jerusalem to wave their Red Cross flags at the lines of armed Jews drawn up to take the zone.[121]

By mid-April – the last month of the Mandate – Jerusalem, the centre of Mandate government, had taken second place in importance to Haifa, the exit gate for 70,000 army and airforce personnel from the country. As the official report on the evacuation commented, the withdrawal plan was 'a complete reversal of all previous plans to build up Palestine as a self-supporting command'.[122] But nothing went according to plan. The Army was unable to carry out successfully the disposal of all the stores and arms accumulated in Palestine during and after the war. The police planned to destroy numbers of armoured vehicles and automatic weapons in 1948, but seventy thousand pounds' worth of ammunition was dumped in the sea. Motor vehicles were sold off equally to Jews and Arabs after some had been handed over to the UN mediators' team. The 6th Airborne Division's headquarters closed down and its radio station went off the air more than a month before withdrawal. The Army left behind hundreds of thousands of tons of stores, and arms dumps which were raided and looted by Arabs and Jews alike. Only the interception of illegal immigrant ships went on efficiently until the last day of the Mandate, because naval forces in the area were maintained at full strength and because both the British Cabinet and the Mandate government agreed that the encouragement of Jewish immigration under British auspices was damaging to British interests in the Middle East as a whole.

The key figure in the evacuation of northern Palestine and the establishment of a clear exit route via Haifa was General Stockwell, who spent much of his time attempting to negotiate cease-fires between Arabs and Jews in Haifa. His strategy was to retain his existing dispositions in the eastern Galilee and redeploy forces in Haifa to secure the route seawards. He refused to allow Arab reinforcements – Iraqis, Syrians, men of the TransJordan Frontier Force and even a handful of European sympathizers – to pass through his lines, and was thereafter accused by Arabs of deliberately helping the Jews consolidate their positions and take over the city. Stockwell's own impression was that the Arabs had used the safeguards afforded by his dispositions to mount an offensive, but had collapsed and panicked because of a 'lack of unity and effort', while the Jews were 'astonished at the speed and success of their operations and dazed by the resultant conditions': their control of Haifa and the flight of much of the Arab population, whose evacuation was overseen by the British forces. While Stockwell's strategy had been influenced by Intelligence reports predicting a Jewish victory, and a situation enabling an orderly British withdrawal, he also anticipated that the result of such a victory would be increased Arab infiltration into Palestine, to gain control of the north. Stockwell was preoccupied above all by the safety of the Haifa enclave, which he did not believe the Arabs would penetrate until after the evacuation of the British troops.[123]

The collapse of Arab Haifa embarrassed the British government and led to an improvised British military attack on Jewish forces. When the Arab states blamed the British government for having let Haifa 'go to the Jews', the Foreign Secretary, Ernest Bevin, instructed the Army to prevent a Jewish capture of Jaffa (allocated to the Arabs under the UN partition plan), and Hagana positions in Tel Aviv were shelled by British artillery brought from Cyprus.

On 15 May 1948, the Mandate was to end. The last Chief Secretary of Palestine, Sir Henry Gurney, recorded its final days in his diary. On 22 April, referred to by Gurney as a 'ridiculous day', the railway head-quarters were burned down in Haifa and all the records were destroyed, including the final pay papers for the railway staff. The Accountant-General's office staff lost £18,000 on the steps of Barclays Bank in Jerusalem. The Hagana took over the Immigration Department and seized 1,500 unused British passports. At this stage Gurney, who had irritated both Jewish and Arab leaders by what they saw as his unnatural and apparently unshakeable calm in the midst of chaos, pronounced a plague on both their houses. On 23 April: 'Jewish plans for the domination of the Holy City are becoming clear, and not a single Christian nation is prepared to do anything to help. The machinery of the Jewish state now seems to be complete on paper with staff for press censorship and all the horrible equipment of a totalitarian regime.' On 27 April: 'All the bad hats of Arabia in Jerusalem. No responsible Arabs to see. They always say it is necessary to refer the matter to Damascus or Cairo and then never produce an answer at all.' On 29 April, the courts had closed down, and nearly all the prisoners in the jails had escaped. Gurney recorded that all the rich Arabs were leaving the country: 'Arab feckleness [sic] at its worst, with black market exploitation and throwing of the blame on somebody other than themselves i.e. the British'. On 5 May, ten days before the end, Gurney wrote: 'Really the Arabs are rabbits. 90% of the population of Jaffa have just run away and only some 5000 now remain.'

On 8 May Gurney listed the Secretariat on the eve of evacuation, the last Mandate roll call: Gibson (who had saved Britain in the Sultan's land case) of Malaya and Trinidad; Stewart of Nigeria and the Bahamas (who believed Western capitalism was doomed and favoured arts and crafts); and Gray, Inspector-General of the police, ex-marine commando; Fox-Strangways of Nigeria, Nyasaland and the West Pacific; Dorman and Butterfield of Tanganyika; and, bringing up the rear with Gurney himself, the Palestine Information Officer Stubbs, one-time advertising manager for Bob Martin dog-conditioning powders. There was no work for any of them. Gurney, cooped up in the Residence, spent his time playing tennis. In his last telegram to London he quoted Isaiah 37:32, casting the British as exiles from the Holy Land: 'For out of Jerusalem shall go forth a remnant, and they that escape out of Mount Zion.'[124]

By then many British military observers, from Basil Liddell Hart, the strategist who knew the Hagana leaders well, to General Stockwell and Cunningham himself, expected the Jews to win the battle for Palestine, even though they realized that Arab armies from the five surrounding states would be sent against them. Liddell Hart told a journalist in May 1948 that he did not think the danger would prove nearly as great in reality as it appeared on paper, given the Arabs' far superior numbers and weaponry, because the Arab states lacked unity and organization, and did not have the scale of weapons to inflict a defeat, and primarily because they would lose heart if they met tough resistance. The Jews' preparedness to sacrifice their lives was, in Liddell Hart's view, their basic advantage.[125] Stockwell, like all the other British officials, had noted the flight of the Palestinian leadership and the disunity of the Arab rank and file; while Cunningham, who had previously anticipated an Arab victory, and had even thought the Jews would ask the British Army to remain, wrote to the Colonial Office, near evacuation, that he did not believe the Arab states would commit full military strength or 'show military sense'.[126]

These assessments proved to be correct. Six thousand Jews, 1 per cent of the total Jewish population of Palestine at the end of the Mandate, died fighting for their newly declared independence.

Palestinian Arab opposition was sporadic – their leadership had fled and the Arab Revolt had drastically reduced their capacity for fighting. The Arab armies did not co-ordinate their strategy. Until 1948, the embryonic Israeli Army, the Hagana, was composed chiefly of infantry, and had waged mainly defensive battles to protect settlements and essential installations. It was only as individuals that they had been recruited into the British Army, and their personal weapons were not superior to those of the Arabs. But the technical knowledge they had acquired under British command enabled them to operate machine-guns, mortars, anti-aircraft and anti-tank weapons and bren guns. The supplies of artillery and armour which reached the Jewish fighters during the war, expertly handled, were decisive.

No British analyst predicted the behaviour of the mass of Palestinian Arabs which – more than any other factor – secured a Jewish majority in that part of Palestine which became the Jewish state. The flight of most of the Arab population during the 1948 war, following the defection of its leadership, ensured Jewish control of a far larger area of Palestine than had been envisaged in the various partition plans. There appears to have been a complex set of reasons for this exodus, varying from district to district and with no single cause or directive. During the first decades after the Mandate contradictory explanations were offered: the Jews argued that the Arabs fled because they were promised return to all Palestine in the wake of victorious armies from the neighbouring states and the annihilation of the Jews; the Arabs, that there was a concerted plan behind the expulsion of a number of refugees from a handful of towns and villages by the Hagana. Recent historical research has questioned both these assumptions. While the Arabs undoubtedly hoped for an early return, and while the Hagana had a contingency plan for the strategic control of Palestine, the flight was spontaneous and the expulsions were ad hoc and uncoordinated.[127] What is undisputed is that the Palestine Arab refugee problem remained for years a basic factor in the Israel–Arab conflict, and one still unsolved.

It was left to Alan Cunningham, in the early stages of the Arab–Jewish war, to make a final, anguished statement:

Tomorrow at midnight the final page of the history of the British Mandate in Palestine is turned. It would be easy in doing so to say sometimes 'here we did right' and no doubt at other times 'there we did wrong' . . . we are more than content to accept the judgment of history. Rather would I wish to say only, if it so be that by our going we bring eventual [underlined] good to the peoples of Palestine, none of us will cavil at our departure.

I have never believed and do not believe now, that the seed of agreement between Jews and Arabs does not exist, even though in all our efforts we have failed to find the soil in which it would germinate.

Cunningham made a plea for the exception of Jerusalem from the conflict and ended:

We who are leaving have experienced great sadness in the latter tortured years. . . . In our hearts will remain the constant desire that co-operation goodwill and amity may be re-established between us to our mutual benefit in the early future. GOOD BYE.[128]

Postscript

BRITISH RULE protected the Zionist beachhead in Palestine during its most vulnerable, insecure period during the 1920s and 1930s. This was, politically, the main legacy of the Mandate, despite the hostility of so many officials to the whole Zionist enterprise and despite the armed confrontations with Jewish militants in the last two years of British rule. The character of the Jewish state which emerged was also influenced by the fact that, when Israel became the 'successor state' to most of British-ruled Palestine, it adopted, without change, so much of the legal and administrative structure of the Mandate. This was to affect the future of both Jews and Arabs in Palestine long after the end of British rule.

Within the first four-and-a-half years of its existence, the Jewish state doubled its population by immigration, bringing in hundreds of thousands of Jews from post-Holocaust Europe and from the Arab states of North Africa and the Middle East. Many of them were destitute, did not speak the Hebrew language, and were not equipped by background or education to function in the modern economy established by the pre-state Jewish population. All the new state's resources were mobilized to provide them with welfare, education and employment. Moreover, the 1948 war had ended in a series of truces, not in peace agreements. The Arab world remained hostile to Israel's existence. Israel reorganized the various pre-state militias into a modern citizens' army and carried out frequent punitive and pre-emptive attacks across its troubled borders. With such challenges to occupy Israel's government, it was not surprising that, despite much new legislation, so much remained of the colonial structure, and even of Ottoman precedent.

There were, however, reasons subtler than the pressures of circumstance and time. The Ottoman 'millet' system, which classified the population according to confessional criteria, allowing autonomy to religious minorities in matters of religion, personal law and education while keeping authority in the hands of the central government, was perfectly suited to Israel's interests. Those Palestinian Arabs who remained after the flight or expulsion of the majority, whether Muslim or Christian, Druse or Bedouin, were considered not as one but several minority groups, and special government advisers were delegated to handle relations with them. Meanwhile, though the official languages of the country remained unchanged, it was Jewish and Hebrew culture which now predominated, with the Arabs living in enclaves as the Jews had done a century earlier. The perpetuation of the millet system had enabled the British in Palestine to postpone the problem of Arab self-determination to an indefinite future date. It enabled Israel to postpone full implementation of the Declaration of Independence – the nearest thing to an Israeli constitution, which promised equality to all its citizens without regard to race, sex or religion – until such time as peace should prevail between the Jewish state and its neighbours. Within the Jewish community itself, it also enabled successive governments to incorporate into Israel's legal system those aspects of Jewish religious law which were anachronistic or actually in conflict with that Declaration. The Ottoman idea of autonomy for different ethnic groups merged with the rationale behind the continued separation of the Jewish and Arab educational systems – which neither side wished to change. There was now no overall Muslim authority with political potential. All members of the Supreme Muslim Council had fled the country in 1948 and its powers were dispersed. The Sharia courts became part of the legal system of Israel, and the Ordinance of 1921 giving power to the Council was revoked in 1961 under the new Qadis law. While some Waqf properties were released to local Arab boards or Trustees, the upkeep of mosques and Holy Places, like the pay of Muslim religious leaders, became the responsibility of the Israeli Ministry of Religious Affairs.

Other aspects of Ottoman law, which had legitimized near-autocratic rule by the Mandate, suited the Israeli Labour party, Mapai, which enjoyed uninterrupted leadership, at the head of successive coalitions, for the first thirty years of Israel's existence. The Ottoman

Land Code and Registry, whose records Israel had inherited from the Mandate, ensured that the Israel government enjoyed control of three categories of land: state lands which had passed from Ottoman to Mandate hands, land abandoned by the Arab refugees (under custody as 'absentee property'), and the small area owned by Jewish land organizations before 1948. In 1961 all these lands became the responsibility of the Israel Lands Authority, which now controlled 92 per cent of the entire territory of Israel – a government asset unparalleled at that time in any country outside the Communist bloc.[1]

The Mandate Emergency Regulations have remained on the statute books unchanged – so unchanged that even references to the Irgun were never actually deleted – and enabled Israel, until 1966, to govern the potentially suspect Arab minority in Israel according to military law, which included strict control over Arab domicile and travel within the country. The Emergency Regulations which helped Britain put down the Arab Revolt and fight the Jewish militias were invoked, unchanged, in the West Bank and Gaza, territories occupied by Israel after the Six Days War. During the Intifada and after, they served Israel (as they had served the Mandate) as the legal basis for imprisonment without trial, the destruction of property, the confiscation of land, and collective punishment.

The British Army in Palestine provided the Jews not just with training in the use of weapons and in mobile warfare, but with a model of how a modern army worked. The interaction of different fighting corps, pincer and outflanking movements versus frontal attacks, many improvised during the fighting itself, had to be learned. The Israeli Army in its formative years owed much to the writings of Basil Liddell Hart, whose theory of the 'indirect approach' and the importance of continual movement in battle were an important influence and contributed to Israel's ability to rebuff Arab invaders. Even while the 1948 war was still raging, there were serious divisions within the Hagana as to the responsibility of staff officers, and the importance of a formal hierarchy and army discipline along British lines. Yet the eventual structure of the Israel Defence Forces owed much to British precedent, though there was opposition to British-style discipline, parade grounds and battle drill, and though officers' clubs, introduced for a brief period, never caught on.

For the Palestinian Arabs, the legacy of British rule was far more ambivalent. The capacity for popular rebellion never recovered from the suppression of the Arab Revolt. The improvement in public health had to be balanced against the frustration of those denied an education and a share in the administration of the country. Yet Arabs who lived through the period recall good administration and a fair system of justice. It was perhaps with a dim memory of British rule in mind, as well as the benefits of British friendship, that in 1997 the Palestinian Authority explored the possibility of whether, when a Palestinian state was eventually established, it should become a member of the British Commonwealth. But what still rankles, among those who remember the period, is the genesis of the Mandate. As Anwar Nusseibeh, the late Palestinian banker and one-time Jordanian diplomat, expressed it in a 1976 interview:

> Without the Balfour Declaration we wouldn't have had the Mandate, without the Mandate we wouldn't have had the British administration, without the British administration we wouldn't have had a situation in which the Jewish presence in Palestine would have developed or did develop into a threat to our existence . . . and our political rights.

Whether this was what the officials in the administration intended is another question. Few appear really to have believed that they could reconcile Arab and Jewish interests, but despite their prejudices and preconceptions they attempted, in the main, to govern fairly. The American historian William Roger Louis has written: 'One of the fascinations of the candid British documentation of the era is the sense of men struggling against overwhelming odds with an acute awareness of moral purpose.' But the challenge that they faced was too complex – and the struggle availed them very little. Cunningham had lamented that he and his colleagues had not found the soil in which Arab–Jewish understanding could germinate; in the absence of that discovery, even the most conscientious colonial Civil Servant was inevitably – as Harris had observed – 'ploughing sand'.

Sources and
Acknowledgements

THE MANDATE ended in chaos, and the primary sources for the period are incomplete. There are several main repositories: the remnant of the Mandate files in the Israel State Archives in Jerusalem, where it is estimated that one fifth of the administration's papers survive, as well as those Samuel papers which relate to his period as first High Commissioner. Much documentation was destroyed when Jewish terrorists dynamited the administrative wing of the King David Hotel in 1946. Other files were destroyed in advance of the British evacuation of Palestine, including much personal material on Mandate employees, though among documents saved for the successor state or states were the all-important Land Registry records. Reports by Mandate officials are to be found in the Colonial Office Palestine files in the Public Record Office (CO 733 and CO 537), and in many collections of personal papers, including those of the third, fifth and seventh High Commissioners, Chancellor, MacMichael and Cunningham, available at the Middle East Centre of St Antony's College, and at Rhodes House Library – both in Oxford. A useful guide to the extant papers, though somewhat outdated, is the British Academy publication *Britain in Palestine*. One gap is partly filled by the records of talks and correspondence between Wauchope, the fourth High Commissioner, and the Zionist leaders, in the Central Zionist Archives in Jerusalem. Records of talks between the Arab Executive and the Arab Higher Committee and high Mandate officials are to be found in all the above collections. I have also consulted the transcripts, now in the Imperial War Museum, of the many interviews carried out twenty years ago by Thames Television researchers during the making of a 1976 documentary on the Mandate.

At the beginning of the notes to each section the general reader will find a list of recent books and articles on the subjects surveyed, for further reading. On some subjects the only research has been published in Hebrew – and I have therefore included a number of key works of this kind. Unfortunately, very little original research on the Mandate, tapping personal archives and oral evidence in Arabic, has as yet been carried out by Palestinian scholars; I have mentioned two: Rashid Khalidi and May Seikaly.

The endnotes refer not only to archival and other primary sources but to subsequently published accounts or memoirs. Where I have referred to rare printed material – for instance, pamphlets put out by the government of Palestine – I have indicated the location. Many footnote references in important scholarly works on the Mandate administration, based on material in the Israel State Archives (for example, Ylana Miller on government and rural Palestine and Kenneth Stein on the land question) are useless. There are two classification systems, and published references can scarcely be correlated with the material. But I hope that by including references to some hitherto untapped primary material, giving as much detail as possible, my account will be useful to future researchers.

Many scholars and archivists have helped me in my search for material. I should like to single out Professor Chedva Ben Israel for her initial encouragement; Clare Brown, archivist at the Middle East Centre, St Antony's College, Oxford; and Melanie Barber, archivist at the Lambeth Palace Archives. Those who answered my many queries included Professor Michael Davies; Dr Peretz (Jack) Yekutieli; Professor Frank Stewart; Jane Fish, Imperial War Museum film library; Dr Michael Heymann; Professor Jonathan Frankel; Dr Sherif Kanaana; Dr Shifra Shvarts; Marcella Simoni; Dr Ron Aharon Fuchs; Professor Yoav Gelber; Dr Dov Gavish; Professor Nathaniel Lichfield; the staff of the Israel State Archives, the Public Record Office, Kew, and the Liddell Hart Centre at King's College, London. The librarians of the National and University Library in Jerusalem were, as usual, unfailingly helpful.

Dr Meron Benvenisti read the book in typescript and corrected a number of factual errors, and Professor Bernard Wasserstein did the same at proof stage. Martin Gilbert corrected errors and omissions in the first two chapters. Professor Michael Davies read the section on the

Department of Health. Helga Keller made valuable suggestions regarding the shape of the Preface and first chapter. All remaining errors are, of course, my own.

Lidia and Dennis Sciama extended their hospitality to me while I was working in Oxford. Zohar Melamed's technical help with computers was, as always, vital. My agent, Gloria Ferris, read the manuscript with an eagle eye and suggested a number of clarifications. Gail Pirkis at John Murray steered the book through a number of revisions. To all, my gratitude and thanks.

Naomi Shepherd
Jerusalem, 1999

Notes

Abbreviations
ISA: Israel State Archives, Jerusalem, Mandate papers (M = Hebrew letter *mem*; G = microfilm)
MEC: Middle East Centre, St Antony's College, Oxford
RHL: Rhodes House Library, Oxford
IWM: Imperial War Museum Library, London
LHC: Liddell Hart Centre, King's College, London
PRO: Public Records Office, Kew
NUL: National and University Library, Jerusalem: Palestine Government Publications

Preface: The Cenotaph and the House

1. Dr Aharon Fuchs, 'The Design History of the British War Cemeteries in Mandatory Palestine' (unpublished article).
2. *Report on Illiteracy in Palestine*, submitted to Members of the British Parliament by the Palestine Arab Party, 10 June 1935 (NUL). For my analysis of Mandate policy on education, and the officials who masterminded it, see Chapter 3, 'Patching up Palestine'. Regarding the abandonment of Palestine, scholars who have surveyed the relevant documentation have found no evidence to confirm the accusation. Despite the chaotic end to British rule, many officials tried to protect documents of use to the 'successor state or states'. See, for instance, Dov Gavish, 'The British Efforts at Safeguarding the Land Records of Palestine in 1948', in *Archives*, vol. 22, no.95 (1996), pp. 107–20.
3. Bernard Wasserstein, *Herbert Samuel: A Political Life* (Oxford, 1992). Only Wasserstein's *The British in Palestine: The Mandatory Government and the Arab–Jewish Conflict, 1917–29* (rev. edn, Oxford, 1991) examines in detail some of the personalities and policies involved, but he limits his study to the 1920s.

Chapter 1: The Genesis of the Mandate

For further reading

The fullest exposition of the Mandate idea is given in Kenneth Robinson, *The Dilemmas of Trusteeship* (London, 1965). See also H. Duncan Hill, *Mandates, Dependencies and Trusteeship* (London, 1948). There is a chapter on international trusteeship in William Roger Louis, *Imperialism at Bay, 1941–45* (Oxford, 1981). The most exhaustive examination of the complex historical background to the Balfour Declaration by a member of the Zionist Commission is Leonard Stein's encyclopaedic *The Balfour Declaration* (London, 1961). A searching reappraisal of the convergence of British and Zionist interests is given in Mayir Vereté's 'The Balfour Declaration and its Makers', in Norman Rose (ed.), *From Palmerston to Balfour* (London, 1992), a collection of Verete's articles. A chapter in Martin Gilbert's *Exile and Return* (London, 1978), 'The Evolution of the Balfour Declaration', pp. 92–108, quotes British archival evidence of the preoccupation of the Foreign Office with the Jews of Russia and their alleged power. Isaiah Friedman's *The Question of Palestine: Britain, the Jews and the Arabs* (rev. edn, London, 1992) provides further British diplomatic references to 'international Jewish power', also mentioned in the same author's *Germany, Turkey and Zionism, 1897–1918* (Oxford, 1977). David Vital's *Zionism: The Crucial Phase* (Oxford, 1987), in one of the final chapters, remarks that Weizmann and other Zionist leaders 'seemed to validate the fundamental assumption on which the association of the Zionists with British interests ultimately turned: that which Robert Cecil had termed "the international power of the Jews".' None of these historians, however, does more than mention the 'assumption', and none gives it prominence. The absurdity of this belief, and its danger for the Jews, are discussed in Jonathan Frankel's thought-provoking article in *Studies in Contemporary Jewry* (see n.12, below, for details).

Notes

1. Iraq became independent in 1932, Syria and Lebanon (mandated to France) were recognized as independent states in 1941 but had to wait for full independence until 1946. Transjordan, originally part of the Palestine Mandate, also gained independence as the Hashemite kingdom of Jordan in that year. The Second World War hastened the process because of promises held out to secure Arab support for the Western Allies.

2. Wyndham Deedes, Chief Secretary to the first administration, quoted in the *Palestine Post*, 20 January 1925.

3. Bishop Graham-Brown to Cash, 10 March 1933, (MEC, Jerusalem and the East Mission Papers, Box XXXVI).

4. PRO CO 537/2320: Lord Tedder, General Montgomery and General J. H. D. Cunningham, memorandum to the Defence Committee of the Cabinet, 19 September 1946.

5. Quoted in Friedman, *The Question of Palestine*, p. 53.

6. A Foreign Office memorandum dated 17 October 1917 links a sympathetic view of Jewish suffering in Russia with Zionism and the need to support it (FO 371/3083, quoted in Gilbert, *Exile and Return*, p. 104). Graham later expressed regret at the delay in the War Cabinet's discussion of the Balfour Declaration on 24 October.

7. For the help afforded by the Rothschilds to the Duke of Wellington during the Napoleonic Wars, see Amos Elon, *The Founder: Meyer Amschel Rothschild and his Time* (London, 1996), pp. 66–8. For the activities of Jewish bankers during the later period, see A. J. Sherman, 'German Jewish Bankers in World Politics: The Financing of the Russo-Japanese War', in *Leo Baeck Institute Yearbook*, 28 (1983), pp. 59–73, quoted in Frankel, n.12, below.

8. Bernard Wasserstein, *Herbert Samuel*, p. 207.

9. The copy of Weizmann's letter to Rosov is in FO 371/3019 F 229217, no.242996. The British belief in the Zionists' power to deny the German supplies of grain is repeated by Elizabeth Monroe in her classic work, *Britain's Moment in the Middle East, 1914–1956* (London, 1956), though Leonard Stein, in *The Balfour Declaration*, dismisses the belief on pp. 570–4, commenting that all his researches 'failed to elicit any evidence that the Zionist appeals to the South Russian Jewish traders had a perceptible effect'.

10. Weizmann to Clayton, 27 November 1919, in J. Reinharz (ed.), *Letters and Papers of Chaim Weizmann*, vol. 9 (New Brunswick, 1977), pp. 41–2.

11. Hannah Arendt, *The Origins of Totalitarianism* (New York, 1965), p. 355.

12. Jonathan Frankel, 'The Paradoxical Politics of Marginality: Thoughts on the Jewish Situation during the Years 1914–21', in *Contemporary Jewry*, vol.4 (1988).

13. Friedman, *The Question of Palestine*, p. 325.

14. Robinson, *The Dilemmas of Trusteeship*, p. 19. See also Sir Anton Bertram, *The Colonial Service* (Cambridge, 1930), Chapter 9: 'Mandated Territories'; and David Meredith, 'The British Government and Colonial Economic Policy, 1919–39', in *Economic History Review*, 2nd series, 28/1–4 (1975), p. 485, for reference to economic benefits.

15. Barbara Smith, *The Roots of Separatism in Palestine: British Economic Policy, 1920–29* (London/New York, 1993), pp. 45–51.

Chapter 2: From Conquest to Colony

For further reading

Studies of the social and economic structure of Palestine as part of the Ottoman Empire include Albert Hourani, 'Ottoman Reform and the Politics of Notables', in W. Polk and R. Chambers (eds), *The Beginnings of Modernization in the Middle East: The Nineteenth Century* (Chicago, 1968), pp. 41–68; Roger Owen (ed.), *Studies in the Economic and Social History of Palestine in the Nineteenth and Twentieth Centuries* (London, 1982); and Beshara Doumani, *Rediscovering Palestine: Merchants and Peasants in Jabal Nablus, 1700–1900* (Berkeley, 1995). Histories of the Palestinian Arabs as a distinct national group include Baruch Kimmerling and Joel Migdal, *Palestinians: The Making of a People* (New York, 1993); and Rashid Khalidi, *Palestinian Identity: The Construction of Modern National Consciousness* (New York and West Sussex, 1997). Demographic statistics were most recently examined in Justin McCarthy, *The Population of Palestine: Population Statistics of the Late Ottoman Period and the Mandate* (New York, 1990). The two British censuses are *Palestine Census Office: Report and General Abstracts of the Census of 1922*, compiled by J. B. Barron (Jerusalem, 1929); and *Palestine: Census of 1931*, report by E. Mills (Alexandria, 1933). Studies of the relationship between Arabs and Jews before the Mandate period have focused almost uniquely on the political conflict, land purchase and its implications; for this, see Gershon Shafir, *Land, Labor and the Origins of the Israeli–Palestinian Conflict, 1882–1914* (Cambridge, Mass., 1989); and Neville Mandel, *The Arabs and Zionism before World War I* (Berkeley, 1976). The standard work on the early period of British administration in Palestine is Bernard Wasserstein, *The British in Palestine*. The same author's *Herbert Samuel: A Political Life* (Oxford, 1992) has a chapter on Samuel's term as High Commissioner. For the Jews in Palestine during the modern period, see David Vital, *A History of Zionism*, 3 vols (Oxford, 1975–87).

Notes

1. Dr Aharon Fuchs, 'The Design History of the British War Cemeteries in Mandatory Palestine'. (unpublished article).
2. W. T. Massey, *How Jerusalem Was Won: Being the Record of Allenby's Campaign in Palestine* (London, 1919). Massey was the official correspondent accompanying the Egyptian Expeditionary Force; his comments (like the main title) convey the propagandist message of the campaign. The most recent biography of Edward Allenby is Laurence James, *Imperial*

Warrior: The Life and Times of Field-Marshall Viscount Allenby (London, 1993).

3. The combatants' account of the invasion of Palestine is taken from George J. Berrie, *Under Furred Hats* (Sydney, 1919, an Australian memoir); James Young, *With the 52nd Lowland Division* (Edinburgh, 1920; Young was a Scottish doctor who treated the wounded during the winter ascent to Jerusalem); Robert Henry Wilson, *Palestine, 1917* (London, 1987); J. W. Wintringham, *With the Lincolnshire Yeomanry in Egypt and Palestine, 1914–18* (London, 1979); Gavin Richardson, *After Gallipoli: The Story of the 14th Border Battalion – the King's Own Scottish Borderers, 1916–18* (London, 1992); C. E. Hughes, *Above and beyond Palestine: An Account of the Work of the East Indian and Egypt Seaplane Squadron, 1916–18* (London, 1930; Hughes was a military observer attached to seaplane reconnaissance units – scarcely mentioned in official reports). Wilson's and Wintringham's accounts may be compared with the Marquess of Anglesey's account in Chapter 18 of *A History of the British Cavalry, 1816–1919* (London, 1982), which is critical of the performance of the British Yeomanry in the war.

4. Wilson, *Palestine, 1917*.

5. A further, unpublished source is in LHC, Clarke Papers, 'The Memoirs of a Professional Soldier in Peace and War' (typescript memoirs of Brigadier Frederick Arthur Stanley Clarke).

6. The *Kia-Ora Coo-ee*, 15 June 1918 (IWM).

7. Milner to Grindle, (PRO FO 371/5282 E 10655/44 and E 15568).

8. Army report on malaria in 'Review of Control of Malaria', 1941 (ISA RG10 M70/35 M321).

9. Richardson, *After Gallipoli*, p.30.

10. Tewfik Canaan, 'The Surrender of Jerusalem', in *Journal of the Palestine Oriental Society*, VIX/1 (1930), p. 27; Canaan reproduces the document of surrender, which was never delivered.

11. Wilson, *Palestine*.

12. For a graphic picture of the Aharonson group, see Anita Engel, *The Nili Spies* (London, 1967); for its connection with British Intelligence, see Anthony Verrier (ed.), *Agents of Empire* (London, 1995). Palestinian oral tradition has it that some Arabs, too, were working for the British. See May Seikaly, *Haifa: The Transformation of an Arab Society, 1918–1939* (London, 1995), p. 43, n.47.

13. Hansard, vol.83, 29 June 1916, col.1084. Wasserstein, *Herbert Samuel*, p. 214ff. See also Sharman Kaddish, *Bolsheviks and British Jews: The Anglo-Jewish Community, Britain and the Russian Revolution* (London, 1992).

14. James Patterson, *With the Judeans in the Palestine Campaign* (London, 1922).

15. Nira Reiss, 'British Public Health Policy in Palestine, 1918–1947', in M. Waserman and S. Kottek (eds), *Health, Disease and Healing in the Holy Land: Studies in the History and Sociology of Medicine from Ancient Times to the Present* (Lewiston, Queenston and Lampeter, 1996), pp. 301–27.

16. *Government of Palestine: Ordinances and Public Notices etc. Issued by the Military Authorities and Government of Palestine Prior to January 1921* (NUL); OETA: *Standing Orders and General Instructions for the Information of Officers, October 1918 (Confidential)*, ibid.

17. Ibid.

18. Zvi Mandel, 'The Machokokocs Pest in the Jerusalem Forests', *Ha'Aretz*, 22 March 1997.

19. See n.16, above.

20. Ronald Storrs, *Orientations* (London, 1943); and Norman Bentwich, *England in Palestine* (London, 1932).

21. Bertram, *The Colonial Service*, Chapter 9: 'Mandated Territories'.

22. Report by Sir Charles Tegart and Sir David Petrie on the Palestine Police, January 1938 (MEC, Tegart Papers, Box II).

23. 'Translation of Hebrew Documents' (PRO CO 733/1721).

24. Edward Keith-Roach, *Pasha of Jerusalem: Memoirs of a District Commissioner under the British Mandate* (London, 1994); Humphrey Bowman, *Middle East Window* (London, 1946); Frederick Kisch, *Palestine Diary* (London, 1938); and J. A. Mangan, *The Games Ethic and Imperialism* (London, 1986).

25. Geoffrey Furlong, *Palestine is my Country: The Life of Musa el Alami* (London, 1956).

26. Transcript of interview with Gershon Agronsky, 16 August 1932 (RHL, Chancellor Papers, Box XVI).

27. Richard Meinertzhagen, *Middle East Diary, 1917–1956* (London, 1959), p. 51.

28. MacInnes to Allenby, 2 May 1917 (MEC, Jerusalem and the East Mission Papers, Box LX, file 1: Allenby–MacInnes, 1918–20).

29. Ibid., Box IV, file 1: Stacy Waddy, 'Suggested Definitions of the Functions of the Jerusalem and the East Mission').

30. Ibid., Box LV, file 2: Record of a Conversation between Bishop MacInnes and Chaim Weizmann, 13 December 1919. For attendance of poor Jewish children at Mission schools, see Hadassah Medical Archives, NY, Series 32, Box XXXII, folder 14: Report by the Va'ad Leumi, 21 March 1934. (Cited by Marcella Simoni, 'At the Roots of Division: A New Perspective

on Arabs and Jews', a lecture delivered at the Association for Jewish Studies conference, Cambridge, 28 June – 3 July 1998.)

31. MacInnes to the Archbishop of Canterbury, Randall Davidson, 24 June 1922 (MEC, Jerusalem and the East Mission Papers, Box IV, file 1).

32. Ibid., Box XIII: Danby's letters to Bickersteth and Matthews, the secretaries of the Mission. The memorandum by Archbishop Douglas on Palestine for the Council for Foreign Relations of the Anglican Church, dated 3 March 1938, is in the Douglas Papers, vol.15, in Lambeth Palace Library, London; there is a note attesting to Danby's dissent.

33. For Graham-Brown's view of Zionism, in the context of Christian doctrine and the future of Palestine, see Graham-Brown to Paton at the Council for Foreign Relations, 11 February 1938 (Douglas Papers, vol. 15, in Lambeth Palace Library, London). A letter from an Evangelical clergyman in Keswick, protesting against Graham-Brown's views of the Return (as stated in a letter to *The Times*, quoting the Report as authority), was published in the *Palestine Post*, 24 January 1939. Copies of the Douglas memorandum and this letter are in MEC, Jerusalem and the East Mission Papers, Box LXII, file 1.

34. The Report of the Archbishops Commission was published by the Society for the Promotion of Christian Knowledge (SPCK) in 1938. The reference to 'Israel in the flesh' having 'forfeited the promises' is in Part 2, 'The Church and the Sacraments', under the subheading 'The Church in Scripture', pp. 101–2. Stewart's letter is in the same volume.

35. For Ashbee and Pro Jerusalem, see C. R. Ashbee, *A Palestine Notebook, 1919–23* (London, 1923); Ashbee (ed.), *Jerusalem, 1918–1920: Being the Records of the Pro Jerusalem Society and Jerusalem during the Period of the British Military Administration* (London, 1921, 1923); and Alan Crawford, *C. R. Ashbee: Architect, Designer and Romantic Socialist* (Newhaven, 1985), pp. 170–93.

36. Ashbee, *A Palestine Notebook*.

37. Ashbee, *Jerusalem*.

38. MEC, H. M. Wilson Papers.

39. Ashbee, *A Palestine Notebook*.

40. Ibid.

41. Benjamin Hyman, 'British Planners in Palestine, 1918–1936' (unpublished PhD thesis, LSE, January 1994).

42. Helen Meller, *Patrick Geddes: Social Evolutionist and City Planner* (London/New York, 1993), pp. 263–82

43. Quoted in Wasserstein, *Herbert Samuel*, p. 250–1.

44. Bernard Wasserstein, 'Herbert Samuel and the Partition of Palestine', 16th Sacks Lecture (Oxford, 1990).

45. Letter dated 21 August 1920 (MEC, Monckton Papers). See also letter to C. P. Cook of 16 August, adding that Samuel 'expected to be assassinated'.

46. Sheila Hattis Rolef, 'The Economic Development Policy of Herbert Samuel in the First Year of Office', *Cathedra*, 12 (English edn), Jerusalem (1979), pp. 70–90.

47. Evyatar Friesel, 'Herbert Samuel's Reassessment of Zionism in 1921', *Studies in Zionism*, 5/2 (autumn 1984), p. 217.

48. ISA M2 RG 2–61 and 62: first meetings of the Advisory Council, 1920.

49. Friesel, 'Herbert Samuel's Reassessment', n.20.

50. Report dated 6 May 1921, 'The Situation in Palestine' (MEC, Brunton Papers).

51. For a thorough examination of the election of the Mufti, see Elie Kedourie, 'Sir Herbert Samuel and the Government of Palestine', in *The Chatham House Version and Other Middle Eastern Studies* (London, 1970). See also Uri M. Kupferschmidt, *The Supreme Muslim Council: Islam under the British Mandate for Palestine* (Leiden, 1987).

52. Wasserstein, *Herbert Samuel*, n.17. Samuel proposed in 1922 that Britain support the integration of Palestine in a confederation of states or countries in the Middle East; he was one of the first British politicians to encourage the involvement of the Arab states in Palestinian politics. In the 1930s, as an elder statesman, Samuel voiced blandly optimistic views of Arab–Jewish co-operation, 'as in the great days of Arab civilization', provoking one member of the House of Lords to comment: 'The difficulty was to get them to co-operate on a Board of Works; are they likely to co-operate in an Arab federation?'

53. Yehoshua Porath, *The Emergence of the Palestinian Arab National Movement, 1919–29* (London, 1974), pp. 152, 200–1 and 347. Deedes, though pro-Zionist, also felt that the system should be changed and proposed abolishing the Jewish Agency entirely.

54. The material on Richmond's appointment, and its opponents, is in PRO CO 733/133/9.

55. Conversation between Sir John Shuckburgh and Sydney Moody, 13 April 1923. Quoted in Friesel, 'British Officials on the Situation in Palestine in 1923', in *Middle Eastern Studies*, 23/2 (April 1987).

56. See the critique of 'confessional communalism' by a contemporary observer, the Australian political scientist W. R. Hancock, in *Summary of British Commonwealth Affairs* (Royal Institute of International Affairs London, 1973), vol.1, 'Problems of Nationality, 1918–36', pp. 435–9. The

entire section on Palestine, pp. 432–85, is a most penetrating analysis of the problems of the Mandate.

57. Samuel, no.895, dated 17 November 1922, Samuel to Duke of Devonshire (ISA RG2 M8 224). In 1931, 79.8% of the population defined themselves as 'Arabs', 18% as 'Jews' and 2.2% as 'other' (Druse, etc.). (Mandate statistics quoted by McCarthy, in *The Population of Palestine*, p. 37.)

58. For a detailed survey of Arabs and Jews in Mandate service, see Wasserstein, *The British in Palestine*.

59. Ernest Richmond to Chief Secretary, 20 January 1920 (ISA M8 RG 2–218).

60. For the social life of the British Mandate, based on material in the MEC Archive, see Derek Hopwood, *Tales of Empire* (London, 1987; two chapters on Palestine) and Joshua Sherman, *Mandate Days* (London, 1997).

61. Hopwood, *Tales of Empire*, p. 131.

62. Shaw to Downie, 9 January 1940 (PRO CO 733/410/21).

63. Thomas Hodgkin's reference to Miss Carey is in his *Letters from Palestine, 1932–1936*, ed. E. C. Hodgkin (London, 1986), p.142.

64. The story of Miss Carey is documented in MEC, Jerusalem and the East Mission Papers, Box XXXV.

Chapter 3: The Law Factory

For further reading

There are sections dealing with the legal system in Palestine under the Mandate in Norman Bentwich's *England in Palestine*, and in Sir Anton Bertram's *The Colonial Service*. The control of immigration until 1937 (including illegal immigration) is discussed in the Palestine Royal Commission Report, London (Peel Commission), July 1937 (Cmd 5479, pp. 279–308), in the Epstein evidence to the Commission and in the perspective of the entire Mandate period in *Survey of Palestine 1947*. The land laws have been given far more detailed attention. See, in particular, A. Granott, *The Land System in Palestine: History and Structure* (London, 1952); Kenneth W. Stein, *The Land Question in Palestine, 1917–39* (Chapel Hill and London, 1984); see also Stein's article, 'Legal Protection and Circumvention of Rights for Cultivators in Mandatory Palestine', in Joel S. Migdal (ed.), *Palestine Society and Politics* (Princeton, 1980); and Yehoshua Porath, 'The Land Problem as a Factor in Relations among Arabs, Jews and the Mandatory Government', in G. Ben Dor (ed.), *The Palestinians and the Middle East Conflict* (Tel Aviv, 1976); and Charles

Kamen, *Little Common Ground: Arab Agriculture and Jewish Settlement in Palestine, 1920–1948* (Pittsburg, 1991). The authoritative work on land survey during the Mandate is Dov Gavish, *Land and Map: The Survey of Palestine, 1920–1948* (Jerusalem, 1991; Hebrew). Pinhas Ofer, 'The Role of the High Commissioner in British Policy in Palestine: Sir John Chancellor, 1928–1931' (PhD thesis for University of London, SOAS, 1971) discusses Chancellor's involvement in the land question and his unsuccessful attempt to alter British policy on Palestine. Barbara Smith, *The Roots of Separatism in Palestine*, deals with the economic aspects of the land question during this period.

Notes

1. Chief Secretary to K. O. Robert-Wray at the Colonial Office (ISA RG3 AG19/148 M720).
2. Bentwich, *England in Palestine*, p. 273.
3. 'Note on Current Legislation in Palestine', dated 24 November 1944 (ISA RG2 J/115/44 G 92–122, p. 550).
4. For the Mandatory debate over child marriage, see ISA RG2 G 92/113 (pp. 1707ff and 1938ff).
5. Bertram, *The Colonial Service*, Chapter 9.
6. *Bon Voisinage* Agreement, Northern Frontier, 1923–4 (ISA RG11 CONT/2/1 11–M1150).
7. Passport Control Officer Samakh to Customs, Haifa, 31 January 1925 (ISA RG11 CONT/3/7 M1150).
8. H. J. Simson, *British Rule and Rebellion*, pp. 176–8.
9. Ibid., pp. 175–7.
10. Minutes of meeting at Government House on frontier control policy, 28 October 1921 (ISA RG11 CONT/2 M1151). A. H. Cashif, report, 25 August 1922 (ISA RG11 CONT/3/7 M1150). Port Officer, Haifa, to Controller of Permits, 31 August 1921 (ISA RG2 CONT/5/1 M1151).
11. District Superintendent of Police, Haifa, to Commandant of Police and Prisons, Jerusalem, 9 November 1931 (ISA RG11 CONT/2 M1150).
12. Edwin Samuel to Edward Keith-Roach, 9 May 1933 (ISA RG11 IMMIG 6–M1174).Wagons Lits Manager to Edward Best, Immigration Officer, Kantara, 20 May 1932 (ISA RG11 CONT/3/13 M1151).
13. Zionist Executive circular letter, dated 23 July 1919, signed by Weizmann, Sokolov and Julius Simon (the Zionist movement's chief economic adviser), warning against the dangers of mass, uncontrolled emigration to Palestine (CZA Z4/523). A similar warning was issued on 18 April of that year (CZA 106/29).
14. ISA RG11 IMM/7/1 M1174.

15. Foreign Office circular letter to chief centres of emigration in Central and Eastern Europe, March 1922 (ISA RG11 IMM/42 11 – M1181).

16. Control of Immigration to Palestine, 1920–1930, dated 16 July 1930 (ISA RG11 IMM/42 11 – M1181.

17. H. M. V. C. Morris, Report on Labour and Unemployment, 17 August 1923, to Chief Secretary (ISA RG11 IMM/6 M1174: 'Schemes for Control of Immigration').

18. Observations by Albert Hyamson on the memorandum by the Jewish Agency, 1930 (ISA RG11 IMM/40/3 11 M1181).

19. Exchange of correspondence between Hyamson and the Histadrut, October–November 1922 (ISA RG11 LAB 4/2 M1184: 'Labour Disputes in the Jaffa District, 1920s').

20. Minute by H. M. V. C. Morris to Hyamson's 'observations'; see n.18.

21. Morris to Chief Secretary, 6 October 1922 (ISA RG11 IMM/6 M1174).

22. *Do'ar HaYom*, 23 February 1921 (Correspondence with Zionist Commission, ISA RG11 IMM 28 M1180).

23. Memorandum on a tour of Eastern Europe, dated 13 July 1926; in Plumer to Amery, 23 March 1926 (PRO CO 733/128/7).

24. Ibid.

25. Sir John Campbell, report on visit to Jewish colonies, in *Joint Palestine Survey Commission: Reports of Experts* (Boston, 1928), pp. 433–78.

26. R. V. Nind Hopkins, Treasury, to Under-Secretary of State for the Colonies, 30 June 1933 (PRO CO 733/230/17249).

27. H. M. V. C. Morris, Report on Labour and Unemployment, 17 August 1923, to Chief Secretary (ISA RG11 IMM/6 M1174: 'Schemes for Control of Immigration').

28. See n.18, above.

29. See 'Immigration of Women as Fictitious Wives', 1934–9 (ISA RG11 IMM/4/42 II M1173.

30. Government Welfare Officer to Chief Secretary, 17 November 1933 (ISA RG11 CONT/6 M1151).

31. 'Egyptian Deportees and Undesirables' (ISA RG11 CONT/ll/1 M1152 N).

32. 'Immigrants from the Soviet Union' (ISA RG11 IMM/7/1 M1174). Quotation translated from *Davar*, 19 November 1927.

33. Hyamson to Nurock, 12 August 1933 (ISA RG11 CONT/6 M1151).

34. Department of Immigration to British Consul General, Beirut, 9 October 1933 (ISA RG11 CONT/6/M M1151).

35. For Hyamson's complaints, see Hyamson to Chief Secretary, 9 December 1932 (ISA RG11 CONT/ll M1152). For estimates of illegal numbers, see ISA RG2 E 212/33 M125/20. The comparative percentages are based on McCarthy, *The Population of Palestine*.

36. Director of Public Works Department to Hyamson, 7 August 1933 (ISA RGII IMM/131 M1183: 'Engineers and Architects'). See also ISA RGII IMM/129 and IMM/153 M1183.

37. Hyamson, minute, 9 April 1929 (ISA RGII LAB 5/3 M1184).

38. 'Admission of Women under the Labour Schedule' (ISA RGII LAB 4/2 M1184).

39. Hyamson to Sawer, 4 October 1922 (ISA RGII LAB 4/2 M1184).

40. Sawer to Hyamson, 10 October 1922 (ISA RGII LAB 4/19 M1184).

41. Passport Control Officer, Paris, to Permits Section, Department of Immigration, 15 January 1926 (ISA RGII LAB 4/2 M1184).

42. Hyamson, confidential report to District Commissioners and Assistant District Commissioners throughout Palestine, 26 March 1924 (ISA RGII LAB 4/19 M1184: 'Employment of Women's Labour in Palestine').

43. Edwin Samuel, Immigration Department, to Chief Secretary, 9 June 1933 (ISA RGII IMM 4/17/4 M1172).

44. 'The Palestine Opera' (ISA RGII LAB 5/40 M1186).

45. Chancellor to Passfield, 10 April 1930 (ISA RGII IMM/6 M1174).

46. Hyamson to Consul General in Alexandria, 23 December 1925 (ISA RGII CONT/11 M1152–21). Some Arab prostitutes married Palestinian citizens in order to remain. Mavrogordato, head of the Police, to Chief Secretary, 1 June 1928 (ibid.), suggested keeping them in jail until deported.

47. 'Deportations:1924–28' (ISA RGII CONT/11 M1152–21); Hyamson to Police, 19 October 1924 (ibid.).

48. Hyamson to Chief Secretary, 9 December 1932 (ISA RGII CONT/11 M1152: 'Deportation from Palestine, May '32 to April '34').

49. R. D. Badcock, Assistant Director of Immigration, confidential dispatch to K. M. Kyles, Haifa Police, 11 February 1932 (ISA RGII CONT/11 M1152).

50. Hyamson, memorandum on deportation, 29 June 1933 (ibid.).

51. Edwin Samuel, *A Lifetime in Jerusalem* (London, 1970), p. 144. See also Keith-Roach, *Pasha of Jerusalem*, p. 158. Keith-Roach refers to a member of the department's being in the pay of a smuggling network, but does not name Msarsa.

52. For the 'Hyamson–Newcombe plan', see S. S. Newcombe, transcript of interview with Sir Cosmo Parkinson, 12 November 1937 (PRO CO 733/75156/33); Michael J. Cohen, 'Secret Diplomacy and Rebellion in Palestine, 1936–39', in *International Journal of Middle East Studies*, 8 (1977), pp. 379–404; and, in far more detail, including references to Bishop Graham-Brown, and comments on his involvement, Herbert Parzen, 'A Chapter in Arab–Jewish Relations during the Mandate Era' in *Jewish Social Studies*, 29 (1967), pp. 203–33.

53. Record of conversation with M(ills) by Bernard Joseph of the Jewish Agency, 1935 (CZA S 25 4314).

54. Wauchope, minute on Hyamson memorandum on deportation, 1 July 1933 (ISA RG11 G/92/101, pp. 1704–5).

55. Wauchope to Arlosoroff at Jewish Agency, 6 April 1933 (CZA S 25/30).

56. Meeting between Wauchope and the Arab Executive, 8 December 1934 (in Wauchope to Cunliffe Lister, 8 December 1934, PRO CO 733/257/37356).

57. Ibid.

58. 'Memorandum on Deportation – Arabs' (ISA RG11 G/92 101, pp. 1710–11).

59. See Suad Amiry and Vera Tannous, *The Palestinian Village Home* (London, 1989) for descriptions of the fellahin culture.

60. Ghazi Falah, *The Role of the British Administration in the Sedenterisation of the Bedouin Tribes of Northern Palestine, 1918–48* (University of Durham, Centre for Middle Eastern and Islamic Studies, 1983); A. Melamed, 'Political Boundaries and Nomadic Grazing', *The Geographical Review*, 15 (1965), pp. 287–90.

61. Stein, *The Land Question*, pp. 19, 143–4.

62. For reference to the 'tree feuds', see Hugh Foot, *A Start in Freedom* (London, 1966), and Edwin Samuel, *A Lifetime in Jerusalem*.

63. 'Anti-Locust Campaign, 1928' (PRO CO 733/149/8).

64. Stein, *The Land Question*, p. 90.

65. Palestine Royal Commission Report (Peel Commission), July 1937 (Cmd 5479, p. 219).

66. Stein, *The Land Question*, p. 137.

67. See cases in ISA RG21 M845.

68. For the role of the mukhtars and legislation, see present volume, Chapter 5.

69. Smith, *The Roots of Separatism*, p. 112.

70. Stein, *The Land Question*, p. 344–9.

71. 'Report on Soil Erosion in Palestine', 1944 (ISA 11/4/1 M4492).

72. Lloyd and Ormsby Gore, minutes to Bentwich draft, 16 November 1927 (PRO CO 733/142/44605).

73. 'Discussion in Chief Secretary's Office (ISA RG 2 J182/32 G92–110, pp. 2405ff).

74. J. H. Stubbs evidence, *Report of the Commission on the Palestine Disturbances of August 1929* (Shaw Report), March 1930 (Cmd. 3530, p. 115).

75. Sawer in *Palestine Annual Report* (1925), p. 8.

76. Smith, *The Roots of Separatism*, pp. 100–5.

77. Hope-Simpson Report, quoted in Peel Commission Report, p. 262.

78. 'Indebtedness of Fellahin, 1933–6' (ISA RG3 AG20/19 M854).

79. Described by Lewis Andrews in his report on the land problem and Mandatory legislation from 1920, 6 February 1934; enclosed in Hathorn Hall dispatch to Cunliffe Lister at the Colonial Office, 27 April 1934 (ISA RG3 AG19/13 M711).

80. In the Qus'qus Tabun case; conversation between Moshe Shertok of the Jewish Agency and Sir Arthur Wauchope (CZA S 25/19).

81. Porath, 'The Land Problem', in Ben Dor (ed.), *The Palestinians*, pp. 518–9.

82. Notes by Chancellor on an interview with Lord Plumer, 15 February 1928 (RHL, Chancellor Papers, Box II).

83. Unsigned report on meeting with Chancellor, 15 October 1928 (CZA S 25/29).

84. Frederick Kisch, transcript of interview with Chancellor, 19 December 1928 (CZA S 25/15).

85. The Wadi Harawith case is described in detail in Stein, *The Land Question*, pp. 76–9.

86. Dispatch of 29 March 1930 to Secretary of State for Colonies (RHL, Chancellor Papers, Box XIV).

87. 'Secret and Confidential Dispatches to Lord Passfield, 1930–31' (RHL, Chancellor Papers, Box XIII, file 3).

88. Chancellor to Passfield, 17 January 1930 (PRO CO 733/183/77050).

89. Morris Bailey, Assistant District Commissioner, Haifa, 'The Indebtedness of the Arab Cultivator', in 'Indebtedness of Fellahin, 1933–6' (ISA RG3 AG20/19 M854); Treasury to Chief Secretary (ibid.).

90. Treasury to Attorney-General, 25 September 1928; Mills, Assistant Chief Secretary, to District Commissioner, Northern District, 8 October 1928 (ISA RG3 AG318 M749: 'Agricultural Loans').

91. Lewis Andrews to Chief Secretary, 16 September 1933 (PRO CO 733/1724).

92. Andrews, in Report of February 1934; see n.79.

93. Keith-Roach, *Pasha in Jerusalem*, p. 150.

94. Abramson, memorandum to District Officials, April 1935 (ISA RG3 AG20/19 M854: 'Indebtedness of Fellahin').

95. Saba to Abramson, 8 April 1935; Kardus to Abramson, 17 April 1935 (ISA RG3 AG20/19); J. E. F. Campbell, memorandum, 19 April 1935 (ISA RG3 AG20/19).

96. Palestine Royal Commission Report, July 1937 (Cmd. 5479).

97. Details of the *fatwa* from Kupferschmidt, *The Supreme Muslim Council*, p. 245, n.128.

98. Lewis Andrews to Chief Secretary, 24 March 1933 (PRO CO 733/17249), in dispatch to Secretary of State for Colonies.

99. Porath, 'The Land Problem', in Ben Dor (ed.), *The Palestinians*, p. 507.

100. Conversation between J. F. Stubbs, of the Land Office, and Bernard Joseph, of the Jewish Agency, 16 June 1939 (CZA S 25/10579).

101. Transcript of interview with Joshua Palmon, in Hadara Lazar, *HaMandatorim* (Hebrew, Tel Aviv, 1990), p. 74 (my translation).

102. 'Note by the Attorney-General', 17 April 1943 (ISA RG3 AG19/13 M711: 'Protector of Cultivators Ordinances').

103. Nathaniel Lichfield, 'Land Ownership and Land Policy for Planned Development in Israel: A Review and Proposals' (unpublished article).

104. G. Mason, Chief Agricultural Officer, to Solicitor-General, 18 December 1933 (ISA RG3 LH 6/49 M754); Attorney-General vs. Mustafa el Khidaish of Ijzim village, 1939 (ISA RG3 43/23 M752).

105. ISA RG3 CH 27 T M2688.

106. Memorandum to Director of Lands, Jerusalem, from District Officer, Nazareth, 7 August 1930 (ISA RG3 LH 6/2 M754).

107. 'Two Bedouin Tribes' (ISA RG3 AG20/35/4 M854).

108. All documents relating to the Sultan Abdul Hamid case are in ISA RG3 AG12/26 and 12/27, M707. The final court hearing and verdict is in 'Selected Cases of the District Courts of Palestine, 1946' (ISA 014/10 M4502).

109. Gibson diary (ISA RG3 12/27).

110. Attorney-General to Chief Secretary, 15 March 1948 (ISA RG3 12/27).

Chapter 4: Patching up Palestine

For further reading

Apart from the Reiss article (see n.1, below), there are only sparse published references in English to Mandate health policy, though much has been published on the Jewish health services. I am indebted to Dr Shifra Shvarts, the leading historian of the Israeli health funds, for enabling me to consult her article 'Health Reform in Israel: Seventy Years of Struggle (1925–1995)' before its publication in *Social History of Medicine* (Oxford, Summer 1998); and to Marcella Simoni, who has allowed me to quote from her as yet unpublished article 'At the Roots of Division: A New Perspective on Arabs and Jews (1930–39)', a lecture delivered at the Association for Jewish Studies Conference, Cambridge, 28 June – 3 July, 1998.

There are two books by officials who played an important role in education under the Mandate: H. R. Bowman (Director of Education, 1920–36), *Middle East Window* (London, 1942); and A. L. Tibawi, *Arab Education in Mandatory Palestine* (London, 1956); Ylana Miller,

Government and Society in Rural Palestine, 1920–48 (Austin, Texas, 1985), Chapter 6, outlines this aspect of Mandate policy as reflected in Mandate archival sources. Colonial Office publications of reports on education, both Arab and Jewish, are referred to in the footnotes.

Notes

1. Reiss, 'British Public Health Policy in Palestine, 1918–1947', in Waserman and Kottek (eds), *Health and Disease in the Holy Land*, pp. 301–27. British statistics give the figure as one half; Jewish statistics as a third: see Hadassah Report, June 1936 (CZA S 49/2872). Statistics in this article – taken from official reports – are usually valuable, but the article itself is vitiated by its facile and often misleading anti-colonial bias; the author exaggerates the political as against the professional orientation of the government's health officials.

2. See Peel Commission Report, pp. 310–18.

3. H. M. O. Lester, The Department of Health: Palestine, 1946–8, 'The Decline and Fall' (RHL, Mss Medit. S.14).

4. Report of Advisory Sub-Committee (Palestine) on Education in the Colonies, 27 January 1942 (MEC, Bowman Papers, Box II).

5. W. J. Vickers (Senior Medical Officer), 'Nutritional Economic Survey of Wartime Palestine, 1942–3' (MEC, Neville Corkhill Papers).

6. 'St Luke's Hospital' (ISA RG10 012/33/66 M4495). See also Chapter 5 of this volume for references to Dr Forster's experiences treating the rebels. The 1932 report on the impossibility of treating Arabs and Jews together in Hebron by I. M. Scott Moncrieff (a British nurse) is also in this file.

7. Department of Health Annual Reports, 1943 and 1946 (NUL).

8. Department of Health Annual Report, 1926. See also: 'Insane Patients, Accommodation for', in Plumer to Amery, 30 March 1928 (PRO CO 733/155/13). For detail of social welfare allocations to both communities, see 'Chief Secretary's Press Conference: Distribution of Funds by the Department of Social Welfare among Arabs and Jews', 24 January 1947 (ISA RG2 E/SW/1/47 M130/38).

9. Hijaz Pilgrimage Agreement, 1933–8 (ISA RG10 M321).

10. 'Transportation of Dead Bodies' (ISA RG10 M1569). M1574 deals with reinterment in Arab countries surrounding Palestine.

11. George Heron, 'Control of Malaria in Palestine', Part I, 11 December 1935, Part 2 (rural areas), 14 January 1936 (ISA RG10 11/70/35 M321); W. J. Vickers (ed.), *A Review of the Control of Malaria in Palestine* (Jerusalem, 1941).

12. Bigger to Senior Medical Officer Nablus, 5 March 1936 (ISA RG23 M2690: 'Anti-Malaria Measures, Tiberias Sub-District').

13. Bigger, 1943 memorandum (ISA RG10 16/20/1 M853–13: 'Anti-Malarial Campaigns, 1938–46').

14. Heron, 'Control of Malaria in Palestine', Part III (ISA RG10 M321).

15. Bigger memorandum enclosed in MacQueen to Acting Chief Secretary, 24 November 1945 (ISA RG10 M1550–2: 'Anti-Malarial Activities, 1942–6'). For an overall view of malarial control, see also Waserman's and Neuman's article, 'The Conquest of Malaria' in Waserman and Kottek, *Health and Disease* (n.1).

16. W. Clayton, Senior Engineer, to Senior Medical Officer, 10 November 1932; Medical Officer of Health, Southern District, to Senior Medical Officer, Jerusalem (ISA RG2/26 M1553).

17. 'Regulations, Inspection of Villages and Upkeep of Village Registers: Public Health Regulations for Villages, 1924–25' (ISA RG10 6/5 M1513).

18. Ophthalmic Hospital, Order of St John, Warden's Report, 1946 (ISA 06/5 M1513). The Report noted over 17,000 Muslim patients as against 3,407 Christians and 627 Jews.

19. All correspondence concerning the various outbreaks are in 'Anti-Plague Measures in Palestine' (ISA RG2 M/260/33 (1947) M221).

20. Head of Haifa Port 'to all concerned', 5 May 1941 (ibid.).

21. Heron to Chief Secretary, 10 December 1932 (ibid.).

22. Monthly Report of Senior Medical Officer, Haifa August 1941 (ibid.).

23. MacQueen to Chief Secretary, 20 January 1942; Macmillan to Secretary of State, 7 February 1942 (ibid.).

24. Chief Secretary to Crown Agents for Colonies, 2 October 1944; MacQueen to Chief Secretary, 3 July 1947; memorandum from Head of Health Department: 'Bubonic Plague in Haifa' (ibid.).

25. 'Anti-Plague Measures in Haifa'; memorandum 'Bubonic Plague in Haifa'; Lester to Chief Secretary, 21 July 1947 (ibid.).

26. Bernard C. Walker, 1938 report in EMMS quarterly paper (ISA RG10 012/3/66 M4495).

27. 'Threshing Floors' (ISA RG26/46 M227).

28. Medical Officer, Hebron, to District Officer, Hebron, December 1927 (ISA 06/5 M1513); Government of Palestine, Department of Health Annual Report, 1925, mentions a special clinic for syphilis; and 'Hebron Boys' School, 1923–47' (ISA RG8 M854), in which Bowman, the Director of Education, recording a visit on 3 December 1924, mentions that his visit coincided with that of the local Medical Officer, who told him that there was a 50% incidence of inherited syphilis among boys in this school. See also 'Prostitutes and Venereal Disease' (ISA RG10 73/2 M1630).

29. Simoni, 'At the Roots of Division'.

30. Tewfik Canaan, 'The Child in Palestine Arab Superstitions', *Journal of the Palestine Oriental Society*, VII (1927), pp. 159–86.
31. 'Maternity and Child Welfare', general correspondence, 1923–7 (ISA RG10 M/4/42 M224).
32. 'Training Centre for Moslem Midwives', 9 December 1925; and Senior Medical Officer to District Officer, 11 February 1926 (ibid.).
33. Heron to Senior Medical Officer, Jerusalem, 26 April 1926; and 'Health Welfare in the Villages' (ibid.).
34. Superintendent's Report, 31 July 1929 (ISA RG10/66/5 M1615); see also 'Maternity and Child Welfare', general correspondence, 1930–46.
35. Note on Inspection of Infant Welfare Centres, 31 July 1929 (ibid.).
36. MacQueen to Heron, memorandum on Infant Welfare Centres, 23 December 1929 (ibid.).
37. MacQueen to Mrs Bowman, 2 June 1927; MacQueen to Heron, 5 November 1927; MacQueen to Heron, 29 August 1929; and MacQueen to Deputy District Commissioner, Jerusalem, 18 May 1929 (ibid.).
38. Report on District Maternity Services, 4 December 1030; Rogers to Medical Officer, 30 May 1935 (ibid.).
39. Numbers quoted from Reiss, 'British Public Health Policy' (see n.1 above).
40. Heron to District Governor, Jerusalem, 21 January 1925; MacQueen to Mayor of Jerusalem, 30 July 1925 (ISA RG10 M853).
41. 'Disturbances in Palestine – Medical Emergencies' (ISA RG10 25/18 M1552).
42. Gawain Bell (RHL, Mss Afr.s.2001: Palestine 1938–40).
43. Lester to District Commissioner, Jerusalem, 21 October 1946; minutes of Secretariat meeting, 2 January 1947 (ISA RG10 M 4/42: 'Hospital Extensions').
44. W. Russell Edmunds, Treasury, to B. J. Surridge, Colonial Office (PRO CO 733/471 (1946).
45. Keith-Roach, *Pasha of Jerusalem*, p. 93. An Israeli television report in the 1990s showed that this tragic custom was still adopted in villages on the West Bank.
46. Government of Palestine Department of Health, Annual Report, 1926 (NUL).
47. Plumer to Amery, 30 March 1928 (PRO CO 733/155/13: 'Insane Patients, Accommodation for').
48. Ibid. See also Chancellor to Colonial Office, 6 January 1930 (PRO CO 733/184/9: 'Lunatics, Foreign, Removal of'). The Jewish Agency applied for a government grant for a mental hospital in 1947 (ISA M29/47 M248).
49. ISA RG10 M 45/5 M1576: 'Lunacy, Correspondence Jerusalem District', 1945–7. See also 'Lunacy in Palestine', quoted in Simoni, 'At the Roots of Division'.

50. Plumer to Amery, 30 March 1928 (PRO CO 733/155/13).

51. MacMichael to Cranbourne, 17 October 1942 (PRO CO 733/155/13: 'Insane Patients, Accommodation for').

52. MacMichael to Colonial Office, 5 March 1942 (ibid., with enclosures from Heron).

53. MacQueen to Chichester, 5 March 1947 (ISA RG10 M 45/5 M1576). For the release of mental patients from prisons at the end of the Mandate, see transcript of interview with Lea Ben Dor, *Palestine Post* journalist, Thames Television, 1976.

54. Dr Eder, transcript of interview with Samuel, regarding Director of Health, 14 February, 20 June and 27 June 1921 (CZA L3/222).

55. Jewish Agency statistics on Jews in Mandate service, 1941 (CZA S 25/7750; 'the religion was judged by the official's name' is the curious observation).

56. Shvarts, 'Health Reform in Israel'.

57. Government of Palestine Department of Health, Annual Report, 1936; MacQueen to R. F. Scrivenor, Assistant District Commissioner, Haifa and Samaria, 4 December 1938 (ISA RG10 79/5 M1642: 'Relief Measures for Jews and Arabs'). See also Heron to Chief Secretary, 27 January 1939 (ibid.).

58. MacQueen to Chief Secretary, 31 May 1945 (ISA RG10 M29/45 M860: chart enclosed).

59. Ibid.

60. Drs Canaan and Dajani to MacQueen, 15 July 1945 (ISA RG10 M32/45 M225).

61. Heron to Chief Secretary, 27 January 1939 (ISA RG10 79/5 M1642).

62. Heron, conversation with Szold and Katnelson, 6 October 1939 (ISA RG10 79/5 M1642).

63. J. Roch, Medical Officer, Settlements, Report on Jewish Destitution, 2 November 1939 (ibid.).

64. V. I. Ferguson, Senior Medical Officer, Jaffa, 'Destitution in Jaffa/Tel Aviv', 13 November 1939 (ibid).

65. George Stuart, Deputy Director of Medical Services, and W. J. E. Phillips, Senior Medical Officer, 'Observations on the Application of Relief Measures to Certain Areas', 31 December 1939 (ibid.).

66. K. C. Tours, 'Tantalus or Wartime Food Problems in Palestine', 1944, fore- word by G. Walsh, Food Controller (ISA o12/3/66 M 4495).

67. Vickers, 'Nutritional Economic Survey of Wartime Palestine', n.5 (MEC, Neville Corkhill Papers).

68. Ibid.

69. Cunningham to Creech Jones, Secretary of State for the Colonies, 20 January 1948 (ISA RG2 E/SW/1/47 130/38). Arabs and Jews did serve together on a handful of committees, including the General Agricultural Council, the Standing Committee for Commerce and Industry, and the Harbour and Road Boards. See Sir Laurie Hamilton, 'Friendship and Co-operation between Arabs and Jews', memorandum prepared for the Peel Commission (PRO CO 733/75550/43). Hammond stressed, however, that both sides regarded themselves as co-operating with government, not with one another. For lepers' reference, see Senior Medical Officer to Director of Medical Services, 4 January 1947 (ISA RG10 M1511).

70. 'Hebron Boys' School, 1923–47'; Bowman, 'Inspection of Boys' Schools', 3 December 1924; 30 April 1926 (ISA RG8 M854).

71. Stacy Waddy, 'Educational Work in Palestine', 1922 (MEC, Jerusalem and the East Mission Papers, Box XXXVII).

72. Quoted in Ylana Miller, *Government and Society*, p. 92.

73. Matiel Mogannam, *The Arab Woman and the Palestinian Problem* (London, 1937). The book gives an unusually full account of the role played by Palestinian women in 1930s politics.

74. Bowman, evidence before Peel Commission, 27 November 1936. (MEC, Bowman Papers, Box II).

75. Stewart Perowne, *The One Remains* (London, 1954).

76. MEC, H. M. Wilson Papers.

77. Bowman's evidence before the Peel Commission, 27 December 1936 (MEC, Bowman Papers, Box II).

78. James Farrell, Circular no.38, 'Secondary Education', 12 February 1941 (ISA RG8 G 92–123, pp. 1882–5). See also Farrell, minute dated 3 February 1945, to Tamimi letter (ISA RG8 M125).

79. Farrell, minute (see n.78, above).

80. Miller, *Government and Society*, p. 154.

81. Wasserstein, *The British in Palestine*, pp. 183–9.

82. For Antonius, see MEC, Antonius Papers, and ISA, Antonius Papers. There is a cameo portrait in Wasserstein, *The British in Palestine*, pp. 183–9; see also Thomas Hodgkin, 'Antonius, Palestine and the 1930s', *Gazelle Review*, 10, (1982), pp. 1–33; Albert Hourani, 'The Arab Awakening Forty Years on', in *The Emergence of the Modern Middle East* (Berkeley, 1981), pp. 193–215; and Susan Silsby, *George Antonius: Palestine, Zionism and British Imperialism* (PhD thesis, University of Georgetown, Washington, 1985).

83. 'The Kadoorie Bequest', 1924 (PRO CO 733/86/16743); see also Miller, *Government and Society*, pp. 92, 110.

84. M. R. Dawe, Director of Agriculture and Forests, to High Commissioner, 27 July 1935; translation of letter from Gaza notables to Dawe, undated; Wauchope minute, 31 July 1935; Farrell, Director of Department of Education, to Chief Secretary, 2 August 1935; 'Proposed Gaza Agricultural School', note of interview between British officials and Gaza notables, 10 September 1935 (ISA RG2 G91–135, pp. 792ff).

85. Greig to Chief Secretary, 20 August 1945; Acting Director of Public Works Department to Chief Secretary, 14 September 1945; Farrell to Chief Secretary, 23 September 1945 (ISA RG2 G91–135, pp. 1346–8).

86. Miller, *Government and Society*, p. 111.

87. W. A. Stewart, 'Arab Technical Education in Palestine', July 1946 (ISA RG2 G91–135, pp. 1996ff).

88. 'Industrial Employment of Women and Children Ordinance Correspondence, 1936'; Postmaster-General to Attorney-General, 27 February 1926; and Farrell to Chief Secretary, 1 March 1938 (ISA AG19/120 M726).

89. A. L. Tibawi, *Arab Education in Mandatory Palestine*, p. 241.

90. 'Elementary School Syllabus: Mandate Government Department of Education' (rev. edn, Jerusalem, 1925; ISA M 4488/010/2). The dearth of Arabic textbooks is mentioned by Bowman in his evidence before the Peel Commission.

91. Perowne to his Aunt Mabel, April 1926 (MEC, Perowne Papers).

92. MEC, H. M. Wilson Papers.

93. 'The Boy Scout Movement', CID Report, dated 25 March 1938 (ISA RG2 G92–123–0875); see also MacLaren to Acting Chief Secretary, 28 June 1937 (ISA RG2 G92–123–0929).

94. For the activities of the Scouts, compare Bowman, in *Middle East Window*, pp. 329–30, with Miller, *Government and Society*, pp. 113–15. May Seikaly, in her *Haifa: The Transformation of an Arab Society, 1918–1939* (London, 1995), notes (p. 266) that the first organized Arab protest against Jewish settlement in the 1930s was a Scout demonstration in Nablus in August 1931. Their militant role is confirmed in Ted Swedenburg, *Memories of Revolt: The 1936–39 Rebellion and the Palestinian National Past* (University of Minnesota Press, 1995), p. 123.

95. Martin Gilbert, *Jerusalem in the Twentieth Century* (London, 1996), p. 104.

96. 'Institute of Higher Studies in Jerusalem'; Eastwood minute; Duke of Devonshire, minute, 15 January 1945; and flyer advertising proposed college (PRO CO 733/470/9).

97. MEC, Jerusalem and the East Mission Papers, Box XXXVII/2 (1935): 'Anglican Schools in Palestine'. It is notable, however, that between a quarter and a third of the pupils in the most prestigious mission schools in Jerusalem (St George's, and the Jerusalem Girls' College) were Jews (ibid.).

98. Notes for a lecture at the Colonial Institute, 1943, by Miss Warburton of the Girls' College (MEC, Jerusalem and the East Mission Papers, Box XXXVII).

99. Letters dated 22 November 1937 and 25 September 1938 (MEC, Emery Papers).

100. Ibid.

101. Farrell memorandum (PRO CO 733/142/4).

102. 'Memorandum on history of relations of Jewish educational heads and departments, 1933–42' (ISA RG2 M125/20 E 212/33).

103. Meeting between Chaim Arlosoroff, Political Secretary of the Jewish Agency, and Mark Young, Chief Secretary (Bowman present), 19 October 1931. See also Hexter, of the Jewish Agency, meeting with Wauchope, High Commissioner, 2 August 1933 (CZA S 25/15/a).

104. Yellin Report, in Farrell to Chief Secretary, 2 May 1932 (ISA RG2 M125/2: 'The Jewish Agency's Educational System').

105. Farrell to Chief Secretary, as minute to Yellin Report for 1933/4 (ISA RG2 E212/33 M125).

106. Farrell to Chief Secretary, 22 December 1933 (ISA RG2 G91–134, pp. 1968ff).

107. 'Inspection of Jewish Schools, 1939–42' (ISA RG2 M851).

108. Farrell, 'Relations between the Government of Palestine and the Jewish School System, 1918–41', 31 December 1943 (PRO CO 733/453/4).

109. Farrell to Chief Secretary, 12 February 1942 (ISA RG2 M125/20 E 212/33).

110. Ibid.

111. Report of McNair Commission on Jewish Education, 1947 (HMSO, COL 201).

112. Farrell, 'Distribution of Educational Benefits in Palestine', 17 December 1945 (MEC, Farrell Papers; also in PRO CO 733/453/4).

113. Farrell, 'Observations on the McNair Report', 30 November 1946 (PRO CO 733/476/2).

Chapter 5: Iron Gloves

For further reading

H.J. Simson, *British Rule and Rebellion* (London, 1938). Brigadier Simson was Chief of Staff to Lieutenant-General J. G. Dill, GOC Palestine from

September 1936 to September 1937, and the book is a devastating critique of the Wauchope administration's responses to the first phase of the Arab Revolt. For the pre-war problems of keeping order, see Michael J. Cohen and Martin Kolinsky (eds) *Britain and the Middle East in the 1930s: Security Problems, 1935–9* (London, 1992), Part 3: *The Mandate for Palestine* (Kolinsky), Chapter 9, 'The Collapse and Restoration of Public Security', pp. 147–68. This analyses the international context of the Revolt and is the most complete review of the various stages of the Revolt and British counter-insurgency measures. For the political context of peace-keeping during these years, see Michael J. Cohen, *Palestine: Retreat from the Mandate* (London, 1987). Kenneth W. Stein, 'The Intifada and the 1936–9 Uprising: A Comparison', *Journal of Palestine Studies*, 19/4, no.76 (1990) underlines the differences rather than the similarities. Kolinsky's article 'Reorganisation of the Palestine Police after the Riots of 1929', *Studies in Zionism*, 10/2 (autumn 1989), pp. 155–76, indicates the problematic nature of policing, scarcely hinted at in the bland picture – as suggested by its title – of the veteran policeman Edward Horne's *A Job Well Done: A History of the Palestine Police* (London, 1982). Another veteran, Douglas Duff, in *Galilee Galloper* (London, 1954), gives a much-embroidered portrait of the maverick police chief Edwin Bryant. David A. Charters, *The British Army and Jewish Insurgency in Palestine, 1945–47* (London, 1989) analyses the reasons for the failure of the British Intelligence services to predict or curb Jewish anti-British activities in the post-war period. Personal memoirs of military and police personnel include Ronald Dare Wilson (Royal Northumberland Fusiliers), *Cordon and Search with the 6th Airborne Division in Palestine* (Aldershot, 1949); General Sir Richard Gale, *A Call to Arms* (London, 1968), Chapter 15: 'Palestine'; Sir Gawain Bell, *Shadows on the Sand* (London, 1983), which has a chapter on his experiences in Palestine in 1938–9; and Bernard Fergusson, who also includes a chapter in *The Trumpet in the Hall*, 1930–58 (London, 1970), pp. 29–51. There are two biographies of Orde Wingate: Christopher Sykes, *Orde Wingate* (London, 1959) and Trevor Royle, *Orde Wingate: Irregular Soldier* (London, 1994). Robert King-Clark, *Free for a Blast* (London, 1988), Chapter 5: 'Palestine 1938', describes the author's experiences in Wingate's Special Night Squads. Israeli assessments of the British contribution to Jewish military skills, in English, include Meir Pail, 'A Breakthrough in Zionist Military Conceptions, 1936–39', in Cohen and Kolinsky, *Britain and the Middle East*; and Yigal Allon, 'The Making of Israel's Army', in Michael Howard (ed.), *The Theory and Practice of War* (London, 1965). However, all the recent, scholarly research on this subject is in Hebrew, most notably Yoav

Gelber, *The Emergence of a Jewish Army: The Veterans of the British Army in the Israeli Defence Forces* (Tel Aviv, 1986). The most authoritative and complete work on the Jewish Intelligence services during the period, also in Hebrew, including information on British/Jewish co-operation during the Arab Revolt, is Gelber, *Growing a Fleur-de-lis: The Intelligence Services of the Jewish Yishuv in Palestine, 1918–1947* (Tel Aviv, 1992). See in particular vol. 1, pp. 147–59 and 236–7, and vol. 2, Part 5, 'Secret Co-operation with the Allies', pp. 456–98, and Part 6, 'Shai in the Anti-British Struggle', pp. 563–76. The fullest account of the suppression of the Arab Revolt by the British Army, written essentially as military history but with some reference to the political background, is also in Hebrew: Yigal Eyal, *The First Intifada* (Tel Aviv, 1998). Shlomo Shpiro, *Building the Foundations of Israeli Intelligence: British–Jewish Intelligence Co-operation in Palestine, 1914–1948* (University of Salford, 1998) relies on secondary Hebrew sources from an earlier period, sometimes uncritically.

Notes

1. Letter by Lieutenant-Colonel F. G. Peake, Resident in Amman, on the causes underlying the 'racial troubles in Palestine', dated 21 September 1929 (RHL, Chancellor Papers, Box II).

2. 'Sealed Armouries, 1928–34' (CZA S 25/4766); see also 'Defence of Jewish Colonies', and Dowbiggin to Mills, 10 February 1930 (RHL, Chancellor Papers, Box XIV, pp. 53–9); Conversation between Frederick Kisch, Political Secretary of the Jewish Agency, and Chancellor, 9 April 1930 (CZA S 25/13); and Kisch and Chancellor, 'Problems of Reopening Sealed Armouries', 4 August 1931 (CZA S 25/14).

3. 'Jaffa Rioting', 29 October 1933 (MEC, Faraday Papers, Box I, file 2).

4. C. H. Imray, 'A Policeman's Story' (RHL, Mss Afr.s.2053).

5. Report by Kisch to Sacher of conversation with Dowbiggin, 25 February 1930, (CZA S 25: 'Reorganization of Police').

6. RHL, Sir William Battershill Papers, Box XV, file 5: Palestine chapter of an unpublished autobiography. Battershill had served in Jamaica, Cyprus and Ceylon before arriving in Palestine to serve as Chief Secretary under Wauchope in 1937, one year into the Revolt.

7. Transcript of interview with Ralph Poston, Thames Television, 1976 (IWM).

8. Edwin Samuel, *A Lifetime in Jerusalem*, and Keith-Roach, *Pasha in Jerusalem*.

9. For instance, see minutes of conversation between Shertok and Wauchope, 27 May 1936 (CZA S 25/30).

10. Conversation between Wauchope and Arlosoroff, 19 February 1932 (CZA S 25/15a). See also record of conversation with Weizmann, in Wauchope to Cunliffe Lister, 8 December 1934 (PRO CO 733/257/37356). The British assurance for 'parity' was given verbally by Ramsay MacDonald to the Jewish leader Ben Gurion at Chequers on 12 July 1931; the Zionist telegram reporting the meeting was not published, in order not to embarrass the Colonial Office. See Norman Rose, *The Gentile Zionists* (London, 1976), pp. 51–2.

11. Minutes of conversation between Arlosoroff and Wauchope, 18 January 1932 (CZA S 25/16).

12. Minutes of interview between leading members of the Jewish Agency and Wauchope, 19 July 1935 (CZA S 25/18).

13. Summary of pre-lunch conversation between Weizmann and Wauchope on 12 April 1936 (CZA S 25/19b); record of telephone conversation between Weizmann and Wauchope, 15 May 1936 (CZA S 25/4314); transcript of interview with Ralph Poston, Thames Television, 1976 (IWM). Poston's recollection was that Weizmann had actually suggested arresting the Arab Strike Committee.

14. 'Events in Palestine', *Labour Monthly* (July 1936). The text of the article is included in an appendix to Hodgkin's *Letters from Palestine*.

15. The exchange of correspondence and Colonial Office minutes on the McDonnell affair are in PRO CO 733/313/1.

16. PRO CO 733/313/1. The only record that I have found of the relevant meeting of the Mandate Defence Committee and its decision to justify demolitions as 'town planning' is in CZA S 25/22768.

17. Ibid.

18. 'Daggers and Knives Ordinance' (ISA RG3 AG19/159 M720).

19. Ralph Poston, transcript of interview for Thames Television, 1976 (IWM).

20. Battershill, memoir (RHL, Sir William Battershill Papers, Box XV, file 5).

21. LHC, Carr Papers. Carr's letters to his wife, nos 240–88, describe his experiences in Palestine.

22. Secret and confidential dispatches to Passfield, Secretary of State (RHL, Chancellor Papers, Box XIII, file 6: 'The Green Hand Gang in Galilee').

23. Bernard Fergusson, *The Trumpet in the Hall*.

24. Al Qassem has been the subject of a number of memoirs. Battat's capture is described in Dr Forster's diaries (MEC).

25. Bell, *Shadows on the Sand*, p. 94; see also in RHL, Mss Afr.s.200: Palestine, 1938–40.

26. Sir John Hackett, transcript of interview for Thames Television, 1976 (IWM).

27. Record of telephone conversation between Hathorn Hall, the Chief Secretary, and Moshe Shertok, of the Jewish Agency, 21 October 1935 (CZA S 25/19).
28. ISA RG3 AG25/6 M736: 'Hot Pursuit'.
29. Bell, *Shadows on the Sand* (see also n.25, above).
30. Lloyd minute, 16 November 1925 (PRO CO 733/98/690–702).
31. For the earliest versions of the Collective Punishment Ordinance, see R. H. Drayton (ed.), *The Laws of Palestine* (December 1933), pp. 147–56. For discussion of the measure at the first meeting of the Executive Council of the Palestine government, see Executive Council minutes, 14 September 1922 (PRO CO 814/18). See n.30, above, for Lord Lloyd's minute, and for correspondence on draft for amendment of the Ordinance, dated 16 November 1925. For 'agrarian crime' in the 1930s, see transcript of interview with Hugh Foot (Lord Caradon) by Thames Television, 1976 (IWM), and Foot, *A Start in Freedom*.
32. Administrative files on the Collective Punishment Ordinance are in ISA RG3 AG19/10 II M711 and ISA RG3 AG19/129 M718. The Palestine Defence Order in Council, Regulations re compensation for demolition, billets, etc., 1936–40, is in ISA RG3 AG19/223 M723. Evidence for widespread demolitions is in ISA M229/1 (secret), and the case of Indur is in ISA RG27 M2660.
33. The Trusted and FitzGerald comments on collective punishment are in ISA RG3 AG19/129 M718.
34. For village administration, see ISA AG19/251 M724: 'Village Responsibility', and the Report of the Committee on Village Administration and Responsibility, 21 November 1941, published as a Palestine government pamphlet (NUL). A full discussion of the issue is to be found in Miller, *Government and Society*, pp. 145–51.
35. Minute of conversation between Kisch and Chancellor, 9 April 1930 (CZA S 25/15).
36. Minutes of conversation between Shertok and Wauchope, 24 August 1936 (CZA S 25 4314).
37. For contacts between British and Jewish intelligence, see Haggai Eshed, *Reuven Shiloach [Zaslani]: The Man behind the Mossad* (London, 1997); Gelber, *Growing a Fleur-de-lis*. The British documents of the SOE/ Hagana co-operation in 1942 were only released in 1997, and so do not figure in either of these accounts. Robert King-Clark's *Free for a Blast* describes the experiences of one of Wingate's British juniors in the Special Night Squad.
38. Transcript of interview with Hugh Foot, Thames Television, 1976 (IWM).
39. Battershill, unpublished memoir (see n.6, above).

40. MEC, H. M. Wilson Papers. Reference to the captured rebel court in MEC, Haining Papers: 'Dispatches on the Operation of British Forces in Palestine and TransJordan in the Command of Lieutenant-General Haining, etc., from 1 April 1938 to 30 July 1939', esp. dispatch of 1 August – 31 October 1938.

41. Lloyd Philips, Assistant District Commissioner, Southern District, Report on Jaffa for 1938 (MEC, Lloyd Philips Papers). See also Report by R. E. H. Crosbie on the Southern District, June–September 1938 (MEC, Tegart Papers, Box III).

42. For the (Trenchard) policy in Iraq, see quote from Sir John Sloesser, *The Central Blue* (London, 1956), p. 51, in Fergusson, *The Trumpet in the Hall*; for interrogations, see Bell, *Shadows on the Sand*; for bombing in Palestine, see correspondence between the Air Ministry and the War Office (PRO CO 733/367/1: 'Security Measures 1938').

43. Transcript of interview with Colonel Harold Bredin for Thames Television, 1976 (IWM).

44. Keith-Roach, *Pasha of Jerusalem, passim*.

45. Memorandum by Inspector-General of Police, enclosed in MacMichael to Colonial Secretary, 20 February 1938 (MEC, Tegart Papers, Box III).

46. Meeting of Sir Charles Tegart and other high-ranking police officials with Battershill, 31 December 1937; Report by Tegart and Sir David Petrie on the Palestine Police; notes of a meeting, 27 January 1938, to discuss the Report (MEC, Tegart Papers, Box II. The same Report is in PRO CO 733/383/1, Wauchope's dispatch of 24 January 1938).

47. 'Dispatches on the Operations of British Forces in Palestine and TransJordan during the Period of Lieutenant-General Haining, etc., from 1 April 1938 to 30 July 1939', esp. dispatch of 1 August – 31 October 1938 (MEC, Haining Papers, p. 3, para. 6).

48. PRO CO 733/372/6, 'Murder of Mr Tobias', 1938. Philip Tobias was the author's uncle.

49. For the gradual dismissal of the Arab Police, see MacMichael to Colonial Secretary, 25 August 1938 (MEC, Tegart Papers, Box II); for problems with British recruits, see A. J. King, for the Inspector-General of Police, to the Chief Secretary, 21 December 1938 (ISA RG3 AG20/23 M731).

50. R. E. H. Crosbie, Report on Southern District, August 1938 (MEC, Tegart Papers, Box III).

51. Forster diaries (MEC, Forster Papers).

52. Reference to the real identity of 'Mansur' is in MEC, Tegart Papers, Box II, file 4: 'Arab Rebel Documents', memo by Kenneth Waring. See also MEC, Forster Papers, diary entry for August 1938.

53. 'An Annex on Bombs', address by E. T. Cosgrove, CID Jerusalem, 25 July 1938 (MEC, Tegart Papers, Box I).

54. Simson, *British Rule and Rebellion*, p. 241.

55. MacMichael to MacDonald, 2 September 1938 (MEC, Tegart Papers, Box I).

56. Transcript of interview with Sir Alec Kirkbride, Thames Television, 1976 (IWM).

57. Keith-Roach, *Pasha of Jerusalem*, p. 196; see also Paul Cotterell, *The Railways of Palestine and Israel* (Abingdon, 1984); Plate 55 (p. 65) has a photograph of one of the double-unit armoured railcars built to combat terrorism 'in the disturbances'. Two Arabs are shown 'being taken for an uncomfortable ride on the ponytruck extension': that is, as hostages in case of bombs on the line.

58. ISA RG10 M155124/2: 'Nebi Musa Festival'.

59. MEC, Haining Papers: dispatch of 1 April to 30 July 1939.

60. Miss Nixon to Chief Secretary, 9 June 1936 (MEC, Jerusalem and the East Mission Papers, Box LXVI).

61. Letter from Archdeacon Stewart to Chief Secretary, 2 June 1936 (ibid., Box LXV, file 4).

62. Wainwright, Deputy Superintendent of Police, to Chief Secretary, 19 June 1936 (ibid., Box LXVI).

63. Bishop Graham-Brown to Chief Secretary, 'April 1938'.

64. MEC, Forster Papers. See also MacMichael to Secretary of State, 24 March 1939 (PRO CO 733/398/1).

65. MEC, Forster Papers.

66. A. T. O. Lees, Assistant District Commissioner, Hebron, Report dated 23 August 1938 (ibid.). according to one of Lees's colleagues, he had been so disaffected that, on his return to England he frequented the British Union of Fascists, and was imprisoned for the duration of the war for his anti-British sympathies. (I am indebted to Professor Joshua Sherman for this information.)

67. MacMichael to Bishop Graham-Brown, 8 August 1938 (MEC, Jerusalem and the East Mission Papers, Box LXVI, file 2).

68. Eric Bishop, enclosure, 5 May 1939 (Washington, NA 867N 4016/86); quoted in Stein, 'The Intifada and the 1936–9 Uprising'.

69. Keith-Roach, *Pasha of Jerusalem, passim*.

70. Transcript of interview with Major-General Bredin, Thames Television, 1976 (IWM).

71. Bigger to Director of Medical Services, 28 December 1938 (ISA RG10 M1642 79/5).

72. Greatrex, Head of SOE in Jerusalem, cable to Cairo, 5 August 1940 (PRO HS 3 207).

73. Memorandum, with comments, of meeting of SOE heads with Shertok, David HaCohen Zaslany and others in London, September 1940 (PRO HS 3 201).
74. Cairo SOE HQ to London, communiqué dated 6 November 1940 (ibid.).
75. These exploits have frequently been described, most recently, in English, in Eshed, *Reuven Shiloach* (see also n.37, above).
76. 'The Relations between SOE and the Jews', memorandum by SOE Controller, 22 June 1942 (PRO HS 209: 'Zionists').
77. 'Comments: Palestine, Syria and Transjordan', memorandum, 1942 (PRO HS 3 207, undated file).
78. Memorandum, SOE Controller (PRO HS 3 209: 'Zionists').
79. Second page of a Report dated 28 October 1942 (PRO HS 3 207).
80. Report headed '115/8/DH/ 224/1', dated 28 September 1942: 'Officer only' (ibid.). This makes it clear that this report contains the only full account of the fiasco, as the relevant documents had been burned during the invasion scare. A cable from Cairo, dated 27 June 1942, refers only to Wilson's dismissal for having mishandled the SOE finances. Wilson is referred to only by his code number, D/H 226; his identity is clear, however, from a key elsewhere in this group of documents. The reference to his character as 'lovable' is in a minute from D/H 224 appended to a report on the trial of Jewish wireless transmitters (see n.79, below).
81. Documents relating to the wireless transmitter affair are in PRO HS 3 209. The quote 'we have been suckers' is in a report on a visit to Palestine and Syria by an 'SOE officer' with Colonel Keble, dated 6 October 1942.
82. Eshed, *Reuven Shiloach*; Gelber, *Growing a Fleur-de-lis*. There appears to be no record of this final débâcle in SOE files, though there are a number of references to Kibbutz Yagur in army files: the kibbutz was frequently the object of arms searches.
83. Details of the recruitment of Palestinian Jews and Arabs in the Second World War are in PRO CO 537/1819.
84. PRO CO 537/1721. The decisions regarding the fate of Jewish recruits, and the partial information given to the Jewish Agency, are in WO cipher 73167 SD ZA, 1 September 1944, in this file.
85. Transcript of interview with Major-General John Cowtan, Thames Television, 1976 (IWM).
86. Gale, *A Call to Arms*, Chapter 15.
87. Transcript of interviews with Rear-Admiral James Munn and John Moore, Major Malcolm Gray and John Waddy, Thames Television, 1976 (IWM).
88. Report by Lieutenant-Colonel D'Arcy, GOC Palestine, G/2018/8/0, 1945 (LHC, Stockwell Papers, 6/1)

89. Sir Henry Gurney, in 'Palestine Postscript: The Last Days of the Mandate', unpublished Ms (MEC, Gurney Papers).

90. Memorandum, headed 'HQ Palestine' and describing confrontation with Jewish militia at Beit Oren on 10 October 1945, G/2018/8/0, signed Lieutenant-Colonel J. C. D'Arcy (LHC, Stockwell Papers, 6/1). His estimate here doubles the actual number of Jewish recruits and exaggerates the strength of the Jewish arsenal – presumably a failure of British Intelligence, which depended for its information on what the Hagana provided.

91. Gale, *A Call to Arms*, Chapter 15.

92. Ibid.

93. Letter from Lieutenant-General Sir Evelyn Barker, GOC Palestine, to Lieutenant-Colonel D'Arcy, 2 July 1946 (MEC, D'Arcy Papers).

94. Conversations between Cunningham and Golda Myerson [Meir], 27 November 1946, and with Ben Gurion, 17 January 1947 (MEC, Cunningham Papers, file 1: 'Meetings with Arab and Jewish leaders').

95. Sir Douglas Harris, memorandum on Palestine to Colonial Office, 25 August 1945; the 'ploughing sand' quote appears in Harris to Secretary of State, 25 February 1945 (both in PRO CO 537/75872/133).

96. Cunningham, letter to Sir Oliver Stanley, circulated to all Ministers in the Middle East, 17 July 1944 (MEC, Cunningham Papers, correspondence).

97. Cunningham to Sir John Shaw, 20 December 1945 (ibid.).

98. Cunningham, transcript of interview with Jamal Bey Husseini, 8 August 1946 (MEC, Cunningham Papers, file I: 'Meetings with Arab and Jewish Leaders'); see also Cunningham, transcript of interview with Eliezer Kaplan, of the Jewish Agency. 23 October 1946 (ibid.).

99. General Dempsey, GHQ ME Land Forces, Cairo, to Lieutenant-General Barker, GOC Palestine, 24 January 1947 (LHC, Stockwell Papers, 6/2).

100. For 'Broadside' leak, see Gelber, *Growing a Fleur-de-lis*, p. 580; for executions, Professor Yoav Gelber, personal communication. Professor Gelber's account of these executions appears in various Hebrew publications.

101. Staff Officer, Report to Stockwell, 15 August 1946 (MEC, Stockwell Papers, 6/2).

102. Sir Harold Pyman, Chief of Staff, Middle East Land Forces, 'C-in-C's Second Agenda on Palestine', 17 December 1946 (LHC, Pyman diaries).

103. Transcript of interview of the High Commissioner (Cunningham) with Rabbi Fishman, and Leo Kohn of Va'ad Leumi, at Cunningham's request, 1 January 1947 (CZA S 25/10551).

104. Transcript of interview with Dr Richard Clutterbuck, Thames Television, 1976 (IWM).

105. 317th Airborne Field Security Section, Report 47 for week ending 30 September 1947, 'Security of Access and Material' (LHC, Stockwell Papers, 6/23).

106. Cunningham, memorandum to Secretary of State, January 1948 (PRO 537/3852: 'Internal Security').

107. Motti Golani, 'The Haifa Turning Point', article to be published in an anthology edited by Professor Anita Shapiro, Shazar Institute, in 1999. (I am grateful to Dr Golani for having allowed me to read the Ms of this article before publication.)

108. Palestine HQ Army document: Secret Appendix A to G/2228/(o), 10 February 1948 (LHC, Stockwell Papers, 6/1: 'Palestine').

109. LHC, Stockwell Papers, 6/26 contains essays and reports by Stockwell, MacMillan, Young, Hackett and Scott, of the 6th Airborne Division on British army morale in Palestine during the last two years of the Mandate.

110. Transcript of interview with Colonel Jack Churchill, Thames Television, 1976 (IWM). Recent Palestinian research puts the actual numbers of those killed at Deir Yassin at 120.

111. Golani, 'The Haifa Turning Point'.

112. LHC, Stockwell Papers, 6/19: 'Evacuation from Palestine, November 1947 – May 1948' (General MacMillan).

113. Conversation between Cunningham and Ben Gurion, 13 October 1947 (MEC, Cunningham Papers).

114. Conversation between Cunningham and Ben Gurion, 1 December 1947 (ibid.).

115. Conversations between Dr Khalidi and Cunningham, 1 and 7 December 1947 (ibid.). The High Commissioner's talks with the Arabs were far more acrimonious than those with the Jews. Cunningham wrote of Khalidi: 'I have always considered him quite unbalanced and nearly mad.'

116. Dov Gavish, 'The British Effort at Safeguarding the Land Records of Palestine in 1948', *Archives*, vol.XXII/95 (1996), pp. 107–20.

117. R. W. Hamilton, *Letters from the Middle East by an Occasional Archaeologist* (Edinburgh, Cambridge and Durham, 1992).

118. 'Ordinances Gambling Machines, Gaming Ordinance' (ISA RG3 AG19/132 M718).

119. H. E. Chudhigh, Report to Chief Secretary, 20 December 1947, in Cunningham to Creech Jones, 20 January 1948 (ISA RG2 M130/38/SW/1/47).

120. H. M. O. Lester, re 'Department of Health: Palestine, 1946–8, "The Decline and Fall" ' (RHL, Mss Medit s.14).

121. Ibid.

122. LHC, Stockwell Papers, 6/19: 'Evacuation from Palestine, November 1947 – May 1948' (General MacMillan).

123. 'Appreciation of the Situation by Major-General Sir Hugh Stockwell, 9.00 hours' 20 April 1948 (LHC, Stockwell Papers, 6/13: Report on Arab–Jewish clashes in Haifa, 21/22 April 1948).

124. Sir Henry Gurney, 'Palestine Postscript', unpublished Ms (MEC, Gurney Papers).

125. Liddell Hart memoranda: diary note: 11/48/116, 22 May 1948; see also transcript of interview with editor of London *Jewish Chronicle* (LHC, Liddell Hart Papers, 11).

126. Letter to J. M. Martin, Colonial Office, 24 February 1948 (MEC, Cunningham Papers: correspondence).

127. The most authoritative and comprehensive work on the subject of the Palestinian refugees is Benny Morris, *The Birth of the Palestinian Refugee Problem, 1947–49* (Cambridge University Press, 1987).

128. MEC, Cunningham Papers. See also Cunningham, 'Palestine: The Last Days of the Mandate', in *International Affairs* (October 1948), pp. 481–90.

Postscript

1. Transcript of interview with Anwar Nusseibeh, Thames Television, 1976 (IWM).

2. William Roger Louis, *The British Empire in the Middle East, 1945–51: Arab Nationalism, the United States and Post-War Imperialism* (Oxford, 1985), pp. 34–5.

Index

Aarohnson, Aaron, 26
Aarohnson, Sarah, 26
Abd'el Hadi, Ruhi Bey, 124, 125
Abdul Hamid, Sultan, 34, 102
Abdul Hamid lands case (1934–48), 121–5
Abdul Rahim, 195
Abramson, Albert, 116
Abu Ghosh, 192
Abu Jildeh, 193
Acre, 88, 138, 212, 214
Acre prison, 146, 147
Aden, 94
Advisory Council, 54, 58, 63
Afghanistan, 90
Afula, 139, 150
Alexander, Mary, 71
Alexandria, 138
Allenby, General Sir Edmund, 6, 21, 26, 28, 41
American Joint Distribution Committee, 128
American University in Beirut, 158, 168
American University in Cairo, 158, 168
Amery, Leopold, 131
Andrews, Lewis, 115, 116; murder of, 117, 191, 193
Anglican Church, 47
Anglican mission schools, 169–71
Anglo-American Commission of Enquiry (1946), 177, 223
Anglo-Egyptian Bank, 29
Anti-Malaria Ordinance (1922), 133
Antonius, George, 160–1
Arab Awakening, The, 161

Arab Census Committee (1931), 65
Arab Executive, 65, 98, 110, 202
Arab Higher Committee, 65, 188, 190, 191, 194, 202
Arab Legion, 236
Arab Revolt (1936–9), 2, 72, 78, 103, 117, 162, 167, 170, 179, 185, 196, 198, 200, 201, 202, 211, 215, 247
Arab (Teachers) Training College (Jerusalem), 42, 156, 157, 166
Arara, 149
Aref el Aref, 41, 69
Arlosoroff, Chaim, 173, 184, 185
Ashbee, Clifford, 49–54, 68, 136
Asquith, Herbert, 14, 56
Athlit, 134
Athlit Kabbara lands, 108

Badcock, R.D., 95
Baghdad, conquest of (1917), 21
Bahamas, 76
Bailey, Morris, 115
Balfour, Arthur J., 7, 11, 14, 58, 156
Balfour Declaration, 7–14, 38–9, 63, 96, 99, 110
Baltic ports, 99
Barbados, 76
Barclays Bank, Jerusalem, 240
Barghuti, Omar el, 69
Barker, Lieutenant-General Sir Evelyn, 225, 228, 229
Basra, 20
Bassa, 214
Battat, Sheikh Aissa, 194
Battershill, William 183, 191, 196, 204

Bedouin, 35, 70, 75, 77, 78, 114, 120–1, 143, 198
Beersheba, 70, 78, 143
Beirut, 89, 108, 158, 167
Beit Jala, 136, 142
Beit Jibrin, 132, 140
Beit Mahsir, 192
Beissan, 150
Beisan land case (1921), 108
Beit Sefafa Hospital, 238
Bell, Sir Gawain, 144, 194–5, 196
Ben Gurion, David, 185, 223, 231, 236
Ben Yehuda, Eliezer, 46, 169
Bengal, 67, 194
Bentwich, Norman de Mattos, 34, 74, 106, 109, 112–13, 188, 196
Bermuda, 76
Bertram, Sir Anton, 76
Bet Oren, 222
Bethlehem, 25, 29, 88, 136, 142, 145, 164
Bethlehem Government Mental Hospital, 145–6, 238
Bevin, Ernest, 240
Bigger, Dr William, 134, 215
Biltmore programme, 223
Bingham, Hugh, 214
Bir Zeit, 158, 167, 204, 205
Bishop, Eric F., 214
Blackburne, Kenneth, 199
Boer War, 24, 195
Bols, General, 41
Bomberg, David, 55
Bon Voisinage Agreement (1926), 77, 78
Bowman, Humphrey, 33, 154, 155, 157, 158, 159, 160, 161, 167, 171, 178
Bowman, Joyce, 143
Bramley, Lieutenant-Colonel Percy, 59, 180
Bredin, Colonel Harold, 205, 214
British Empire Exhibition (1924), 66
British Guiana, 76, 141
British Labour party, 149
British National Health Service, 150
Brunton, Captain William, 59–60
Bryant, Edwin George, 181
Buchanan, Sir George, 9
Burnet, John, 20
Butlin, Emily G., 71

Cafferata, Raymond, 181
Cairo, 28, 49, 216, 240
Cairo School of Arts and Crafts, 164

Campbell, Sir John, 86–7, 93, 111
Campbell, J. E. F., 117
Canaan, Dr Tewfik, 69–70, 141, 151
Carey, Alice May, 71–3
Carr, Lieutenant-General Lawrence, 190–1, 192
Cecil, Lord Robert, 9
Ceylon, 31, 76
Chancellor, Sir John (third High Commissioner), 38, 94, 105, 110–13, 149, 192, 193, 201
Chauvel, General, 23
Chaytor, General, 25
Chichester, Major O. R. H., 147
Church Missionary Society, 43, 71, 129
Churchill, Colonel Jack, 234
Churchill, Sir Winston, 10, 216, 224
Churchill White Paper (1922), 63, 82
Clay, Albert T., 69
Clayton, Brigadier-General Sir Gilbert, 161
Clutterbuck, Major-General Richard, 230
Collective Punishment Ordinance (1925), 197, 198, 201–2
Collective Responsibility Ordinance (1924), 197
Committee on Village Administration and Responsibility, 201
Confraternity of the Holy Sepulchre, 45
Constantinople, 31, 81
Constanza, 79
Cosgrove, Edward T., 209
Cowtan, Major-General John, 220, 221
Creech Jones, Arthur, 154
Cromer, Lord, 74
Crosbie, Robert H. E., 204, 208
Crusaders, 1, 6
Cunningham, General Sir Alan (seventh High Commissioner), 3, 226–8, 230, 232, 236, 238, 242–3
Curzon, Lord, 57
Cyprus, 7, 29, 31, 76, 99, 199, 221, 222, 226, 240

Daily Telegraph
Dajani, Dr Fouad Daoudi, 151
D'Arcy, Lieutenant-General John C., 222, 223
Damascus, 88, 94, 203, 210, 240
Danby, Revd Herbert, 46–7, 69
Davar, 89

Dawe, Morley T., 163
Dayan, Moshe, 217
Dead Sea, 68
Deedes, Sir Wyndham, 60
Deir Dibwan, 121
Deir Yassin, massacre at, 234
Dill, Lieutenant-General John G., 189
Disraeli, Benjamin, 56
diyet (blood money), 75
Doar Hayom, 85
Dorot, 220
Dowbiggin, C. H., 181, 182
Dowson, Sir Ernest, 103, 104
Drayton, Robert H., 113
Duff, Douglas, 212
Dura, 162

Ed-Duyuk tribe, 121
Eder, Dr David, 148
Edinburgh Medical Mission, 214
Ein Karem, 71
Egypt, 7, 67, 96, 132, 147
Egyptian Expeditionary Force, 21
Egyptian Labour Corps, 77
El Alamein, battle of (1942), 219
El Hammeh hot springs, 77
Emergency Regulations (1936), 198;
    (1940), 246
Emery, Espie, 170-1
Epstein, Jacob, 27
Eugster, Lieutenant-Colonel, 235-6
Evelina de Rothschild (Girls') School,
    (Jerusalem), 168
Exodus (ship), 221
Ezrath Nashim Mental Hospital,
    Jerusalem, 146, 147, 230

Fahoum, Rafi Bey el, 198-9
Falastin, 138
Faraday, Commander J. E. M., 181
Farhan, Sheikh, 193
Farrell, Wilfred Jerome, 157, 158-9, 160,
    161, 163, 164, 165, 168, 171, 174-8
Federated Malay States, 67, 112
Feisal, Emir, 57
Ferguson, Joy, 178
Ferguson, Vivian L., 152
Fergusson, Bernard, 193
First World War, 1, 5, 8, 9, 13, 20, 80,
    182, 203
FitzGerald, William J., 119-20, 199-200
Fitzmaurice, Gerald, 9

Foot, Hugh, 197-8, 204
Forster, Dr E. D., 129, 208, 213
Fox-Strangways, V., 241
France, 216
Frumkin, Gad, 196-7, 201

Gale, Sir Richard, 221, 229
Galilee, 30, 42, 78, 118, 193, 204, 205,
    206, 232
Galilee, Sea of, 134
Gaza, 22-3, 26, 29, 78, 123, 143, 150,
    154, 162, 189, 190, 246
Gaza Government Hospital, 143
Geddes, Sir Patrick, 54-5
Germany, 97, 185
Gibson, Leslie, 74, 99, 123-5, 241
Goitein, S. D., 174
Golinkin, Mordechai, 93
Gordon School (Khartoum), 161
Gort, Viscount (sixth High
    Commissioner), 226
Government House (Jerusalem), 1-2
Grabbski, Polish finance minister, 85
Graham, Sir Ronald, 9, 10
Graham-Brown, Bishop George, 7, 47,
    48, 96, 169, 212
Gray, Major Malcolm, 221
Gray, Colonel W. N., 241
Greatrex (SOE officer), 216
Greece, 86
Greek Orthodox Church, 45, 71
Greek Refugee Settlement Commission,
    86
Green Hand Gang, 193
Greig, R. H., 163
Gruner, Dov, 229
Gurney, Sir Henry, 223, 240-1

Ha'Aretz, 89
Haan, Jacob de, 39
Hackett, Lieutenant-General Sir John,
    195, 233, 235
Hadaad, Elias, 69
Hadassah Hospital, Jerusalem, 144, 234
Hadassah Medical Association, 128, 130
Hagana, the, 195, 201, 202, 211, 215,
    216, 217, 218, 219, 220, 224, 225,
    228, 232, 234, 235, 240, 242
Haifa, 77, 78, 79, 110, 112, 128, 137,
    138, 144, 147, 170, 182, 202, 212,
    232
Haifa Government Hospital, 143, 238

Haining, Lieutenant-General R. H., 205, 206, 208, 211
Hall, Reginald, 9
Hamilton, Robert, 237
Harris, Sir Douglas, 226, 247
Harrison, Austen St Barbe, 66, 71, 183
Hashem Effendi, 207
Hashim, Ibrahim Pasha, 124
Hathorn-Hall, John, 188
Hauran Arabs, 77
Haycraft, Sir Thomas, 197
Hebrew University, 55, 113, 156, 169, 234
Hebron, 42, 129, 132, 139, 150, 154, 162, 208, 213; massacre of Jews in (1929), 114, 181, 201
Heron, Colonel George, 32–3, 133, 135, 137, 142, 144, 145, 147, 148, 150, 151, 215
Hilmi Pasha, Ahmad, 162
Histadrut (General Federation of Labour), 129, 149
Hitler, Adolf, 97
Hodgkin, Thomas, 72, 187
Hogan, Sir Michael, 124
Holliday, Clifford, 144
Holocaust, 220, 227, 228, 244
Howard League for Penal Reform (London), 214
Huleh region, 78, 136
Husseini, Abd'el Khader el, 208–9
Husseini, Haj Amin el (see also the Mufti), 41, 61, 65, 117, 184, 191, 210
Husseini, Hussein Bey el, 25
Husseini, Jamal Bey el, 227
Hyamson, Albert, 34, 38, 83–96, 97

Ijzim, 212
Imray, C. H., 181–2
India, 21, 106, 110, 207
Indur, 199
Industrial Employment of Women and Children Ordinance (1936), 164
International Labour Organisation (ILO), 149, 164
Intifada, Palestinian, 246
Iraq (see also Mesopotamia), 21, 54, 57, 157, 161
Iraq Petroleum Company, 190
'Irgun' (Irgun Zvai Leumi), 224, 225, 228, 229, 230, 231
Irish Guards, 230, 235

Ironside, General Sir Edmund, 210
Isaacs, Sir Rufus, 11
Israel, 244–6
Israel Lands Authority, 246
Israeli–Arab War (1948), 73
Israeli Army (Israel Defence Forces), 242, 246

Jaffa, 25, 29; riots of 1921 in, 58–9, 78, 112, 128, 138, 143, 152, 163, 181, 187–8, 195, 202, 213, 232, 240, 241
Jaffa Bakeries, 84
Jaffa Government Hospital, 238
Jaffa–Jerusalem railway, 29
Jenin, 150, 195
Jericho, 237
Jerusalem, relics of British rule in, 1; strategic unimportance of, 21; 'Jerusalem by Christmas' (1917), 21; winter ascent to (1917), 23; water supply of, 24; as religious centre for Jews and Arabs alike, 41–2; Western (Wailing) Wall problem, 42, 56, 111, 181; as centre of Mandate administration, 30; restoration of Old City by 'Pro Jerusalem Society', 49–54; during the Arab Revolt, 179, 209; Noble Sanctuary as a refuge in, 191; during the 1947–8 civil war, 232, 239
Jerusalem and the East Mission, 43, 139, 140
Jerusalem Girls' College, 170
Jerusalem Sports Club, 68
Jewish Agency, 16, 17, 61, 64, 66, 82, 83, 94, 148, 172, 173, 180, 184, 186, 195, 196, 201, 202, 216, 217, 218, 219, 223, 224, 228, 231
Jewish Brigade, 219–20
Jewish educational system, 171–8
Jewish National Fund, 87, 111, 118, 120
Jordan river, 57, 78
Jordan valley, 24, 28, 67, 77, 118, 150

Kadoorie, Sir Ellis, 161
Kadoorie schools, 161–2
Kagan, Helena, 28
Kantara, 78, 80
Kantrovitch, Henry, 34
Kaplan, Eliezer, 227–8
Kardus, Abdallah, 116
Kaukji, Fawzi el, 193

Kawkab Abu Haija, 214
Keith-Roach, Edward, 6, 31, 33, 67, 116, 141, 145, 182, 183, 193, 199, 206, 214
Kenya, 200
Kfar Yasif, 214
el Khalidi family, 147
Khalidi, Dr Walid, 236
Khartoum, 161
Khatib, Nafi, 134
Kia-Ora Coo-Ee
King David Hotel (Jerusalem), 16; explosion in (1946), 225
King-Clark, Robert, 203
Kirkbride, Sir Alec, 210–11, 212
Kisch, Brigadier Frederick, 33, 111, 201
Klausner, Yosef, 46, 169
Kristallnacht, 98
Kupath Holim (Jewish health insurance fund), 130, 148–9

League of Nations, 5, 14, 15, 39; covenant of, 14, 15, 16
Lebanon, 77, 78, 79, 164
Lees, A. T. O., 213–14
Lehrs, Dr, 238
Lester, Dr H. M. O., 127, 238–9
Levant Fair (1932), 94
Liddell Hart, Colonel Basil, 241
Lloyd, Lord, 85, 106, 197
Lloyd George, David, 7, 11, 14, 21, 83
London Mission to the Jews, 43
Louis, William Roger, 247
Lutyens, Sir Edwin, 1, 54
Lydda, 80, 163, 192

Maccabiah Games (1932), 94
McConnell, General, 219
MacDonald, Ramsay, 114, 185
McDonnell, Sir Michael, 187–9
McDonnell Pensions Ordinance (1936), 188
MacInnes, Bishop Rennie, 28, 42–3, 44–5, 46, 166, 168
MacLaren, Stuart, 168
McMahon letters (1916), 2
MacMichael, Sir Harold (fifth High Commissioner), 32, 118, 147, 175, 191, 194, 205, 209–10, 217, 219, 226
Macmillan, Lieutenant-General G. H. A., 233
McNair Report (on Jewish education in Palestine), 177–8

McNeill, Brigadier Angus, 68, 180
MacQueen, Dr John, 135, 137, 138, 142, 147, 149, 150
Magnes, Rabbi Judah, 47, 113
Malaria Research Unit, 128, 133
Malaria Survey, 133
Malay Peninsula, 217
Malouf, Dr Mikhail Shedid, 238
Mandate, the British for Palestine, 3, 4; origins of, 5–19
Mandate system, 15
Manning, Olivia, 138
'Mansur' (*non de guerre* of Abd'el Khader el Husseini), 208
Mapai (Israel Labour Party), 245
Margolin, Eliezer, 58–9
Massey, W. T., 26
Mauritius, 76, 99, 110, 221
Mecca, 77, 132
Meinertzhagen, Richard, 12, 39, 41
Mendelssohn, Erich, 144
mesh'a land system, 103, 105, 106
Mesopotamia (*see also* Iraq), 21, 141, 161
Meyer, Dr, 149
Middle East Department (of the Colonial Office), 57, 62
Mildmay Mission, 129
'millet' system, 245
Mills, Eric, 32, 97
Milner, Lord, 41
Mishmar HaEmek, 218, 219
Mogannam, Matiel, 75, 156
Montgomery, Major-General Bernard, 205, 214, 218, 229
Moody, Sydney, 63–4
Moore, John, 221
Morris, H. M. V. C., 84
Morris, William, 49
Moscow, 89
Motza, 201
Moyne, Lord, 224
Mufti, the (Haj Amin el Husseini), 114, 117, 190, 191, 193, 194, 208, 210
Muhurraqa lands, 121–2
Munn, Rear-Admiral James, 221

Nablus, 143, 193, 195
Napoleon, 21
Naser, Nabiha, 158
Nashashibi family, 61
Nation, The, 23

National Council for Civil Liberties (London), 214
Nazareth, 45, 117, 150, 164, 191, 199, 214
Nebi Musa festival, 41–2, 167, 211
Negev desert, 118, 220
Nepal, 67
Netanya, 150
Newcombe, Colonel S. F., 96
Newton, Frances, 70–1
Nicholas II, last Russian Tsar, 8, 9
Nicholson, Arthur, 9
Nigeria, 67
Nixon, Margaret, 70, 92, 140, 212
Noble Sanctuary (Jerusalem) 191, 209, 211; see also Temple Mount
North-West Frontier Province, 194, 203, 206
Novomaisky, Moses, 58
Nurock, Max, 34
Nusseibeh, Anwar, 247

O'Beirne, Hugh, 9
O'Connor, Major-General R., 205
OETA (Occupation of Enemy Territories Administration, 1917–20), 28–30, 40–1
'Operation Agatha', 228
'Operation Elephant', 229
Ormsby Gore, William, 181

Palestine, as a British strategic asset, 5–7, 21, 63, 231; as a 'National Home' for the Jews, 2, 7, 80; and self determination for the Arabs, 2, 14–16; post WWI devastation in, 27–8; Arab population of, 3, 16, 18, 20, 34–6; Jewish population of, 36, 152; population in British eyes, 37–8; censuses during British rule, 65, 94; colonial precedents and administration of, 21, 33, 67, 96, 106, 110, 132, 141, 147, 207, 217; legal system, 74–6; immigration laws in, 76–99; land laws of, 99–125; Zionist rural economy in, 87; Arab peasant culture in, 100–1; health care in, 126–54; as British military base, 153; education system in, 154–78; policing of, 180–2; British proposal for partition of, 6, 191, 210; UN proposal for partition of, 231; civil war in, 231–2; abandoned by British, 243
Palestine Arab Medical Association, 151
Palestine Citizenship Order (1925), 88
Palestine Electric Corporation, 91, 170
Palestine General Agricultural Council, 198
Palestine General Council of Social Services, 238
Palestine Land Court, 122, 125
Palestine Land Settlement Ordinance (1927), 106
Palestine Land Transfer Ordinances (1920, 1921), 107
Palestine Order in Council (1922), 62, 75
Palestine Oriental Society, 69–70
Palestine Police, 182, 206–8
Palestine Scheme, 217–19
Palmach, the, 215, 217, 228
Palmer, Major Anthony, 217
Palmerston, Lord, 8
Paris Peace Conference (1919), 10, 11
Passfield, Lord (Sidney Webb), 114
Passfield White Paper (1930), 114, 190
Paterson, Dr, 129
Patterson, Colonel James, 27, 203
Peake, Lieutenant-Colonel Frederick G., 179, 180, 227
Peel (Royal) Commission (1937), 61, 103, 117, 127, 157, 158, 191
Peirse, Air Commodore Sir Richard, 189
Perowne, Stewart, 42, 111, 157, 166
Petach Tikva, 229
Philips, Ivan Lloyd, 204
Plumer, Viscount (second High Commissioner), 16, 86, 87, 109, 110–11, 114, 131, 145, 147, 155, 189, 197
Poland, 81, 85, 152
Police Ordinance (1921), 208
Polish army units in Palestine, 153
Pollock, Lieutenant-Colonel Sir John, 216, 217
Pope, Margaret, 214
Poston, Ralph, 182–3, 186, 190
Prevention of Crimes Ordinance, 200
Privy Court of St James (appellant court for Palestine), 123, 125
Pro Jerusalem Society, 49–54
Protection of Cultivators Ordinances, 109, 118–20
Public Health Ordinance, 140

Qala, 192
Qassem, Izzedin el, 193
Quakers, 141

Rafa, 80
Ramallah, 141, 156, 204
Ramat Gan, 229
Ramle, 150, 204
Rantis, 192
Raratonga islanders, 21
Ras el Naqura, 78
Reading, Lady Stella, 134
Rhodesia, 110
Richardson, Gavin
Richmond, Ernest, 32, 49, 59, 60–2, 67
Rishon-le-Zion, 24
Rockefeller Foundation, 133
Rockefeller Museum, Jerusalem, 237
Rogers, V. W. E., 143
Rosh Pina, 78, 207
Rosov, Israel, 12
Rothschild, Baron Edmond de, 24
Rothschild family, 10
Royal Engineers, 230
Ruhama, 220
Russia, Tsarist, 7, 8, 9, 10; Soviet Russia
    12, 81, 89
Rutenberg, Pinhas, 57

Saba, Nicola, 116
Safed, 114, 181, 201, 237
Said, Nuri, 96
St John's Eye Hospital (Jerusalem), 129,
    137
St Luke's Hospital (Hebron), 129
St George's Cathedral (Jerusalem), 43,
    68
St George's School (Jerusalem), 43, 155,
    170
St Vincent Hospice (Jerusalem), 146
Salt, es, 57
Samakh, 78, 79
Samaria, 206
Samuel, Edwin, 34, 101, 182
Samuel, Sir Herbert (first High
    Commissioner), 3, 13, 27, 38, 56–62,
    65, 66, 74, 81, 82, 83, 109, 110, 148,
    160, 161, 185
Sawer, Edward, 33, 92, 101, 107–8
Schiff, Jacob, 11
Schmerl, Walter, 88
Scott, H. S., 175

Scott, Lieutenant-Colonel M. F., 233
Scouting movement, 34, 157, 167–8
Sea of Galilee, 79, 207, 237
Second World War, 7, 18, 99, 103, 104,
    119, 123, 128, 144, 153, 179, 200
Selim Abdul Hamid, Prince, 122
Seychelles, 76
Shai (Intelligence service of the
    Hagana), 211
Shaw Commission (1930), 190
Shefa Amr, 138
Shertock, Moshe, 186, 195, 202, 216
Shuckburgh, Sir John, 63
Sinai desert, 21, 80
Six Days War (1967), 2
Sixth Airborne Division, 221, 228, 231,
    233, 239
Sodom and Gomorrah Golfing Society,
    68
Special Night Squads, 202–3, 220
Special Operations Executive (SOE),
    216–19
Stanley, Sir Oliver, 175, 226
Starkey, J. L., 206
Stephan, Hana, 69
Stern, Abraham ('Yair'), 229
Stern Gang, 224, 234
Stewart, Bishop Weston, 48, 213
Stewart, William A., 164, 241
Stockwell, General Sir Hugh, 228, 233,
    239–40, 241
Storrs, Colonel Ronald, 30, 32, 42,
    48–54, 66, 68, 168
Strathearn, Dr John, 144
Stuart, Dr George, 153
Stubbs, James N., 107, 118
Stubbs, R., 241
Sudan, 33, 67, 106, 110, 161
Sudan Land Settlement Law, 106
Sudanese Civil Service, 33
Suez Canal, 6, 7, 20, 21, 78, 80, 132
Supreme Muslim Council, 61, 64, 65,
    147, 184, 191, 245
Sursock lands, 108
Sykes-Picot Agreement (1917), 13
Syria, 57, 75, 77, 78, 79, 164, 216

Tafish, Ahmed, 193
Tahkemoni School (Jerusalem), 175
Tamimi, Rafiq Bey, 159
Tancred, 56
Tanganyika, 67, 112

Tanner, Lord, 190
Tarazi, Wadia, 158
Tayyiba, 167
Technion, the (Haifa), 162
Tegart, Sir Charles, 32, 206, 208
Tel Aviv, 85, 86, 112, 138, 147, 152–3, 182, 218, 219, 224, 228, 229, 240
Temple Mount (Jerusalem), 191, 209
Thomas, J. H., 186
Tibawi, A. L., 165
Tiberias, 79, 134, 236, 237
Tidhar, Jacob, 39
Tireh, 202
Tobias, Philip, 207
Town Planning Ordinance (1920), 54
Transjordan, 51, 54, 57, 59, 63, 71, 77, 78, 111
TransJordan Frontier Force, 181, 193, 239
Treaty of Lausanne (1923), 122
Trieste, 79, 81
Trinidad, 76
Trusted, Harry, 199
Tulkarm, 140, 150, 159, 162, 167
Turkey, 76, 123–4

Uganda, 141, 200
United Nations, 1, 2, 231, 236
United States, 85
UNSCOP (United Nations Special Commission on Palestine), 225–6, 231

Va'ad Leumi (Jewish National Council), 66, 172–3, 177, 230
Victoria College (Alexandria), 160
Village Congress, 162

Waddy, Colonel, 222
Waddy, Stacy, 43, 155
Wadi Hawarith land case (1929), 111, 114
Wailing (Western) Wall (Jerusalem), 42, 56, 111, 181
Wainwright, Major William F., 212
Walker, Bernard, 139–40
Wallach Hospital, 128

Waqf, Muslim, 51, 110, 184
War Graves Commission (Cairo), 49
Warsaw, 94
Waters-Taylor, Colonel, 41
Watson, General, 40
Wauchope, General Sir Arthur (fourth High Commissioner), 17, 38, 97–8, 105, 115, 162, 163, 173, 182–9, 191, 192, 193, 194, 202
Wavell, Major-General Sir Archibald, 189
Webster, Charles, 10
Wedgwood, Josiah, 131
Weizmann, Chaim, 11, 12, 42, 44, 58, 184, 185, 186, 223, 227
West Bank (of Jordan river), 246
Whitaker, Miss, 145–6
White Paper (1939), 99, 118, 215
Wilson, General B. T., 218–19
Wilson, Helen, 167, 204
Wilson, Robert Henley, 22–3, 26
Wilson, President Woodrow, 5
Wingate, Colonel Orde, 202–3, 211
Wintringham, J. W., 22
Wise, Rabbi Stephen, 12

Yagur, 219
Yalu, 192
Yellin, Avinoam, 174
Yellin, David, 168
Young, Lieutenant-Colonel P. G. F., 233
Young Men's Muslim Association, 193
Young Turk Revolution, 9, 123

Zangwill, Israel, 55
Zaslani, Reuven, 202
Zichron Ya'akov, 149
Zilka, Renee, 139
Zinoviev letter, 89
Zion Mule Corps, 27
Zionism, 8–14
Zionist Executive, 80, 89, 146, 169, 224
Zionist Organization, 54, 55, 80, 81–2, 90, 111, 145, 148
Zionist Commission (1918), 39–40, 58, 62, 136, 148